HIGH-PERFORMANCE TRAINING FOR TRACK AND FIELD

Second Edition

William J. Bowerman

William H. Freeman

Leisure Press
Champaign, Illinois

Library of Congress Cataloging-in-Publication Data

k and field / by Bill Bowerman

Based on the author's Coaching track and field, 1974.
Includes bibliographical references.
ISBN 0-88011-390-1
   1. Track-athletics--Training.   2. Track-athletics--Coaching.
I. Freeman, William Hardin, 1943-   .   II. Bowerman, William J.
Coaching track and field.   III. Title.
GV1060.675.T73B69   1991
796.42--dc20   90-36286
                                                                        CIP

ISBN: 0-88011-390-1

Acquisitions Editor: Brian Holding; **Developmental Editor:** Peggy Rupert; **Managing Editor:** Robert King; **Assistant Editor:** Julia Anderson; **Copyeditor:** Peter Nelson; **Proofreader:** Pam Johnson; **Production Director:** Ernie Noa; **Typesetter:** Kathy Boudreau-Fuoss; **Text Design:** Keith Blomberg; **Text Layout:** Jill Wikgren and Tara Welsch; **Cover Design:** Jack Davis; **Cover Photo:** Will Zehr; **Illustrations:** Glenn Amundsen and David Gregory; **Printer:** Versa Press

Leisure Press books are available at special discounts for bulk purchase. Special editions or book excerpts can also be created to specification. For details, contact the Special Sales Manager at Human Kinetics.

Printed in the United States of America   10   9   8   7

Leisure Press
A Division of Human Kinetics
Web site: http://www.humankinetics.com/

United States: Human Kinetics, P.O. Box 5076, Champaign, IL 61825-5076
1-800-747-4457
e-mail: humank@hkusa.com

Canada: Human Kinetics, Box 24040, Windsor, ON N8Y 4Y9
1-800-465-7301 (in Canada only)
e-mail: humank@hkcanada.com

Europe: Human Kinetics, P.O. Box IW14, Leeds LS16 6TR, United Kingdom
(44) 1132 781708
e-mail: humank@hkeurope.com

Australia: Human Kinetics, 57A Price Avenue, Lower Mitcham, South Australia 5062
(08) 277 1555
e-mail: humank@hkaustralia.com

New Zealand: Human Kinetics, P.O. Box 105-231, Auckland 1
(09) 523 3462
e-mail: humank@hknewz.com

Dedicated to
Bill Hayward
and the
Men of Oregon

Contents

Foreword

In 1962, when I was an Oregon freshman and dedicating myself to distance running, I didn't have this book. I had the man who wrote it, Oregon coach William J. Bowerman. There were a lot of times I'd rather have had the book.

Bill Bowerman was, and is, and ever shall be a generous, ornery, profane, beatific, unyielding, antic, impenetrably complex Oregon original. As a freshman, I found him deeply disturbing. One of my best friends was his middle son, Jay, who became an Olympic biathlete. That didn't matter. We both found him disturbing.

The principles of high performance training set down in this book (with a clarity traceable to a collaborator named Freeman) had long been assembled and put into practice when I joined Bowerman's team, but he was, and is, and ever shall be working on refinements. We paid our freshman dues by being guinea pigs in experiments that compared different sorts and intensities of training.

On the fundamentals, Bowerman delivered a 40-second speech. "You stress an organism, for example a freshman," he told us, "and you let it rest. What happens? It responds by overcompensating. It becomes some increment stronger, faster, or more enduring. That's all training is. You'd think any damn fool could figure out how to do it. The only trick is finding what works best for a specific athlete."

I still share some of Bowerman's amazement that so few damn fools do learn to train to optimum effect. This general ignorance is something I've always been grateful for, given that I've had to race athletes more talented than I. The equalizer has always been there, the fact that talent can almost be counted on to blunder in training. But if we were to gain an edge from that, Bowerman had to teach us to prepare intelligently.

Stress. Rest. Response. Individuality. They seem dry, clinical terms. But Bowerman hurled them upon us—not with the reasoned good humor of this book, but with all the force of his Old Testament personality.

STRESS: The actual workouts were the least of our worries. The man was the thing, the man in all his mystifying incarnations. He spoke in parables, in Hammurabi's Code, in ringing declamations from Delphi. (I think the only one that survives in this book is the big one: "Know Thyself"). He made us study. Instead of giving any of us full scholarships, he made us work weekends on the graveyard shift in Eugene's plywood mills. When we were new, he would assign an interval workout and, standing in the infield, call out our times civilly enough but completely ignore us otherwise. If you asked him a question—Was your form correct?—he would stonily, silently lift his gaze to the swallows in their flight above Hayward Field.

He made our shoes. He was disdainful of the excessive weight and nonexistent cushioning of the shoes then on the market, so he improved them. As you sat, a little weary, at your locker after a long run, a bear would suddenly loom up before you; no, a man, covered in black hoarfrost, smelling evilly of burned rubber. It was Bowerman, fresh from grinding down the rough edges of the rubber soles he'd cemented to your training shoes. He either never ground them enough (so you had to finish the job) or ground holes in the uppers. Had we known these were the beginnings of Nike's vast success, would we have been more respectful of his cobbling?

Bowerman seemed to glory in the tyranny permitted a head coach. He played with us, yanking us from races on the starting line because the dual meet score was growing lopsided, kicking people off the team because they ran unauthorized mileage behind his back.

Once he bet me a case of Nutrament that I couldn't break 2:00 for the 880 on a freezing Saturday morning. I ran with control, hitting the 440 in 60. I could feel myself accelerating in the last lap. Near the finish I knew I'd done it. I heard him stop the watch. I slowed and turned, gasping, to hear the time. "2:00.3," he said. "Good try." I leaped upon him, screaming, made insane by outrage. He allowed me to wrestle the watch away from him. It read 1:56.6.

He loved to sit in the sauna until his heavy ring of brass keys had been heated to 180 degrees, then brand us with them. And when we yowled that nowhere in Plato or Isaiah was his behavior justified, he answered us with the defining parable. All of this, ALL of it, was in the manner of the two-by-four.

''Farmer couldn't get his mule to work,'' he'd say. ''Couldn't even get him to eat or drink. Mule just stood there. Finally he brought in a mule expert who took a look, went in the barn, and came out with a six-foot two-by-four. HIT that mule as hard as he could between the eyes.

'' 'THAT's supposed to get him to DRINK?' said the farmer. 'THAT's supposed to TEACH him something?'

'' 'Well, ' said the mule expert, 'first you have to get his attention.'' '

REST: ''Are you in this to do mindless labor?'' he asked when I announced my lunatic intention of running 200 miles per week over the summer after my first year. ''Or do you want to improve? You can't improve if you're sick or injured.''

Before June was half over, I was sick and injured. Bowerman, fed up by the spring of my sophomore year, forced me—by threat of bodily harm—to do two or even three easy days between each remotely taxing workout. My schedule seemed little more than a life of 3-A and 3-B. You can look it up. In three weeks I improved from 9:30 to 8:48 in the two-mile.

That was my personal two-by-four. It finally began to penetrate my thick skull that I had to rise above the world's fixation with work. I had to attend to my own slow-recovering physiology. I had to rest.

RESPONSE: Work for its own dumb sake is a hard habit to break, but slowly I embraced those deceptively simple basics. I accepted easy days into my life. I stopped counting miles. I grew stronger, gradually extending the one long run permitted me every 10 days from 20 to 25, to 30, even 35 miles. Over time, those runs transformed me into a marathoner capable of running 2:11:36 in 1970 and of finishing fourth in the 1972 Olympic marathon.

Coming to terms with my individual raw material also had a wider liberating effect. Eccentricity—and in Bowerman I sure had an example of that—no longer seemed all that silly. Quitting Stanford law school and trying to be a writer no longer seemed an imbecilic thing to do.

Now, looking around at a world largely inhabited by people who have never learned how to compete without letting it take over their life, people who've never learned how to peak when it counts, or take a joke, or stand up to a tyrant, or have faith in their thinking even if it is kind of strange, I begin to appreciate my good fortune in having been born into the Bowerman Kingdom.

INDIVIDUALITY: How much of what the man did to and for me can his book of training principles do for you? It's a good question. The technical instruction Freeman and Bowerman provide in these chapters is first-rate. Yet, as I found, a lot of what seems common sense is hard to apply. It goes against the damn fool compulsive achiever's grain. ''Rest?'' ''Have fun?'' ''Finish your training feeling exhilarated, not exhausted?'' Those are fighting words, and this book has no two-by-four.

I feel a lot more like a farmer than a man who knows mules. All I can say is, Here is the water. Drink.

Kenny Moore

Preface

This book grew from *Coaching Track and Field*, which described Bill Bowerman's Oregon training system, the most influential in the United States today. It presents

- the theory of training,
- how the theory is applied in the training program, and
- extensive real-life daily training schedules for each event.

Use *High-Performance Training for Track and Field* for a training year, even if you do no more than copy the workouts, and we guarantee that your athletes will perform well. Most training books cover either the "why" (the latest training theories) or the "how" (applying the theory to an actual training program). This text gives *both*, blending them into the single most useful text available for track and field coaches and athletes.

The earlier book included a training year of workouts for each event. All of the schedules were used by national or world-class American athletes, some of them U.S. and world record holders. The result was the most comprehensive set of real-life training schedules in any track and field book.

This book adds the theoretical bases that underlie training, summarizing what researchers know about training and competition and discussing the most advanced, scientifically monitored foreign endurance training system in the world. It tells, briefly and simply, what you need to know about periodization in training, overload theory, and the effects of nutrition and psychology on today's training.

Our scientific knowledge of training has expanded during the last decade, but today's knowledge has not changed the principles that underlie the Oregon System. Our training patterns reflect the latest scientific training methods.

The heart of the Oregon System is intact, including the training schedules, with a minimum of 6 months of daily training sessions per event. Although the schedules have indeed been used by elite athletes, they can be used as they appear by almost any healthy athlete, male or female. As these schedules demonstrate, there is an art to coaching. The schedules were carefully crafted to develop athletes without losing them to injury or burnout.

The schedules emphasize developing the fundamental skills and necessary conditioning of the events, with performance levels scaled to individual abilities. They are most appropriate for junior and young senior athletes (high school and university athletes, ages 14-22).

High-Performance Training for Track and Field is a step-by-step guide for teacher-coaches in their first years, who will find it to be a model for success. Experienced coaches will find its systematic analyses of training methods an invaluable addition to their own expertise.

Experienced coaches can use the schedules as an example and a starting point in developing or modifying their own training systems. Less experienced coaches can use them as models. Some coaches have simply copied and posted the schedules for their athletes to follow. Although we do not recommend that method, it will work. An individual athlete can adapt the schedules to a training program tailored to his or her own goals.

No other text has ever been so usable for coaches and athletes alike. By studying and using this book properly, even the most inexperienced coach can produce well-prepared athletes.

Whether you are a coach or an athlete, a beginner or an expert, *High-Performance Training for Track and Field* will be more useful to you than any other track text in print.

Bill Bowerman
Bill Freeman

Introduction: How to Use This Book

This text has two parts. Part I summarizes what coaches and scientists know and believe about training and conditioning, emphasizing the scientific basis that underlies training in all events and all sports. Part II covers specific event training, with each chapter beginning with an overview of the science that affects training and performance in that event. The training methods are studied and the most common training techniques for the event are explained, showing how the fundamentals of training are actually applied.

The training schedule sheet for the event is shown next, and the meanings of the symbols are defined. In addition, the origin of the schedule sheets and a presentation of their use and interpretation appear in chapter 5.

The training schedules are the most valuable portion of the book; the schedules for all events have been proven effective. The workouts are taken from real training files; they follow athletes through daily training for at least 6 months of a training year until May or June, when the most important meets are contested. These workouts have been used by national and world-class athletes, Olympic team members, sub-4:00 milers, 1:45 800-meter runners, 60-foot shot-putters, 10.0-to-10.2-second 100-meter runners, 13.3-second high hurdlers, and so on.

Because those competitors were advanced athletes, the coach or athlete should experiment with the workouts and adapt them to the athlete's own capabilities when actual times and paces are given. The quantity of work should also be adapted for younger athletes. With those precautions, the workouts are absolutely usable by any athlete. They solve a great problem for the inexperienced coach or athlete: *What* should an athlete do to train well?

The training schedules are preceded by a list of resources for more information about each event (materials, mostly periodical articles, the majority of which have appeared in print since 1980). We do not agree with the content of every article, but we stress that there is no single way to achieve success.

The schedules in this text can be used as is. Some athletes may need to modify the workouts, but this will not often be the case. Some coaches have simply copied the workouts and told athletes to follow the schedules, with no explanation. Although athletes can progress even with that method of coaching, we do not approve of it. We prefer that the coach and athlete first learn what the parts of the schedule mean. In addition, they must

- learn the scientific principles of training (discussed in chapter 1). These principles provide the foundation for wise training.
- practice and develop the performance techniques, the skills needed for good form. Those skills make performance more effective while making the likelihood of injuries much smaller.
- study how the training patterns are organized, how each part of the pattern fits with the other parts, and why each part of the pattern is used.

Coupled with a knowledge of the scientific background, this understanding will allow you to adapt training more effectively to your athletes. Good coaches and athletes are always experimenting with new ideas in training. Useful experiments require a thorough understanding of these foundations.

PART I

Foundations for the Training Program

CHAPTER 1	# The Foundations of Sport Training

Though many athletes compete in sports, only a few reach the highest performance levels. Why is that true? Certainly not everyone has the same potential when beginning. Even so, many athletes who seem only ordinary in their early years later blossom into national- or world-class performers. Why are they able to make it to the top when initially more talented athletes are not? The answer lies in their training.

The Three Cornerstones of Training

Training and competition are complex activities; many variables contribute to success. However, three very basic rules should always be followed in training. These cornerstones of any successful system of training are

- moderation,
- consistency, and
- rest.

Moderation

Moderation is the first cornerstone of training. It means not going to extremes in any aspect of training. Inexperienced distance runners should not run 100 miles a week in training because they may develop serious injuries that could end their running careers early. Extended hours of training are not nec-

essary. Athletes at most levels of competition can compete successfully with 2 hours of daily training if it is well planned and seriously conducted. Only at the most advanced levels of sport (after 6 to 10 years of training) does the need for more extensive training appear.

Athletes in some events have trained more than this, it is true. However, the long-term results of more extreme training programs are inconsistent, with more athletes failing than succeeding in reaching the top. Some athletes develop serious injuries, and many become burned out, psychologically drained by the heavy training loads.

The human body can take far more stress than we generally give it. However, it needs to adapt to heavier stresses gradually. Moderation means a carefully planned training program that avoids extremes in physical or psychological stress. Training and competing can be a beautiful, exciting part of life, but they are not all there is to life. The principle of moderation permits the athlete to enjoy the other parts of life as much as sport.

Consistency

Consistency is the second cornerstone of training. One way to avoid extremes in training is to train at a reasonable level every day. This does *not* mean using the same training load each day. When an athlete trains consistently, the body has more time to adapt to the stress of training, easing its way to higher levels of fitness. If a few days of training are missed, the body loses tone and endurance. A day or two of extra-hard training does not make up for that loss. In fact, the athlete may overstress the body, resulting in an injury or an illness. Extra physical strain does more than simply tire the body, so the consistency of training is critical. The athlete who trains daily at a moderate level will outperform the equally talented athlete who trains extremely hard at times and skips training at other times.

Consistency has another reward for the athlete. As training continues, a solid fitness base develops. The longer the time used to develop the base, the less effect an interruption of training has. Athough any athlete loses conditioning when training is interrupted, an athlete with a long-term base loses condition more slowly and regains it more quickly.

Rest

Rest is the third cornerstone of training, perhaps the most important one for younger athletes. An athlete *must* get enough rest. This may be the training rule least followed by young athletes. A simple rule of training: When in doubt, get more rest. Athletes feeling tired or weak shouldn't try to have hard training sessions. Instead, they should have very light training sessions or simply skip sessions. Athletes must be aware of how much sleep they are getting. Athletes in training need more rest and sleep than nonathletes.

Why do they need more rest? First, the extra work creates extra physical stress, which calls for more recovery time. Second, the body makes its adaptations to stress when the body is at rest rather than during the stress. This is part of the overload aspect of training. If the body does not have enough rest, it cannot recover and adapt fully, so it does not benefit fully from the training.

The body is like a massive computer, with many complex working parts. When it is worked very hard, occasionally it tires or overloads, becoming less efficient. With a computer, a problem requires "down time," a "rest" period while the operators repair the problem. The body repairs its own problems (unless they are extreme), but it requires its own down time every day. The amount varies from one person to another, but most athletes need at least 8 to 10 hours of sleep each night.

Generally speaking, the younger the athlete is, the more rest that is needed. An athlete must learn to be "tuned in" to his or her body; it tells when it needs more rest and when it has had enough. The body runs on rest, just as it runs on fuel. If it has too little rest, it begins to run poorly.

These three cornerstones are critical to any training plan that a coach or an athlete may use. If an athlete trains consistently at a moderate level while getting enough rest, his or her performance should continue to improve for years. The principles of the training system described in this book are built around these cornerstones.

The Principles of Training

Training is based on a set of principles, fact-based beliefs that are followed in deciding how the athlete's training should be carried out. These basic principles set the tone for the whole program. Developed over a period of years, each principle plays an important part in helping to plan an effective program. No set of principles is sacred in training, but the following discussion covers the principles adhered to in the Oregon System (Table 1.1).

Table 1.1 Foundations of Training

The Three Cornerstones of Training
- Moderation
- Consistency
- Rest

The Principles of Training

Principle 1: Each person is an individual
Principle 2: Set reasonable (but challenging) goals
Principle 3: Have a master plan
Principle 4: Base the plan on event-specific abilities
Principle 5: Be flexible in the plan
Principle 6: Develop good mechanics
Principle 7: Variety is the spice of life
Principle 8: Follow the hard-easy approach
Principle 9: It is better to undertrain than to overtrain
Principle 10: Observe the rules of good nutrition
Principle 11: Use recreation for the "whole" person
Principle 12: Get enough rest

The Overriding Principle: **Make It Fun**

Principle 1: Each Person Is an Individual

The entire training program is built on this principle. Though all people have common structural and physiological characteristics, each has his or her own particular talents, strengths, and weaknesses. In planning the program, take advantage of and develop the strengths, even as you strive to strengthen the weak areas. The program should meet the athlete's personal, specific needs. For this reason, never simply copy another person's training: The strengths and needs may not be the same; what is good for one person may not be appropriate for others. Therefore, find what makes that person's program successful, then decide whether such factors might work well within your own program.

Principle 2: Set Reasonable (but Challenging) Goals

To get anywhere, you must know where you are going. Goals should be a challenge, for life is a process of rising to meet challenges. At the same time, goals need to be reasonably attainable. An athlete's goals should be based on what the athlete can do now (or has done recently). If the athlete's best mile is 5:00, a goal of 4:00 or even 4:30 is not reasonable. A goal such as breaking 4:50 is still a challenge, but it is one that a good training program may deliver. A person moves by steps, not by leaps. The purpose of setting reasonable goals is to help lead the athlete in a gradual progression toward larger goals. We need goals that challenge the athlete but are not discouraging because they are too extreme.

Principle 3: Have a Master Plan

Every athlete needs a master plan. The plan sets goals and shows how the athlete will progress toward them. A master plan looks at the total picture and takes the long view. For a young or beginning athlete, the plan may simply be for a season or a year. For a more experienced athlete, the plan should set broad goals for several years. Where does the athlete want to be next year and the year after that? A master plan is the competitive road map; it shows where the athlete is going and how to get there.

Principle 4: Base the Plan on Event-Specific Abilities

For an athlete to be better in any event, the physical traits that are specific to that event must be developed. One of the components of a good periodized training program is the development of a model of the event. Coaches and scientists try to determine what measurable physiological and psychological traits are found in elite performances in each event. Training is planned to develop those traits. The model is improved each year, and the training plan is modified to conform to the performance model. For example, if the anaerobic component is extremely important to success in a running event, the plan should empha-

size training of that type. The athlete should be trained very specifically for the event.

Principle 5: Be Flexible in the Plan

We cannot control nature, nor can a training plan result in a perfect progression mapped across a sheet of graph paper. The master plan must be flexible enough that it can be adapted to changing conditions or needs. Unusual weather may affect training or force a temporary change in the training site. The master plan must be able to meet changing circumstances, just as the athlete must prepare for changing situations in competition. This is why athletes need to learn to be independent, for in major meets they are not allowed to communicate with their coaches.

Principle 6: Develop Good Mechanics

Good performance mechanics should be developed early in an athlete's career. For an athlete, good mechanics means easier, more effective training and competing. The time spent in perfecting the performance mechanics will be repaid again and again in competition. A noticeable characteristic of the world-class athlete is a high level of technical skill.

Principle 7: Variety Is the Spice of Life

A good training plan uses a variety of training methods. The more predictable the training program is, the duller it will be. This trait leads to staleness in the athlete because it lessens the challenge of training. This is one reason that the Oregon System developed as an eclectic training system, one that took its methods from several different systems. The more variety a training program has, the more challenging and interesting the training will be for the athlete.

Principle 8: Follow the Hard-Easy Approach

A day of hard training should be followed by a day of easy or recovery training. Though the Oregon System has used this method for decades, East German research has proven its worth only recently. Using daily blood tests on their athletes to determine how they responded to training (when they should train hard and when they needed rest), the Germans also came up with a hard-easy pattern, with light training on every other day, for most athletes. The body needs about 48 hours for full recovery from very hard exercise. To stress this idea, we use Arthur Lydiard's watchword for joggers: Train, don't strain. Moderation requires recovery periods.

Principle 9: It Is Better to Undertrain Than to Overtrain

Because moderation is needed, every athlete must avoid the temptation to train ever harder. Human nature tells us that if so much work results in so much progress, twice as much work should yield twice the progress. However, human nature neglects mentioning that the athlete may break down under the increased training load.

The use of very heavy training leads to effects of the law of diminishing returns. As the work load continues to rise, the results begin to flatten out, eventually giving worse results for the increased loads. The results of overtraining are staleness, fatigue, and a loss of interest in training or competing.

Principle 10: Observe the Rules of Good Nutrition

Proper energy intake is very important to successful sport. The term *good nutrition* (rather than *diet*) is used deliberately because strange or fad diets need to be discouraged. A normal, well-balanced eating plan will meet most athletes' nutritional needs for successful competition. The only real difference is in quantity, rather than in magic foods. At the same time, the idea of dieting should be discouraged, especially with female athletes. Women distance runners too often are encouraged to maintain very low body weights, which is unhealthy. Most athletes who train intelligently and eat sensibly gradually reach a reasonable competition weight. An athlete who is overweight may have unaddressed problems that are not physical.

Principle 11: Use Recreation for the "Whole" Person

Every athlete needs to develop a balanced approach to life to learn to enjoy it more fully. Recreation specialists like to use the term *re-creation*, for recreation helps rebuild us after the stresses of life take their toll. Recreation is not simply killing time, nor does it necessarily mean doing "useful" work. Everyone needs time spent in escaping the routine pattern of life, adding variety to life. The key is enjoying the gift of life. An athlete who has no dimensions other than being an athlete and student or worker misses much of the interest of life. An athlete should be a whole person.

Principle 12: Get Enough Rest

Rest is one of the most neglected needs of less successful or younger athletes. For an athlete in doubt, rest will probably be more useful than an extra workout. Although many experienced athletes train twice a day, younger athletes need to approach this practice with caution. Students often keep late hours while studying. The extra sleep in the morning (to ensure adequate rest) may be more useful than an extra training session. Younger athletes need more rest than older athletes. The athlete should never neglect rest because, like oxygen debt, such neglect always catches up with the body.

The Overriding Principle: Make It Fun

People develop an interest in sport because it is fun. The coach should strive to make training and competition fun, regardless of the athlete's level of ability. Even very hard training can be enjoyable if it is not monotonous or an unattainable challenge. By making the sport fun, the coach helps the athlete maintain an appetite for training and competing. Maintain that appetite, and the athlete will continue to train and improve.

CHAPTER 2	# The Basics
	## of Sport Training
	## and Conditioning

Though a great coach is always an artist in arranging a training system, the sport sciences are the underlying foundation of any successful training program. An overview of training science basics is the best starting point for every coach who wants to be a success.

The Physiological Laws of Training

All training systems are affected by three physiological laws:[1]

- Law of overload
- Law of specificity
- Law of reversibility

Law of Overload

Any improvement in fitness requires an increased training load. That load is a stimulus to which the athlete's body reacts. If the load is greater than normal, the body becomes fatigued and its fitness level falls. As the body recovers, though, its fitness level returns to normal. If the training load is optimal, the athlete will be more fit after recovery (overcompensation) than before the load was applied (Figure 2.1).

Overcompensation is the central purpose of training. The coach plans a training load that produces a fitness increase after the athlete recovers. If the training load is too small, the training effect is less. If the load is too great, the athlete will not even rise to the original fitness level. Because each athlete reacts differently to training stimuli, training must be planned in terms of the individual's abilities, needs, and potential.

The most effective training develops a base of general skills and fitness before developing the more specialized skills of each event. This is the major goal of the early part of the training year. The more balanced the body's early development is, the higher the performance levels it can attain later. This fact should be the major focus in training children and junior athletes.

Law of Specificity

The nature of the training load determines the training effect. An athlete needs training methods tailored to the specific demands of the event. The training load becomes specific when it has the proper training ratio (of load to recovery) and structure of loading (of intensity to load).

Intensity is the quality of the training load. Running speed is measured in meters per second (m/sec) or stride rate (s/sec). Strength is measured in pounds, kilograms, or tonnage moved. Jumps and throws are measured by height, distance, or number of efforts. The heart rate is a good guide for endurance running. The intensity of the effort is based on the percentage of the athlete's best effort (Table 2.1 and Figure 2.2).

The *extent* of the training load is the sum of training in terms of time, distance, accumulative weight,

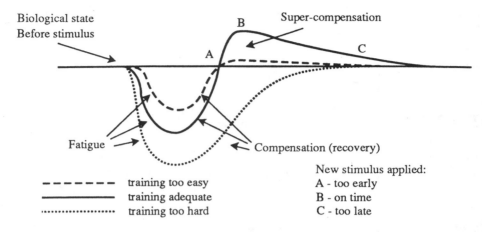

Figure 2.1   Effective and ineffective training loads. From "Planning the Training Schedule" by B. Klavora, 1980, Coaching Association of Canada: Bridging the Gap Unit, package 7, item 3, pp. 1-14. Adapted with permission.

Table 2.1   Estimating the Intensity of Effort

Intensity	Work (% of max)	Strength (% of max)	Heart rate* (BPM)	Endurance (%$\dot{V}O_2$max)
Maximum	95-100	90-100	190+	100
Submaximum	85-95	80-90	180-190	90
High	75-85		165	75
Medium	65-77	70-80	150	60
Light	50-65	50-70		
Low	30-50	30-50	130	50

*Heart rate should be based on a percentage of the athlete's maximum heart rate, which varies considerably among individuals.

From William H. Freeman. (1988). *Peak when it counts: Periodization for the American coach* (p. 10). Los Altos, CA: Tafnews. Reprinted with permission.

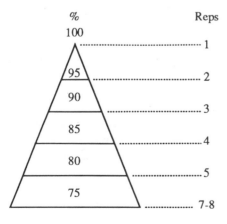

Figure 2.2   Intensity of effort for strength. From William H. Freeman. (1988). *Peak when it counts: Periodization for the American coach* (p. 10). Los Altos, CA: Tafnews. Adapted with permission.

or other measures, while the *duration* is that part of the load that is devoted to a single unit or type of training. An athlete may run for 75 minutes (extent) yet elevate the heart rate over 150 beats per minute (BPM) for only 10 minutes (duration) of that time.

Specialization refers to training exercises that develop the capacities and techniques needed for a specific activity or event. A thrower needs strength in specific areas of the body, while more specific motor skills are needed for each different throwing event. A runner needs speed and endurance, but their ratio depends on the length of the race. A runner must develop a technique that is most efficient for the racing distance. All of these traits are developed by using specialized training. Elite training gradually changes the emphasis from general to specific training as the athlete ages.

Modeling is developing a model of the competitive event. This model is then used to develop a training pattern that simulates the competitive requirements of the event. Many years are needed to develop and perfect the model. It begins with the coach's analysis of the competitive event, but afterward the emphasis is upon trial and error refinement of the model.

Law of Reversibility

The training effect can reverse itself. If the training does not become more challenging, the fitness level plateaus (flattens out). If the training ends, the fitness level gradually falls. In fact, the training load must continue to increase if the athlete's general and specific fitness are to improve. If the training load remains at the same level, the fitness rises for a time, then begins to fall. The training load must increase regularly (*progressive overload*) for the performance level to improve (Figure 2.3), though the load may rise and fall (allowing recovery and compensation) across a given period of time. The training ratio (of load to recovery) is critical. The coach must determine how much recovery is needed within a session and between sessions.

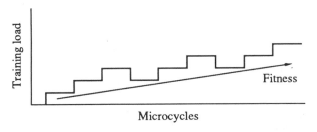

Figure 2.3 Progressive overload. From William H. Freeman. (1988). *Peak when it counts: Periodization for the American coach* (p. 11). Los Altos, CA: Tafnews. Adapted with permission.

At the same time, the planned training load must be *realistic*. The demand should not exceed the athlete's capabilities or rise too quickly, or it may be psychologically (and perhaps physically) destructive to the athlete's progress. The object of training is improvement, not discouragement or defeat.

Restoration is recovery from a high training load. Restoration is just as critical to the training effect as the training load itself. If too little restoration is allowed, the athlete will gradually lose fitness.

Active rest is a form of restoration (also used in the transition phase) that includes light physical activity. It may be jogging, or it may be participating in other sports. It allows the athlete to recover, yet it helps maintain a base of general fitness.

The Components of Sports Fitness

Sports fitness has four basic components:

- Endurance
- Strength
- Flexibility
- Speed

Endurance

Endurance must be developed first, for without it most other types of training cannot be repeated enough to develop the other components of fitness. The amount of this emphasis depends on the event, with the short races and field events requiring considerably less endurance than the longer runs. Too much endurance training can hamper performance in some events.

Endurance can be aerobic or muscular. The most common method of developing aerobic endurance is with steady-state running for a length of time on a regular basis. It should be fast enough to raise the pulse to the 130- to 150-BPM range and should be maintained for at least 20 to 30 minutes. Muscular endurance is developed by many repetitions of low-resistance exercises. Circuit training can be used to combine the two types of endurance. Endurance training should not overwhelm the need for specific speed.

Strength

Strength can be whole-body strength, as in general conditioning, and specific strength, most effective within the range of motion of a given event. Strength is critical to every track and field event for both men and women. The level of strength has a positive effect on both speed and endurance.

Flexibility

Sometimes called "mobility," flexibility determines the body's range of motion. The stretching exercises of the warm-up are designed to improve the athlete's flexibility. Because strength training results in shortening of the muscles, flexibility work is needed to keep the muscles loose through their full range of motion. The ability to hold stretched positions permits higher levels of performance, so stretching is a critical part of the training program.

Speed

Speed is critical to elite performance in every event. A thrower must be very quick, and even male marathoners at the world-class level can usually run a mile in about 4:00. While speed comes from the contractile quality of the muscles, the efficiency of movement comes from specific training, leading to improved speed. Though the basic quality of speed (reaction time) is largely inherited, it can be improved through training.

Types of Running Training

All types of running training are used to some degree in any training program, depending upon the athlete's needs. The basic types of running training are

- overdistance training,
- interval training,
- repetition running,
- fartlek,
- sprint training, and
- time trials.

Overdistance Training

Overdistance training is the essential element in the development of the endurance base. Coaches and athletes are learning that the intensity of training is more important than mileage. The heavy training loads of the 1960s and 1970s declined during the 1980s. During the 1990s a typical training load for a world-class runner at 10,000m and the marathon may be 80 to 90 miles per week, with considerably smaller loads for less experienced athletes.

Today overdistance runs are becoming shorter and more intense. Runners use *tempo running*, shorter runs at a pace that causes an optimal pulse reading for a length of time, rather than "grinding out the miles" on long, slow runs. The training effect is much greater.

Interval Training

Interval training means running short distances (intervals), usually on a track. Interval training has five variables:

- Length of the interval
- Speed or intensity of the interval
- Number of intervals
- Length of the recovery
- Nature of the recovery

Though interval training traditionally involves distances and times for those distances (such as 300m in 45 seconds), the work may be in terms of running set lengths of time at a given pulse rate or intensity

level (such as 30 seconds at 170 to 180 BPM). The length of the work interval depends on the type of physiological improvement needed. The energy reserve of the muscles comes from ATP (adenosine triphosphate). It is produced by three pathways:

- ATP-PC (phosphocreatine) system
- Lactic acid (LA) system
- Oxygen (O_2) system

The ATP-PC and LA systems are anaerobic, working with little or no oxygen, while quickly producing ATP for a short time. The O_2 system is aerobic (using oxygen) and produces ATP for a longer period of time. The choice of the interval depends upon the length of the race (Table 2.2).

Table 2.2   Racing Time and Energy Systems for Training

Race length	Major energy system	Race distance
Under 30 sec	ATP-PC	100m, 200m, high hurdles
30-90 sec	ATP-PC, LA	200m, 400m, intermediates
1:30-3:00	LA, O_2	800m
More than 3:00	O_2	1,500m and longer

From Edward L. Fox and Donald K. Mathews (1974). *Interval training* (p. 35). Philadelphia: Saunders.

Repetition Running

Repetition running is a more intensive version of interval training. The intervals are run at a faster pace, with a nearly complete recovery between repetitions. Some coaches define intervals and repetitions according to their training emphasis: An interval focuses on the stress created by the pace and short recovery, while a repetition focuses on the pace itself, thus allowing a fuller recovery. In some training systems, repetitions are longer intervals, such as 800 meters or more.

Fartlek

Fartlek (speed play) is a less formal version of interval training that is especially suited to training away from the track. It mixes bursts of faster paced intervals of work with slower running within the context of a longer run on trails or a golf course. The length and the intensity of the faster runs are decided by the runner, depending upon what he or she needs and feels at the time. For more speed, shorter and faster bursts are used, whereas longer and less intense intervals are used for more endurance. Ideally, the training takes place on relatively soft surfaces, such as grass or sawdust trails.

Fartlek is a valuable training method because it allows a wide range of intensities, while also helping prevent the stress injuries that can come from training on pavement or running tracks. At the same time, it gives a more relaxing psychological setting and a chance to avoid the monotony of the track. It is more difficult for less experienced athletes, however, because they tend to turn it into a long, easy run with a few short accelerations. It has to be carefully taught to young runners. The use of pulse monitors allows structured fartlek, a highly controlled training process, by monitoring and limiting the effort and recovery levels.

Sprint Training

Sprint training involves very short bursts of very fast running used primarily to improve the athlete's speed. It is also used for technique training. The recovery interval is almost complete, much like a short form of repetition running. Only a small number of repetitions are used because fatigue changes the nature of the training. For distance runners this is used in the final stages of sharpening or peaking.

Time Trials

Time trials are mentioned because they are an easily abused aspect of the training program. Time trials have two functions: assessing progress and simulating competition. They should be conducted under meet conditions, more formal than a training session. They should be held no more often than 2 to 3 weeks apart, or they become meaningless. Unless a trial serves a specific training function, it should not be used, because it reduces the number of effective training days. Frequent time trials are a sign of insecurity: The coach wants reassurance that the training system is working.

Strength-Development Programs

The order of strength-training exercises is critical in two respects. First, the larger muscle groups should be exercised before the smaller ones. Otherwise, overloading the large muscles is difficult because the smaller muscle groups tire more quickly. Second, no two exercises should train the same group of muscles consecutively, for the muscles will have too little recovery time.

The principle of specificity is extremely important. Strength development is specific to both the muscle group exercised and the pattern of movement used. You should duplicate the event movement pattern as closely as possible in the strength-training program. This specificity includes the joint angle at which the muscle is exercised and the type of contraction performed. This affects isometric training the most because the major strength gain in isometrics is only at the angle used in exercising the muscle.

Resistance-Training Procedures

Exercises are measured in repetitions (reps), usually divided into larger groups called sets. One set is a number of reps performed without interruption. Three sets of five reps (3×5) means to repeat the exercise five times without stopping, take a recovery rest, perform the exercise five more times, take a rest, then perform the exercise for a final five times, completing the three sets.

Resistance exercises are generally used three times a week, on alternating days to permit the muscles to recover. Strength specialists may train every day, but the muscle groups are divided so that no muscle group is trained on consecutive days. During the early competitive season, strength work drops to 2 days per week, then to once a week as the season nears its peak. At that stage the emphasis is on maintenance of strength. Improved technique makes up for any loss of strength. If strength training stops when the season begins, much of the strength gain will be lost before the end of the season.

Intensity is also a factor in strength activities. To lessen fatigue and improve efficiency, active rest is useful between lifts at higher intensities. This involves light or nonlifting movements directed toward other parts of the body after an intense exercise is completed.

Every athlete encounters "sticking points," performance plateaus that the athlete cannot easily pass. These can result from both overtraining and undertraining. Often a change in the workout load helps. Other causes may be poor diet or physical or mental fatigue (often called "staleness").

Starting weights are largely a matter of opinion and personal feeling. The coach or athlete should check the more scientifically oriented strength-training books. Starting weights may be based on a percentage of either the athlete's body weight or his or her best performance in each exercise. Strength training emphasizes either body development (hypertrophy) or strength, depending upon the weight and number of repetitions of an exercise (Table 2.3).

Table 2.3   Weight Training Load and Emphasis

Load	Percentage of maximum	Number of repetitions	Training emphasis
Heavy	90	1-3	Strength
Medium	80	5-6	Muscular endurance
Light	70	8-12	Muscular endurance

A General Weight-Training Program

We prefer not to suggest specific strength-training programs at this point, but rather suggest that it's better for coaches and athletes to develop their own programs. A number of publications are available that deal primarily with such programs, and we refer readers to the Additional Readings at the end of this chapter. A few recommended texts include Fox and O'Shea. In general as athletes become more experienced, they will learn which exercises are most helpful for their own events.

Plyometrics

Plyometrics (jump training) is used to develop leg strength and resilience for explosive power. The most common forms of training are with multiple jumps (on one or both legs) on the ground and with jumps using boxes of varying heights. The training involves work with the muscles' stretch reflex. There is a high injury risk if too many jumps are attempted, so caution is important.

Circuit Training

Circuit training uses a series of resistance exercises and calisthenics that follow a sequence, usually within an indoor area. The athlete moves quickly from one exercise station to the next, performing each exercise within a time limit. The circuit is finished when the performer completes the sequence. This approach is good for physical conditioning in limited areas, when bad weather conditions force athletes indoors, and for group exercises (athletes start at different stations, then move to the next station on a signal).

The parcourse is an outdoor version of circuit training, an exercise trail laid around a park or wooded area, with jogging or running between the stations. One Olympic 800m champion used a similar course for his base conditioning, with a 10-station circuit at 100m intervals around a kilometer sawdust loop.[2]

Concerns in Training and Conditioning

Sex Differences in Sport Training

The training for both sexes is largely the same, differing primarily in terms of the loading. Until puberty, boys and girls have essentially the same abilities and capacities. During puberty, the differences are as great within a single sex as between the sexes. From about ages 10 to 16, students show widely varying body sizes, strength, and levels of coordination, depending upon when a child goes through puberty and how quickly it happens. At this time (about the 5th through 10th grades), a teacher or coach needs to be as careful with single-sex classes as with a mixed class. However, both sexes can work at the same relative intensity.

After physical maturity (about age 18), several differences between the sexes affect physical capacity and performance. The typical male has about 12 to 15% body fat, compared to 26% for females. Women have more difficulty in reaching higher levels of performance because the additional body fat is "drag weight;" that is, it limits performance.

Body fat levels may be very low in elite distance runners (2 to 6% in men and 6 to 15% in women). Menstrual irregularities may occur when a woman drops below 15% body fat, though recent research suggests training intensity or stress causes this effect.[3] We do not yet know whether this effect is harmful.

Women are more likely than men to suffer from anemia (iron deficiency). Heavy training increases this deficiency, so women in training may need iron supplements, though supplements should not be taken without medical consultation.[4] Women's performances at different times in the menstrual cycle may vary, but the effect is highly individualized. Olympic medals have been won at all stages of the cycle.

Another major difference is the higher proportion of muscle tissue in men (about 60%) compared to women (about 40%). Because male hormones are a major factor in the development of muscular strength, women do not have the same potential for strength development that men have. Also, because of female hormones, it is very difficult for women to develop the "bulky" muscles associated with male athletes.[5] However, though a woman athlete can become much stronger through training, even heavy weight training will not result in a "masculine-looking" woman. Women are both shorter and lighter than men, which has many effects in terms of biomechanics and potential power.

Although coaches are aware that some athletes may take steroids to help increase their strength, they should not forget a common hormonal treatment used by many women: birth control pills. Younger women may be placed on the Pill by a physician to control menstrual disorders. Among the Pill's effects are an increase in weight. Nausea may be a side effect when treatment starts, so the coach should be cautious in any interpretation of physical problems. However, never assume that any athlete's problem is only in the head.

Remember that the differences between the sexes are based on averages. An elite female athlete may be more capable than the average male athlete. Both women and men can benefit from intensive training programs; their capacities to endure such training are essentially the same. Some male coaches suggest that female athletes are less likely than men to complain about heavier training loads.

Men and women who perform at the same level can be trained together, for their abilities are essentially the same. Coed teams have many benefits; the men's and women's teams may be very supportive of each other, particularly if they are coached and trained together.

Warm-Up: Prelude to Exercise

A careful warm-up raises the body and muscle temperatures, which increases their working effectiveness. A warm-up stretches the muscles, which helps prevent injury. It should not be done to the point of fatigue, however. Because long-distance runners use a more limited range of motion than athletes in other events, they often do minimal warming up.

The athlete should wear a sweatsuit to promote the warming effect. Rubber suits should *never* be used because they prevent normal evaporation of sweat. This raises the body temperature and can result in heat exhaustion or heart attacks (even in teenagers) in some situations.

A warm-up begins with a short, light jog, just long enough to raise the muscle temperature. Then stretching exercises are used, beginning with light, gradual stretching and progressing over 10 to 20 minutes to more thorough exercises. All of the major muscle groups should be stretched. No sudden movements (such as bouncing or jerking) should be used, so the muscles are never strongly forced to stretch. The progress should be gentle and gradual. Brief calisthenics may follow stretching. The athlete should be warm and sweating after the warm-up but not tired.

The closing part of the warm-up should be event-specific. All runners do a bit of running, with a few short bursts of faster runs. Sprinters take a few easy-to medium-effort starts, while hurdlers begin to work with lower hurdles. Throwers simulate parts of their throwing routine.

Warm-Up Exercises

Stretching improves performance because loose muscles perform more easily and are less prone to injury. Relaxation is a part of stretching. No sudden pulling or yanking motions should be used. Be careful of pairing athletes for stretching; there should be no fast moves or forcing of stretching. Lasting injuries may result from sudden stretching. The final stretched position should be held for 20 to 30 seconds, keeping in mind that it is a *relaxed* extension of the muscles, not a forced one. Edward L. Fox, Richard W. Bowers, and Merle L. Foss suggest 10 stretching exercises for class instruction and team training (Table 2.4).[6]

Table 2.4 Warm-Up Stretching Routine

1. Achilles tendon and gastrocnemius
2. Back
3. Hamstring
4. Groin
5. Spine and waistline
6. Quadriceps
7. Shoulder and chest
8. Ankle
9. Abdominal
10. Hip

Some calisthenics are also useful as warm-up and conditioning exercises. They should not be used too much because younger athletes quickly become bored with them. The following are suggested exercises for specific body areas:[7]

Shoulders and groin: jumping jacks

Ankles, toes, and gastrocnemius: toe raises and running in place

Quadriceps: half-squats (no weights)

Shoulders, arms, and chest: push-ups

Abdominals: bent-knee sit-ups and bent-knee leg-raises

Straight-leg sit-ups and leg-raises should not be used because they create back strain rather than help develop the abdominals.

Special Environments

Much of the American training year involves dealing with weather that interferes with training. The most common concerns are heat and cold.

Heat.   Much of the general or base training occurs during the hot summer months and is unsupervised. Only a few places in the United States do not have some problems of extremes in heat and humidity. In many heat conditions, the athlete's sweat does not evaporate quickly enough, which limits the ability to cool the body and may result in heat stress.

Heat alone, common in the Southwest, can be dangerous; combined with high humidity, as in the Midwest, East, and South, it can be deadly. If the humidity is high, heat stress can appear in athletes before the temperature reaches 70 °F (22 °C). Even with low humidity, temperatures above 80 °F (27 °C) can create the risk of stress. Symptoms of heat stress include headaches, dizziness, sudden tiring or weakness, a pounding sensation in the head, tingling or goosebump sensations across the body, or the cessation of sweating.

The five levels of heat effects are cramps, syncope, exhaustion (water depletion), exhaustion (salt depletion), and stroke. Muscle cramps result from excessive loss of salt through sweating. Taking salt tablets may increase the problem unless enough fluid is taken at the same time. In most cases, an athlete can eat enough salt with meals to avoid this problem.[8]

Heat exhaustion causes collapse or fainting as the body tries to end the work that is causing stress. It results from severe loss of fluids, salts, or electrolytes that the body uses to assist in cooling itself.

Heatstroke is most noticeable when sweating stops. Failure to cool the body quickly may result in brain damage, coma, or even death. Although it does not commonly happen, runners die every year from heat stress, usually because proper caution is not taken.

Sweating is the body's way of coping with heat and humidity. The humidity is important because the higher the level of water in the air, the less sweat that evaporates from the athlete. The evaporation does the actual cooling, not the act of sweating. The athlete must stay aware of these two concerns:

- Is my sweat evaporating?
- Am I getting enough fluids?

In warm or humid training conditions, fluid intake is extremely important. The best, most easily, and most quickly absorbed fluid is water. Waiting until the training session is completed to drink fluids is extremely dangerous and does not help an athlete adapt to heat.

Adapting to heat is done best under natural conditions. To be able to race in heat, an athlete must train in heat. An athlete can train harder and longer, and run faster, in cooler conditions. However, if an important race will be run in hot or humid conditions, the athlete needs to train under those conditions. Adapting to heat takes about 10 to 14 days. The most useful training is to take longer, easier runs, being careful to drink enough fluids. However, as much as 50% of the body's adaptation to heat may come from the heat generated by interval training, regardless of the climate.

Cold.   Cold weather creates its own training problems. Athletes must dress carefully for protection. Modern fabrics and layering allow less bulky training dress than in the past.

The most vulnerable parts of the body are the extremities. Thermal socks or layers of socks are needed for the feet, just as gloves are used for the hands. The material should absorb sweat so the body can cool itself properly within the warm bundles of protective gear (an athlete can suffer from heat exhaustion even in very cold weather). A cap that can cover the ears, or added earmuffs, helps protect the head. In extreme climates, an athlete may wear a ski mask to protect the face from frostbite.

A sunny, cold day or a windy day can create special problems. A warmly-dressed runner may overheat if the sun is out and the air is calm. The same effect is possible with a strong tailwind. On windy, cold days, an out-and-back run is best. The athlete is dressed to begin facing the wind, removing clothing while returning with the wind. If the process were reversed, the athlete would overheat early, then chill and tire rapidly when running into the wind.

Athletes should be aware of the effects of the windchill factor: A strong wind in cool conditions may create far harsher conditions than expected. Cold is as deadly as heat, and strong winds heighten the effect. Insisting on an outdoor run regardless of the weather conditions is not a virtue. It may be far wiser to skip a session or train indoors than to risk injury or worse. The smart coach and athlete always consider the possible effects of weather conditions on training and racing.

Sport Psychology and Motivation

Sport psychology is critical to the preparation of elite athletes. Psychology is used for more than just motivation. As Thomas Tutko noted, "On the whole, the psyching-up idea is more part of the problem than a solution"[9] because often it simply increases the athlete's anxieties, reducing performance effectiveness. Performers simply try *too* hard.

Richard M. Suinn's training book for athletes recommends a seven-step program of mental training to prepare athletes for competition[10]:

1. Relaxation training
2. Stress management
3. Positive thought control
4. Self-regulation
5. Mental rehearsal (visual motor behavior rehearsal)
6. Concentration
7. Energy control

The focus is upon learning to control one's emotions and channel them, dealing constructively with stress and maintaining a positive focus on training. The old concept of *psyching up* acted more as sensory overkill, putting some athletes almost out of control. Elite performance requires very calm, deliberate control of one's energy and skills, while a heated, emotional approach provides an unstable platform for performance. Thus, much of the focus of sport psychology is on relaxation, or stress and tension control.

The other aspect is the accent on the positive. The old coaching approach was to criticize and pressure athletes, forcing them to improve. It was similar to the old Theory X in business, the idea that people were inherently lazy and unwilling to perform unless threatened and forced to do well. The emphasis on the positive skips past Theory Y (people do want to perform well) to Theory Z, a cooperative approach to training and performance.[11] The coach tries to reinforce the positive aspects of training, encouraging and supporting the athletes as they proceed. Confident athletes perform far better than insecure ones.

The coach should evaluate athletes' performances objectively but should conclude with and emphasize the positive. Encourage the athletes and show them how they are progressing. An athlete who faces constant criticism will eventually quit and will leave with a poor self-image. Every performance has some positive aspects. The coach who encourages the athletes will generally be the most successful coach in the long run.

The Goal: Consistency in Training

Ultimately, the most successful training program is the one that is most consistent. Athletes must train for weeks, months, and years at a consistent, moderate level. This stability creates a solid foundation for future success. The athletes are not forced up and down the emotional scale by extreme psyching or negative criticism. They are not put through destructively hard

training sessions as "character-builders." Instead they are brought along with a carefully designed, positively oriented program that gives them emotional support, encouragement, and pride at every step along the way. This is what good training is all about; it is the heart of sport for life.

References

1. William H. Freeman. (1989). *Peak when it counts: Periodization for the American coach* (pp. 9-13). Los Altos, CA: Tafnews.
2. Bill Dellinger & Bill Freeman. (1984). *The competitive runner's training book* (pp. 49-55). New York: Collier.
3. Edward L. Fox, Richard W. Bowers, & Merle L. Foss. (1989). *The physiological basis of physical education and athletics* (pp. 401-402). Dubuque, IA: Wm. C. Brown.
4. Ibid., pp. 393-394.
5. Ibid., p. 405.
6. Ibid., pp. 190-193.
7. Ibid., p. 299.
8. Ibid., pp. 492-493, 499.
9. Thomas Tutko & Umberto Tosi. (1976). *Sports psyching* (p. 11). Los Angeles: J.P. Tarcher.
10. Richard M. Suinn. (1986). *Seven steps to peak performance: The mental training manual for athletes*. Toronto: Hans Huber.
11. William G. Ouchi. (1981). *Theory Z: How American business can meet the Japanese challenge* (pp. 48-49, 58-59). Reading, MA: Addison-Wesley.

Additional Readings

Barr, Susan I. (1988). Athletic performance and nutrition. *Track Technique*, **105**, 3353-3354, 3364.

Brook, Norman. (1986). *Mobility training*. London: British Amateur Athletic Board.

Carlisle, Bob. (1987). Quality of preparation and performance: The significance of "R and R." *New Studies in Athletics*, **2**(3), 49-55.

Coleman, Ellen. (1988). *Eating for endurance*. Palo Alto, CA: Bull.

Costill, David L. (1986). *Inside running: Basics of sports physiology*. Indianapolis: Benchmark Press.

Dare, Bernie. (1979). *Running and your body*. Los Altos, CA: Tafnews.

Dyson, Geoffrey, Woods, B.D., & Travers, Peter R. (1986). *Dyson's mechanics of athletics* (8th ed.). New York: Holmes & Meier.

Ecker, Tom. (1985). *Basic track and field biomechanics*. Los Altos, CA: Tafnews.

Elliot, Rich. (1984). *The competitive edge: Mental preparation for distance running*. Englewood Cliffs, NJ: Prentice-Hall.

Fox, Edward L. (1984). *Sports physiology* (2nd ed., pp. 123-124). Philadelphia: Saunders.

Haymes, Emily M., & Wells, Christine L. (1986). *Environment and human performance*. Champaign, IL: Human Kinetics.

Horrigan, Joseph, & Shaw, David. (1989). Plyometrics: Think before you leap. *Track and Field Quarterly Review*, **89**(4), 41-43.

Kubistant, Tom. (1987). *Performing your best*. Champaign, IL: Human Kinetics.

Lundin, Phil. (1987). Plyometric training loads for youths and beginners. *Track Technique*, **101**, 3211-3213, 3218.

Martens, Rainer. (1987). *Coaches guide to sport psychology*. Champaign, IL: Human Kinetics.

Moody, Jim. (1981). Incorporating Olympic lift training into a weight program for high school track and field athletes. *Track and Field Quarterly Review*, **81**(1), 57-62.

Nideffer, Bob. (1985). *Athlete's guide to mental training*. Champaign, IL: Human Kinetics.

Orlick, Terry. (1986). *Psyching for sport*. Champaign, IL: Leisure Press.

O'Shea, John P. (1976). *Scientific principles and methods of strength fitness* (2nd ed.). Reading, MA: Addison-Wesley.

Radcliffe, James C., & Farentinos, Robert C. (1985). *Plyometrics: Explosive power training* (2nd ed.). Champaign, IL: Human Kinetics.

Roscoe, Dennis. (1988). Principles of strength training. *Track Technique*, **105**, 3361.

Schmidtbleicher, Dietmar. (1987). Applying the theory of strength development. *Track and Field Quarterly Review*, **87**(3), 34-44.

Schmidtbleicher, Dietmar. (1988). Strength training programs. *Track Technique*, **104**, 3330-3331.

Scholich, Manfred. (1986). *Circuit training*. Berlin: Sportverlag.

Shangold, Mona, & Mirkin, Gabe. (1985). *The complete sports medicine book for women*. New York: Simon & Schuster.

Subotnik, Steve. (1986). The ten most common running injuries. *Track and Field Quarterly Review*, **86**(3), 43-45.

Suinn, Richard M. (1986). *Seven steps to peak performance: The mental training manual for athletes*. Toronto: Hans Huber.

Syer, John, & Connolly, Christopher. (1984). *Sporting body, sporting mind: An athlete's guide to mental training*. Cambridge, UK: University Press.

Tenisci, Toni, & Ubel, Ralf. (1985). A Soviet approach to weight training. In Jess Jarver (Ed.), *The throws* (3rd ed., pp. 32-37). Los Altos, CA: Tafnews.

Walker, Moya. (1987). Dietary planning for performance. *New Studies in Athletics*, **2**(1), 73-85.

Wilmore, Jack H., & Costill, David L. (1988). *Training for sport and activity* (3rd ed.). Dubuque, IA: Wm. C. Brown.

Young, Warren. (1988). An evaluation of strength training methods. *Track Technique*, **102**, 3267-3268.

CHAPTER 3	# Designing the
	# Training Program

A major concern for coaches is the process of designing a training program. How do you plan the training year? What factors determine the training emphases? How are training sessions designed? This discussion is adapted from *Peak When It Counts*,[1] a detailed explanation of periodization and how to apply it to the American training year.

Periodization Defined

The term *periodization* simply means dividing the training process into periods of time with different training emphases, goals, and lengths. Each period prepares the athlete for the next, a more advanced training period, until the athlete peaks at the most important competition of the year.

Periodization is an attempt to make training an objective process. It points the training effort toward the major goal. Training is a very complex process, involving both internal and external variables. It is affected by the quantity and quality of training, by rest, and by the competitive experiences of the athlete.

Training graphs show the training emphases at different times during the training year. Periodization tries to quantify training in a meaningful way so you can summarize it in tables and charts. This allows you to see more clearly how the athlete is expected to progress.

An athlete uses periodized training so he or she can

- peak at the ideal moment,
- achieve the optimal training effect from each phase of training, and
- make training a more objective process.

Also, because the training plan produces objective records of training and progress, it can be compared to future training. The coach can objectively measure how much more training is being done in the new year, what types of training are different, and the amount of improvement in the performance characteristics along the way. It gives more objective standards to measure how improvement in the control tests translates into event success.

The Language of Periodization

The training periods in periodization are called *cycles*. A training year contains seven categories of cycles (from the largest unit of time down to the smallest):

1. Macrocycle
2. Mesocycle
3. Period
4. Phase
5. Microcycle
6. Training session
7. Training unit

A training year with a single macrocycle (primary goal or training emphasis) leads to a single peak competition (*single periodization*, Figure 3.1). Although the single training emphasis often is appropriate, many training years include two major competitions or peaks (*double periodization*), such as the indoor and outdoor seasons in American track and field.

Although some distance runners may try for three peaks (cross-country, indoor track, and outdoor track), this is very difficult to achieve against elite competition. Proper preparation for elite competitive efforts requires too much time for an athlete to achieve a true peak three times a year. Most athletes who have been able to perform at that level maintain such a high training load that they cannot really predict a peak; a peak is more a matter of chance.

Triple periodization is more appropriate for explosive technical events (jumps, throws, sprints, and hurdles). Indeed, European athletes commonly divide their long summer season into two mesocycles of competition separated by a mesocycle of transition, regeneration, or modified base training lasting for 2 to 4 weeks.

The Periodization Training Cycle

A *macrocycle* is a complete training cycle, from the start of training to a peak at a major competition, then through the concluding transitional or recovery period. A calendar year consists of one to three macrocycles.

A *mesocycle* is a subdivision of a macrocycle. It means a middle (in length) cycle between the long cycle (macrocycle) and the short cycle (microcycle). The term is not used consistently in the literature. It can include periods and phases but is often used as a subdivision of a phase.

A typical macrocycle includes three *periods*,

- preparation,

- competition, and
- transition or recovery.

Each period is a different training emphasis and load within a macrocycle. A period lasts for 1 to 6 months.

The *preparation* period prepares the athlete for competition. In traditional terms, it includes the preseason training. The second period of the cycle is the *competition* period, including the athlete's competitive season. The meets are chosen to prepare the athlete for the single meet selected as the goal of the season, where the athlete expects to peak.

The third period of the cycle is the *transition* period (sometimes called recuperation or regeneration), a bridge between competition and the start of the next preparation period. It allows the athlete to recover from the physical and psychological stress of competition. This period does not include any event-training activities; it is a time of active rest, designed as much for the psychological change as for the physical recovery.

Each training period consists of one or more *phases*. For example, the preparation period includes two phases. The first phase emphasizes general conditioning, while the second phase emphasizes the special conditioning needed for the event. A phase usually lasts between 2 weeks and 4 months.

Each phase consists of a number of *microcycles* (usually from two to six). A typical microcycle lasts for 1 week, though it can be as long as 3 weeks or as short as 3 days.

A *training session* (also called a *lesson*) is a single workout with a single training focus, such as the afternoon workout at the track. An athlete might have from zero (on a rest day) to three training sessions in a single day.

Each session includes a number of *training units*. A training unit is a single component of the training session. Usually a training session includes between one and five training units.

Macro-cyle						
Periods	Preparation		Competition			Transition
Phases	General 1	Specific 2	Precompetition 3	Comp. 4	Peak 5	Transition 6
Micro-cyles						

Figure 3.1 Single periodization. From William H. Freeman. (1989). *Peak when it counts: Periodization for the American coach* (p. 6). Los Altos, CA: Tafnews. Adapted with permission.

The Types of Periodized Training

Periodized training falls into three categories: general, special, and competition specific. *General training* (basic conditioning) is "training for the general functioning capacity of the athlete. It is the foundation of endurance, strength and mobility through training units. . . . The objective here is to ensure that the athlete will be fit to accept and benefit from special training."[2]

Special training develops the conditioning, traits, and technique that are specific to success in the athlete's event. The terms *special training* and *specific training* can be confusing. Special training uses partial movements involving the technical skills being learned. Specific training involves the whole action.

Competition specific training is "training where technique and conditioning are completely rehearsed by applying the fitness acquired through special training to the event itself."[2] It is done either within competition or with special simulations that are similar to competition.

Planning Periodized Training Programs

Periodized training is planned from the top down, beginning with a period of several years and moving downward to the components of a single training session. Experienced athletes should plan their training from the multiple-year perspective. Younger or less experienced athletes should plan their training for only 1 year at a time because they have less predictable improvement curves. A young athlete may suddenly mature physically, with a sharp rise in performance over a very short time. Also, the early learning and performance curve is steep for athletes in a new event. Major improvements are rare for more experienced, older athletes, so their training needs can be planned farther ahead.

Long-Term Planning

A long-term training plan must consider these four factors:

- Number of years of organized training needed to achieve a high performance level
- Average age when high performance is achieved
- Amount or degree of the athlete's natural ability
- Age that the athlete began specialized training

Long-term training plans change the proportions of general training and specialized training. An effective long-term plan includes the following objective criteria:

1. It relates the performance objectives to factors specific to the sport.
2. It increases the training and competition load in successive training years, assuming that the athlete improves. At the highest stages of development, the number of major competitions should level off; it may even decrease.
3. It forecasts the annual increase of volume and intensity of training according to the event's dominant component and the athlete's needs.
4. It changes the emphasized training exercises yearly.
5. It specifies the control tests and standards to be met.
6. It specifically covers all of the needs of the event.
7. It shows the progression of the number of training lessons and hours per year.

Long-term training requires much careful thought. It requires good training records for the athlete, with the control tests spread carefully across the training year. Well-planned training is measurable, so tables, charts, or graphs of the training progress can be made. The coach should be able to show how much of the training load (time and percentage) was devoted to developing each performance component.

A record sheet can list the objectives for each year in a 4-year (Olympiad) plan. The coach and the athlete work together to develop the long-term plan, though the coach's role is larger with younger athletes (because of their lack of practical experience).

The basic steps in developing the long-term plan are these:

- Set performance goals (the athlete's time, distance, or height) for each year.
- Set the objectives of each type of preparation (physical, technical, tactical, and psychological) for each year.
- Select the control tests that will be used to evaluate the athlete's progress, along with the standards that will show whether the athlete is making satisfactory progress.
- Graph the athlete's training factors (training volume, training intensity, and progress toward peaking) across the bottom of the plan. This gives a condensed version of each year's training plan.

An example of a hypothetical 4-year plan for an 800m runner (Figure 3.2) shows how a 4-year plan is constructed. It lists the objectives planned for each

Club: _____ _____

Athlete: _____

Event: 800m

	OBJECTIVES			
	Year 1	Year 2	Year 3	Year 4
Performance	2:14	2:06	2:01	1:58-1:59
Physical preparation	• Develop general physical preparation • Develop aerobic endurance	• Improve general physical preparation • Develop muscular endurance • Improve aerobic endurance • Develop anaerobic endurance	• Improve specific physical preparation • Improve muscle endurance • Perfect aerobic endurance • Improve anaerobic endurance	• Perfect specific physical preparation • Perfect aerobic endurance • Perfect anaerobic endurance
Technical preparation	• Correct arm carriage • Correct position of head	• Efficient stride length • Minimum vertical bouncing	• Relaxed running • Efficient technical movement	↑ ↑
Tactical preparation	• Steady pace throughout the race	• Fast, alert in the first 400m • Steady pace in the body of the race	• Secure good position before the finish • Perfect the start	• Cope with various strategies • Perfect the finish
Psychological preparation	• Develop mental awareness • Attempt to modify the above	• Develop self-concept	• Identify anxieties and stressors and how to handle them • Relaxation techniques	↑
Tests and standards	100m = 12.4 400m = 57.0 1500m = 4:22 VO$_2$max = 3.08L	12.0 55.5 4:16 3.7L	11.7 53.0 4:09 4.1L	11.5 51.5 4:04 4.5L

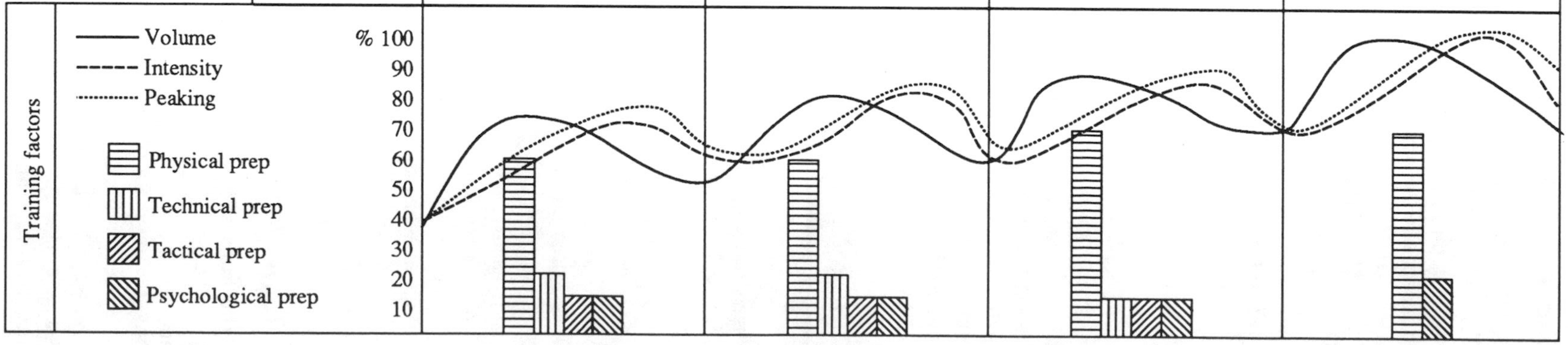

Training factors

% 100 90 80 70 60 50 40 30 20 10

——— Volume
– – – Intensity
········· Peaking
▥ Physical prep
▤ Technical prep
▨ Tactical prep
▩ Psychological prep

Figure 3.2 Hypothetical four-year training plan for 800m runner. From Tudor O. Bompa: *Theory and methodology of training*. Copyright © 1983 by Kendall/Hunt Publishing Company. Adapted with permission.

year, with the performance goals, the tests and standards, and a rough graph of the training progress and periods of training over the 4-year period.

Annual Planning

Planning the competitions. You can design a rough pattern for the year by fixing the date (or dates) when the athlete must peak, then developing a training curve similar to that in Figure 3.3. The entire year's program is simply a process of preparing for that peak. It is a cycle of training, competition, and regeneration (recovery). Meets are classified into two groups, the main competitions and the preparatory meets.

Concern about win-loss records may be a factor in the process, so no meet that is important this way should be scheduled for the last 2 or 3 weeks before the season's main competition; the effort affects the season's final preparation. Preparatory meets are tests to assess the athlete's progress. The coach should include meets that create the same meet conditions (time schedules, level of competition) and meets at the same facility (track) or course (cross country, road racing). At those meets, the primary goal is to adjust to the environment for the sake of future success rather than to win at that time.

The number of competitions is critical because the athlete should peak at the proper time rather than compete too often and lose fitness. Table 3.1 suggests the number of meets per year by event.

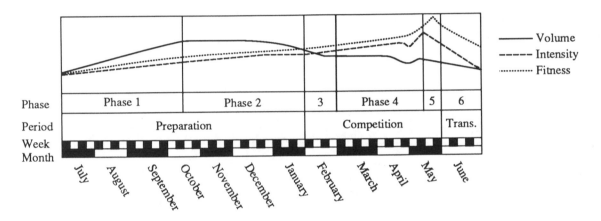

Figure 3.3 Hypothetical training curve for one year. From Tudor O. Bompa: *Theory and methodology of training.* Copyright © 1983 by Kendall/Hunt Publishing Company. Adapted with permission.

Table 3.1 Suggested Number of Meets per Year

Event	Beginning athletes		Elite athletes	
	Winter	Summer	Winter	Summer
Sprints, Hurdles, Jumps, and Throws				
Primary event	3-4	12-16	3-5	16-20
Secondary event	2-3	4-6	1-3	3-5
Middle Distances				
800-1,500m	—	4-8	2-3	10-16
Shorter distances	2-3	8-10	2-4	8-10
Marathon	—	1	—	2-3
50km Walk	—	6-8	—	8-10
Combined Events				
Decathlon	—	1-2	—	2-3
Heptathlon	—	2	—	2-4
Individual events	2-4	10-12	3-5	12-16

From Tudor O. Bompa: *Theory and Methodology of Training.* Copyright © 1983 by Kendall/Hunt Publishing Company. Reprinted with permission.

Consider these factors in planning the athlete's meet schedule:

- The most important meet of the year is the *only* one that determines the athlete's ranking. All other meets are steps to prepare the athlete for that one competition.
- If the meets are planned properly, the athlete will peak at the most important meet of the year.
- Having too many meets interferes with the balance of competition and training. This lessens the athlete's physical and psychological potential.
- The athlete should compete *only* when capable of meeting a meet's objectives for each training factor (physical, technical, tactical, and psychological).
- Each meet should be a more difficult competition for the athlete than the previous meet.
- A meet with too little competition provides no motivation.
- Superior opponents should not be avoided.

Planning the training year. The training year is divided into one or more macrocycles, with one macrocycle for each peak. Each macrocycle has three periods: preparation, competition, and transition. If an athlete peaks for both indoor and outdoor track, there should be several weeks of low-key transitional activities following the major indoor competition. The athlete's fitness level will drop during this period, but that drop enables the athlete to undertake more effective training later, resulting in improved performances during the outdoor competitions. If the transition period were *not* included, the athlete would "hit the wall" at some point, ending further progress and effectively ending the season.

Records for the annual plan. The annual planning process begins by planning the year's competition schedule. This gives a starting point to the training structure. It is combined with the 4-year plan's objectives for that year, which is then modified based on the evaluation of the previous year. Then the annual training plan is developed, giving the year's plans, control tests, and progression. Next, detailed exercises and tests are placed into the training plan. As the year progresses, the coach keeps a record of the athlete's performances on the control tests and in the meets.

Planning the macrocycles. The macrocycle is planned to result in a peak performance at a major meet. Explosive events (such as sprints, jumps, and throws) may allow up to three major peaks (therefore, three macrocycles in a year), but for other events only one or two peaks are possible. The greater the part that the influence of endurance (the aerobic component) plays in the performance, the fewer peaks that

are possible in a year. For the highest possible performance level, a marathoner should plan only one major peak in a year.

The schedule of macrocycles is largely a function of the meet schedule that you develop. After you choose your most important meets of the year, you will know when your macrocycles will occur. Each major meet (one to three in a year) requires a macrocycle. The macrocycle ends after the transition period that follows the major meet (1 to 4 weeks after the major meet). At that point, the next macrocycle begins.

*Planning the training period*s. Each of the three training periods should have specific training objectives consistent with the annual plan. The objectives should be listed in the order of their importance to performance so you can assess the relative training time that is applied to their development. The athlete's success or progress in meeting the goals or objectives should be evaluated and recorded at the end of each period.

The preparation period develops the basic conditioning and technique that is needed for competition. The length of this period depends on the athlete's fitness level. A more fit, more highly skilled athlete needs much less preparation time than a young, inexperienced, or unfit one.

The competition period tests the athlete in steps along the way toward the season's major meet. This progress is evaluated after each meet, refinements are made in the next microcycle's training, and the athlete trains to improve again. The goal of the entire macrocycle is the major meet at the end of the competition period.

The transition period provides recovery from the competition season and prepares the athlete to start the next macrocycle. If the year includes more than one macrocycle and peak, the midyear transition periods may be as brief as a week or so. The transition period at the end of the training year should last for at least 1 month.

Planning the phases. A macrocycle is usually divided into six subdivisions called *phases* (Table 3.2). A phase usually lasts for 3 to 6 weeks. Table 3.3 shows the primary objectives of each phase.

For training programs that stress a repeated cycle based on the biological model, a phase is divided into three parts, each lasting for one to four microcycles:

- **Preparation:** general conditioning for the phase goal
- **Adaptation:** specific conditioning for the phase goal
- **Application:** control testing, simulations, or competition

Table 3.2   Phases of the Macrocycle

Period	Phase	Phase type	Length
Preparation	1	General preparation	3-6 weeks
	2	Specific preparation	3-6 weeks
Competition	3	Precompetition	3-6 weeks
	4	General competition	3-6 weeks
	5	Special competition	2 weeks
Transition	6	Transition or recovery	1-4 weeks

From William H. Freeman. (1989). *Peak when it counts: Periodization for the American coach* (p. 24). Los Altos, CA: Tafnews. Reprinted with permission.

Table 3.3   Objectives of the Phases

Period	Phase	Objectives
Preparation	1 General preparation	1. Diagnose problems from competition. 2. Develop endurance, strength, mobility. 3. Fine-tune technical model. 4. Prepare for Phase 2.
	2 Specific preparation	1. Develop event-specific fitness. 2. Develop the advanced technical model. 3. Prepare for Phase 3.
Competition	3 Precompetition (if appropriate) (if appropriate)	1. Experience progressive intensity of meets. 2. Improve meet performances. 3. Make technical evaluation in meet setting. 4. Expand meet experiences. 5. Qualify for advanced meets.
	4 General competition	1. Refine the advanced technical model. 2. Prepare for the peak performance.
	5 Special competition	1. Achieve peak performance at major meet.
Transition	6 Transition	1. Have active recovery from season. 2. Prepare for Phase 1.

From Frank W. Dick. (1978). *Training theory* (pp. 60-61). London: British Amateur Athletic Board. Reprinted with permission.

This pattern repeats from the level of the individual training session up to that of the macrocycle. It can be applied to multiyear training plans, with a year devoted to each part.

Phase 1 (*general preparation*) improves the athlete's base fitness and technique levels. This "training to train" requires up to one-third of the macrocycle and prepares the athlete for the training in Phase 2.

Phase 2 (*specific preparation*) prepares the athlete for the third phase, but it also develops event-specific fitness and models the advanced technique in the athlete.

Phase 3 (*precompetition*) takes up the majority of the competitive season. It uses a series of meets that

increase in intensity or in the opponents' skill, challenging the athlete to improve his or her performance.

The whole point of training is to achieve excellence in the major meet. The athlete's technical performance in these early meets is a critical indicator of progress. The use of inexpensive videotaping tools helps immensely in this area because coaches can more easily evaluate the performances later on tape.

Phase 4 (*general competition*) has two tasks: refining the advanced technical model and preparing for the peak performance. For elite athletes, this may be a time with no meets, lasting for 4 to 6 weeks. It is used as a breather from competition, a time to concentrate on the final adjustments in the technique and fitness levels. The training reaches its peak intensity (quality) at this time, but the loading (quantity) will be falling sharply.

Phase 5 (*special competition*) is the peak of the season, with the most important meet of the year. The training load is very light, allowing the athlete to be rested and fresh, so the highest level of performance is possible. It may include one or more final tune-up meets before the major meet. This phase usually lasts for only 1 or 2 weeks.

Phase 6 (*transition*) is also called the recovery or regeneration (rebuilding) phase. It involves active recovery from the season, with other physical activities in low-key, relaxing situations. The activity level is high enough that the athlete will be physically ready to begin general training with Phase 1 after Phase 6 is ended. At the same time, the activity level is low enough for the athlete to be physically and psychologically rested and recovered, thus enthusiastic to return to Phase 1.

Planning the Microcycles

Characteristics of microcycles. Each phase is divided into a series of microcycles. A typical microcycle is 1 week long, though it may vary in length from 3 to 21 days. Microcycles have four features:[3]

1. The structure (the volume relative to the intensity) of the load demand changes during the cycle.
2. The load degree differs from one training session to the next, alternating between lower and higher loads according to the athlete's load tolerance and ability to recover.
3. The training sessions have differing main tasks, which use either special or general training exercises.
4. The training load rises for as long as is necessary to meet the objectives of the training phase.

Each training session is followed by a recovery period long enough to remove the fatigue that prevents the athlete from meeting the required standard of performance in the next training session. Sessions with general exercises are useful as active recovery, which makes the recovery process shorter than passive rest does. Depending on the activity, an athlete may not need a full recovery before the next training session. This is possible if the coach plans sessions with varying tasks, methods, and loads, so the stress on a given bodily system is not consistently high. The coach may plan some training sessions that focus on a single task, rather than trying to mix conflicting systems (such as speed and endurance) during the same session.

The cycle should be planned so that sessions with special demands on speed, speed-strength, and high-level technique are performed before sessions that emphasize endurance. Generally, more than 24 hours of recovery is needed after very hard training. Meets should occur during the overcompensation phase that follows such recovery (usually 2 or 3 days after the optimum load training session). However, no pattern of training microcycles has proven to be infallible.

Following is the optimum succession (best order of training activities) for a microcycle:[4]

1. Learn and perfect technique with medium intensity.
2. Perfect technique at submaximal and maximal intensity.
3. Develop speed of short duration (up to personal limit).
4. Develop anaerobic endurance.
5. Improve strength with a load of 90 to 100% of personal maximum.
6. Develop muscular endurance with medium and low loads.
7. Develop muscular endurance with high and maximal intensity.
8. Develop cardiorespiratory endurance with maximal intensity.
9. Develop cardiorespiratory endurance with moderate intensity.

This succession of training is very similar to Korobov's recommended progression for the single training session, which is to develop technique and/or tactical training, speed and/or coordination, strength, and general endurance.

You should use the following factors to plan the content of a microcycle:

1. Set the objectives, particularly the dominant training factors.
2. Decide the type of microcycle:
   a. development microcycle (improves fitness),
   b. tuning microcycle (maintains fitness), or
   c. unloading microcycle (peaking cycle).
3. Set the absolute level of work:
   a. number of training sessions,
   b. volume of training,
   c. intensity of training, and
   d. complexity of training.
4. Set the relative level of effort (how many peak sessions, which alternate with less intensive training sessions).

5. Decide on the character of training (training methods and means for each training session).
6. Set control testing or meet days.
7. Begin with low- to medium-intensity sessions, progressing to more intensive sessions later.
8. Before an important meet, use a microcycle with only one training peak, occurring 3 to 5 days before the meet.

Microcycle patterns. A 1-week microcycle usually has two peak sessions. Training lessons should be repeated two or three times per microcycle for each different objective. Learning technical skills requires much repetition. The frequency of repetition varies, depending on the type of training, like so:

- Daily training:
    General endurance
    Flexibility
    Strength in small-muscle groups
- Every other day:
    Strength for large-muscle groups
- Three sessions per week:
    Specific endurance (submaximal intensity)
- Two sessions per week:
    Specific endurance (maximal intensity)
    Maintenance of strength
    Maintenance of flexibility
    Maintenance of speed
- Two to three sessions per week:
    Bounding drills and speed exercises under strenuous conditions (sand or snow)

During the competitive period, the microcycles should include some modeling of the conditions of the most important meet of the year. If the athlete must compete for 2 days in a row, this practice should be simulated every 2nd or 3rd week. In some cases, an athlete qualifies in the morning, then competes in the finals in the afternoon.

Planning the Peak

Peaking is as much a psychological state as a physical one, "with an intense emotional arousal. . . . An important attribute of peaking seems to be the athlete's capacity to tolerate various degrees of frustration which occur before, during and after competition."[5]

Although peaking is a very complex process, the primary factors that facilitate it are the athlete's high working potential, quick rate of recovery, near-perfect neuromuscular coordination (technical skill), overcompensation, unloading, recovery, psychological

factors (motivation, arousal, and psychological relaxation), and nervous cell working capacity (increased only for the last 7 to 10 days before main meet).

The peaking process involves a final use of overcompensation in the training schedule. Overcompensation usually occurs from 24 to 36 hours after an optimal training session. During the racing season, the training plan may alternate maximal- and low-intensity stimuli, resulting in a wavelike pattern of fitness. This approach helps prevent exhaustion from overtraining while competing.

The correct unloading (tapering) procedure is critical to performance in the major meet. The training load during the last five microcycles (Figure 3.4) before the main meet shows the increase of the training load from low to medium to high (causing fatigue), with a drop back to medium and then low loads that results first in compensation, then in overcompensation for the main meet.

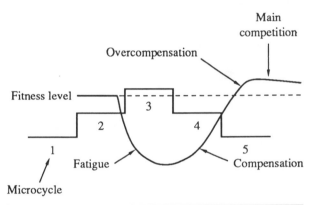

Figure 3.4 Loading for peaking. From William H. Freeman. (1989). *Peak when it counts: Periodization for the American coach* (p. 31). Los Altos, CA: Tafnews. Adapted with permission.

Recovery and regeneration are extremely important during the competitive season. Massage and sauna are useful, and proper diet is also a critical factor in the energy level.

The psychological aspects of training are also critical at this time. Although the athlete may be motivated to perform at a high level, reasonable goals and expectations should be set. Otherwise, unnecessary frustration will become a postmeet factor. The athlete should not be overmotivated or too aroused; his or her psychological state will already be "on edge." At this time the coach is more useful in the role of encouraging and providing relaxation than in "pumping up" the athlete.

The length of time that a peak can be maintained depends upon the length and quality of the underlying preparation period, as well as other factors that are very individualized. The Zone 1 level (performance within 2% of one's best) may last as long as 2 to 3-1/2 months, with three to five minor peaks during that time, if the preparation period was long enough and the training process during the competition period is handled properly. The peaking process itself is about 7 to 10 days in length, after which the performance level falls off.

Maintaining that performance level requires a short phase of regeneration after each peak for a major meet, followed by more training. If those conditions were not met, the peak period would be shortened considerably. The number of competitions is also a factor; too many competitions cause a performance plateau, instead of improving performances.

To avoid the onset of fatigue during the competitive season, the training plan should follow this constant pattern:

- Competition
- Regeneration
- Training
- Unloading
- Next competition

An athlete usually needs four to six microcycles to rise from the precompetition phase to the Zone 1 performance level. Extending the Zone 1 performances beyond the eighth microcycle of competition (2 months) requires careful planning and monitoring of the athlete's training.

In deciding how many meets an athlete can compete in during a season, note that the events fall into four groups according to their recovery needs: the throws, the short sprints and jumps, the long sprints and middle distances, and the long distances and combined events. The stress of competition rises from the first group to the fourth. Table 3.4 shows the recommended number of meets and recovery time for each group.

Planning the Training Sessions

The training session has three or four primary parts. A three-part session includes the preparation (usually the warm-up), body (content), and conclusion (usually the cool-down).

A four-part session adds an introduction before the preparation. The three-part session is used by more advanced athletes. It is the dominant form during the competition period. The four-part version is best for beginners and group sessions, because it allows the goals of the lesson to be explained.

Earlier we outlined Korobov's four-step progression for the body of the training session, from learning or perfecting technique and/or tactics, to developing speed and/or coordination, then strength work, and finally training for general and specific endurance. Technique and tactics are practiced first because they require a rested body. If other types of training were performed first, fatigue would interfere with the learning rate. When perfecting technique that is fatiguing or heavy in its work load (such as in the throwing events or weight lifting), the speed and coordination exercises should be performed before the technique development exercises. When developing maximum speed, the speed training should be performed first, immediately after the warm-up.

In learning or perfecting technique, the sequence of learning should be to

1. consolidate the skills learned in the last session,
2. perfect the skills that are most important to the event, and
3. apply the skills under simulated competitive conditions.

The complete training session should not last more than 2 hours. Younger athletes may improve more rapidly with shorter training sessions. This time includes the warm-up and the cool-down, leaving 90 minutes or less for the body of the training session. With less skilled athletes, the concluding part of the training session may include supplementary conditioning exercises, especially if the entire session is not too demanding and the athletes are not exhausted.

The conclusion, or cool-down, is often neglected by coaches. It is critical in enhancing the body's recovery. Light running, jogging, and walking help to clear the lactic acid from the muscles so they will be less tight or sore at the start of the next training session. Light stretching aids the body's recovery from weight-training sessions. Every athlete should learn a relaxing cool-down procedure and follow it after every training session. It is even more critical following intensive competition. Even 10 minutes of cool-down activities are very helpful to the athlete's recovery.

A lesson plan for a group of athletes has four parts, beginning with an introduction. It includes notes of points that the coach wants to stress, including points relating to individual athletes. Not only does such a plan help the coach focus the training session, but it provides a good record for reviewing the training process later in the year or during later years.

Each athlete should keep a training diary as a record of his or her individual training. The coach and the athlete can decide what information should be included in the diary. Various versions of training diaries have included the morning's resting pulse, details of diet and sleep, fatigue indexes, and other items in addition to the workout details themselves.

Table 3.4 Recommended Competitions by Event Groups

Event group	Time to overcompensation	Meets per year
Throws	2-3 days	16-20
Short sprints	3-5 days	16-20
Jumps	3-5 days	16-20
Long sprints	6-7 days	16-20
Middle distance	6-7 days	10-15
Long distance	2 weeks or more	6-10
Marathon	More than 2 weeks	3-5
50km walk	More than 2 weeks	3-5
Combined events	2 weeks or more	3-5

From Tudor O. Bompa. (1987). Peaking for the extended athletics calendar. *New Studies in Athletics*, **2**(4), 41. Adapted with permission.

Remember that thorough planning combined with good records of what was actually done are essential if you are to make the training process optimally effective.

Changing Approaches to Periodization

Periodization is *not* a rigid approach to training. More advanced training patterns use more frequent variations in the volume and intensity of training while keeping the overall training level relatively high until unloading for the peak meet. This pattern is more useful for elite competitors than for average athletes because it addresses the need for more intensified challenges for a high-level athlete who wants to improve.

Remember that even though the Russians have experimented with this type of training for 25 years, they have warned their own coaches against applying the research in too rigid a manner.[6] It is preferable to accept a slightly slower rate of improvement in performance than to try to force the athlete to progress too quickly. A physical breakdown from overtraining can cost the athlete a season, and it may even result in 1 or more years of lost progress. For younger athletes (into their early 20s), mononucleosis sometimes occurs during times of overstress (too much training combined with too many other activities or needs). It most often appears in the first 2 years of college as young athletes make the transition to harder training, along with their new academic demands, increased personal responsibilities, and wider social opportunities.

References

1. William H. Freeman. (1989). *Peak when it counts: Periodization for the American coach* (pp. 4-34). Los Altos, CA: Tafnews.
2. Frank W. Dick. (1978). *Training theory* (pp. 56-81). London: British Amateur Athletic Board.
3. Dietrich Harre (Ed.) (1982). *Principles of sports training: Introduction to the theory and methods of training* (2nd ed., pp. 80-87). Berlin: Sportverlag.
4. N.G. Ozolin. (1971). Athlete's training system for competition. In Harre, ibid. (p. 210).
5. Tudor O. Bompa. (1987). Peaking for the extended athletics calendar. *New Studies in Athletics*, **2**(4), 29-43.
6. Yevgeniy Kashkalov. (1971). Varying work loads in middle distance training. *Track Technique*, **43**, 1375-1377.

Additional Readings

Andersen, A.B., Froberg, K., & Lammert, O. (1987). Should we revise our ideas of the effectiveness of youth training? *New Studies in Athletics*, **2**(1), 65-72.

Bompa, Tudor O. (1983). *Theory and methodology of training: The key to athletic performance.* Dubuque, IA: Kendall/Hunt.

Bondarchuk, Anatoliy. (1988). Constructing a training system. Parts 1 and 2. *Track Technique*, **102**, 3254-3259, 3268; **103**, 3286-3288.

Fleck, Steven J., & Kraemer, William J. (1988). *Designing resistance training programs*. Champaign, IL: Human Kinetics.

Gambetta, Vern. (1989). Planned performance training: The application of periodization to the American system. In *The Athletics Congress's Track and Field Coaching Manual* (2nd ed., pp. 37-45). Champaign, IL: Leisure Press.

Garhammer, John. (1979). Periodization of strength training for athletes. *Track Technique*, **75**, 2398-2399.

Kemp, Merv. (1989). Specific strength. *Track Technique*, **108**, 3458-3459.

Kipke, Lothar. (1987). The importance of recovery after training and competitive efforts. *Track Technique*, **98**, 3128-3135.

McDonald, Craig, James, Steve, & Kutschkau, Tom. (1989). Elements of a successful prep track program. *Track Technique*, **107**, 3403-3408.

McInnis, Andrew. (1981). A research review of systematized approaches to planned performance peaking with relation to the sport of track and field. *Track and Field Quarterly Review*, **81**(2), 7-12.

Poliquin, Charles. (1988). Variety in your strength training program. *Track Technique*, **106**, 3383-3386.

Raiport, Grigori. (1989). *Red gold: Peak performance techniques of the Russian and East German Olympic victors*. New York: St. Martin's.

Zalessky, M., Sobolevsky, V., & Khomenov, L. (1988). Basic restoration procedures. *Track Technique*, **106**, 3381-3382, 3396.

CHAPTER 4	# Locating and
	# Testing Candidates
	# in School

Few coaches have the good fortune to inherit a team of good athletes. Most coaches begin each year needing new athletes to fill at least several of the events, if not all of them. Do not overlook any prospect in this search. The physical education classes are an excellent source of prospects whether you coach in high school or college.

Coaches benefit from regularly testing the physical education classes in several events. The tests can be mixed with the normal start-of-the-year testing in the classes. The tests described here are proven indicators of talent in untrained athletes, though other tests can be used as well.

General Comments on Testing and Recruitment

Tests may not be absolute indicators of talent. Some athletes have off days; others are late bloomers. These tests try to discover native ability without requiring the prospect to have prior training in the events. For that reason, the coach can test prospects on their first day of practice or test everyone in a physical education class during the first week of school. Athletes do not always realize that they have the talent for a given event, so all prospects should be tested for all events.

If the tests are given in a brief period and several teachers or assistants are available to record the results, the tests can be given quickly to many students. Table 4.1 gives the testing order, Table 4.2 lists the test standards for high school students, and Figure 4.1 (page 31) shows how to organize a playing field for the tests.

Students can move from one station to the next as they complete each test, except that the 800 meters is run last in one or two large groups. Athletes or managers can direct some of the events to lessen the number of persons needed to administer the tests. A coach can give all of the tests in one afternoon if the procedure is well organized and carefully explained to the prospects.

Do not consider these tests as the only possible selection factors; a student's strong interest in an event may overcome an early lack of talent for that event. Never underestimate human drive and willpower. Many other tests are also used to indicate event-specific talent. This list is simply one we have found useful for many years.

The coach should try to make the sport popular with the students. He or she should try to see that it is enjoyed, for this is an important criterion for a young person in trying out for a team. No matter how "in" a sport may be at first, if the coach does not make it an enjoyable experience, he or she will lose many prospects and eventually lose any vestige of status that

Table 4.1 Testing Organization

Event	Test number	Test	Site
High jump	1	Jump and reach	Gym
Long jump	2	Standing long jump	Gym
Sprints, long jump	3	40-yard dash	Field
Hurdles	4	40-yard low hurdles	Field
Javelin throw	5	Ball throw	Field
Triple jump	6	Standing triple jump	Field
Shot put	7	Shot put	Shot area
Distance runs	8	800m run	Track

Table 4.2 Summary of Test Standards

Event	Test	Performance Male	Performance Female
Sprints	40-yard dash	5.2 sec	6.2 sec
Distances	800m run	2:30	3:00
Hurdles	40-yard low hurdles	6.2 sec	7.5 sec
High jump	Jump and reach	30"	20"
Long jump	Standing LJ	7'6"	6'0"
	40-yard dash	5.2 sec	6.2 sec
Triple jump	Standing TJ	24'	19' (high school)
	Rhythm and balance characteristics (observable)	28'	22' (college)
Pole vault	All-around gymnastic ability		
Shot put	Standing put	20'	18'
Discus	Shot-putters		
Javelin	800-gram ball	Good javelin distance	Good javelin distance
	Softball throw	200'	150'

the sport might have carried. If a sport becomes popular, three quarters of the recruiting problem is solved.

Convincing a Prospect to Come Out for the Team

Every coach wonders how great an effort to make to get a prospect to come out for the team and convince the prospect to stay if he or she shows signs of quitting. Athletic competition has many benefits, but we do not know whether those benefits are realized if an athlete stays on a team when he or she prefers not to be there.

Is it worth the continual effort to convince a hesitant athlete to stay on the team? We suspect that it is not. The coach is going to waste much time that

is better spent on athletes who appreciate the attention. Also, the team risks losing a valuable member late in the season with no trained replacement. If that loss occurs before the meets begin, however, it might be covered by other athletes. Thus, the effect of a potential dropout on team morale can be minimized. Finally, an athlete may threaten to quit simply to get attention from the coach. Most coaches have enough work to do without pampering prima donnas.

Athlete Tests and Selection Standards

The purpose of these tests is to help select your most likely prospects for each event as quickly as possible. They allow you to locate talent in unsuspected places

Football field with yard lines

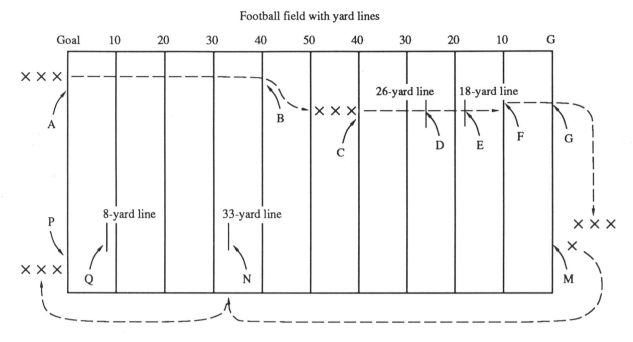

Test 1: 40-yard dash, A to B
Test 2: 40-yard hurdles, C to G (hurdles at D, E, F)
Test 3: Ball throw from M, prospects throwing to N (if softball)
Test 4: Standing triple jump, P to Q (high school prospect)

Figure 4.1 Field testing with several teachers available.

and begin more specific training earlier in a program that has a very short season. If you have only two athletes interested in the shot put, you have no trouble deciding who your shot-putters are. However, if all of your athletes complete the battery of tests, you may discover other potential putters to add to the group.

The distances for the running tests are not the usual racing distances; they simply lend themselves well to testing on a typical, lined football field. Other testing distances may be equally valid. However, our goal is to test the maximum number of prospects in a minimum of time and with a minimum of personnel and equipment.

Sprint Test

The first test is for sprinters. Time each person in a 40-yard dash. Give the test on the football field, starting on the goal line and finishing where the coach is standing on the 40-yard line (Figure 4.2). This site minimizes the risk of injury if prospects fall while running. Have each person go down in a three-point stance (both feet and one hand on the ground) for the start. No one is needed to start the students, if they run one at a time, because the timer starts the watch when the athlete lifts the hand from the ground. Each person is given only one trial because untrained

Football field with yard lines

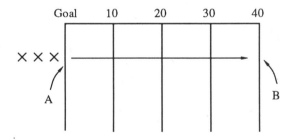

A   Starting line
B   Finish line, position of timer
X   Students lined up to run

Figure 4.2 Test for sprinters.

runners rarely improve their sprint times on later attempts.

Hurdling Test

For hurdling prospects a 40-yard distance is also used, but three hurdles are added to the course (Figure 4.3). The first hurdle is 14 yards from the start, and the other two hurdles are at 8-yard intervals past the first one. If you are starting the runners on the goal line,

Football field with yard lines

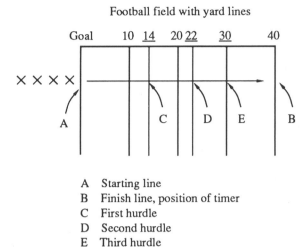

A   Starting line
B   Finish line, position of timer
C   First hurdle
D   Second hurdle
E   Third hurdle
X   Students lined up to hurdle

Figure 4.3 Test for hurdlers.

for example, the hurdles will be on the 14-, 22-, and 30-yard lines, with the finish on the 40-yard line. The hurdles are set at low hurdle height (30″). For females, reduce the hurdle separations slightly, setting them at 13.5, 21, and 28.5 yards.

Distance Run Test

Find distance runners with an 800m run. Divide the class into two groups, one group lined up facing the other and numbered in sequence, with each member of Group 1 having a counterpart in the student with the same number in Group 2. Each runner gets the finishing time of his or her counterpart and reports it to the recorder, the first runner in Group 1 reporting the time of the first runner in Group 2, and so forth. After one group runs and has its times recorded, the second group runs and has its times reported by the first group. If only runners with the best times are of interest, everyone can run at the same time, with the coach pulling the top runners to the side as they finish.

Other testing distances are equally valid, such as 1,500m, 1 mile, or Cooper's tests (12-minute run or 1.5-mile run). However, the 800m run is sufficient and saves time (and no prospect gets lapped).

High Jump Test

For high jumpers, use the jump and reach (Sargent jump) test. A strip of masking tape can be placed on the wall, running upward from about 6 feet to 11 feet above the floor. It should be marked at 1-inch intervals over that distance, with larger marks and numerals every 6 inches. Each jumper stands flat-footed next

to the wall at the tape and raises an arm so the observer can note how high the jumper can reach with the fingers. He or she then crouches and jumps, reaching with the hand to touch as high up the strip of tape as possible, while the observer notes the new height (Figure 4.4). Thus, a person with a standing reach of 7′3″ and a jumping reach of 9′10″ has jumped 31 inches, the difference between the two marks.

Reach   Ready to jump   Jumping reach

Figure 4.4 Test for high jumpers.

This test was more meaningful before the back layout (Fosbury Flop) style of jumping appeared in the late 1960s. For "floppers," sprinting speed is as important as the leg spring tested by the Sargent jump. Many elite floppers have tested poorly on the vertical jump, so consider any prospect with moderate spring and good leg speed.

Long Jump Tests

Two tests are used in conjunction for long jump prospects. The first is the sprint test, and the second is the standing long jump. This can be done into the long jump pit, or it can be done indoors on any floor that provides nonslip footing. A strip of masking tape can be placed upon the floor, running outward at a right angle to the takeoff point, beginning 4 feet from the takeoff point and marked at 1-inch intervals to 11 feet. Each jumper stands directly behind the takeoff line with the toe of each foot touching the line, then leaps as far forward as possible (Figure 4.5). The leap

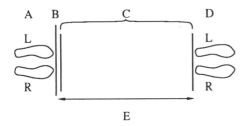

L   Left foot
R   Right foot
A   Starting position for jump
B   Foul line
C   Jump
D   Landing position
E   Distance jumped

Figure 4.5 Test for long jumpers.

can be into a pit or onto a tumbling mat (mark where the mat's corners should be on the floor because it moves with each landing). A combination of jumping and sprinting ability is desired in long jumpers.

Triple Jump Test

The standing triple jump is used to find triple jump prospects. Have a jumper demonstrate the technique first because it may seem strange to the students. The jumper takes off from one foot, lands on the same foot, goes into a step, landing on the other foot, then makes a long jump to conclude the sequence (Figure 4.6). Use the same takeoff line as for the standing long jump, but make chalk or masking tape marks at 6-inch intervals from 15 to 32 feet away from the takeoff point. If this is not done with the landing in a jumping pit or on a mat, it should be done on a grassy area, such as the football field. The jumper can "swing" into the jump, starting with one foot behind the takeoff foot to provide some push into the

jump. The coach is looking for athletes with good rhythm and balance, so hurdlers are often good prospects.

Shot Put Test

We find shot putters with the standing put. Mark a throwing line on the ground with chalk, then make lines at 10 feet, at 15 feet, and at 1-foot intervals from 15 to 30 feet from the throwing line. The prospects take turns throwing from a standing position facing the direction of their throws (no turns are used).

Javelin Throw Test

Javelin throwers test by throwing a softball, a football, or an 800-gram weighted ball (about 1-3/4 pounds). These throws indicate talent (and add years to the life expectancy of the person marking the distances of the throws). The goal line of the football field is used as a throwing line, with the 150-foot mark at midfield and the 200-foot mark at the far 33-yard line (Figure 4.7). The throwers run up to the line however they wish, as long as they do not cross it. The distance an 800-gram weighted ball is thrown gives the closest approximation of how far the javelin can be thrown.

Locating Prospects for Other Events

We have no test that we use to discover discus throwers or pole vaulters. Shot putters usually throw the discus, eventually showing themselves stronger in one event or the other as they become more competent in their skills. Pole vaulting requires a unique combination of skills that shows most readily in skilled gymnasts. The vaulter is invariably a risk-taker at physical stunts. A pole vaulter may be an athlete who is a fair sprinter, long jumper, and hurdler.

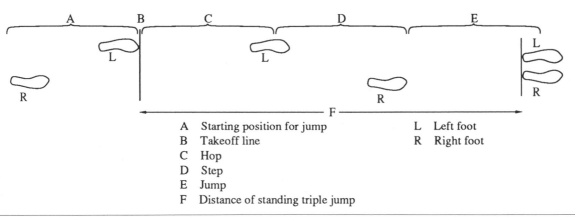

A   Starting position for jump   L   Left foot
B   Takeoff line   R   Right foot
C   Hop
D   Step
E   Jump
F   Distance of standing triple jump

Figure 4.6 Test for triple jumpers.

Football field with yard lines

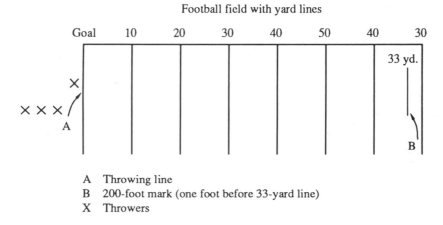

A Throwing line
B 200-foot mark (one foot before 33-yard line)
X Throwers

Figure 4.7 Test for javelin throwers.

Readings

Arbeit, E., Bartonietz, K., Borner, P., Hellmann, K., & Skibbia, W. (1988). The javelin: The view of the DVfL of the GDR on talent selection, technique and main training contents of the training phases from beginner to top-level athlete. *New Studies in Athletics*, **3**(1), 57-74.

Bartonietz, K., Hinz, L., Lorenz, D., & Lunau, G. (1988). The hammer: The view of the DVfL of the GDR on talent selection, technique and training of throwers from beginner to top level athlete. *New Studies in Athletics*, **3**(1), 39-56.

Foreman, Ken. (1989). The use of talent-predictive factors in the selection of track and field athletes. In *The Athletics Congress's Track and Field Coaching Manual* (2nd ed., pp. 31-36). Champaign, IL: Leisure Press.

Freeman, William H. (1986). Decathlon performance success: Progress and age factors. *Track Technique*, **96**, 3050-3052.

Henson, Phil. (1983). Predictive tests for track and field. *Track and Field Quarterly Review*, **83**(4), 60-61.

Jones, Max. (1988). The test quadrathlon. *Track and Field Quarterly Review*, **88**(3), 43-46.

Pintaric, Ivan. (1984). Norms for discus throwers. *Track Technique*, **87**, 2786.

Riordan, Jim. (1987). Talent spotting in Eastern Europe. *Track Technique*, **101**, 3214, 3220.

The tests of equivalence [throws]. (1984). *Track and Field Quarterly Review*, **84**(1), 50-53.

CHAPTER 5	# The Oregon
	# Training Schedule
	# Sheets

The Oregon workout sheets were first developed while Bill Bowerman was coaching in Pakistan for the U.S. State Department. He needed to communicate with coaches and athletes who spoke several different languages. To save time and improve the coaches' understanding, he had an interpreter translate a single list of fundamentals for each event into the coaches' native languages. Those charts were copied, together with weekly training schedules.

Then Bowerman could refer to each exercise by its number. For example, if he wanted the runners to run 8 × 440 yards in 70 to 73 seconds, he wrote "8 × 5E1." The number 5 was "Intervals," E was "440," and 1 was "70-73" (see Figure 5.1). He knew what he was assigning because his copy was in English, and the runner knew what the coach wanted because each coach's copy, with the same numbering system, was printed in Urdu or Hindustani or his other native tongue. Thus, the coach could communicate with the athletes in another language "by the numbers." The system worked so well that he used it with his own athletes when he returned to Oregon.

The format of the charts was revised slightly every year, so there are slight variations from year to year. Figure 5.2 shows the February 1960 workouts of Jim Grelle, who made the U.S. Olympic Team at 1,500m that year. As an example, look at his workout on the 10th of that month. He warmed up, then ran 4 × 440 yards in 64 seconds. The current versions of the schedule sheets, which appear at the ends of chapters 6 through 20, represent workouts of real

athletes who trained under Bowerman at Oregon.

These workout schedules can be viewed as historical records (of sorts), and they can be saved. The coach can compare the progress of an athlete against his or her previous progress or that of any earlier athletes in that event, giving a more accurate picture of the athlete's progress. We believe that this is the quickest way to communicate with large numbers of athletes.

Periodization and the Oregon System

The Oregon System is an early form of periodized training. Its laws and principles are consistent with those of periodized training. From the start, the athletes' goal was to peak for the outdoor track conference meet and the NCAA Championships. All other goals were secondary to that goal. Cross country served primarily as base training and technique work for distance runners rather than as a major competitive season. Indoor track was a short season (one to two meets), used primarily to maintain training interest during the chilly, wet Oregon winter.

The training patterns used by the distance runners (chapters 10 and 11) show the same wavelike hard-easy pattern used by elite athletes in an intricate periodized system of training. Regular testing measured each athlete's progress toward the peak goals. Meet conditions were simulated on a regular basis.

Runner's Schedule   NAME   DATE

1 A. Jog 1 to 3 miles B. Weights & jog	M

2. Fartlek
    A. Varied   (1) 30 min. (2)
    B. Steady (1) 2-4 mi. (2) 4-6 mi. (3) 7-10 mi.
	T

	W
3. Weights	T
4. High knee and power run	F

5. Intervals
    A. 110   (1)18-16-14 (2) 17-15-13
    B. 165   (1) 25   (2)
    C. 220   (1) 35   (2)
    D. 330   (1) 52   (2) 48   (3) 45   (4)
    E. 440   (1) 70-73   (2)
    F. 660   (1) 1:45   (2)
    G. 880   (1) 70   (2)
    H. 3/4   (1) 70   (2)
    I. Mile (1) 72   (2) 68-70   (3) 64-67   (4)
    J.
    K.
    L.
	S

	S
	M
	T
	W

6. Sets
    A. 660-440-330-220-110   (1) 1:45-68-49-32-15   (2)
    B. 440-660-440-220   (1) 63   (2)
    C. 550-165-165   (1) 55 pace   (2)
    D.
	T

	F
7. Squad meeting	S
8. Special A. Sauna B. Swim C.	S

9. Drills
    A. Sprint-float-sprint (165)
    B. 1-step acceleration (165)
    C. 40-30 drill   (1) 4 laps   (2)
    D. 70-90 drill   (1) 1-1   (2) 2-1   (3)3-1   (4)
    E. Cut downs   (1) 110   (2) 165   (3) 220
                      (4) 330   (5) 440   (6) 880
                      (7)
	M

	T
	W
	T
	F
	S

F. Simulate   (1) 1st 220-   (2) 2 1/2-   (3) 10 miles-
        race drills   last 220   1 1/2   3/4 drill
                      (4)
     G. 2-4 miles at (1) 80   (2) 75   (3)
	S

10. A. Test B. Trial C. Compete (1) 3/4 date pace (2) Over (3) Under	M
11. Hill interval A. 110 B. 220 C.	T
12. With coach (A) Bill B. (B) Bill D. (C)	W
14. A. Wind sprint B. Hurdle drill C. Spring and bound D.	T
	F
15. Finish work	S
16. Acrobatics or apparatus	S
17. 3/4 effort	
18.	
19.	
20. Secondary event	
21. A. Pictures B. Film	

Figure 5.1 Sample of an original training schedule.

DATE

			2x	2x	2x		
Feb.	1	1	9D	6C	5D	12	11
	2	1	3				
			10x				
	3	1	7F	11			
	4	1	3				
	5	1	3				
	6-7	2	Saturday and Sunday				
			1x	2x			
	8	1	10	4D	11		
	9	1	3				
			4x	4x	4x		
	10	1	7F	6C	5D	3	
	11	1	3				
	12	1	3				
			1x		1x		
	13	1	3/4	64s	660	29s	
	14	1	16	2			
	15	1	2				
	16	1	3				
			10x				
	17	1	7F	3			
	18	1	3				
			1x				
	19	1	9D				
	20–21	2	Saturday and Sunday				
			4x	4x			
	22	1	6C	5C	12	9	
	23		3				
			1x	1x	4x		
	24	1	9	14	5C	9	
	25		3				
	26		3				
			1x		1x		
	27	1	3/4	64s	660	29s	
	28						

1. Warm-up weight work or arm and shoulder work on rope, rings, or apparatus.

2. Fartlek

3. Light fartlek

4. Repeats. 110, A.20; B.18; C.16; D.14; E.12; F.11

5. Repeats. 220, A.38; B.35; C.33; D.31; E.29; F.28; G.27; H.26

6. Repeats. 330; A.54; B.51; C.48; D.45; E.42; F.39; G.38; H.37

7. Repeats. 440, A.75; B.72; C.70; D.68; E.66; F.64; G.62; H.60; I.58

8. Selected longer distance repeats.

9. Sets.

	660 —	440 —	220
A.	1:50	70	34
B.	1:45	68	32
C.	1:42	66	30
D.	1:39	64	29
E.	1:36	62	28
F.	1:33	60	27
G.	1:30	58	26

10. Bunches. 2 or 3 660s; 3 to 6 440s; 6 to 10 220; Use same time as (9) A, B, Etc.

11. Run ot after each competition or workout

12. Wind sprints

14. Reduced interval 440s. Run 440, rest, 440, run 440, rest, 220; 440, rest 110, run 440. Use letters as (7).

15. Alternate sprint 55, shag 55.

16. Up and down hill.

Figure 5.2 Early Oregon training schedule sheet.

Training and progression were recorded and charted in written records. Though the basic patterns were the same for each athlete, the workouts themselves were highly individualized. The end result was almost 100 all-American athletes and dozens of Olympians across a wide range of events.

How to Interpret the Training Schedules

Later chapters discuss how to train for each individual track and field event. The daily training schedules in each chapter are not written in the form of today's periodized training patterns. Few examples of such genuine (rather than theoretical) training schedules are available. Instead of designing sets of theoretical periodized workout schedules, we have given real training schedules of athletes, each of whom was a national- or world-class athlete at the time that the schedules were used. Those athletes include Olympic champions and world-record holders in the 400m and discus, and national champions (sometimes national-record holders) in most other events.

Though the workouts are the originals, the schedule sheets have been revised slightly and redesigned to make the numbering system more consistent from one event to another. Also, the running distances were converted to the metric system. For easy reference, these schedules appear at the end of each event chapter.

Coaches who use the training schedules can write workouts for every athlete. A full month of training can be assigned, and saved, on one sheet. Because of the numbering system for the training fundamentals, the coach can easily review the program to see whether each training element is included or left out. An individual athlete's training needs can be easily met by modifying the sheet.

The numbering system allows the training to be recorded in a form of shorthand. Repetitions of an activity are numbered above the code for that activity. For example, in some cases a "6C" refers to running a 200m interval. A notation of "4×" above the "6C" means four repeats of 200m. If the assignment is "6C(2)," then the 200m pace is given in the "(2)" space on the schedule sheet.

Many of the numbered activities are essentially the same for every event (see Table 5.1). This makes the job of writing the workouts easier, and it shows a foundational core of training that is common to every athlete. The activities that are specific to an event are discussed in the appropriate event chapters. Following is an explanation of the fundamentals common to all schedules.

1. Warm-up routine.
The first activity on every schedule sheet is the warm-up. It includes jogging for every athlete. For the sprinters and jumpers, it includes easy work on the relay pass, described in the sprinting chapter. Except for distance runners (who cover from 1 to 3 miles), the athletes jog about two laps on or near the track. Jogging on grass or some other softer surface is easier on the legs than running on the track.

All athletes follow the jogging with their stretching routine. Then sprinters do the high-knee, fast-leg drill, while hurdlers go through the X drill (hurdle warm-up). Sprinters and hurdlers finish with a few easy starts.

A few other activities may be used instead of or following the warm-up. Field-event athletes might be assigned to run to Hendricks Park,* a tree-covered park on a nearby ridge (completing a 3-mile running loop) or to the hilly golf course 1 mile away. These may be conditioning runs themselves, or the athletes may run a hill-training session at the golf course. They may run steps at the track stadium. Usually, such other activities complete the training session, except for a cool-down.

Table 5.1   Common Activities on Training Schedules

1. Warm-up routine
    A. Jog 1-2 laps with relay pass
    B. Slow, high knee, fast leg
2. Fartlek
    A. Varied pace: stride, sprint, recover; stride, meet a challenge, recover; finish feeling exhilarated, not exhausted
        (1) 10 minutes   (2) 30 minutes   (3)
    B. Steady pace: slow, 10 to 30 minutes
        (1) Hendricks Park   (2) golf course   (3)
3. Strength and flexibility
    A. Weights and jogging
    B. Jogging and stretching
7. Team meeting
8. Special activities
    A. Sauna   C.
    B. Swim
10. Progress assessment
    A. Meet   C. Simulation
    B. Trial   D. Control test
12. With Coach
    A. (n a m e)   B. Leader
14. A. Wind sprints (1) straight (2) curve
    B. Hurdle (X) drill
    C. Spring and bound
    D. Alternate run/jog, at least 800m
    E. Hills with (1) coach (2) leader
15. Plyometrics
    A. Jumps (1) 1 leg (2) both legs (3)
    B. Bounding (1) 1 leg (2) both legs (3)
    C.
20. Work on second event
21. Visual aids
    A. Videotape   C. Photos
    B. Film
        (1) record performance   (2) study
30. Experimental work

2. Fartlek.
Fartlek has been an important part of distance training since the late 1940s, when it first came to the United States. Done properly, it has the advantages of interval training but without the boredom of laps on the track or the stress risks of working on harder surfaces.

With fartlek all of the elements of a race are mixed with periods of rest or partial recovery. The length of the training session depends upon the runner's time and energy, though few quality fartlek sessions last

---

*Because the schedules provided represent actual workouts, the authors have opted to keep Hendricks Park (near the University of Oregon) as an entry. Coaches may assign a comparable "park run" for their athletes.

more than 45 minutes. Fartlek sessions are usually done on soft surfaces, such as grass or sawdust.

The runner begins by jogging slowly for 2 or 3 miles as a warm-up, preparing the cardiovascular and respiratory systems for hard work. The runner then accelerates to race pace or to a planned effort level, running for 400 to 800m or until fatigue is felt. When fatigue appears, the athlete sprints for 50 to 150m until it begins to ''hurt.'' This is followed by a very slow jog or a walk to recover. Next comes a series of short sprints of perhaps 50 meters, alternating sprinting and walking or jogging equal distances until the effort becomes difficult, then recovering with another jog or walk.

Next, the runner imagines a racing setting. He or she strides at racing pace up to the shoulder of an imagined opponent, passes with a quick burst, then settles into racing pace for 200 to 400m, followed by a recovery jog or walk. Next comes another imaginary race, with the opponent approaching from the rear. The athlete accelerates enough to hold off a challenge or a series of challenges, then finishes with another jogging or walking recovery. Anything that can happen or be imagined in a race can be practiced in a fartlek session. Fartlek is a personal, *not* a group, tool.

In the past we have referred to Holmer and Lydiard fartlek. This is changed on the schedule sheets to avoid confusion. Holmer fartlek, named for Swedish coach Gosta Holmer (who made fartlek famous), is the traditional varied-pace running, or true fartlek. Lydiard fartlek, named for New Zealand coach Arthur Lydiard, is not really fartlek; it is steady-paced running. In the early stages of training, such steady runs may last from only 20 to 30 minutes, enough for general conditioning and a change of scene. Distance runners eventually run from 45 minutes to 1 hour or more. The value of Lydiard's contribution is its emphasis on the aerobic component of conditioning.

3. Strength and flexibility.

Few elite athletes fail to include strength training in their training program. This listing is used for ''easy day'' training, so we give two variations. The first variation is for weights and jogging, or a strength-training session, followed by easy jogging (preferably on a soft surface). The second variation does not include weights, calling simply for a light session of jogging and stretching.

Traditionally, we do not assign a set weight-training program. Strength training is specific to both the athlete and the event. Although we offer some general suggestions in the event chapters, we highly recommend that the coach and the athlete study the writings of strength-training specialists. The athlete's input is critical in developing a good strength-training pro-gram. The psychological or mental aspect is as important as the physical aspect in strength training.

7. Team meeting.

Team meetings should be a regular feature of the training sessions. These should not be daily events, nor should they interrupt training. They should be held either before the warm-up or after the training session and cool-down are completed. They should, above all, be *brief* because the student's time is far more limited than the coach's. An *effective* team meeting should not last longer than 10 to 15 minutes.

These meetings are to give *vital* information, such as future meets or changes in schedules or arrangements, or to ensure that team members are working toward the same goals. Short meetings can help draw the team together, but they are not pep rallies. An athlete who must be pumped up to train well has a limited future as a performer.

8. Special activities.

These activities are primarily alternate training or recovery activities. The two listed activities are sauna and swimming. The sauna can be a useful relaxation experience during a long, dreary winter's training. It also has some benefits in preparing athletes for dealing with heat in summer racing.

Swimming is an excellent easy day activity because it exercises the muscles without putting any body-support strain on the joints or feet. It provides all-around conditioning. It is also popular as a training activity for injured athletes (in such forms as running in place in deep water, including fartlek-type workouts).

10. Progress assessment.

We have listed several variations of the meet or time trial. Our version of the time trial is more properly called a ''*test effort*'' because it is never a full-effort attempt. Arthur Lydiard spoke of three-quarter—effort trials, where the athlete runs an even-paced effort at a planned pace that is slower than an all-out effort. The aim of these trials is for the athlete to perform each trial better than the previous trial, but always within limits, *knowing that he or she can perform even better when the time comes.*

The *simulation* is an imitation of the racing situation, with some changes made so that it will not be a full effort. Bill Dellinger uses a series of simulations for distance runners,[1] having them run the full racing distance at a mixture of the goal pace and slower paces. The athlete becomes accustomed to running the full racing distance, to running an increasingly faster overall pace, and to varying and monitoring the running pace carefully. These simulations are especially useful with younger athletes or with athletes changing to a new event.

Control tests are widely used in Eastern Europe. They are standard tests that indicate some aspect of the athlete's fitness in relation to their actual performance in the event. They are most useful in the field events.

12. With Coach *(name).* At times an athlete may be assigned to work with a specific or different coach for a training session or part of a training session. The coach's name is written in the blank space.

14. Miscellaneous training. Several different basic training activities are listed here. Wind sprints, usually about 100m each, are sometimes run on the straight and other times run on the curve (the latter for sprinters in the 200 and 400 or for intermediate hurdlers). The hurdler's drill, which we call the X drill, may be run by steeplechasers as technique work or by jumpers to help regulate their stride patterns.

Springing and bounding activities were once a smaller part of the training, but are growing for jumpers as plyometrics (next section). The alternate run and jog, done for at least 800m, is used primarily as a cooling-down activity. Hill training is used most in the fall and winter base-training phases, sometimes directed by a coach and sometimes led by one of the athletes.

15. Plyometrics. Plyometrics are jumping and bounding activities performed on one or both legs, sometimes across the open ground and sometimes on the track. It can include jumping from, onto, or over boxes or platforms of different heights. It improves the strength and resilience of the leg muscles. The result of a good plyometric program is stronger legs with more spring. It must be planned carefully, beginning with a very light load of activities, because the stress on the legs is high. We strongly recommend that any program be developed carefully, using expert information.[2]

20. Work on second event. Many school-age athletes compete in a second event. This number assigns a specific time to train for that event. An athlete should not try to train for too many events, but younger athletes may not be sure of their best event. An athlete's potentially best event may still be hidden at the start of the collegiate experience.

21. Visual aids. Visual aids are extremely useful to athletes in the technical events. Athletes can learn and imprint proper techniques by studying photos, films, and videotapes of the world's best athletes. The advances in videotaping over the last 2 decades have made this task far simpler for today's coaches and athletes. Tape is inexpensive and many machines allow frame-advance viewing for super—slow-motion technique studies.

All athletes should be videotaped regularly so their technique can be studied. Ideally, each athlete should be on a tape devoted to him or her so progress from one taping to the next can be studied. At the same time, the field-event athletes should study the performances of champion athletes on a regular basis.

30. Experimental Work. Every coach sometimes wants to experiment with a new idea in training or technique. This number assigns such activities. Athletes at the university level may be involved in a research study by faculty or graduate students, particularly outside the competitive season.

Other activities. You will notice in the event chapters that each event has some numbered activities that no other event has. At the same time, some numbers may be listed without including an activity. This allows for activities that are new or are not used regularly. Also, each activity in the schedules isn't necessarily included in every month of workouts. However, coaches should still consider these as they design their own programs. The coach or the athlete may have his or her own special drills or workout segments, which can be assigned one of those open numbers. The ''Experimental work'' listing is ''30,'' so open numbers are available to the coach and the athlete.

Figure 5.3 shows two types of boxes in which coaches can record an athlete's progress during the season. These boxes are useful additions to the training schedules for the high jump, long jump, pole vault, shot put, discus, and javelin.

Above all, the schedule sheets are not meant to be static. Just as an athlete's training and a good coach's training system are modified after each year's new experiences and learning, so will the schedule sheets be modified slightly each year. They should change

Date	Result	3/4	Date	Goal

Date	3/4	7/8	Goal	Date

Figure 5.3 Two types of abbreviated progress records.

to reflect the needs of your own program. They should be as dynamic as the training process itself.

Adapting the Training Schedules to Your Program

Although the training schedules are highly usable as they are, we prefer that each coach adapt them to his or her own program. This requires you to study the workouts and compare their objectives and progression to your own needs. Keep in mind that the training schedules were used by male college-age athletes. However, the original program emphasized moderation in training. Thus, the overall training loads are not high. As a result, there is little need to lessen the work load. Consider the following differences in adapting the schedules to your own program.

Age Differences

Older athletes can use higher work loads and more training sessions, while younger athletes cannot effectively train as often or as long. The coach must watch the recovery carefully because less experienced athletes may overtrain, not being as observant of their bodies' reactions to training stresses.

The coach can set a time limit on training sessions for young athletes, such as 1 hour for the middle schooler and 1-1/2 hours for the high school athlete (a heavy training day might add 1/2 hour to those figures). In addition, easy days should be clearly specified so young athletes are aware that such days are as important to the training process as the hard days.

Interval training and distance-running loads are the only areas in which the training schedules' load might be too high for younger athletes. We usually limit intervals to three times the racing distance, with a maximum load of three miles or 5,000m of intervals (not including recovery jogs). Those figures are reasonable for well-trained high schoolers. For middle school athletes, we suggest an interval limit of twice the racing distance, with 2 miles or 3,000m as an absolute limit. For middle schoolers, the long runs can be up to 6 miles, but 3 to 4 miles should be sufficient for most such runs.

Sex Differences

We do not recommend changing the training loads for females, compared to male work loads. Athletes' best marks are the truest gauges of their tolerance for given training loads. Two athletes with a best mark of 5:00 for the mile are essentially the same physio-

logically, regardless of their sex. Certainly no reason exists for giving one of them a lesser (or greater) training load. Instead, base any reductions on their age or skill levels, as described here.

Skill or Fitness Differences

The primary modification needed for the training schedules is a change in the suggested times for interval training sessions. All of the paces given in the training sheets are based on male college athletes in a national-level program. However, the interval times are also based on a standard progression of paces, based on each athlete's goal pace and date pace.

The *goal pace* (GP) is the pace that the athlete hopes to run for the peak race at the end of the season. For example, if the athlete's goal is to run 800m in 1:48, the GP is 27 seconds for 200m (54 seconds for 400m), the pace that will result in a time of 1:48. For races longer than 800m, the GP is usually the 400m pace. If an athlete hopes to run 5:20 for 1,600m, the GP is 80 (the pace time for 400m).

The *date pace* (DP) is the pace that the athlete can run the race in *at this date*. If the 800m runner can run 1:54 now, the DP is 28.5 for 200m. If the 1,600m runner runs 5:40, the DP is 85 seconds for 400m.

When using an interval workout from the schedules, compare the suggested interval times to the time of year and the schedule's GP (during the last month of the year). Translate that figure to your own GP and DP. The typical progression is to try to improve by 1 second per 400m per month of training. Thus, 2 months before peaking, an athlete may be running DP intervals about 2 seconds per 400m slower than the GP. This allows the athlete to gradually adapt to the faster racing paces.

GP and DP are discussed in more detail in the distance-training chapters.

References

1. Bill Dellinger & Bill Freeman. (1984). *The competitive runner's training book*. New York: Collier-Macmillan.
2. James C. Radcliffe & Robert C. Farentinos. (1985). *Plyometrics: Explosive power training* (2nd ed.). Champaign, IL: Human Kinetics.

Additional Reading

Bowerman, William J., & Freeman, William H. (1974). *Coaching track and field*. Boston: Houghton Mifflin.

PART II

The Training Programs

CHAPTER 8	# The High Hurdles

Hurdlers are usually agile people with quick reactions. They should be strong and fiercely competitive, and usually they are not easily agitated or distracted. Do *not* expect hurdlers to fall into a single physical group. Though most hurdlers are tall and tend toward ranginess, there have been world-class male hurdlers as short as 5′8″ and successful high school hurdlers even shorter.

Because the women's races use lower hurdles, only a woman who is unusually short or has very short legs may be at a disadvantage. Tanya Davis (5′1″ tall) of Nevada–Las Vegas ran the 100m hurdles in 13.40 seconds in 1986, and Gail Devers (5′2-3/4″ tall) of UCLA ran the race in 12.61 in 1988. Leg speed can overcome a height disadvantage.

Always remember one thing where hurdlers are concerned: They are sprinters first and hurdlers second. A slow person on the flat will be slow over the hurdles. Though your hurdlers may not be as fast as your best sprinters, they will not likely be far behind. In 1962 the University of Oregon set a world record of 40.0 on a cinder track for the 440-yard relay (39.7 for 400m) with a team of three hurdlers and one sprinter. Because hurdlers must be able to sprint to be successful, you should study the chapters on sprint training as a part of hurdle preparation.

In the beginning God did not create hurdlers. They either develop themselves or are developed by the teacher-coach. If the coach has to develop hurdlers, an organized training plan is needed. We will look at teaching athletes to hurdle, then we will discuss training methods and procedures for the high hurdles.

Teaching the Hurdles

Teaching prospects to hurdle can be discouraging to them, because it is human nature to avoid anything that might hurt. The prospect of hitting a hurdle and perhaps falling on the track may cause runners to shy away from trying to hurdle. The athletes cannot fear the hurdles. You can do two things to minimize their fears: (a) Perform most hurdle practices, at least in the learning and early practice stages, on the grass; and (b) use soft-top hurdles. Those simple precautions do much to limit the fears of athletes.

You must know the difference between the lead leg and the trail leg. The leg that goes over the hurdle first is the lead leg, while the leg that follows the body over the hurdle is the trail leg.

It makes no difference which leg the high hurdler uses as the lead leg. Athletes find that they naturally prefer one leg to the other. For a race that goes around a turn on the track, there are advantages to leading with the left leg. However, not all of the best runners of such races lead with the left leg.

The arm opposite the lead leg is called the "lead arm" because it leads over the hurdle in conjunction with the lead leg. If a person leads with the right leg, the left arm is the lead arm, and the right arm is the trail arm.

The hurdler should be observed regularly from three different vantage points. The common one is from the side. Many problems can be detected from this angle, but the coach should also watch from in front of and behind the hurdler. Balance and mechanical problems that are too subtle to detect from the side can be seen from the front or the rear.

The hurdler should at all times remember that the primary objective is to get to the finish line as quickly as possible. This is a sprint race with obstacles in the way. The hurdling form should not be developed in a way that gains beauty only to lose speed.

Learning to Hurdle With the X Drill

The athletes should first try walking over the hurdles. Pull three hurdles over backward and place them 5 yards apart. Boxes or other objects about 12 to 15 inches in height can be used as well. Have the hurdlers walk over the obstacles, concentrating on lifting the lead knee. After several repetitions of this exercise, they should walk through while concentrating on the trail leg and turning the trailing toe outward and upward, until they have the feel of the basic hurdling action. Then they will be ready to learn the X drill, used to teach hurdling and review the basic techniques regularly.

The term *X* has no meaning other than as a name for the routine. We begin with three hurdles set at the low height (30 inches). If lower hurdles are available, they may be preferable for women candidates. The high hurdle settings are shown in Table 8.1. For the teaching drill, begin with closer hurdle settings. For men, use 14 yards to the first hurdle and 8 yards between the hurdles, then move to 14 and 9 yards, then finally to 15 and 10 yards. For women, use 12 yards to the first hurdle and 7 yards between the hurdles, then move to 13 and 8 yards, then move finally to the full distances.

The first step in the X drill is walking to the side of the hurdles. The athletes walk past the hurdles, keeping them on their lead-leg side. As they approach each hurdle, they lift the lead knee and step over the hurdle with that leg only, keeping the trail leg out to the side of the hurdle. This exercise is repeated, then the athletes move to the other side of the hurdles to practice with the trail leg. Again they walk past the hurdles, taking care to place the lead foot past the hurdle, then bring the trail leg over the hurdle with the toe turned out so the foot crosses the hurdle parallel to its top. This exercise is also repeated.

The hurdlers next progress to trotting past the hurdles, using the same exercises as above, but taking only five steps between each hurdle. After they acquire the habit of leading with the knee, we no longer use the lead-leg exercises as part of the X drill. First they trot through two repetitions to the side, exercising the trail leg, then they complete this stage of the drill by five-stepping over the top of the hurdles, using all aspects of correct form. This is also repeated twice.

The final stage in the drill is a switch to using three steps between the hurdles. First, two repetitions are run to the side using the trail leg, then two are run straight across the tops of the hurdles. While the previous exercises must be rather slow, the three-stepping exercises must be rather fast.

Training With the X Drill

We emphasize several points of form when using the X drill:

1. The lead leg is directed by lifting the knee. If the knee is lifted in the approach to each hurdle, the foot almost automatically reaches out to clear the hurdle, and it is less likely to be directed off to the side. The leg can also be raised more quickly than if the hurdler led with the foot because a short pendulum (the thigh) can move more swiftly than a longer one (the whole leg). The knee of the lead leg should not lock while crossing the hurdle because this slows the step to the ground.

Table 8.1 High Hurdle Settings*

| | | | Hurdle spacing | | |
Gender	Distance (m)	Hurdle height	Start to first hurdle	Between hurdles	Last hurdle to finish
Men	110	1.067 3'6"	13.72 45'0"	9.14 30'0"	14.02 46'0"
Women	100	0.840 2'9"	13 42'8"	8.50 27'10-3/4"	10.50 34'5-1/2"

*Settings are given first in meters, with equivalents in feet and inches underneath.

2. The hurdler should pull the trail knee through and into sprinting position. The trail foot does not have to be thrust forward to reach into the next step if the knee is brought through properly and the hurdler keeps on the toes and tries for a quick-stepping rhythm.

3. The toe of the trail foot must be rotated upward (everted) until the foot clears the hurdle in a position parallel to the top, rather than hitting the hurdle.

4. The shoulders must be kept level. To do this the trail hand (on the side of the lead foot) reaches about as far forward as the lead knee (but straight ahead, not across the knee), while the lead arm extends fully straight ahead and downward across the hurdle (we call this combination "a hand and a half"). If either hand comes across the body, the hurdler will tend to land off balance, moving toward the side of the track.

5. The hurdler should work to stay up on the toes, trying not to run flat-footed or land on the heels before or after clearing the hurdle.

6. The dive, the lean over the hurdle by the upper body, should be held until the toe is almost on the ground. The trailing foot can then be pulled straight forward, clearing the hurdle with less effort.

The X drill is the conclusion of the warm-up exercises on each day when the hurdlers practice their hurdling, which is usually two or three times a week. When working on technique with the X drill, they practice only one fundamental at a time, such as running through the drill while concentrating on keeping on the toes or getting the rhythm of the dive. Working on everything at once can be too confusing to the athlete (and the coach).

Training Theory for High Hurdles

The fitness characteristics for the hurdle races are the following:[1]

General conditioning
    aerobic endurance
    strength endurance
    mobility
    maximum strength
Special conditioning
    speed endurance
    special mobility (flexibility)
    speed
    elastic strength
    special strength: relative
    special endurance: 200m and 400m

Competition-specific conditioning
    hurdles technique
    sprint technique
    start technique
    stride patterns
    time trials

The key to hurdling is speed, with technique following closely. The athlete's height is a factor but not in the expected way. Just as being short creates difficulties for the hurdler, being tall also creates problems.[2] For men, 6'0" to 6'2" seems to be the ideal height, give or take an inch. For taller athletes, the tendency is to shuffle (rather than sprint) between the hurdles. Otherwise, the hurdler will overrun the barriers. For women, the ideal height seems to be 5'7" to 5'9". However, elite performers appear across a wide range of heights.

The first training emphasis should be speed, with much mobility work to improve flexibility at the hip.[3] Bounding, hill running, and strength work are used to develop leg power. Wilbur Ross notes that optical fatigue is a factor that limits performances. He also recommends using music in developing the hurdler's all-important running rhythm.[4]

As in sprinting, no widely accepted general theory of hurdle training has appeared yet. We have a contrast between the United States, with its seemingly bottomless pool of raw talent, and the rest of the world. American hurdlers have superior speed but poorly developed technique. European hurdlers, who are gaining ground on the Americans, have superior technique but lack the raw speed.[5] Speed is still the bottom line.

Coaches can evaluate the weak points in an athlete's endurance by recording touchdown times off the hurdles. For example, the start is critical in the high hurdles. How does the athlete's time from start to landing after the first hurdle compare to his or her flat start for that distance? An athlete's total time can be predicted from the touchdown time after one hurdle, assuming no endurance weaknesses. Recording times is much easier now that miniature stopwatch-timers are widely available. The coach can easily record the touchdown time after all 10 hurdles while watching the full race. This is an extremely valuable coaching tool. Tables 8.2 and 8.3 give samples of projected touchdown times for the high hurdles.

Applying the Theory

The warm-up routine of the hurdler should ensure that the circulation is moving well, the body temperature is adjusted, and the runner feels warm but not tired. Extreme stretching should be avoided. If extreme or

Table 8.2　Men's 110m Hurdle Touchdown Times

Target time	H1	H2	H3	H4	H5	H6	H7	H8	H9	H10	Finish time
12.8	2.4	3.4	4.3	5.2	6.2	7.2	8.2	9.2	10.3	11.2	12.8
13.0	2.4	3.4	4.4	5.4	6.4	7.4	8.4	9.4	10.5	11.6	13.0
13.2	2.5	3.5	4.4	5.4	6.4	7.4	8.5	9.6	10.7	11.8	13.2
13.6	2.5	3.6	4.6	5.6	6.6	7.7	8.8	9.9	11.0	12.2	13.6
14.0	2.5	3.6	4.6	5.7	6.8	7.9	9.0	10.1	11.2	12.4	14.0
14.4	2.6	3.6	4.7	5.8	6.9	8.1	9.3	10.5	11.7	12.9	14.4
14.6	2.6	3.7	4.7	5.8	7.0	8.2	9.4	10.6	11.8	13.0	14.6
15.0	2.6	3.7	4.9	6.0	7.2	8.3	9.5	10.7	12.0	13.2	15.0
15.5	2.7	3.8	5.0	6.2	7.4	8.6	9.8	11.0	12.3	13.6	15.5
16.0	2.8	3.9	5.1	6.4	7.6	8.8	10.1	11.3	12.6	14.0	16.0

From Brent McFarlane. (1981). Hurdles touchdown times. In Jess Jarver (Ed.), *The hurdles: Contemporary theory, technique and training* (2nd ed., p. 34). Los Altos, CA: Tafnews. Reprinted with permission.

Table 8.3　Women's 100m Hurdle Touchdown Times

Target time	H1	H2	H3	H4	H5	H6	H7	H8	H9	H10	Finish time
11.8	2.2	3.2	4.1	5.0	5.9	6.9	7.9	8.9	9.9	10.9	11.8
12.0	2.3	3.3	4.2	5.1	6.0	7.0	8.0	9.0	10.0	11.1	12.0
12.3	2.3	3.3	4.2	5.1	6.1	7.1	8.1	9.1	10.2	11.3	12.3
12.8	2.4	3.4	4.4	5.4	6.4	7.4	8.4	9.5	10.6	11.7	12.8
13.2	2.4	3.4	4.4	5.5	6.6	7.7	8.8	9.9	11.0	12.1	13.2
13.8	2.5	3.5	4.6	5.7	6.8	7.9	9.1	10.2	11.4	12.6	13.8
14.0	2.5	3.5	4.6	5.7	6.9	8.1	9.3	10.4	11.6	12.8	14.0
14.3	2.5	3.6	4.7	5.9	7.1	8.3	9.5	10.7	11.9	13.1	14.3
14.8	2.6	3.8	4.9	6.0	7.2	8.4	9.6	10.9	12.2	13.5	14.8
15.0	2.6	3.8	4.9	6.1	7.3	8.5	9.7	11.0	12.3	13.6	15.0

From Brent McFarlane. (1981). Hurdles touchdown times. In Jess Jarver (Ed.), *The hurdles: Contemporary theory, technique and training* (2nd ed., p. 34). Los Altos, CA: Tafnews. Reprinted with permission.

violent stretching exercises are performed in practice, the extra adrenalin flowing on the day of competition makes the hurdler more liable to pull or strain a muscle before the competition ever starts. No muscles need to be stretched any more in warming up than they will be stretched in performing the competitive activities.

From the dressing room, the hurdler jogs to the track, then covers about 800m while alternating jogging and stretching easily. He or she finishes with another 400m of jogging and is then ready for the day's activities. Note that the X drill is a graduated warm-up routine as well as a training routine.

Practice shows that if an athlete works hard on one day, a recovery period will probably be needed the

next day. This is generally true for all athletic events. By alternating hard and easy days of training, the athlete can prepare well for the competitive events and at the same time use the easy days to benefit from activities such as easy jogging, weight training, and swimming. Often the hurdlers may work with the sprinters on activities such as relay work on the easier days.

For a hard day, the hurdler begins with warm-up jogging and stretching, then goes through the X drill, working perhaps on the trail leg. He or she progresses from five-stepping to the sides and over the top to three-stepping to the sides and over the top. The X drill begins with the hurdles set at lower heights, the hurdle gradually being raised as the athlete warms up (such as 30 inches, then 36, 39, and 42 inches for men). Such a range of heights is not as necessary for women athletes because their hurdles are lower relative to their height. The hurdler might then run several intervals, followed by easy fartlek, with the workout concluded by four progressively faster 100s.

As the athlete becomes more fit, the coach will realize that there are competitive situations where the hurdler may race on 2 or even 3 consecutive days. If this is so, preparation for such a situation should begin about a month ahead of time. On one day the athlete might warm up with the usual routine, do the X drill, then simulate a racing situation, such as running through a full set of hurdles, running five hurdles back to back, or perhaps running the first three hurdles and the last three hurdles, striding from hurdle 3 to hurdle 8. This is followed by a cool-down at the end of practice. It is neither a hard nor an easy day, but the runner is being conditioned mentally and physically for the big races that are coming.

The next day, rather than taking it easy, the hurdler again warms up, perhaps takes three or four starts, works on the hurdles as on the previous day (going through a full flight either in part, in segments, or in the first and last parts), then cools down again.

The third day (when preparing for three consecutive racing days) begins with a warm-up, then simulates the racing situation again. Following this is the hardest workout of the week. When athletes get into shape by planned work, they do not want to rest so much when preparing for the meets ahead that they become less fit. The continuation of this procedure might be to run a series of 100s or 150s, or perhaps do enough relay work to run 800m, then finish with a jog through the hills or a series of moderate wind sprints.

As a final note on training, a good practice is to have regular test efforts every 2 weeks until the competitive season begins. These usually are not over the full distance. For the high hurdles, they are usually at 60m (four or five hurdles), 70m (five or six hurdles), or 80m (seven hurdles, 3/4ths of the racing distance). These might be all-out trials, but more often they are aimed at running at a set pace or at a rate of gradual improvement from one trial to the next. Also, they are usually run over hurdles set below the regular competitive height during the winter (36 or 39 inches for men, 30 inches for women).

The Training Schedules: Special Fundamentals for High Hurdles

Many of the fundamentals on the high hurdle schedule sheet are common to the sheets for other events (chapter 5). We need to look at the activities that are different.

5. Starts.   Starts are done as in the sprints, moving from relaxed effort to harder effort but never making an all-out effort. Starts may be over 30 or 50m, either on the flat or over the high or intermediate hurdles. 5E and 5F develop the endurance. The back-to-back hurdles are starts from the blocks over the first five hurdles, a walk back to the starting line, and a repeat start over five hurdles. The first three, last three drill runs over the full high hurdle race, without the middle four hurdles. The athlete drives through the first three hurdles, slows to stride through the middle of the race with no barriers, then accelerates to finish strongly over the last three hurdles and through the finish line.

6. Intervals.   Intervals may include some variations in their emphasis. They may be run with a fast 20 to 50m in the middle. They may be run over the intermediate hurdles for strength and endurance work. Shorter intervals may be run on the straight or around the curve. Any situation that the athlete might encounter in a race should be practiced repeatedly in training.

10. Progress assessment.   Meets, time trials, and simulations can involve a variety of distances and conditions. For high hurdlers, the most common testing distance is the indoor race of 55m, though a trial may range from 40m to the full outdoor distance.

11. Bunches.   Bunches, unlike intervals, are usually run in pairs. An 11A (500m) means to run 500m two times. An 11BC means to run 300m twice, then run 100m twice. The 11D is a set rather than a bunch, running 300m, 200m, and then 100m.

16. Finish work.   These exercises strengthen the finishing endurance and skills. The first three, last three drill is the same as 5F under "Starts." The 16B is run over the full 10 hurdles, but simply with floating or running easily over the first five barriers, then finishing strongly over the last five. The 16C is run like the 16B, but with the first five hurdles removed from the lane.

17. X drill.   This calls for parts of the X drill to be run at different heights, such as rising from the intermediate hurdle height to the high hurdle height. The different focal points of the body are numbered. For example, 17B(7a) means to run across the top of the hurdles, using the 30-inch low hurdle setting and working on staying up on the toes. The athlete might work on one or two aspects of technique during a workout. He or she cannot effectively focus on every aspect in sequence because fatigue will interfere with proper performance. However, every part of the technique can be practiced at least once in a week. During the late season, only the weaker points are practiced.

The training schedules for 10 months follow. The school notes are based on the university quarter system. When these schedules were written, the NCAA Meet was held in mid-June instead of the current late May. The higher numbers in parentheses indicate the speed in seconds.

References

1. Frank W. Dick. (1978). *Training theory* (pp. 64-65). London: British Amateur Athletic Board.
2. NSA Round Table: The sprint hurdles. (1988). *New Studies in Athletics*, **3**(2), 14-17.
3. Jess Jarver. (1981). Hurdling in a nutshell. In Jess Jarver (Ed.), *The hurdles: Contemporary theory, technique and training* (2nd ed., pp. 9-13). Los Altos, CA: Tafnews.
4. Wilbur L. Ross. (1978). *The hurdler's bible* (3rd ed., pp. 44-50). San Juan, PR: Santana.
5. Frank Lehmann. (1987). Development of hurdle technique. *Track Technique*, **99**, 3172-3173.

Additional Readings

Arnold, Malcolm. (1988). Time analysis of the sprint hurdle events at the II World Championships in Athletics: Interpretation from the point of view of training practice. *New Studies in Athletics*, **3**(2), 72-74.

Cornachia, G. (1983). Hurdle exercises. *Track and Field Quarterly Review*, **83**(2), 55-56.

McFarlane, Brent. (1987). Hurdle periodization. *Track Technique*, **101**, 3219-3220.

McFarlane, Brent. (1988). High performance hurdling: The women's 100m hurdles. *Track and Field Quarterly Review*, **88**(1), 31-37.

McFarlane, Brent. (1989). Hurdle fault analysis and correction chart. *Track Technique*, **108**, 3445-3448.

McFarlane, Brent. (1989). *The science of hurdling*. Ottawa: Canadian Track and Field Association.

May, Willie. (1990). Developing high school high hurdlers: Progression phase. *Track and Field Quarterly Review*, **90**(1), 24-25.

Mulqueen, Michael. (1985). Hurdles. *Track and Field Quarterly Review*, **85**(2), 44-45.

Poquette, Jean. (1981). Nehemiah's high school training. In Jarver, pp. 67-72.

Rose, Peggy A. (1986). *A technical training manual for beginners and intermediate level female high school hurdlers*. Unpublished master's thesis, Texas Woman's University, Denton.

Saraslanidis, Plutarchos. (1988). Trends in juniors' training in 110m hurdles research from the 1st World Junior Championships: Athens, 1986. *Track and Field Quarterly Review*, **88**(1), 38-41.

Szczepanski, Tadeusz. (1984). The women's 100m hurdles. *Track and Field Quarterly Review*, **84**(2), 34-37.

Warden, Peter. (1988). Planning training for the sprints and hurdles. *Track Technique*, **105**, 3351-3352, 3363-3364.

Winckler, Gary. (1989). Hurdling. In Vern Gambetta (Ed.), *The Athletics Congress's track and field coaching manual* (2nd ed., pp. 73-87). Champaign, IL: Leisure Press.

High Hurdle Training Schedule

ATHLETE

1. Warm-up
   A. Jog 1-2 laps with relay pass; hurdle X drill at lower height
   B. Slow, high knee; fast leg drill
   C. 2 starts to first hurdle
2. Fartlek
   A. Varied pace: stride, sprint, recover; stride, meet a challenge, recover Finish feeling exhilarated, not exhausted
      (1) 10 minutes (2) 30 minutes (3)
   B. Steady pace: slow, 10-30 min
      (1) Hendricks Park (2) golf course (3)
3. Strength & flexibility
   A. Weights and jogging
   B. Jogging and stretching
4. High knee and fast leg
5. Starts: 2 at 1/2 speed, 2 at 7/8 speed
   A. 30m
   B. 50m
   C. HH
   D. IH
   E. Back to back highs, 5 hurdles
   F. First 3, jog, last 3
      (1) on your own (2) gun
6. Intervals X. Over IH
   Z. Fast 20-50m in middle
   A. 100
      (1) 18-16-14-12 sec (2) 17-15-13 sec
      a. curve b. straight c.
   B. 150 (1) 22 sec (2) 20 sec (3)
   C. 150-100-50
      (1) 22-16-6 sec (2)
   D. 200 (1) 30 sec (2) 28 sec (3)
   E. 300 (1) 3/4 effort (2)
   F. 500 (1) 3/4 effort (2)
7. Team meeting
8. Special
   A. Sauna   C.
   B. Swim
9. Relay work
   A. Routine   C. Trial
   B. 50m
10. Progress assessment
    A. Meet   C. Simulation
    B. Trial   D. Control test
       (1) 40m (2) 60m
       (3) 80m (4) full distance
11. Bunches
    A. 500 (1) 75-80 sec (2)
    B. 300 (1) 45-48 sec (2)
    C. 100 (1) 12 sec (2)
    D. 300-200-100 (1)
12. With Coach
    A. (name)   B. Leader
14. A. Wind sprints (1) straight (2) curve
    B. Hurdle X drill
    C. Spring and bound
    D. Alternate run & jog, at least 800m
    E. Hills with (1) coach (2) leader
15. Plyometrics
    A. Jumps (1) 1 leg (2) both legs (3)
    B. Bounding (1) 1 leg (2) both legs (3)
    C.
16. Finish work
    A. First 3, jog, last 3
    B. Full 10: float for 5, then go last 5
    C. Last 5 hurdles
17. X drill a. 30" b. 33" c. 36" d. 39" e. 42"
    A. 5-step to side   C. 3-step to side
    B. 5-step to top   D. 3-step to top
       (1) lean (2) lead leg (3) trail leg
       (4) lead arm (5) off arm (6) quickness
       (7) on toes
    G. On grass
18.
19. 5 hurdles
    A. First 5   B. Last 5
20. Work on second event
21. Visual aids
    A. Videotape   C. Photos
    B. Film
       (1) record performance (2) study
30. Experimental work

DATE September/October

M	Organization—lockers—equipment
Tu	Meet on the use of weights
W	Discuss off-campus courses—14A
Th	3A
F	1A—1B—2A(1)
Sa	
Su	Recreation
M	1B—19—2A—$\overset{4x}{6A(1)}$—14D
Tu	3A
W	14E
Th	3A
F	10B(200m at 7/8-9/10 effort)
Sa	
Su	
M	1A—19—$\overset{2x}{6A(1)}$—14D
Tu	3A
W	12—jog
Th	3A
F	1A—$\overset{2x}{11A,B,C}$—1B
Sa	
Su	
M	1A—1B—17A,B,C,D(6" and 3" below race height)
Tu	3A
W	14E
Th	3A
F	
Sa	
Su	

DATE October/November

M	1B—5A—21A(1)—11A—$\overset{2-4x}{6A(1)}$—2B(1)
Tu	3A
W	12 or 8—6A(1)
Th	3A
F	$\overset{2x}{6E}$—$\overset{4x}{100m}$—2A(1)
Sa	3B
Su	
M	1A—5A—17G—$\overset{4x}{6A}$—2A(1)
Tu	3A—21A(1)
W	12 or 8—6A(1)
Th	
F	10B(100m flat or 5 hurdles)
Sa	10B(300m flat)
Su	
M	1A—5A—$\overset{1x}{100m}$—$\overset{2x}{6E}$—$\overset{2x}{6D}$—6A(1)
Tu	3B—21A(1)
W	12 or 8
Th	3A
F	10B(100m or hurdles)—2A(1)
Sa	
Su	
M	1A—5A—17G—$\overset{3x}{6B}$—10B(1)
Tu	3A
W	8 or 12—$\overset{3x}{6B}$
Th	
F	10B(100m and relay)
Sa	10B(relay and 300m)
Su	

DATE November/December

M	1A—17A,B,C,D—$\overset{2x}{6XB}$—$\overset{2x}{11A}$
Tu	3A
W	8 or 12
Th	
F	$\overset{2x}{10B(100m}$—$\overset{1x}{300m)}$—14A
Sa	
Su	2A
M	1A—1B—5C—11A—$\overset{2x}{6XB}$
Tu	7—3A—21A(1)
W	1—5A—9A—6D—11A
Th	
F	10B (relay)—10B(3)—2B(1)
Sa	10B(100m—300m)
Su	
M	
Tu	
W	
Th	
F	
Sa	
Su	
M	
Tu	
W	
Th	
F	
Sa	
Su	

DATE January

M	Register—lockers—2B
Tu	3B
W	1A—4—17A,B,C,D—⁴ˣ6A(13-15)—14E or 12
Th	9A—3A—4—6C
F	1—5A—17A,B,C,D—³ˣ6B—2B(1)
Sa	11 or 2
Su	
M	1A—4—17—²ˣ6A(2)(a)—²ˣ6A(2)(b)—⁴ˣ6A(13)
Tu	3A—4—7
W	1A—5A—²ˣ4 hurdles—14E or 12
Th	3A(grass)
F	1A—4—5B(2)—jog—²ˣ6A(2a)—²ˣ6A(2b)—²ˣ2A(1)
Sa	
Su	
M	1—5A—6A(1)—6B—2B(1)
Tu	1—3(grass)
W	1—5B(2)—17(2,3)(d,e or a,b)
Th	1—3—jog
F	10B(relay—hurdles)
Sa	
Su	
M	1—5A(2)—17(2,3)—11A
Tu	3A
W	1—5A(2)—10B(2)—6B
Th	3A
F	Gear ready—jog
Sa	10A at Portland, or 3B
Su	

DATE February

M	1A—4—5A(2)—²ˣ17B,C—6B—²ˣ6A—jog
Tu	3—8A or 8B
W	1A—4—11A(1)—14E
Th	3A—3B
F	1A—5A(2)—17B,C—5A—²ˣ6D(2)—⁴ˣ6A(14)—2B(1)
Sa	14E—3
Su	Recreation
M	1—4—17B,C(5)—²ˣ11A—11B—2B(1)
Tu	3A—8A or 8B
W	1—⁴ˣ6A(2)—14E
Th	3A—8A or 8B
F	1—jog
Sa	10B(4)(36" and 39" or 30" and 33")—relay—jog
Su	Jog
M	1A—17B,C(1)—³ˣ6B(3)—²ˣ6D(2-1)—2B(1)
Tu	1A—²ˣ6D(2-1)—⁴ˣ6A(13)—11A,B,C
W	14E
Th	1A—4—5B—²ˣ6A(13)—2B(1)
F	10B(relay—70m highs)—11A,B,C
Sa	3—2B(1)
Su	Recreation
M	1—4—17B,C(4)—²ˣ11A—11B—2B(1)
Tu	3A—8A or 8B
W	⁴ˣ6AX—14E
Th	3A—8A or 8B
F	2A(1)
Sa	10B(3)—10B(300m IH)
Su	Recreation

DATE March

M	1A—4—⁴ˣ6A(12-13)—11A(2)—2B(1)
Tu	9A—3A
W	1A—17A,B—⁴ˣ6A(12-13)—14E
Th	9A—2B(1)
F	10B(relay)—6E—2B(1)
Sa	10B(4)—6E—2B(1)
Su	Study—jog
M	Exam week—jog, study, rest
Tu	
W	1—4—5A—17A,B,C,D—¹⁻²ˣ6A(2)—jog
Th	
F	1—4—5B—²ˣ6A(1)(a)—²ˣ6AX(1)(a)—6D(grass)
Sa	10A(1 race)
Su	Jog—spring trip—settle in
M	a.m. Jog p.m. Hill jog
Tu	Jog 4—²ˣ5A(2)—6B—⁴ˣ6A(12-13)
W	Jog 9A
Th	Jog 1A—³ˣ5B—6D(grass)
F	Light—gear ready
Sa	10A
Su	Home
M	Register—1A—9A—6C—⁴ˣ6B—6A
Tu	9A
W	1A—5A—5A(2)—5B—6A(1)—6E or 6F
Th	Light—9A
F	Gear ready
Sa	10A(relays)
Su	Jog

DATE April

M	1A—4—5A—17—6A—7
Tu	9—3A
W	9A—1A—1B—14E—6A(2)
Th	17A,B,C,D(e or b)
F	5A—9A
Sa	10A(relay—highs)
Su	Home—loosen up
M	9A—17—6D
Tu	4x 1A—5A(2)—6A—11B—7
W	9A—6F(easy grass)
Th	1A—5A(1)—5B—5C—6B
F	Travel—loosen up
Sa	10A(dual)
Su	Home—loosen up
M	4x 9A—1A—6B—6A—6E—jog
Tu	9A—jog
W	9A—1A—3A—16B—16C—2B(1)
Th	9A
F	Light
Sa	10A(home)
Su	Jog
M	2x 1—5A—17—5B—6B—light jog
Tu	9A—3A
W	1—5A—5B—12—8
Th	Relay and jog
F	5(2 starts)—9A—gear ready
Sa	10A(dual)
Su	Loosen up

DATE May

M	2x 1A—5A—17—5B—6AX
Tu	9A—14A
W	7—5A,B,C—jog
Th	Gear ready
F	Light
Sa	10A(dual)
Su	Light
M	a.m. 9A | p.m. 1—17—5B—5C(grass)—6D
Tu	3A
W	1—5A,B,C—6BX—jog
Th	Light
F	Travel
Sa	10A(Invitational)
Su	Home—loosen up
M	9A—17G—14A
Tu	1A—5A—17—5B—5C—6B
W	1—9A—6A
Th	1—5A—17—14A
F	Gear ready
Sa	Northern Division Meet
Su	
M	
Tu	
W	
Th	
F	
Sa	
Su	

DATE June

M	1A—4—14A
Tu	5(easy)—9A(easy)
W	9A
Th	Easy jog
F	10A(prelims)
Sa	10A(conference finals)
Su	Picnic
M	Exams—light—study
Tu	Light—study
W	1A—5A—5B—14A
Th	1A—5A—5B—14A
F	1A—5A,B,C—14A
Sa	Light
Su	9A
M	Light
Tu	9A
W	Light
Th	NCAA Meet: heats
F	NCAA Meet: semis
Sa	NCAA Meet: finals
Su	
M	
Tu	
W	
Th	
F	
Sa	
Su	

CHAPTER 9	# The Intermediate
	## Hurdles

The 180-yard low hurdles used to be the odd American race for high schools, but fortunately the 300m hurdle race has replaced it. The women's race is at the low hurdle height, so the primary requirement of the race is someone who can run a good flat 400 or 800 and lift her feet, as long as she is not too short-legged. The race requires only moderate hurdling skills at the younger age levels, for with moderate training a good sprinter can beat a good hurdler 9 times out of 10.

Training Theory for 400-Meter Hurdles

Training theory for the 400m hurdles is consistent with training for the 400m flat race and the high hurdles; that is, no consistent agreement exists on training methods. This has always been a strong American event because of the mass of raw talent in sprinting and hurdling. One area of agreement is on the importance of developing a sense of rhythm for approaching the hurdles. Overemphasis on the step pattern can cause difficulties for the athlete if race conditions cause the athlete to break stride. The hurdle distances and rough step pattern are shown in Tables 9.1 and 9.2. The number of steps depends on the athlete's speed and body structure.

Coaches and researchers in the Russian system made these recommendations for improving women's performances in the intermediate hurdles:[1]

- Use double periodization for advanced athletes (allows better distribution of conditioning).
- Use more long runs over the intermediate hurdles (set at the standard distances, these develop specific endurance and rhythm between the hurdles).
- Use more bounding against the clock for 30m to 100m (develops specific power).
- Run more intermediate hurdle races (competition is an excellent preparation method). *Note*: This may be unnecessary for an athlete on a school team with long competitive seasons.

Applying the Theory

The intermediate hurdler should think of him- or herself as having the speed of a sprinter, the skill of a high hurdler, and the endurance of a half-miler. The athlete who has the courage to believe this has the potential to become a great intermediate hurdler. The intermediate hurdle race, although related to the highs, is an entirely different event. In tough competition, it is a most unusual person who can do both events

Table 9.1 Intermediate Hurdle Settings*

| Gender | Distance | Hurdle height | Hurdle spacing | | |
			Start to first hurdle	Between hurdles	Last hurdle to finish
Men	400 meters	0.914	45	35	40
		3'0"	147'8"	114'10"	131'3"
Women	400 meters	0.762	45	35	40
		2'6"	147'8"	114'10"	131'3"

*Measurements are first given in meters, with equivalents in feet and inches underneath.

Table 9.2 Intermediate Hurdle Step Pattern

Strides to first hurdle	Strides between hurdles
21	13
21-22	14
22	15
22-23	16
23-24	17

with the utmost skill. The danger is that the athlete may put so much into the preliminary races that he or she will be totally exhausted after 3 days of competition in each event, particularly after meeting other outstanding athletes who are competing in only one event.

It is very difficult to accomplish the double in national competition. Some high hurdlers are unable to cover the entire distance of the intermediates, possibly because physiologically they cannot accommodate the lactate buildup or perhaps because they are mentally lazy and do not want to prepare themselves to run this tough event. When Jerry Tarr won both events for Oregon in the 1962 NCAA Meet, he would not have run both events except that the competition in the highs was limited, with few rounds to race. Most important, only eight intermediate hurdlers declared, allowing him to go through the high hurdle qualifying rounds without having to run an all-out race before the finals in either race.

What does the intermediate hurdler do? Run off the starting block, attempting to reach the first hurdle in 6 seconds. This is, of course, after developing the stride to the point that it is reached quickly but comfortably. From the first to the second hurdle takes about 4 seconds for most world-class males. It is not realistic for a beginning hurdler to try to run fast splits over the early hurdles, as a world-class performer might try to do. Instead, the touchdown tables (Tables

9.3 and 9.4) give a rough idea of projected times at different points in the race, based on the time that the hurdler is trying to run.

Imagine you were a beginning male hurdler. You should start from a standing start, or down in the traditional sprint start, and run the first hurdle comfortably but quickly in about 7 seconds. Next, trot back and cover the same distance again, but this time going over the first three hurdles. Take a recovery, jogging completely around the track; then when you reach the head of the last straight, run the last three hurdles down the straight, trying a pace of between 4 and 5 seconds between each hurdle. Take another full-lap recovery jog, then run the three hurdles on the bend, again trying to get between 4 and 5 seconds between each hurdle. Complete another lap recovery jog, then run the last two hurdles, for about 80m and try to finish up as you would in the 400m hurdle race.

A variation of this exercise is to run the first 100m, recover with a quarter, run the middle 200m of the race, jog another lap, then finish with 100m over the hurdles. Another exercise is to run 100m over the hurdles, jog back to the start, run 200m over the hurdles, jog back to the start, then run 300m over the hurdles.

Too much hurdling can produce sore knees and ankles from hitting the hurdles, so the intermediate hurdler should run through the X drill over the low and high hurdles, then run through intervals of low or intermediate hurdles totaling once or twice the racing distance, and then think like an 800m runner. Use what we call step-down sets, running one or two sets of 600-400-200. This consists of 600m at a pace of 30 to 35 seconds per 200m for men (1:30 to 1:45 total), 35 to 40 seconds for women (1:45 to 2:00), then a recovery of 600m (or however much is needed). This is followed by 400m at a slightly faster pace, perhaps at a pace 2 seconds faster per 200m. After a 400m jog, the set is concluded with a 200m at about 2 seconds faster than the 400m pace, then a 200m recovery jog. The runner might then run a second set,

Table 9.3 Men's 400m Hurdle Touchdown Times

H1	H2	H3	H4	H5	200m	H6	H7	H8	H9	H10	Finish time
5.8	9.5	13.2	17.0	20.8	22.5	24.7	28.7	32.9	37.3	41.8	47.0
5.9	9.7	13.5	17.4	21.3	23.0	25.3	29.5	33.8	38.2	42.7	48.0
6.0	9.9	13.8	17.7	21.7	23.5	25.8	30.1	34.5	39.1	43.6	49.0
6.0	10.0	14.0	18.1	22.2	24.0	26.4	30.8	35.3	39.9	44.5	50.0
6.1	10.2	14.3	18.5	22.7	24.5	27.0	31.4	35.9	40.6	45.9	51.0
6.1	10.4	14.7	19.0	23.3	25.0	27.7	32.2	36.8	41.6	46.5	52.0
6.3	10.7	15.1	19.5	23.9	25.5	28.4	32.9	37.6	42.5	47.5	53.0
6.4	10.9	15.4	19.9	24.4	26.0	29.0	33.7	38.5	43.4	48.4	54.0

From Brent McFarlane. (1981). Hurdles touchdown times. In Jess Jarver (Ed.), *The hurdles: Contemporary theory, technique and training* (2nd ed., p. 35). Los Altos, CA: Tafnews. Reprinted with permission.

Table 9.4 Women's 400m Hurdle Touchdown Times

H1	H2	H3	H4	H5	200m	H6	H7	H8	H9	H10	Finish time
6.1	10.3	14.5	18.8	23.1	25.0	27.5	32.0	36.7	41.4	46.3	52.0
6.3	10.7	15.1	19.6	24.1	26.0	28.7	33.4	38.2	43.2	48.2	54.0
6.5	11.1	15.7	20.3	25.0	27.0	29.8	34.7	39.7	44.9	50.1	56.0
6.7	11.5	16.3	21.1	25.9	28.0	30.8	35.9	41.1	46.2	51.8	58.0
6.9	11.9	16.9	21.9	26.9	29.0	32.0	37.2	42.5	47.9	53.4	60.0
7.1	12.3	17.5	22.6	27.8	30.0	33.1	38.4	43.9	49.5	55.2	62.0
7.3	12.6	17.9	23.3	28.7	31.0	34.2	39.8	45.4	51.1	57.0	64.0

From Brent McFarlane. (1981). Hurdles touchdown times. In Jess Jarver (Ed.), *The hurdles: Contemporary theory, technique and training* (2nd ed., p. 35). Los Altos, CA: Tafnews. Reprinted with permission.

or else take a run for a few miles through the local countryside or on other softer surfaces. Two courses through rolling hills are used at Oregon. Hill running is exhilarating, and it is also an excellent resistance exercise, just as is weight training.

The hurdlers also follow a regular schedule of weight training. It is identical to the one used by the sprinters and longer distance runners. Ten exercises are used that exercise the entire body. Runners can develop their own routines beyond those basic exercises as they become familiar with the training. That is the prerogative of the individual athlete. The basic routine can be done in 10 minutes, so the athlete can benefit without feeling that excessive time is required.

The most important thing for the hurdler is to establish a routine that looks after the various parts of the race, giving enough attention both to the mechanical fundamentals of the event and to the pleasures of the preparation, so the athlete goes into the competition with the belief that he or she is fully prepared to turn in the very best effort.

The primary differences in the hurdling form of the intermediate hurdles from that of the high hurdles are few. They result in large part from the lower hurdle height, requiring less lift and effort to clear the hurdle and, therefore, less technical excellence. Because the intermediate race is longer, the pace is slower and the hurdler may be a bit more upright in clearance posture. The additional race length adds a considerable fatigue factor, which further modifies the hurdler's form late in the race.

The Training Schedules: Special Fundamentals for Intermediate Hurdles

The fundamentals on the intermediate hurdle schedule sheet are essentially the same as those on the high hurdle sheet (explained in chapter 8). There is more emphasis on specific endurance by dividing the race into segments of 100, 150, and 200m or more. The start, middle, and finish of the race are practiced. The athlete should practice working in different lanes because the race can be far different in Lane 1 than in Lane 8. Different lanes have varying physical and tactical considerations. The athlete should practice leading with either leg so an interruption in the pace will not result in stutter-stepping to hit the hurdle with the preferred leg. The schedules give 10 months of training. The higher numbers in parentheses give the target speed in seconds.

Reference

1. V. Brezier, et al. (1985). 400m hurdles training for women. *Track Technique*, **93**, 2976-2977.

Additional Readings

Bulanchik, E. (1983). 400 meter hurdles: Beginning training. *Track and Field Quarterly Review*, **83**(2), 49-50.

McFarlane, Brent. (1989). *The science of hurdling*. Ottawa: Canadian Track and Field Association.

Ross, Wilbur L. (1978). *The hurdler's bible* (3rd ed.). San Juan, PR: Santana. [The classic text on hurdling.]

Stepanov, V. (1989). Women's 400m hurdles problems. *Track Technique*, **108**, 3457.

White, Bill. (1983). Technical aspects of the 300 meter hurdles. *Track and Field Quarterly Review*, **83**(2), 51-52.

400 Meter Hurdle Training Schedule

ATHLETE _____

1. Warm-up
   A. Jog 1-2 laps with relay pass; hurdle X drill at lower height
   B. Slow, high knee; fast leg drill
2. Fartlek
   A. Varied pace: stride, sprint, recover; stride, meet a challenge, recover
      Finish feeling exhilarated, not exhausted
      (1) 10 min (2) 30 min (3)
   B. Steady pace: slow, 10-30 min
      (1) Hendricks Park (2) golf course (3)
3. Strength & flexibility
   A. Weights and jogging
   B. Jogging and stretching
4. High knee and fast leg
5. Starts: 2 at 1/2 speed, 2 at 7/8 speed
   A. Over 2 hurdles (1) LH (2) IH
   B. Back to back (1) 3 hurdles (2)
   C. First 3, slow jog, fast last 3
6. Intervals X. Over hurdles Y. On flat
   Z. Fast 20-50m in middle
   A. 100 (1) 18-16-14 (2) 13 sec
      (3) 12 sec
   B. 150-100-50 (1)   (2)
   C. 200 (1) 30 sec (2) 3/4 effort
      (3) 28 sec (4) 26-28 sec
   D. 300
   E. 150
   F. 400
   G. 500
   H. 600
7. Team meeting
8. Special
   A. Sauna   C.
   B. Swim
9. Relay work
   A. Routine   C. 100m
   B. 50m
10. Progress assessment
    A. Meet   C. Simulation
    B. Trial   D. Control test
       (1) 400m (2) 300m (3) first 3, last 3
       CA. simulate 200m race
       CB. simulate 400m race
       CC. parts of race
    F. On the flat
11. Sets (bunches)
    A. 500-300-100
       (1) 70-75, 42-45, 12-13 sec
    B. 300-200-100
       (1) 39-42, 25-27, 12-13 sec
12. With Coach
    A. (name)
    B. Leader
14. A. Wind sprints (1) straight (2) curve
    B. Hurdle X drill
    C. Spring and bound
    D. Alternate run & jog, at least 800m
    E. Hills with (1) coach (2) leader
15. Plyometrics
    A. Jumps (1) 1 leg (2) both legs
    B. Bounding (1) 1 leg (2) both legs
    C.
16. Finish work
    A. Jog first 300, go last 100
    B. Jog first 200, go last 200
       (1) lanes 2-5-8
17. X drill (a) 30" (b) 33" (c) 36"
    (d) 39" (e) 42"
    A. 5 steps to side   C. 3 steps to side
    B. 5 steps over top   D. 3 steps over top
       (1) on toes (2) shoulders level
       (3) lead arm (4) off arm
       (5) hand and a half
18. Parts of race X. Hurdles Y. Flat
    A. 100s: 1st, 2nd, 3rd
    B. 150s: 1st, mid, last
    C. Last 200   D.
19.
20. Work on second event
21. Visual aids
    A. Videotape   C. Photos
    B. Film
       (1) record performance (2) study
30. Experimental work

DATE September/October

M	Organization—equipment—lockers
Tu	7—use of weights—information
W	7—running courses—procedures—14A
Th	1A
F	1A—1B
Sa	1A—1B
Su	Recreation
M	1A—11A—14A
Tu	3A(light)
W	14E—6A(easy on grass) [4x]
Th	
F	10B(200m at 7/8-9/10)—14D
Sa	
Su	
M	1A—11A—11B—6A(1)—14D [4x]
Tu	
W	12—14E
Th	3A
F	1A—11A,B—1B
Sa	
Su	
M	1A—1B—11A,B—6B—2B(1) [1-2x, 3x]
Tu	3A
W	14E
Th	
F	10B(100m—300m)
Sa	
Su	

DATE October/November

M	1A—4—5A(easy)—11A,B—14D [4x]
Tu	3A
W	1B—5A(easy)—17(a or c)—14E
Th	21A(1)—3A
F	1A—17A,C(a or c)—6D—14A [3x]
Sa	1A—1B—5—10B(500m)—2B(1)
Su	Recreation
M	1A—1B—11A,B—2A(1)
Tu	3—14A
W	1A—6A—14E—6A [4x]
Th	3A
F	10B(relay—300m or 500m)
Sa	Your choice
Su	
M	1A—4—5A—11A—2A
Tu	3A
W	1B—4—14E—6A [4x]
Th	1B
F	1A—6B—jog [2x]
Sa	10B(relay—350m)—2B(1)
Su	
M	1A—1B—5—11A—2B [1-2x]
Tu	1B—8B
W	14E
Th	3A
F	1A—9A—2B(1)
Sa	Go with or observe runners
Su	Recreation

DATE November/December

M	1A—17A,C(a-b or c-d)—11A—11B—2B
Tu	3A
W	1A—6C(3)—6A(2)—14E [4x, 4x]
Th	3A
F	1B—6E(9/10 effort)—2B—6A(7/8 effort) [3x, 4x]
Sa	
Su	Recreation
M	1A—1B—17A,B,C,D(ab or cd)—11A,B—2B(1)
Tu	3A
W	1A—5A—14E—6A(2) [4x]
Th	3A
F	10B(relay—800m or 400m)
Sa	
Su	
M	
Tu	
W	
Th	
F	
Sa	
Su	
M	
Tu	
W	
Th	
F	
Sa	
Su	

DATE January

M	Class or squad organization—4—3
Tu	Complete registration—7(procedures)—2B
W	1A—4—1B—5B(1)—4E
Th	7—3A—4—6YB
F	1—5A—4—11A—2A
Sa	Workout
Su	
M	1A—4—4—5B—18A(2x)—6C(4)(4x)—2B
Tu	1—4—3A
W	1A—5A—4—18B—11A—jog
Th	3A—14E
F	1—4—5A—18B—11B—jog
Sa	10B(high hurdles—60m)
Su	
M	1—5A—18A—18B—11B—2A
Tu	3A
W	1—5A—6A(2)(4x)—6XB(2x)—jog
Th	3A—grass run or 14E
F	1—4—5A(2x)—6XA(2x)—6XB(2x)—2B
Sa	10B(high hurdles—60m)
Su	
M	1—5A—18A—18B—11B—jog
Tu	7—3A
W	1—5A—18B—11B—8A
Th	3A
F	Gear ready
Sa	10A or B(indoor meet)
Su	

DATE February

Day	a.m.	p.m.
M		1A—17—4—5A—6A(2)(4x)
Tu		1A—4—6E(18-19)(3x)—6A(3)(4x)—4
W		7—1A—17(ab or cd)—4(4x)—6A—14E
Th		1A—3
F		Jog and gear ready
Sa		10B
Su		Easy jog
M	1B	3A—6XC(4x)
Tu		1A—18XB—6D—2A(2x)—6D(37-38)(2x)
W	1B	1A—6A—14E—4(4x)—6A
Th		1A—17—18B—2B(2-4x)—6A
F		Jog
Sa		Jog
Su		10BF(600m)
M	1B—6A(3x)	2B—6A(4x)
Tu		1A—17—11B—2B(2x)—14A
W	1B	1A—6F(54-56)(3-4x)—2A
Th		1A—6C(4)(6-8x)
F	1B	
Sa		1B—(600-400-200)(1x)—2A
Su		
M	1B	17(ab or cd)—18A—6C(2-4x)—2A—6A(4x)
Tu		1A—4—18B—6C(2-4x)—2A—6A(4x)
W		3—14E
Th	1B	6C(4)(6-8x)—2A—6A(4x)
F		17(ab or cd)
Sa		10BF(1) & 10B(1) or 10B(highs) & 10B(1)
Su		2A

DATE March

Day	a.m.	p.m.
M	1A	17(ab or de)—10HH—18(D)—18A—jog (1x)
Tu		18B (2x)
W	1B	17(ab or cd)—1x/10HH—1x/last 250m/200pace—2A—4x/6A
Th		9B
F	1B	5A(2) (3x)
Sa		10B(full HH—full IH)
Su		
M	1B	17(ab or de)—18B—11B—2A
Tu	1A	1B—3
W	1B	17(ab or cd)—5C—16B—2A—6A (4x)
Th		1A—3
F	1B	5A—jog
Sa		10A(IH and 4x400 relay)
Su		Travel—spring vacation
M	1B	17(ab or cd)—18B—(600-400-200)—2A—jog (1x)
Tu	1B	17(ab or cd)—16(last 300)—16A—6C (2-4x)
W	1B	17(ab or de)—2A—6A (4x)
Th	1B	17(ab or de)—5—18B—16B—6A (4x)
F	1B	3A
Sa		10A(dual)
Su		Travel home—register
M	1B	17(ab or cd)—5B—16(last 250m)—6G—6H—jog
Tu		9—3A
W	1B	17(ab or cd)—5C(HH)—16(last 250m)—2A—6A (4x)
Th	7	Light
F		Gear ready
Sa		10A(IH and IH)
Su		Jog

DATE April

M	1A—4—5—18C—11A—jog
Tu	9B—2A
W	1A—17(ab or de)—18B—6D(39-42)—14E [3x]
Th	9B—1A
F	Gear ready—14A(grass)
Sa	10A(dual)
Su	Loosen up
M	1A—17(ab or cd)—18C—(600-400-200)—2B [1x]
Tu	3—9A—jog(20 min.)
W	1A—5A—18C—6D—14E—grass 50m [2x 4x]
Th	9A—18A
F	Gear ready—jog
Sa	10A(dual)
Su	Loosen up
M	1A—4—17(ab or cd)—5C—18B—jog—6G [1x]
Tu	3A
W	1A—5—5A—17(ab or de)—16B—6D—6A(grass) [1x 4x]
Th	3A
F	Gear ready
Sa	10A(dual)
Su	1A—10B—2A
M	1A—17(a or c)—jog
Tu	1A—4—17(ab or cd)—18A—16B—18YA—jog
W	3—grass hurdle—6YB—jog [4x]
Th	1A—5A—17(ab or de)—10B(HH at IH)—18XAB—2A
F	Easy
Sa	10B(quadrangular)
Su	Jog

DATE May

M	1A—5A—17(ab or cd)—5B—18B—jog—6A [4x]
Tu	Grass hurdle—5
W	5—5C—4 (grass)
Th	5—18A—jog (grass)
F	Gear ready
Sa	10A(dual)
Su	Loosen up
M	1B—6A—4—grass hurdle [4x]
Tu	1A—17(ab or cd)—6XE(1st)—6XA(last)—2A [2x 2x]
W	3B
Th	1—17—grass hurdle—jog
F	Gear ready, grass hurdle
Sa	10A(Northern Division Meet)
Su	6G—2B [1x]
M	1B—3A—2A
Tu	1A—17(ab or cd)—5B—18B—jog—14A
W	7—light grass
Th	Grass hurdle—14A(grass)
F	Prelims—PAC 8 Meet
Sa	Finals—PAC 8 Meet
Su	Loosen up
M	
Tu	
W	
Th	
F	
Sa	
Su	

DATE June

M	Light and 9B
Tu	1A—5—18CX—6G—2A [1x]
W	1A—5—18BX—6D—2A [2x]
Th	Light—14A
F	Jog
Sa	1A—5—18CX—6G—2A [1x]
Su	1A—5A—18AX—2A
M	1A—5A—10B(10HH—30" or 36")—18B—2A
Tu	Light—gear ready
W	Travel—loosen up
Th	NCAA Heats—14D—14A
F	NCAA Semis—14D—14A
Sa	NCAA Finals
Su	
M	
Tu	
W	
Th	
F	
Sa	
Su	
M	
Tu	
W	
Th	
F	
Sa	
Su	

CHAPTER 10	# Middle Distances:
	## 800 and 1,500 Meters and the Mile

The training principles and science described in the early chapters of this book apply to all middle distance races. At the elite level, an 800m race requires about 70% anaerobic endurance (to 30% aerobic), while the 1,500m requires about a fifty-fifty mixture of aerobic and anaerobic. However, as Jess Jarver notes, "While there appears to be general agreement that aerobic and anaerobic endurance capacities play the most important role in the training of middle distance runners, exactly how this can be best achieved still remains rather vague. This applies, in particular, to the best distribution of work to develop these capacities, as well as the limits of their trainability."[1]

Two points are of particular interest. First, over the last two decades, international training theory has moved away from high-mileage training, becoming closer to the Oregon System. Indeed, there is no principle of the Oregon System that is inconsistent with the most advanced training in the world today.

Second, there is now general agreement that heavy training loads (even of aerobic training) should not be used with young athletes. Low-mileage aerobic training is the best focus for precollege athletes, with some speed training but only limited training for anaerobic endurance. Early age-group training programs and serious competitions are not recommended. Instead, a junior high school student should develop a moderate aerobic base and a basic level of general skills, with a moderate number of meets. High school students can become more specialized, using slightly more intensive training and more meets.

Jarver also points out that "the majority of world-class middle distance runners have used very little planned training during their years of growth." Indeed, Russian researchers recommend that serious training for anaerobic endurance not begin before the age of 18.

The Oregon System

The Oregon System of training began with Bill Hayward, Oregon track coach from 1904 to 1947. He stressed a program of gradual conditioning and a reasonable limit on the number of competitive races. It was continued by one of his athletes, Bill Bowerman, track coach from 1948 to 1973. Bowerman was succeeded by Bill Dellinger, one of Bowerman's own Olympians, in 1973.

The basic system is a combination of interval training and fartlek. It has been developing around those basic concepts for four decades now, and it is still developing. It has been synthesized through years of coaching practice into the present system. We have found no better system for the athletes for whom it was developed: college students between the ages of 17 and 24. Here the work level is lower than that cited for many world-class athletes. Keep in mind, however, that those athletes are often 5 or more years older than college students and 10 years older than high school athletes.

The basic principles are simple. The first is to "train, don't strain." An athlete should enjoy training. A runner should complete the workout feeling exhilarated, not exhausted. Training must be fun, or else why do we train?

It is better for a runner to undertrain than to overtrain. Overtraining results in staleness, a loss of interest in practice and in competition. Staleness also results from competing too often, which interferes with the best performances and progress of our athletes. An ideal situation for distance runners is competition every 10 to 14 days, occasionally every 3 weeks. It is difficult to understand how a team or a coach can accomplish much in the school season with two meets a week. When do they learn or teach?

To those coaches who prefer two or three meets a week and point to the summer European programs where American athletes have performed outstandingly, we emphasize that those distance runners are usually mature, experienced athletes, 25 years old or older. Furthermore, during that time all they do is compete, eat, and rest. The school athlete is not only competing; he or she is also getting an education, which should be the first concern. This requires considerable study time and energy.

The Hard-Easy Training Approach

No athlete should compete before being properly conditioned. Competing too soon causes the athlete to risk injury because the body is not properly prepared for the stresses of competition. For that same reason, neither the coach nor the athlete should use meets as a means of conditioning.

The training pattern follows a hard-easy sequence, with each day of hard training being followed by a day of easy, or light, training, primarily jogging and light fartlek. The reason for this cycle is basic to all training: The body must have rest. Rest is always necessary for the body to recover and replenish itself. Furthermore, taking light days allows more work in the training sessions on the hard days, giving greater progress in the long run. This cycle is basic, but it is not inflexible. Some runners are strong enough to take 2 hard days for every easy day; others can take only 1 hard day and then need 2 easy days.

We prefer to keep the runners short of their peak, not over the hill. Once an athlete has been properly conditioned and has a good background of training, it takes little extra work to bring him or her to a peak. However, an athlete cannot remain at a peak for very long. For that reason, we prefer to hold the athletes short of their peak and sharpen them at the end of the season for the most important meets. Many athletes are world-beaters in the early season but cannot make the finals in the national meets. We want to avoid such a situation.[2]

Athletes work toward objectives and goals in their training. If they don't know where they are going, how will they get there? How will they know how close they are? The athletes and the coach set personal goals for the end of the year, then gradually progress toward those goals through training sessions and test efforts run at the 3/4ths–effort level.

The athlete must also train to the competition. No athlete can train without taking account of the competitors. This involves training to reach the same level, or a better one, as the competitors and also includes training in tactics and their uses.

One of the purposes of training is to improve the runners' strengths, so that their assets become greater assets, and to overcome their weaknesses, so that those handicaps are removed or minimized.

The athlete should continue with light exercise after hard training or competition. This is sometimes called "cooling down." The reason is quite simple: During strenuous exercise the body builds up lactic acid, a by-product of muscular activity, in the muscles. If the lactic acid is not removed from the muscles, it can result in cramping and possibly muscular injury. Easy jogging after heavy exercise keeps the blood circulating rapidly, gradually drawing the excess lactic acid from the muscles. For this reason, also, an easy trot on the morning after heavy exercise is beneficial to the body.

The morning run is now considered an essential of distance training. The practice is excellent, if the runner can handle it. It helps the athlete wake up in the morning and get the metabolic processes started for the day. It also encourages going to bed earlier. If the runner does not get the rest, however, it becomes a destructive process. A runner with heavy studies or involved in a romance should not try the morning run, nor should the coach force the attempt. The athlete is going through the biology of youth. It must be accommodated because it cannot be changed.

Compared to the programs of other world-class athletes, ours does not recommend very hard training. At one time 100 or more miles a week was believed necessary for success in distance running. Experience proved otherwise. We recommend from 60 to 80 miles a week in training for elite college males. This program produced several dozen sub-4:00 milers. Although mileage helps, it is far from the only variable involved in training. Certainly, it is not the most important one.

Every athlete's training methods should be taken with a grain of salt, experimented with, and then adapted to the specific needs and abilities of the individual who wishes to use them. The coach must keep in mind that the student-athlete is supposed to be studying and there are other things in life besides running.

The athletes should learn to maintain their appetite for running, not make it the most important thing in their lives. If athletes pass up other things in life, they will be isolating themselves, which is not good.

The age at which training should begin is simple to pick: the age at which the youngster wants to train. A 4-year-old who likes to run is old enough to train (not *be* trained). An 18-year-old who must be driven out to the track and flogged around it either is too young to train or has lost the appetite for it. The key is *enjoyment*: Athletes should enjoy what they are doing; they should not have to be forced into training.

Principles and Physiology of Distance Running

The principles of training are discussed in detail in chapter 1. The major emphases are moderation, consistency, and rest. The scientific foundations that underlie the system are described in chapter 2. However, we need to discuss a few points in greater detail.

Of the physiological phenomena that are a measure of a person's ability to run a race of over 100 yards, one of the best indicators is oxygen debt and its related reactions. When running, a miler is burning internal fuels and using oxygen for the burning, just as a car burns fuel that consumes oxygen. If the lungs can supply enough oxygen as fuel to carry the runner for a mile at a comfortable pace, there is no distress. If there is insufficient oxygen supplied to maintain the pace, or if the pace is too fast for the amount of oxygen supplied, the runner goes into oxygen debt.

Other related biochemical factors produce the same sort of inability to maintain pace. Producing carbon dioxide and related wastes in greater quantities than can be eliminated by the cardiorespiratory system interferes with oxygen exchange and contributes to oxygen debt, just as too much smoke in the chimney prevents good combustion in the stove.

Some coaches speak of fatigue tolerance or tolerance to oxygen debt. Is it a superior level of fitness that permits an athlete not only to turn in a world-record performance but to do it repeatedly? We suspect that it is a combination of fitness, tolerance, the coach, and, of course, the runner's superior physical equipment.

Other Distance Training Practices

We believe in weight training for runners. By "weight training" we do not mean developing Olympic weight lifters or spending hours weekly. We use a short list of exercises that concentrate on the upper body, the back, and the arms, all of which tend to be neglected by most runners. Strengthening those areas, particularly the back and the abdomen, assists in improving the posture, which in turn permits the body to take in more oxygen, permitting the athlete to run faster and farther.

Swimming is also beneficial to runners. It is good for relaxing and loosening tight muscles. It is very helpful for a runner with knee or ankle problems because the muscles can be exercised without irritating the joints. In fact, one varsity swimmer at Oregon (Scott Taylor) came out for the mile during his 5th year of school. At the end of the year, he ran a 4:05.2 mile, followed by a 1,500m race at a faster pace. He later became an Olympic performer in the modern pentathlon.

A final distance running practice is primarily for college athletes. During their early season training, all of our distance runners practice steeplechase techniques occasionally. Few of them have ever encountered this event before coming to college, so this finds runners who show natural ability or interest in this event. Those athletes continue to work on steeplechase activities. The work consists primarily of practicing clearance of the barriers, pace work over the barriers, and work on the water jump, begun with stepping onto and then over sections of logs.

Components of Running Ability

The three essential components to successful racing over the middle distances are endurance, pace judgment, and speed. The first two are of equal importance, and the third is nice to have but not absolutely necessary. A possible fourth essential was added by Emil Zatopek and Vladimir Kuts in the 1950s: varied-pace or aggressive tactics.

Endurance is needed to withstand the continued stress of a distance race. Runners must develop the strength to endure before becoming able to compete well. Endurance is not solely physical or physiological; it is also a state of mind and a function of willpower. Champions have not only greater physical endurance, but also greater mental endurance. They can drive themselves closer to their true capacities before their minds tell them to stop. Tolerance to stress requires much mental training along with the physical training.

Pace judgment is extremely important. Most inexperienced runners begin their race at a very fast pace, slow down too much during the race, then try to sprint at the finish. That tactic is not only painful but also physiologically foolish. The easiest way to run a given time, physiologically, is at an even pace. The ability to run any pace requires training in pace judgment. The world's best distance runners are all excellent judges of pace. It results from years of training and racing experience, and it is essential to success.

The third component of success is *speed*. Although it is not the most important factor, it is still very helpful. Speed can be improved in runners in most instances. Where it can be improved, it should be improved.

The tentative fourth essential is *varied-pace* or *aggressive tactics*. This is the method of changing quickly from one pace to another during the race: throwing in a short sprint here, a quick extended surge there, and attempting to hold a reasonably fast pace for the rest of the race. It is a difficult type of race to run, physiologically much more difficult than an evenly paced race. The runner has the disadvantage of having to lead the race, while hoping to "kill off" the opponents without exhausting his or her own physiological resources. However, it is as psychologically exhausting on the opponents as it is physically exhausting, for they never know when a fast burst may be used or how long it will last; thus, they are unsure how to cope with it.

Introducing the Runners to Training

Champions must be serious, with abundant energy and tenacity. They must be willing to endure grueling daily workout schedules, regardless of weather conditions, year after year. They must be eager to push themselves to the limit of their capacities as well as eager to defeat their opponents. The two greatest characteristics of champions have always been dedication and hard work.

Equipment

The runner's equipment is almost as meager as the swimmer's, with one exception: the shoes. Every experienced runner should have three pairs of shoes, if possible. One is for wearing to and from the track and during roadwork, the second is for regular practice, and the last is for competition.

For practice sessions, a sturdy but comfortable shoe is essential. A four-spike model is a frequent choice. It must be comfortable and light because every ounce counts. If a pair of shoes weighs 4 ounces more than another pair of shoes, that extra 4 ounces amounts to the runner literally lifting 220 extra pounds in the

course of a mile race (4 ounces × 880 strides). That energy can be more profitably spent running faster than in dragging an anchor.

For training clothes, lightweight materials that protect from the weather yet still "breathe" should be used. The running trunks and jersey should also be very light. Names or emblems can be silk-screened rather than sewn on, avoiding useless, weighty junk. The only necessary stripe across the chest is the one at the finish line.

Practice gear can be inexpensive. Cotton long johns can be substituted for lycra tights or sweatpants, not only for economy but also because they do not get clammy when wet and can be worn in competition during cold weather.

Stocking caps are good protection against the cold, but a sweatshirt with a hood attached is probably more practical because the hood cannot be forgotten or lost. All of the training clothing should be kept clean, washed as often as possible.

Work on Mechanics and Posture

We try to improve our runners' mechanics because they gain much from it. A champion can do the job with less effort than a nonchampion. The reason for this is that his or her body has been trained to do that task more efficiently. We want to improve the mechanical efficiency of our runners so they can do the same amount of work with less effort. Thus, they will be able to devote the saved energy to running a faster race. The effort expended will be the same, but the time will be faster because the body works more efficiently, yielding greater output without requiring greater effort.

Good posture comes from good muscle tone. If the muscles of the stomach, the lower back, and the hips are well developed, they assist in maintaining an upright posture. Weight lifting and other exercises can help in this regard.

The best postural position for the middle distance runner is an upright one. A line from the ear straight down to the ground should show that the back is perpendicular to the ground during running. The widely accepted belief that the body needs to lean forward to run well is *not* true. Research by Dr. Donald Slocum[3] shows that such a belief is incorrect. Champion runners have an upright posture while striding at racing speed. This is true even for sprinters, once they have finished accelerating.

Figure 10.1 is a side view of a group of runners in an 800m run. Times on this lap varied from 51 to 53 seconds, so they are running at race pace. Notice that they are all running erectly, with little or no body lean, though there are some personal eccentricities

Figure 10.1 Upright running posture. Photo by William H. Freeman.

of form. The upright posture is simply more efficient because when any body part is out of alignment, some muscles must strain to keep the body balanced, diverting part of the body's energies from the task of running a fast race.

In our work with runners, we try to point out the mechanical advantages of this upright form. We have the runners practice their form during fartlek and interval training, so it becomes part of their natural technique. We try to remember that there are individual variations to this "perfect" form. There are very few "picture" runners, for most people have some physical characteristics that require minor technical compensations.

Our research found that the pelvic position is the key to control of the runner's posture. The pelvis should be "tucked under," or brought forward in relation to the rest of the body. This assists in straightening the spine, which helps maintain an upright posture. The chest is directly in line above the hips, keeping the back in a straight line perpendicular to the ground. The head is up, the chest is raised, and the arms are swung slightly across the chest. This basic running form permits easier use of the leg muscles and aids in taking air into the lungs. If the horizon seems to be moving up and down, the runner may be overstriding.

The arm carry and swing also affect the posture. We teach an angle of 60 to 90 degrees at the elbow as optimal, though an athlete with very muscular arms might need to use a more open angle. This angle contributes to running efficiency in three ways. First, it improves the circulation. The little bit of downward

flow from hand to elbow makes the heart's job that much easier. There is also centrifugal force to be considered. Like the water in the bucket swung at arm's length, centrifugal force will act to keep the blood from returning from the hands if the arms are carried very low.

Second, there is a mechanical advantage. The lower the arms are carried, the longer the stride tends to be. The longer the stride, the greater the energy output required to maintain the pace and stride length. Because the arms and legs work in opposing pairs, we try to develop a short, quick, economical stride by keeping the arms moving in a shorter working radius.

Third, the arm swing contributes to the athlete's balance or imbalance. Exaggerated swinging of the arms must be compensated for by shifting the weight on the opposite side of the center of gravity or by expending more energy. A fresh runner can swing an arm way out of line and get away with it. However, coming down the home stretch, fatigued and tense, he or she may wander all over the track, or if too fatigued may even fall.

We recommend that runners use their arms in this manner: With an elbow bend of 60 to 90 degrees, swing the hand in an arc from about the top of the hipbone to the breastbone in the center of the body, with the arms naturally alternating this movement. Swing the hand and arm from the shoulder; the elbow does not open and close. At times the runner may want to rest or save the arms for the final drive by carrying them for a while. This motion is one where the hands remain about 3 to 6 inches apart and swing in a rhythmical tempo back and forth across the chest.

A quick, light stride is the most economical. It is more easily maintained when running upright rather than leaning forward. The leg swing should be as effortless as possible. The knee lift is moderately high, but there is no conscious effort to reach with the knee. The leg and foot are dropped directly under the body for the stride, and the leg is not fully extended in front of the body. A slightly short stride is the most efficient.

It is better to understride than to overstride. The runner should watch an object on the horizon to see whether it appears to be moving up and down. If the object is bounding, then the runner is bouncing, lifting the body on every stride. He or she is probably overstriding, a very common fault, or at least running inefficiently.

There are three ways to plant the foot while running: heel to ball, flat-footed, and ball to heel. The ball-to-heel plant is basically running on the toes, as sprinters do, and is out of place in distance running. It is less efficient for a runner because it requires more energy and puts additional strain on the calf muscles. Most great runners use either the heel-to-ball or the flat-footed stride. Runners should experiment to see which is most comfortable for them. The flat style involves landing flat-footed and rocking forward; the heel-to-ball style lands in the area of the heel of the foot and rolls forward, pushing off with the toes.

Three of the items we have discussed—stride length, body mechanics, and body posture—are worth repeating. Stride length is important because it, combined with stride cadence and economy of energy, determines in part how soon the race will be finished. The "long, beautiful stride" is often a disadvantage because it acts as a brake when the foot lands ahead of the center of gravity. Also, it requires more energy because it lifts and drops the body with every stride. Overstriding is the most common fault of high school distance runners. A short, economical, quick stride is better and more efficient.

Body mechanics are important because improper mechanics create a much greater energy drain. The body should be moved as efficiently as possible so the energy saved by good mechanics can be diverted to faster running. Posture is also critical to efficiency. If the mechanical and postural advantages are ignored, there are still two advantages of the upright running posture:

1. The body can take more air into the lungs because the upright trunk allows the lungs more space in the body cavity.
2. The knees can be lifted higher, allowing the runner to swing the legs more freely and easily while running.

Work on Pace Judgment

Pace judgment is a critical ability of the champion runner. The most efficient way to run a race is with even pacing. Pace judgment is not inherent—it is learned. Once it is acquired, the athlete can plan the race more easily and can better utilize his or her strengths. The significant thing is that pace judgment is one of the weapons with which an athlete is armed. The athlete knows what his or her pace is and deviates from it only as a weapon.

Poor races result from an inability to judge pace. By running too fast in the early stages of races, athletes build up an oxygen debt that they cannot repay without slowing down greatly. Practice perfects rhythm at any pace. A person can be strong of wind and heart and in good condition, but not have practiced pace work long enough to establish his or her rhythm.

To start teaching pace to our runners, we put a small stake in the middle of each straight and each turn of the track, dividing the track into four 100m segments. The runners are shown a pace card with the 400, 200, and 100m splits for 1,600m times of 4:32, 5:00, 6:00, 7:00, and 8:00, which looks like this:

1,600	4:32	5:00	6:00	7:00	8:00
400	68	75	90	105	120
200	34	37.5	45	52.5	60
100	17	19	22.5	26.25	30

Practice consists of watching a large pace clock and jogging into a paced 100m when the second hand reaches any of the quarter-circle points: 0, 15, 30, or 45 seconds. Men try to reach the 100m in 20 to 25 seconds (25 to 30 seconds for women), then walk or jog a 100m, and repeat the paced run until they have run ten 100s. It is interesting how many men run at a pace faster than a 4-minute mile on the first 100m, but reassuring to see how soon pain teaches the first lesson of 20 to 25 seconds per 100m. When the runners can do this, we drop down to the 5-minute 1,600m pace for men or 6-minute pace for women and increase the distances to a 200m, a 300m, or even a 400m.

It is doubtful that any runner can be dead sure of the pace. Our runners have a margin of error of 2 seconds per 400m in the 1,500m, the mile, and the 5,000m, and of 1 second per 400m in the 800m. Our pace chart for men looks like Table 10.1.

In practicing pace, we not only expect errors in judgment, but we permit runners to be off a bit, as long as they remain within allowable limits. We expect the margin to appear in any of the segments of the race, but we do not want a big deviation, for example, in the third or fourth quarter of the race. If a male runner is trying for 1:56 in the 800m and he hits 28 and 29 for a 57 at the 440, that is acceptable. If he then rests with a 32, he is running like a beginner and either is not capable of running a 1:56 or has not yet found the courage to pour it on and make his own race.

It is frustrating to see a well-conditioned good judge of pace hold back and save something for the last 100m against a competitor who is known to have a better kick. If the other athlete is going to win, make him or her *earn* it. Through pace judgment, the weapons for the slower, stronger athlete are to either

1. build a lead that a sprinter cannot overcome or
2. force the opponent into a pace that will remove his or her kick.

Table 10.1 Theoretical Race Paces

100	200	400	1,600m and 1 mile		
			800	1,200	1,600
18-19-20	36-37-38	73-75-77	2:26-2:30-2:34	3:39-3:45-3:51	4:52-5:00-5:08
17-18-19	34-35-36	68-70-72	2:16-2:20-2:24	3:24-3:30-3:36	4:32-4:40-4:48
16-17-18	33-34-35	66-68-70	2:11-2:15-2:19	3:16-3:22-3:28	4:22-4:30-4:38
16-17-18	32-33-34	63-65-67	2:06-2:10-2:14	3:09-3:15-3:21	4:12-4:20-4:28
15-16-17	30-31-32	60-62-64	2:00-2:04-2:08	3:00-3:06-3:12	4:02-4:10-4:18
14-15-16	29-30-31	58-60-62	1:56-2:00-2:04	2:54-3:00-3:06	3:52-4:00-4:08
Margin of error					
−1 +1	−1 +1	−2 +2	−4 +4	−6 +6	−8 +8

100	200	800 meters		
		400	600	800
15-17-18	33-34-35	66-68-70	1:39-1:42-1:45	2:11-2:15-2:19
15-16-17	31-32-33	63-65-67	1:34-1:37-1:40	2:06-2:10-2:14
14-15-16	30-31-32	60-62-64	1:30-1:33-1:36	2:01-2:05-2:09
14-15-16	29-30-31	58-60-62	1:27-1:30-1:33	1:56-2:00-2:04
13-14-15	28-29-30	56-58-60	1:24-1:27-1:30	1:52-1:56-2:00
13-14-15	27-28-29	54-56-58	1:21-1:24-1:27	1:48-1:52-1:56
Margin of error				
−1 +1	−1 +1	−2 +2	−3 +3	−4 +4

The General Training Patterns

The annual cycle. A master plan is developed for each 3-month period. The early training during October, November, and December consists of conditioning, cross country, and testing. The pretrack and long-distance training in January, February, and March stresses fundamentals and increasing strength. During the competitive season (April, May, and June) all efforts are directed toward keeping the athletes in top physical and psychological condition.

The volume of work is rather modest at the start of a training period. It builds up as the year progresses, reaches a peak just before the competitive season, and then is somewhat reduced as the weekly competition demands maximum energy and attention. During all the seasons, the schedules generally follow a pattern of a hard day (1 to 2 hours of work) followed by an easy day (about 30 minutes of work).

During the early season, group assignments are made to the runners. During the competitive season, each person has a separate workout sheet on which his or her workouts are written for 1 week at a time.

An example of the rough progression of training throughout the year for a male miler who can already run in the 4:00 range is shown in Table 10.2. The pace given is for a 440-yard interval, the volume is the workout mileage in terms of the number of times the racing distance ("2" for a miler would be 2 miles), and the rest interval is proportionate to the interval being run. If the athlete is running 400s and the interval is 1/2, the rest interval is 200 yards of walking or jogging.

This general workout pattern can be adapted to the individual runner in both pace and volume. The goal pace (60 seconds per lap) is scheduled for May, so time adjustments can easily be made. For a woman with a goal of 5:00 for 1,600m, the May pace for 400m is 75, which is 15 seconds more than the 60 pace in the table. Thus, all of the 400m paces are increased by 15 seconds, starting with 90 seconds in October, dropping to 85 seconds in November, and so forth.

Above all, the runners must have variety. The pleasurable variety offered by fartlek, the discipline of interval training, some special speed work, and regular

Table 10.2   Oregon Training Schedule Outline (for a 4:00 Miler)

Month	Week	400m Pace	Volume	Rest interval
Oct	1	75	2	full
	2	75	2-3	1/2
	3	75	2	1/4
	4	75	2-3	1/4
Nov.	1	70	2	full
	2	70	2-3	1/2
	3	70	2	1/4
	4	70	2-3	1/4
Dec.	1	68	2	full
	2	68	2-3	1/2
	3	68	2	1/4
	4	68	2-3	1/4
Jan.	1	66	2	full
	2	66	2-3	1/2
	3	66	2	1/4
	4	66	2-3	1/4
Feb.	1	64	2	full
	2	64	2-3	1/2
	3	64	2	1/4
	4	64	2-3	1/4
March	1	62	2	full
	2	62	2-3	1/2
	3	62	2	1/4
	4	62	2-3	1/4
April	1	61	2	full
	2	61	2-3	1/2
	3	61	2	1/4
	4	61	2-3	1/4
May	1	60	2	full
	2	60	2-3	1/2
	3	60	2	1/4
	4	60	2-3	1/4
June	1	59	2	full
	2	59	2-3	1/2
	3	59	2	1/4
	4	59	2-3	1/4
July	1	58	2	full
	2	58	2-3	1/2
	3	58	2	1/4
	4	58	2-3	1/4
Aug.	1	57	2	full
	2	57	2-3	1/2
	3	57	2	1/4
	4	57	2-3	1/4

exercises all increase the runner's strength. The runner needs a bit of almost everything, including a balanced training diet, both for overall improvement and for the prevention of the boredom that is sometimes called "staleness."

Date pace and goal pace should be defined again at this point. *Date pace* (DP) is the actual pace at which the runners are clocked in a test effort or time trial that they try to run at 3/4ths effort. This is usually expressed as their pace for 400m. If the runner can already run 4:24 for 1,600m, the DP is 66. After the next test effort, the DP is adjusted to reflect the runner's improvement. We try to get the runner to improve by 1 second per 400m during each training period (2 to 3 weeks).

Goal pace (GP) is the 400m pace that the runner wants to run at the peak of the season. If the athlete wants to run a 4:08 1,600m, the GP is 62. If the goal is 5:24 for the 1,600m, the GP is 81.

The 10-day, 14-day, and 21-day schedules are named for the times that their training cycle requires at a set pace. Each pattern concludes with a test effort. The test effort, often marked simply as "test," is a time trial run at 3/4ths effort. It is *not* an all-out effort.

The Running Patterns

We have already mentioned that the athletes' schedules should be tailored to fit their needs, ambitions, and goals. These schedules are a mixture of training methods that we have tried and found helpful. The first pattern was a 7-day pattern. It was developed years ago simply as a way to plan ahead where to put the training emphasis for a given period. At that time, most runners did not begin regular training until the 1st of January or February, and they did not train or compete with any regularity after mid-June.

The pattern, based on the hard-easy sequence, looked like this:

(1) Monday: heavy training
(2) Tuesday: light training
(3) Wednesday: heavy
(4) Thursday: light
(5) Friday: heavy
(6) Saturday: light
(7) Sunday: heavy

You will notice that this schedule throws 2 hard days, Sunday and Monday, together. In applying the principle of hard-easy, or heavy-light, training, we must recall that every person is different. Some runners benefit from the 2 heavy days, but others need to make Sunday a light or rest day also.

The idea of the 10-day pattern came from Sweden. It fits the progress of conditioning, testing, and preparation better than the one that most of us are forced into by the Gregorian and school calendars of 7 days to a week, which usually puts us into a 14-day training period. A 10-day schedule looks like this:

(1) Monday: heavy training
(2) Tuesday: light training
(3) Wednesday: heavy
(4) Thursday: light

(5) Friday: heavy
(6) Saturday: light
(7) Sunday: heavy
(8) Monday: light
(9) Tuesday: light
(10) Wednesday: test effort

This schedule points out another principle: Usually there should be at least 2 days of light training before a hard test effort or a competition. Our school calendar being what it is, we must use the 14-day training pattern. This 2-week pattern also brings up our strong belief that runners compete best if their major efforts are at least 2 weeks apart.

We recognize that major meets may have trials and final races over a period of 2, 3, or even 4 days. We plan and train for such situations with the individual runner. The basic 2-week pattern calls for alternating days of heavy and light training, beginning with a hard day on the first Sunday and including 2 light days, the second Thursday and Friday, before the competition or test effort on the second Saturday. The specific 14-day pattern that we follow is like this:

(1) Sunday: steady fartlek: 6 to 15 miles
(2) Monday: varied fartlek (light)
(3) Tuesday: goal; date; light fartlek
(4) Wednesday: steady fartlek (light)
(5) Thursday: rhythm or quick; fartlek; cutdowns
(6) Friday: light fartlek
(7) Saturday: overdistance; underdistance; date; fartlek
(8) Sunday: steady fartlek: 6 to 15 miles
(9) Monday: varied fartlek (light)
(10) Tuesday: goal; steady fartlek; light running
(11) Wednesday: steady fartlek (light)
(12) Thursday: quick, light fartlek; cutdowns; or simulated race
(13) Friday: light fartlek
(14) Saturday: test effort (date pace); steady fartlek; cutdowns

Some of the above words will be clearer if we elaborate a bit. *Overdistance work* is understandable. *Goal* refers to intervals run at the goal pace. The athlete runs intervals totaling the racing distance at that pace. For example, a 1,600m runner with a goal pace of 60 seconds per 400m would run four times 400m in 60 seconds each as the "goal" part of the workout; perhaps run a set of 600, 400, 300, 200, and 100m intervals all at that pace; or run any other combination totaling 1,600m.

Date refers to intervals run at the date pace. If a runner is at 5:20 in the date pace, he or she might next run 1,600 to 3,200m of intervals on a pace of 80 seconds per 400m. The workout session would conclude with some fartlek.

Some schedules include sprints, which consist of a small number of fast, short intervals. They are followed by a moderate to heavy amount of fartlek. The workout is concluded with increasingly fast, short intervals, or *cutdowns*. These are usually 100s run at a pace that gradually quickens, such as 4 × 100 in 16, 15, 14, and 13 seconds

The *overdistance* or *underdistance* in the schedule for the first Saturday refers to a test effort at either a longer or a shorter distance than the usual racing distance. For example, 1,600m runners might run an 800m, or they might run 3,000m or 5,000m. The workout for the second Thursday consists of a small number of short, quick sprints, followed by a moderate, but not heavy, fartlek workout. The final day is a test effort conducted at the date pace.

The 21-day pattern combines two 10-day patterns, with a day of rest tossed in at a convenient spot. Most of our training before the meets begin is just this type of pattern. The schedule progresses like this:

(1) Sunday: steady fartlek: 6 to 15 miles
(2) Monday: varied fartlek (light)
(3) Tuesday: goal; date;
    light fartlek; cutdowns
(4) Wednesday: steady fartlek (light)
(5) Thursday: rhythm; light fartlek; cutdowns
(6) Friday: light fartlek
(7) Saturday: overdistance trial; steady fartlek;
    cutdowns
(8) Sunday: steady fartlek: 6 to 15 miles
(9) Monday: varied fartlek (light)
(10) Tuesday: heavy intervals; light fartlek;
    cutdowns
(11) Wednesday: steady fartlek (light)
(12) Thursday: quick intervals; light fartlek;
    cutdowns
(13) Friday: light fartlek
(14) Saturday: underdistance; date;
    light fartlek; cutdowns
(15) Sunday: steady fartlek; 6 to 15 miles
(16) Monday: varied fartlek (light)
(17) Tuesday: goal; steady fartlek; cutdowns
(18) Wednesday: steady fartlek
(19) Thursday: quick intervals; light fartlek;
    cutdowns; or simulated race
(20) Friday: light fartlek
(21) Saturday: date pace trial; steady fartlek;
    cutdowns

Rhythm is simply the opposite of lack of rhythm; it is not a pace. *Tempo* is similar to rhythm, but we

use it as an action (an exercise in which the hands are held about 6 inches apart and swung quickly back and forth across the chest as a break in the monotony of running, a breather or a wake-up exercise).

Sometimes speed is listed—short sprints that are done as speed work. We might do 4 × 50m fast sprints, or one or two 150s with the middle 50 extremely fast. There should not be many intervals of this type because the risk of injury is high.

Trials and What They Mean

We use test efforts or time trials to assess the runners' progress at different points throughout the year. However, our trials are not all-out efforts. Our trials are similar to the system of trials used by Arthur Lydiard, 3/4ths-effort trials in which the runner tries to achieve a predetermined time (the date pace) by running an evenly paced race.

For example, if a female ran 4:56 for 1,600m in her trial 3 weeks ago, her present goal (date pace) would probably be 4:52 (73 pace). Actually, to avoid trying to push her along too fast, we average several times to get her new goal. We add twice her previous trial time to her new tentative goal (4:52) and divide by three, yielding a more accurate goal for her new pace (4:54).

She runs her trial as closely as possible to an even pace (73.5, 2:27, 3:50.5), following the suggested limits of variance in Table 10.1. Her run is a controlled effort in which she knows she could have run faster and in which she kicks or runs under her date pace only in the last 1/4th or less of her racing distance. The race thus shows how far she has progressed toward her goal, while giving her practice in the most efficient way of running her race: even pace.

Setting Goals

Each individual should have a goal, and for a good runner the goal should be high. If a young man was a 4:28 high school miler, we sit down with him and ask, "How fast do you want to run next year?" Too many freshmen say, "Four minutes." That is a good goal, but we want to know what to aim for during the immediately coming year. After all, 4:28 is only 4 × 67 seconds.

Let us assume that 4:16 is a reasonable goal for this 18- or 19-year-old freshman. Let us make two more assumptions: (1) If he is capable of better than 4:16, let's help him as far as his ability will carry him; and (2) if he falters somewhere in his progress toward 4:16, we will adjust the schedule to the slower time of 4:20 or 4:24 or possibly 4:28, which may be as fast as he will ever run.

Each runner should have a goal. It should be a good goal, but it should be realistic. We want our runners to make steady progress year after year, rather than progress rapidly 1 year only to stagnate or regress during the next several years. Now that we have given the rudiments of our distance training system, we will get down to the specific training for the individual middle distance and distance races.

Training Methods

The basic training methods were discussed in chapters 2 through 4. Try to fit the workout to the individual. Some athletes can handle more work than others. Some show more improvement with intervals, others with fartlek. The two are combined with a little speed work until we learn what kind of fertilizer makes our flowers grow best.

For interval training, 1 to 2-1/2 times the racing distance, preceded by a warm-up and followed by some fartlek or speed work, is a heavy workout. Experience shows that 1/4th of the racing distance is the ideal distance for practicing intervals for shorter races. Distances shorter and longer than the 1/4th distance are used, and the intensity is increased by reducing the rest or recovery intervals.

A male runner working toward a 4:40 1,600m would run 4 to 12 × 400m in 70 seconds each, whereas a female trying to run 5:40 would run 4 to 12 × 400m in 85 seconds each. For variety, they might run some 200s at a slightly faster pace or some 600s at a slightly slower pace. The total distance covered during a workout would be one to three times the racing distance, or 1 to 3 miles (1,600 to 5,000 meters) total (we prefer not to go over 3 miles of intervals). Their full rest would be an equal interval. If they want the workout to be a bit more intense, they shorten the rest interval to 200 or even 100m.

Experience suggests that you gain nothing by training ahead of pace (such as a 4:40 1,600 runner training at a 65- or 60-second pace for 400m). The runner will reach higher goals by getting in a greater volume of work than by trying to carry too fast a pace and not completing the workout. How many freshmen males have said, "But I can run faster than 75s (or 70s). I can run 10 400s in 64 seconds."

The answer should be a question: "But can you run a mile in 4:16?" The courage of the young athlete who wants to try is admirable, but after he tries and finds himself wanting, we question his judgment if he will not turn himself over to his coach.

Besides roads and trails in the woods, runners might use local golf courses. However, you should get written permission to use the courses from the presi-

dent and board of each course every year. The ground rules for the runners are simple:

1. Always stay on the outside of a fairway and "run with the grain," or direction of play.
2. Do not cut across a fairway.
3. Go behind the tees and around the greens.
4. If a player is addressing a ball, stop until it is hit.

Steady-paced running is also very valuable. Runners are not ready to start training until they can run steadily without stopping for 45 to 60 minutes. How does a runner reach that stage? The runner wears a watch and starts at 8 to 10 minutes per mile (60 to 75 seconds per 200m), heads down the street for 10 minutes, then returns, all at that same pace. The runner adds time gradually until he or she can go out for 30 minutes and return, a total of 1 hour. Then the runner is ready to begin a distance-training schedule.

Overdistance training is essential to a balanced program of training for the distance races. This consists simply of long runs, usually at a steady pace. As for what constitutes a "long" run, it depends to some extent on the athlete's normal racing distance. To most 800m runners, a 6- or 8-mile (10 to 12km) run is a long distance, but for a 5- or 10km racer, it is not long at all. Generally speaking, a long run would be any distance over 10 kilometers. The longest distance any of our runners uses with any regularity is 14 to 16 miles (23 to 26km).

We have a series of "loops," training courses laid out around the town and surrounding countryside. They are mostly on roads because the local climate is very wet for 6 months of the year. The shortest loop is 3 miles (5km) through Hendricks Park on a low ridge near campus, and our longest loop (16 miles) wanders around nearby Spencer's Butte, a small mountain south of town. Local training loops should include both easy and difficult terrain, depending upon what the training program needs.

We are not entirely convinced that runs of more than 10 miles at a time are necessary to successful running. We definitely do not believe that over 70 or 80 miles a week are needed for success on the international level.

One cardinal principle should never be forgotten: Variety is the spice of life. Every runner needs variety, if for no other reason than to prevent mental staleness. The system must always recognize that individuals are different. Schedules are only guides. Just as a balanced diet makes for a healthier, happier person, so does a varied and balanced training schedule make for a more efficient, eager runner. A continuous, nonvaried schedule usually makes an automatic, unimaginative runner.

The Distance Runner's Sprint and the Golden Mile

Training for the 800m run and the 1,500m and mile are essentially the same. The first object of the training is good, solid cardiovascular work that will permit the athlete to run up to 6 miles in a session. The longer training runs take away the athlete's basic speed, but it can return to its maximum level with 3 to 6 weeks of quality, or "sharpening," work. However, no athlete can build up the cardiovascular system in 6 weeks.

The training program should combine the speed-developing training activities and the conditioning training from the fall of the year to the end of the racing season. Although this is contrary to some training theories, experience has proved it to be as successful as any other system. Now it is supported by more recent training theory. It has a further advantage, largely psychological, but still important: The athletes get more pleasure out of their training if the quality and the quantity training are combined, rather than used separately at different times in the year.

The training cycle for 800m and 1,500m runners should begin in the fall and continue throughout the year for the best results. After school begins, the athletes participate in the cross-country training described in chapter 11. The fall training concentrates on cardiovascular development. At the end of the cross-country season, in late November, the athletes begin training patterns aimed at their track racing distance.

Some athletes prefer interval training, while others like the long runs. Some do not thrive on the "who can get in the most miles" philosophy. Men have run a 4:00 mile on as little as 30 miles a week or less in training. Those "quick types" usually perform best on 50 to 80 miles per week in training. Other athletes may be the slower "warriors" who love the long distance training and destroy an opponent with work, trying to set a devastating pace to get out of the range of the sprinter. Teacher-coaches must know their runners, just as the athletes must know themselves. In training, there are many roads from A to B, and the shortest is not always the quickest or the best, any more than is the longest.

Racing Tactics

An athlete who wants to run the best possible time for a race is usually better off running as closely as possible to even pace for the entire distance. However, many racing situations call for tactics that consider not what will yield the fastest time but what will give the greatest chance of victory against a particular opponent. A knowledge of tactics is vital.

To use tactics well, the runner must know two things. The first was inscribed at the entrance to the temple of the Delphic Oracle: "Know thyself." What are the athlete's personal strengths and weaknesses as a racer? Can he or she carry a solid pace for the entire racing distance? How far can he or she carry a final sprint? This is learned in the test efforts, then put to practice in racing situations. The athletes must learn their capabilities and weaknesses well, both to know how they can use them to their advantage and to know how their opponents might use those weaknesses against them.

The second thing that athletes must know is their opponents. What are their strong and weak points? Those point the way to how they can be beaten. The comparison between the athlete and the opponent indicates which of the following tactical considerations might be of the greatest value.

If the athlete is clearly better than the opponent, then practice some facet of the race during the competition. This work on strengthening one particular phase of the race helps in an obvious way, but it also serves another purpose: It conceals the athlete's strengths. Athletes should no more show all of their racing weapons against a weak opponent than they should use a sledgehammer on an ant. Instead, concentrate on some section of the race, such as the first, middle, or last part.

This concealment of the athlete's weapons leads to another aspect of tactics: An athlete should not always run the same kind of race. He or she should have a plan for *every* race, and it should be a different one in some respect. If the athlete runs only one kind of a race, a good tactician will notice it, analyze it, and beat that runner. Being obvious is never a tactical virtue, unless it is a deliberate effort to mislead an opponent.

An athlete whose strong point is the last part of the race should work to make it his or her best weapon. The athlete should work to improve what he or she is endowed with, rather than accepting it as it is and working only on other areas of ability. This does not mean to work only on the strengths; the runner must also train to overcome the weaknesses. A person with only one weapon in the bag may meet someone else with the same weapon, only to find that the other weapon is bigger. Again, an athlete should beware of tipping his or her hand. The athlete might in fact use his or her greatest weapon only once in a year, at the time of the most important race.

One artificial tactic is varied-pace running. It is also a tactic of which the runner should beware. Some athletes can use it, but other runners are destroyed by it. It is a very big weapon for the person who can use it. However, the athlete who knows that he or she cannot use it should beware of a contest with someone who can use it. He or she must let the other runner go, then reel him or her in like a fish, making sure not to let the opponent get too far ahead. A runner should not at any time go when the opponent surges. Rather, as soon as the runner is close enough to the finish to hold it to the end, he or she should go into the sprint finish. An athlete who runs the opponent's race will have a very bad experience because it is a devastating way to run a race. An athlete should not offer him- or herself as a lamb for the slaughter. One should never try to fight an opponent on his or her own choice of battleground.

Whenever an athlete is tempted to try to beat an opponent while letting the opponent use his or her favorite club in the contest, the athlete should remember one thing: Wisdom and judgment are a great deal more important than determination. There is more pleasure in being a wise victor than a determined loser.

The runner must be cautious in the first part of the race, for it is very important. It is easily the most dangerous part of the race. Most athletes tend to start too fast, which puts them quickly into oxygen debt and makes the late stages of the race very difficult. Few athletes are strong enough to lead all the way. Pace judgment is extremely important in this case, for by running too fast in the first 1/8th to 1/4th of the racing distance, the runner stands the greatest chance of looking like a fool. The runner with good pace judgment should be onto the correct pace by the end of the first 1/4th of the racing distance. A runner without good pace judgment need not worry because he or she has little chance in top competition anyway. When tempted to overwhelm the opponents with a fast start, the runner must remember one vital fact: All of the points are awarded at the finish line.

Every runner, no matter how good, *must* know what is going on at the front of the race. If an athlete trots along in the rear of the pack, someone may break away and not be noticed until it is too late. A runner probably has some advantage in running in the rear for the first half of the racing distance, but he or she must progress to one of the first three places by the halfway point in the race to keep an eye on what is going on at the front. To stay in the first three places, an athlete must be careful not to get "boxed in," or blocked, as other runners move up in position. Each time a competitor moves up to go by, the athlete should "take one," moving out a lane or so and going with the new competitor to ensure a place at the front of the race. Moving out from the curb also helps prevent being boxed in and unable to move if an opponent tries to break away from the leaders.

In the last 300 meters of the race, a good competitor should attempt to get in front, *if* he or she can sprint that far. Once in front, the runner becomes the other runners' problem. The runner should use up to 9/10ths of his or her effort to get in front. The runner should not use 100% because there needs to be a bit of reserve to avoid being passed in the last 50m of the race. A runner should not try to win from fifth place on the last straight of the track, a very foolish tactic. Someone who prefers to race with that tactic should enter the 100-meter dash instead.

The Training Schedules: Special Fundamentals for 800 and 1,500 Meters

In using the training schedules, which have been used by successful athletes, remember that they should be viewed as a starting point, an example of how the theories of training have been applied, rather than seen as "the" way to train. The training schedule sheets were interpreted in chapter 5. The only different activities are the warm-up, fartlek, and drills (Numbers 1, 2, and 9).

The *sprint-float-sprint* goes for 150m, the runner sprinting for the first 50m, then relaxing and "floating" for the middle 50m, before sprinting again. The runner is learning to take a breather without slowing down during a race.

The *150, middle one-step acceleration* is a paced 150m run, with an attempt to sharply increase the pace within a single step. It helps develop the ability to "change gears" quickly to react to a racing situation, whether it is a chance to move quickly or a response to another runner's move.

The *40-30 drill* and the *70-90 drill* are used to practice varied-pace racing. The 40-30 drill divides the run into 200m segments. The athlete runs continuously for a set number of laps, alternating between 40-second and 30-second 200s. The 70-90 drill alternates 400s of 70 and 90 seconds. The 1-1 option calls for an even mix of the paces, while 2-1 and 3-1 mean to run either two or three of the fast 400s for each slow 400m. This type of mixed-pace training session can also be used to simulate racing at the goal pace, mixing goal pace running with slower paces.

Cutdowns are a series of intervals run at increasing speeds. For instance, "4 × 100 cutdowns" might mean running the first 100m in 18 seconds, the next one in 17 seconds, the third one in 16 seconds, and the last one in 15 seconds. A set of 6 × 300 cutdowns might be run in pairs, with the first two 300s in 54 seconds, the next two in 51 seconds, and the last two in 48 seconds. It helps to accustom the runner to finishing strongly. It is also a refreshing way to finish a training session.

Simulated race drills are used to practice race situations. The *first 200, last 200 drill* practices running the first 200m of the race, followed by the finishing 200m. Racers in the 800m should practice starting in different lanes for the run around the first turn.

The *2-1/2, 1-1/2 drill* breaks the mile or 1,500m/1,600m race into two parts. The athlete runs the first 2-1/2 laps (1,000m) of the race at pace, strides 400m, then runs the last 1-1/2 laps (600m) at pace. This simulates the race and is long enough to require specific endurance for the event.

The *15km, 1,200m drill* (10-mile, 3/4 drill) is a 10-mile run on the roads. At some point during the run the coach appears and has the athlete run a timed 3/4-mile (1,200m) at close to mile pace. This teaches the runner to combat a long, hard surge by an opponent or else to be able to drop an opponent by forcing the pace for a very long surge. Runners such as Steve Prefontaine sometimes ran the 1,200m in 3:05 or faster. Note that after the 1,200m, the athlete slows down only to the earlier running pace, *not* to a slow jog. That is what makes the drill very difficult. It is primarily a drill for runners of the 5,000m or longer distances.

An athlete may run *2 to 4 miles* at a moderate (but not taxing) pace, such as 80 seconds per 400m for a male college runner. This is a good drill to simulate trial heats for longer distance runners. For example, a 3,000m runner who must run a qualifying race on Friday, followed by a final on Saturday, can use this as a Friday workout before Saturday meets. It is run at a pace fast enough to require more than just a light effort, but not a moderate effort. A variation is to run the drill on the day after a meet instead of the day before.

References

1. Jess Jarver. (1985). What is new in middle distance running? In Jess Jarver (Ed.), *Middle distances: Contemporary theory, technique and training* (2nd ed., pp. 6-8.). Los Altos, CA: Tafnews.
2. William H. Freeman. (1989). *Peak when it counts: Periodization for the American coach*. Los Altos, CA: Tafnews.
3. Donald B. Slocum & William J. Bowerman. (1981). The biomechanics of running. In *Proceedings of the Second National Conference on the Medical Aspects of Sports* (pp. 55-58). Chicago: American Medical Association.

Additional Readings

Alford, John W. (Ed.) (1983). *Running: The IAAF Symposium on Middle and Long Distance Events.* London: International Amateur Athletic Federation. Also in *Track and Field Quarterly Review*, **83**(3).

Bompa, Tudor O. (1989). Physiological intensity values employed to plan endurance training. *Track Technique*, **108**, 3435-3442.

Costill, David L. (1986). *Inside running: Basics of sports physiology*. Indianapolis: Benchmark Press.

Dellinger, Bill, & Freeman, Bill. (1984). *The competitive runner's training book*. New York: Macmillan.

Diemer, Brian. (1988). Progressive training towards a peak. *Track and Field Quarterly Review*, **88**(2), 32-33.

Flanagan, Cheryl. (1981). Thoughts on training female distance runners. *Track and Field Quarterly Review*, **81**(3), 28.

Frederick, Sue. (1987). Why altitude training doesn't work. *Track and Field Quarterly Review*, **87**(2), 30-31.

Freeman, William H. (1985). Concerns in training women distance runners. *Track and Field Quarterly Review*, **85**(3), 29-36.

Galloway, Jeff. (1987). Learning from our ears. *Track and Field Quarterly Review*, **87**(2), 4-5.

Gladrow, Walter. (1983). Establishing training loads for women's middle distance. *Track and Field Quarterly Review*, **83**(3), 47-50.

Groves, Harry. (1987). Tactics and strategy. *Track and Field Quarterly Review*, **87**(2), 11.

Humphreys, John, & Holman, Ron (Eds.) (1985). *Focus on middle-distance running*. London: Adam & Charles Black.

Maplestone, Bob. (1981). Coaching junior college freshmen and sophomore middle distance runners. *Track and Field Quarterly Review*, **81**(3), 12-14.

Martin, David E. (1985). Distance running: The Elite Athlete Project. *Track Technique*, **93**, 2965-2969.

Ramos, Juan G. Bacallao. (1987). Planning middle and long distance training programs. *Track Technique*, **99**, 3154-3158.

Snell, Peter, & Vaughan, Robert. (1990). Longitudinal physiological testing of elite female middle and long distance runners. *Track Technique*, **111**, 3532-3534.

Sunderland, David. (1986). Progressions and methods of training for young 800 metre runners. *New Studies in Athletics*, **1**(4), 65-70.

von Papen, Henning, & Nellesen, Manfred. (1985). 1500m starting tactics. *Track Technique*, **93**, 2977.

Watts, Denis, Wilson, Harry, & Horwill, Frank. *The complete middle distance runner*. London: Stanley Paul.

Williams, Keith. (1990). Biomechanical relationships in distance running. *Track Technique*, **110**, 3499-3502.

Zajac, Adam, & Prus, Gregory. (1988). Training for middle distance. *Track Technique*, **102**, 3250-3253.

800 Meter Training Schedule

ATHLETE _____

1. Warm-up
   A. Jog 1-3 miles, stretch
2. Fartlek
   A. Varied (1) 30 min (2) 45 min (3) 60 min
   B. Steady (1) 2-4 miles (2) 4-6 miles (3) 6-10 miles (4) 10 miles (5) 45 min
3. Strength & flexibility
   A. Weights and jogging
   B. Jogging and stretching
4. High knee and power run
5. Intervals
   A. 100 (1) 18-16-14 sec (2) 17-15-13 sec (3) 12.5 sec (4) 12.0 sec (5) 11.5-12 sec
   B. 150 (1) 25 sec (2) 7/8 effort (3) 22.5 sec (4) 19.5 sec (5) 19 sec
   C. 200 (1) 35 sec (2) 28 sec (3) 25-26 sec (4) 27 sec (5) 26-28 sec
   D. 300 (1) 52 sec (2) 48 sec (3) 45 sec (4) 42 sec (5) 39-42 sec
   E. 400 (1) 70-73 sec (2) 59 sec (3) 58 sec (4) 59-62 sec (5) 65-70 sec (6) 63 sec (7) 53 sec
   F. 600 (1) 1:45 (2) 1:39 (3) 1:27
   G. 800 (1) 70 sec pace (2) 68 sec pace
   H. 1200 (1) 70 sec pace (2)
   J. 1600 (1) 72 sec pace (2) 68-70 sec pace (3) 64-67 sec pace
   K. 700 (1) 58 at 400 (2) race pace
   L. 2-1/2 laps (1) 60-65
6. Sets
   A. 600-400-300-200-100 (1) 1:45-68-49-32-15 sec (2) 1:42-66-46-30-14 sec
   B. 400-600-400-200 (1) 63 sec (2) 28-30/200 pace
   C. 500-150-150 (1) 55 sec (2) date pace (3) 52 pace
   D. 400-300-200
   E. 200-400-200 (1) 29 sec pace (2) 26/200 pace
7. Team meeting
8. Special
   A. Sauna
   B. Swim
   C.
9. Drills
   A. 150 sprint-float-sprint
   B. 150 middle 1-step acceleration
   C. 40-30 drill (1) 4 laps (2) 6 laps (3)
   D. 70-90 drill (1) 1-1 (2) 2-1 (3) 3-1 (4)
   E. Cut-downs (1) 100 (2) 150 (3) 200 (4) 300 (5) 400 (6) 800 (7)
   F. Simulated race drills (1) 1st 200, last 200 (2) 2-1/2, 1-1/2 (3) 15km, 1200 (4)
   G. 2-4 miles at (1) 80 per lap (2)
10. Progress assessment
    A. Meet   C. Simulation
    B. Trial   D. Control test
    (1) 3/4 date pace (2) over (3) under
11. Hill intervals
    A. 100
    B. 200
    C.
12. With Coach
    A. (name)
    B. Leader
14. A. Wind sprints (1) straight (2) curve
    B. Hurdle X drill
    C. Spring and bound
    D.
15. Plyometrics
    A. Jumps (1) 1 leg (2) both legs (3)
    B. Bounding (1) 1 leg (2) both legs (3)
    C.
16. Finish work
17. Acrobatics or apparatus
18. 3/4 effort
19. Steeplechase
    A. Hurdle drill   B. Water jump
20. Work on second event
21. Visual aids
    A. Videotape   C. Photos
    B. Film
    (1) record performance (2) study
22. Park
    A. Around
    B. Hill
23. Golf course
    A. Around   C. Long
    B. Short
30. Experimental work

DATE September/October

Day	a.m.	p.m.
M		7 (organization, lockers, equipment)
Tu		3—2B
W		1—5D—5C—2A(1) (2x, 2x)
Th		3—2B
F		1
Sa		10 a.m.: 3-mile or 6-mile fall road run
Su		
M		3
Tu		1—19A—5G—5A—5F—5E—6D (2x 2x 2x 3x 2x 4x)
W		Light and 3
Th		22A (45 min.)—5A
F		Light
Sa		2A(2) (park)
Su		
M		1—5D—22A—5A(16-18) (4x, 10x)
Tu		3
W		1—5C(2)—6A(1)—23A (8x, 3x)
Th		17 (rope climbing)—3—2 (20 min.)
F	3x 5A(1)	30 min. out—30 min. back—5A (4x)
Sa		6A(1) (grass)—easy jog
Su		
M	Jog	5C or D (100 rest—20 secs.) (6-10x)
Tu		17—3 (20-min. jog)
W	Jog	5D(2-3) (200 rest)—6A(1)—1 (6x, 3x)
Th		17 (rope and parallel bars)
F	Jog	3x/5A(1)—30 out—30 back (7-10 min./mile)
Sa		1
Su		

DATE October/November

Day	a.m.	p.m.
M	1	5H(1)—2—5A(1) (4x)
Tu		3—8A
W		1
Th		6A(2)—2A(3) (3x)
F		1—3
Sa		400-400-400-200-200 = 1600 / 10B(68—68—34—9/10)—2A(1)
Su		
M		1—5G(2)—5F(2)—2A(3) (2x, 2x)
Tu		1—3—8A
W	3-6x 5A(1)	Mile(80—80—29—9/10)—2A(1) [400-400-400-200-200]
Th		Jog and stretch
F	1	9A(600 to 1200)—2A—9A(300 to 600)
Sa		6A(2)—6E(1)—2A
Su		
M	1	1—5G(2)—1 (4x)
Tu		3—8A
W	3-6x 5A(1)	1—6E—6A(1)—2A(3) (3x)
Th		9A(800-1200)—2A
F		1—3
Sa		
Su		10B(800)(30-30-28-9/10)—2A—5A(1) [200, 6x]
M		1—2A—5A(1)
Tu	1	6C(2)—5E—6A(1)—1 (4x, 2x)
W		3—8A
Th	5A(1)	1—6B(2)—2A—5A(1) (4x)
F		3—8A
Sa		1—6A(60-sec pace)—6A(1)—1A (2-3x)
Su		

DATE November/December

Day	a.m.	p.m.
M	1	1—5F(3)—5E(2)—5D(1-2)—1—5A (2x, 8x, 4x)
Tu		3—8A
W	5A	2A(3)(grass)
Th		Light jog
F		10B(800 date pace)—2A(45 min.)—5A(1)
Sa		2B(3)(7 to 9 min. pace per mile)
Su		
M	1	1—5K(1)—5E(3)—5D(3-4)—6A(1)—1—5A(1) (2x, 2x, 3x)
Tu		3—8A
W		9A(600)—2A(45 min.)—5B(2) (2x)
Th	1	1—3—8A
F		10B(mile)(68—68—9/10 effort) [400-400-400-400]
Sa		2B(4)(8 to 10 min. pace)
Su		
M		
Tu		
W		
Th		
F		
Sa		
Su		

DATE January

	a.m.	p.m.
M		Recheck organization—1 or 3
Tu		2B—3—8A
W		5J or 5G(3/4 effort)—2A—8A
Th		3—8A
F		1—8A
Sa		reestablish date pace 5J or 5G(1/2 effort)—2A(3)—8A
Su		
M		4x 3x 2x / 1—5C—5D—6A(1)—2A(1)—5A(1)
Tu		Jog and stretch—8A
W		3—6B—2B—5C(1)
Th		1—3—8A
F		8x 4x / 1—5C(2)—9A—2A—5C(1)
Sa		10B(1)
Su		
M	1	11x 2x / 1—5B(3)—2A(1)—5C(1)
Tu	Jog	2x 6x 2x / 6A(1)—1A—5B(4)—5C(1)
W		3—8A
Th	1	5x / 5B(4)—2A or B—5A(3)
F	Jog	3—8A
Sa		Mile(80-80-60-9/10 effort)—2A
Su		
M	Jog	4x 3x / 5E(2)—5B(4)—2A—8A
Tu	Jog	9A(600)—2A(1)—8A
W	2x 5A(1)	3
Th		6x 4x / 1—5B—2A—5A(3)
F	Jog	Check indoor gear—1
Sa		Indoor 1,000 or 2B(1)
Su		

DATE February

	a.m.	p.m.
M	Jog	4x 2x / 1—5E(2)—5C(2)—6A(1)
Tu	2x 5A(1)	1—4—3—8A
W	Jog	2A
Th		2x 4x 2x 2x / 10B(1500)—5B—5D—5B—2A—5A(1)
F	5x 5A(1)	2A(1)—3—8A
Sa		2x / 10B(500 or 1,000)—2A—5A(1)
Su		2B(3)
M	Jog	3x 4x / 3—5C(1)—2A(1)—50
Tu	2x 5A(1)	2x 4x / 1—6E—6A(1)—2A(3)—5A(grass)
W	Jog	3—8A
Th	2x 5A(1)	1—6C—9A(800)—2A(1)
F		Light jog—5B(7/8 effort)
Sa		10B(1,000 or 500)—2A
Su		2B(3)
M	Jog	2x / 1—5B(9/10 effort)—2A
Tu	2x 5A(1)	2x 2x / 1—5C(3)—6C—6B—6A(1)—5A(1)
W	Jog	3x 3x / 1—5A(1)—2B(2)—5A(1)—8A
Th	Jog	3x / 2A—5A(1)
F	2x 5A(1)	2x 2x / 1—9A—9A(200)
Sa		2A(3)
Su		Country jog
M	Jog	3-6x 3x / 2A(3)—5A(1)
Tu	2x 5A(1)	2x 3x / 1—6C—2B(2)—5A(1)
W	Jog	3x / 1—5B(9/10 effort)—2A(1)—5A(1)
Th	2x 5A(1)	1—3—8A
F		1
Sa		10B(600)
Su		Run—choice

DATE March

	a.m.	p.m.
M	1	3x 3x / 9E(3)(33-30-27)—2A(1)—5A(1)
Tu	2A(2)	4x 4x / 1—5A(3)—5C(2)—6A(1)—2A(3)
W	1	2x / 2A(1)—3—5A(1)
Th	2A(1)	2x / 1—5B(9/10)—2B(5)—9E(4)(48-45-42)
F		4x / 1—3—9E(3)(36-33-30-27)
Sa	1	2-3x / 1—6C—2A(3)—5C(1)
Su		Runner's choice
M	2x 5A(1)	3
Tu	1	10B—800m(300 at pace,200 jog, 300 at pace)—2x/6A(2)—3-5x/5A(1)
W	2x 5A(1)	1—3—8A
Th	1	6x 2-3x / 5B(2)—2A(3)—9F(4)(51-48-45)
F	3x 5A(1)	4x / 5B—2A—5A(3)
Sa	2A	10B(800 at date pace)—2A(3)
Su		Runner's choice
M	1	4x 2x / 1—5E(5)—5C(4)—2A(3)—9E(4)(48-45-42)
Tu	2B	4x 3x / 5A(4)—2A—5A(1)
W	1	2x / 1—5E(5)—5B(9/10 effort)—2A
Th	2A	2A or 2B—5A(1)
F	1	2x 2x / 5A—3—5A
Sa		10A or 10B
Su		Travel to spring trip
M	2A	2x / 1—2A or 2B—5A(1)
Tu	2B(1)	4x 4x / 1—5E(6)—6E—2A(1)—5A
W	2A	2x / 2A or 2B—5A(1)
Th	2x 5A(1)	4x / 5C(4)—2A
F	2x 5A(1)	Jog
Sa		10A
Su		Home and re-register (spring term)

DATE April

Day	a.m.	p.m.
M	1	1—9A—6E(2)³ˣ—2A(2)⁴ˣ—5A(1)³ˣ
Tu		3—2A
W	5A(1)³ˣ	1—6E—9E(4)(50-47-44)³ˣ—2A—5A(1)³ˣ
Th		Light
F	1	10B:800/200 in 35; go last 500: 13-26-52-65)—2A
Sa		10A or 600 at date pace—2B
Su		Runner's choice
M	5A(1)²ˣ	1—5C—6E—6A(2)⁴ˣ—2A(1)²ˣ
Tu		3—1A—8A
W	1	6C—23A or B—5A(1)³ˣ
Th		5B(9/10 effort)²ˣ—2B
F		Gear ready—light jog
Sa		10A—800 and relay
Su		Runner's choice
M		1—5C—5C—2A(1)⁴ˣ—9E(4)(48-45-42)²ˣ
Tu	1	5A(5)⁴ˣ—2A(1)³ˣ—5A(1)
W		1—6B—5B(9/10 effort)²ˣ—2B
Th	5A(1)²ˣ	9A—2B
F		5A(quick)⁴⁻⁶ˣ—relay work
Sa		10A(1500 and relay)
Su		Runner's choice
M	1	2A—5A(1)²⁻³ˣ(grass)
Tu		1—6E—5D(2-3)—6A(1)⁶ˣ—2A(2)²ˣ—5A(1)
W	5A(1)²ˣ	3—2A—8A
Th		1—5F(14-26-54-68-1:22)—6x/5C—2A—2x/5A(1)
F	1	Jog
Sa		10A(easy, perhaps relay only)
Su		Runner's choice

DATE May

Day	a.m.	p.m.
M	5A(1)²ˣ	1—5C(4)⁴ˣ—2A(2)
Tu	1	1—5B(9/10 effort)²ˣ—8A—8B
W	5A(1)²ˣ	1—5K(2)—6A(1)
Th	1	5C—5B(9/10 effort)⁴ˣ²ˣ—2A(1)
F		Gear ready—1A
Sa	5A(1)²ˣ	10A(800 and relay)
Su		Runner's choice
M	2A	3—1—8A—8B
Tu	5A(1)²ˣ	5D(5)—6A(1)³ˣ—23—5A(1)²ˣ
W	2A	5C(4)⁴ˣ—2B—5A(1)²⁻³ˣ
Th	5A(1)²ˣ	5B(7/8 effort)²ˣ—2A
F		Gear ready—baton work
Sa	2A	10A(400 or 1500 and relay)
Su		Runner's choice
M	1	1
Tu	5A(1)²ˣ	1—6E—6B—6A(2)—2A
W	1	Light—8A—8B
Th	5A(1)²ˣ	Gear ready—5C—5B—5A—2A
F		2A(1)²⁻⁴ˣ—5B(quick)
Sa	1	10A(800) Northern Division
Su		Runner's choice
M	1	6C(3)—2A(1)²⁻⁴ˣ—5B
Tu	1	5C(4)—5D(5)—5C(4)—5B(9/10 effort)²ˣ—2B
W		Jog—5B—2A(1)¹⁻²ˣ
Th		Jog—5A(quick)
F	1	10A—trials—PAC 8 Meet
Sa	1	10A—finals
Su		2A or 2B

DATE Late May or June

Day	a.m.	p.m.
M	5B—1	Jog
Tu	1	Twilight meet
W	5A	2A
Th		5C(5)—6A(2)⁴ˣ²ˣ—2A
F	5A⁴ˣ	2A—8B
Sa	2A	5E(2) or 5C(5)—2A(3)⁶ˣ—5B(4)
Su		Jog
M	Jog	5C(9/10 effort)—2A—5A(1)⁶ˣ
Tu	Jog	5L(1)—2B—5C⁴ˣ
W	Jog	4—1—8A and B
Th	Jog	6C—5B—2A—5A(1)³ˣ
F		5C(3)—5E(3)—5C(9/10 effort)—1—5A²ˣ
Sa		5B(4)—2B—5A(7/8 effort)⁶ˣ²ˣ
Su		Jog
M		5B(4)—2A—5A(7/8 effort)⁶ˣ⁴ˣ
Tu		Light
W		Light
Th		Trials
F		Semifinals
Sa		Finals
Su		Jog
M		
Tu		
W		
Th		
F		
Sa		
Su		

1,500 Meter Training Schedule

ATHLETE _____

1. Warm-up
   A. Jog 1-3 miles, stretch
2. Fartlek
   A. Varied (1) 30 min (2) 45 min
   B. Steady (1) 2-4 miles (2) 4-6 miles
      (3) 6-10 miles
      (4) 45 min out, 45 min back
      (5) 12-15 miles
3. Strength & flexibility
   A. Weights and jogging
   B. Jogging and stretching
4. High knee and power run
5. Intervals
   A. 100 (1) 18-16-14 sec (2) 17-15-13 sec
   B. 150 (1) 25 sec (2)
   C. 200 (1) 35 sec (2) 32-35 sec
      (3) 28 sec (4) 29 sec (5) 27 sec
   D. 300 (1) 52 sec (2) 48 sec (3) 45 sec
      (4) 42 sec
   E. 400 (1) 70-73 sec (2) 65-70 sec
      (3) 60 sec (4) 62 sec (5) 66 sec
      (6) 58 sec
   F. 600 (1) 1:45 (2) 1:30 (3) 1:27
   G. 800 (1) 70 sec pace
      (2) 61 sec pace (3) 63 sec pace
      (4) 59 sec pace (5) 60 sec pace
   H. 1200 (1) 70 sec pace (2)
   J. 1600 (1) 72 sec pace (2) 68-70
      (3) 64-67 (4)
   K. 1000 (1) 60
   L.
6. Sets
   A. 600-400-300-200-100
      (1) 1:45-68-49-32-15 sec
      (2) 1:42-66-46-30-14 sec
   B. 400-600-400-200 (1) 63 sec (2) 59 sec
   C. 500-150-150 (1) 55 sec (2)
   D. 200-400-200 (1) 29-58-29 sec (2)
   E. 800-600-200
   F. 300-600-300
7. Team meeting
8. Special
   A. Sauna   C.
   B. Swim
9. Drills
   A. 150 sprint-float-sprint
   B. 150 middle 1-step acceleration
   C. 40-30 drill (1) 4 laps (2) 6 laps (3)
   D. 70-90 drill (1) 1-1 (2) 2-1
      (3) 3-1 (4)
   E. Cut-downs (1) 100 (2) 150 (3) 200
      (4) 300 (5) 400 (6) 800 (7)
   F. Simulated race drills
      (1) 1st 200, last 200
      (2) 2-1/2, 1-1/2 (3) 15km, 1200
   G. 2-4 miles at (1) 80 sec/lap (2)
10. Progress assessment
    A. Meet   C. Simulation
    B. Trial   D. Control test
       (1) 3/4 date pace (2) over (3) under
11. Hill intervals
    A. 100   C.
    B. 200
12. With Coach
    A. (name)
    B. Leader
14. A. Wind sprints (1) straight (2) curve
    B. Hurdle X drill
    C. Spring and bound
    D.
15. Plyometrics
    A. Jumps (1) 1 leg (2) both legs (3)
    B. Bounding (1) 1 leg (2) both legs (3)
    C.
16. Finish work
17. Acrobatics or apparatus
18. 3/4 effort (1) 1500m
19. Steeplechase
    A. Hurdle drill   B. Water jump
20. Work on second event
21. Visual aids   C. Photos
    A. Videotape
    B. Film
       (1) record performance (2) study
22. Park run
    A. Around   B. Short hill
23. Golf course run
    A. Around
30. Experimental work

DATE September/October

Day	a.m.	p.m.
M 1	Jog in the mornings, if time permits	Organization—lockers—equipment—1A
Tu 1		3—2B
W 1		2x / 1—5D—5C—2A(1)
Th 1		3—2B
F 1		2x / 1—6D(1)—9A(800-1600)—2B
Sa 1		2A(1)
Su		2B(3)
M 1		3
Tu 1		2x 2x 3x 4x / 1—19A—5G—5A—5F—5E,D,C—7
W 1		1
Th 1		19—18
F 1		2(light)
Sa		2A(2)
Su		2(light)
M 1		4x 10x / 1—5C—22A—5A(16-18)
Tu 1		1B
W 1		4x 3x / 1—5D(1-2)—6A(1)—5A(1)
Th 1		1B
F 1		4x 3x / 1—5C(2)—2A(2)—5A(1)
Sa		2(light)
Su		2A(2)—22A
M 1		2(light)
Tu 1		2-3x / 10B—6A
W 1		2B(1)—3
Th 1		2A(2)
F 1		2(light)
Sa		10B or cross-country
Su		2(light)

DATE October/November

Day	a.m.	p.m.
M 1		2—22A—2B(3)(7-8 min. pace)
Tu 1		2B(1)—3
W 1		2x 4x 1-2x / 2—19A—5D(2-3)—22A—22B—2A(2)
Th 1		2A(1)
F 1		9A(1200-1600)—4
Sa 1		3
Su		6A—2A(2)
M 1		3
Tu 1		10B(18)—2A—22A
W 1		3
Th 1		10B(18)—22
F 1		2(light)
Sa		5-9x / 23A
Su		2A(light)
M 1		2A(light)
Tu 1		2x / 1—4—6A(1 or 2)—2A(2)
W 1		3
Th 1		1
F 1		Light
Sa		10A—cross-country regional meet
Su		2(light)
M 1		3—2A
Tu 1		4x 2x / 5E(2)—6A(1)—2B(2)
W 1		3
Th 1		6-10x / 23A
F 1		2(light)
Sa		4x 2x 5-6x / 5E(2)—5H(1)—5A—2A
Su		2(light)

DATE November/December

Day	a.m.	p.m.
M 1		2A(1)—3
Tu 1		4x 4x 3-5x / 5E(2)—19A—6A
W 1		3
Th 1		9A(1-1.5 miles)—2B
F 1		3
Sa		4x / 6A—22A
Su		Pleasant jog
M 1		10A—area cross country race
Tu 1		Home—1
W 1		4x 6-10x / 19A—5G(1)
Th 1		3
F 1		2A or 2B
Sa		Light
Su		10B(6 laps)—22A
M		Vacation:
Tu		Fartlek runs
W		+ rest
Th		+ recreation
F		
Sa		
Su		

DATE January

	a.m.	p.m.
M		Class or squad organization
Tu		Register and 1B
W		2-3x 1—19A—5D(2-3)—4x 5G—2x 6A—1
Th		2B(1)
F		3—2B
Sa		2B(4)
Su		Recreation
M		3—2B
Tu	1	11x 7—5B—4x 9A—22B—2x 5A(1)
W		1B—2B
Th		10x 1—9A—3x 6A(1)—2x 5D—2B
F		1—3
Sa		Easy 200s
Su		2
M	1	3—1A
Tu	1	10x 5D(3)—8x 5F—2B
W	1	3
Th	1	1
F		Gear ready—1
Sa		10A—indoor mile or 10B
Su		Pleasant jog
M	1	3
Tu	1	10x 1—5B—4x 5C—14A
W	1	3
Th	1	7
F	1	Gear ready—1
Sa		10A—2 miles indoors
Su		Recreation

DATE February

	a.m.	p.m.
M	1	4x 22A—2x 5A(1)
Tu	1	4x 5E(2)—6x 5D(3)—5A(9/10)—4x 5C(3)—2B(1)
W	1	3
Th	1	2-4x 22A—2x 22B—2-3x 5A(1)
F		2
Sa		10A
Su		2B(3)
M	1	1
Tu	1	4-6x 23A—3x 5A(1)
W	1	3—1
Th	1	3x/5F(2)—2x/5A(9/10 effort)—4x/5E(4)— 2x/5A(9/10 effort)—2x/6A(2)
F		1
Sa		2
Su		1
M	1	3x 5A(1)—2B(1)
Tu	1	2A(1)—6B—5D(2-3)—4x 5C(4)—9A(800)
W	1	3x 5A(1)—2B(1)
Th	1	1—6D—23A—5C(1)
F		Light
Sa		10B(18)—22A—22B
Su		2
M	1	2B—4x 19A—19B—4x 5E—2x 5A—4x 5D(4)—3x 5A(1)
Tu	1	6x 2A—22A
W	1	2A
Th	1	2B(5)
F		4x 19A—4x 19B—12x 5D(3)(9/10 effort every 3d)—2B
Sa		2A(1)—3
Su		2

DATE March

	a.m.	p.m.
M	1	[—4—2B(1)
Tu	1	2-6x 1B—22B—4-6x 22A—2x 5A(1)
W	1	1—3
Th	1	4x 19A—19B—4x 9A(1200)—2B(1)
F		Light
Sa		10B(17)—2
Su		2
M	1	1B—4
Tu	1	2
W	1	3—4
Th	1	2-4x 6B—19AB—6A(2)—2A
F		3—4—2B
Sa		Light
Su		2
M		Exam week—2A(1)
Tu		2x 5G(3)—2x 5A—3-4x 5F(1)—2x 5A—4-6x 5E(5)—6x 5D—2A
W		3—2B(1)
Th		2B
F		Gear ready—14A
Sa	Travel	10A—dual meet
Su		Travel—spring trip
M	1—14A	4x 5E(3)—2A(1)—3x 6A(1)—2A(1)
Tu	3—14B	3x 5D(4)—2x 5A(9/10 effort)—2
W	1	Light
Th	1—14A	2(hills)
F		3
Sa		10A—triangular meet
Su		Travel home—registration

DATE April

Day	a.m.	p.m.
M	2A	1—3
Tu	2B	1—6A(4-6x)—9G(1)—2A
W	2A	1—3
Th	2B	1—19
F		Gear ready—1
Sa		Relay meet—10A(2 mile)
Su		2
M	2A	7—1—5F(2)(4x)—5F(3)(4x)—6A(2)(4-5x)—2B(1)
Tu	2B	3—9F(2)(60's)—22
W	2A	Light
Th	2B	14A
F		Gear ready—1
Sa		10A—dual meet—1500
Su		2
M	2B	1—2(easy)—3
Tu	2A	5A(1)(2-3x)—5K(1)(3x)—5F(2)—2B
W	2B	1—3
Th	2A	2(easy)
F		Gear ready
Sa		10A—dual meet
Su		2(easy)
M	2A	7—2B(grass)
Tu	2B	1—5E(3)(4x)—6A(3x)(1:39-64-45-29-13.5)—2A(1)
W	2A	2—3
Th	2B	2(easy)
F		Travel—1
Sa		Dual meet—10A(2 miles)
Su		Home—loosen up

DATE May

Day	a.m.	p.m.
M	1	7—19A(4x)—5E(3)(4x)—2A
Tu	2A	1—6B(2x)—6E(2:14-1:37.5-63-30)—2A(1)
W		1—5A(1)(2x) Light
Th	2A	14A—2 (easy)
F		Gear ready—1
Sa		10A—dual meet—1500
Su		2
M	7	1—5D(3)(3x)—5A(2x)(9/10 effort)—2A(1)
Tu	1	2A(1)—5E(3)—5G(2)—5E(3)(2x)—6A(2)—2B
W	2A	Light
Th	1	2B (easy)
F	2A	Gear ready
Sa		10A—traditional dual meet
Su		2
M	2A	1—5E(3)(4x)—5E(3)(2x)—9B—2A(1)
Tu	1	1—6F(2x)—6A
W	2A	1—3—2A(1)
Th	1	2
F		Travel
Sa		10A—relay (4 x 1 mile)
Su		Home—2
M	1	7—19AB—2A(2)
Tu	2A	19A(2-4x)(300's)—6B(2)—2A(1)
W		1
Th		2B(easy)—14A
F		Gear ready
Sa		10A—Division championship
Su		2

DATE June

Day	a.m.	p.m.
M	1	1—3
Tu	2A	5G(4)—5F(2)—5E(3)—5C(5)—2A(1)
W	1	1
Th	2A	22(easy)
F		Travel
Sa		10A—1500
Su Home		19A(2x)—19B(2x)—5A(1)(3x)
M	2A	2A
Tu	1	1
W		10A—twilight meet (3,000)
Th		3
F		17—2A
Sa		6C(2x)—2B
Su		2
M	5A(1)(2x)	5G(5)—5F(3)—5E(6)—5D(4)—5C(5)—2A(1)
Tu	1	2B—14A
W	5A(1)(2x)	1
Th		Trials—NCAA Meet
F		Semifinals
Sa		Finals (1500)
Su		
M		
Tu		
W		
Th		
F		
Sa		
Su		

CHAPTER 11	# The Longer
	# Distances: Cross Country,
	## Steeplechase, 5,000 Meters
	## and Longer

As an athlete moves on to the longer races, the aerobic component of training becomes more important. However, speed is a factor even in the longest races. Today's world-class marathoner is also a world-class 10,000m runner. For men, that means sub-28:00 for the track race, while for women it means sub-32:00 speed. For an athlete to maintain that speed for an extended distance requires good leg speed. The top male marathoners can run close to 4:00 for a mile or under 3:45 for 1,500m. Though that high-speed component in the short races is not yet vital for women, it will be within a decade, as a larger talent pool enters the arena.

This discussion of speed points out a critical fact: The long distances and the steeplechase are not refuges for the athlete with no talent. The races do allow more progress based on extended hard work, so they are excellent frameworks for the traditional work ethic. However, at the world-class level, there are no weak events. Through 1988, the world records at 10,000m require paces of just over 65 seconds per 400m lap for a man and 72 seconds per lap for a woman, both maintained for 25 laps. The marathons require paces of 72.5 and 80.5 seconds per 400m lap for almost 105 laps (though not run on the track) for a man and a woman, respectively.

More attention is now paid to developing the anaerobic threshold. The idea of very high mileage at a relatively easy pace is discredited as an effective training method for the distances.[1] As David Martin of the USOC's Elite Athlete Project says, "This 7:00 a mile stuff for a hundred miles a week isn't necessarily going to hack it."[2] Instead, higher intensity training at lower mileages is more effective.

The most effective training depends upon paces based on the athlete's aerobic and anaerobic thresholds, the levels at which the athlete accumulates certain levels of lactic acid:

- Aerobic threshold: 2mmol per liter of lactate
- Anaerobic threshold: 4mmol per liter of lactate

These thresholds are "breaking points" on the rising curve of lactic acid produced by the body as exercise becomes more strenuous. The *aerobic threshold* is the point at which the athlete is beginning to "work," having to use more oxygen to maintain the training effort. The *anaerobic threshold* is the point at which the athlete can no longer take in enough oxygen to fuel the exercise, thus beginning to go into oxygen debt (recovery oxygen) and drawing on the body's reserves to maintain the effort.[3] This discussion is based on Finnish research and practice, but some exercise physiologists question the meaning of the thresholds.[4]

The most effective training speeds are in the transitional range between those two levels. Although an athlete's potential $\dot{V}O_2$max has genetic limits, the ability to race at a given level (percentage) of that figure is not so limited. In other words, the $\dot{V}O_2$max is not the only factor limiting an athlete's potential. As an example, Steve Prefontaine had a $\dot{V}O_2$max of above 80, compared to about 70 for Frank Shorter, yet both had roughly the same best marks at 5,000m (both world class). Shorter had more efficient running technique and was able to run at a higher percentage of his maximum than was Prefontaine.

Thus, we see two important aspects of long distance training: proper running technique and training at more effective levels of effort. We discussed the proper technique in chapter 10. The more intensive training sessions that theory recommends make the hard-easy principle even more important.

The benefit of (and reason for) the hard-easy principle is that the body needs time to recover from a work load. The recovery time that is needed depends on the intensity of the work load. A light run may require only a few hours of recovery. A 10-mile run at close to the anaerobic threshold may require from 1 to 3 days of recovery, depending on the athlete's background.

With that understood, how do we determine the most effective training levels? While the $\dot{V}O_2$max and the aerobic and anaerobic thresholds are best determined by treadmill tests in a lab setting, rough measures can be made by two other methods. Italian researchers have developed a noninvasive test (no blood samples needed) that can be used on the track.[5] The athlete runs 8 to 12 laps of a 400m track while wearing a recording heart rate monitor. Each segment of the run is timed, and the heart rate at the last part of each segment is noted. The athlete accelerates to the next speed, then holds steady at the new pace. The heart rate and the running velocity are graphed to show a sharp change from the gradual rise of the heart rate.

Finnish researchers have suggested that when more scientific testing is not possible, the thresholds can be estimated from the beats per minute (BPM) of the maximum heart rate (HRmax, which can also be estimated).[6] The training zones are as follows:

- $\dot{V}O_2$max training: within 5 BPM of the HRmax
- Anaerobic training:
  20 to 30 BPM below HRmax for long distance runners
  15 to 25 BPM below HRmax for middle distance runners
- Aerobic training:
  40 to 60 BPM below HRmax for long distance runners
  35 to 50 BPM below HRmax for middle distance runners

Table 11.1. gives an example based on a maximum heart rate of 200 BPM. The maximum rate varies by age, sex, and fitness.

Table 11.1 Estimating the Heart Rate for Training Levels

Training zone	Heart rate (BPM)	
	Middle distance	Long distance
Maximum	200	200
$\dot{V}O_2$max training	195-200	195-200
Anaerobic training	175-185	170-180
Aerobic training	150-165	140-160

Adapted from John Underwood, personal communication, June, 1985.

After the limits are set for each type of training, the athlete can easily find the most effective training speeds for steady runs. By running at varied paces on the track and taking the pulse, the runner can find what speed gives a pulse of 150, 160, and so forth. Those speeds will be the training speeds. The theory suggests the following types of training during the base conditioning period:

> $\dot{V}O_2$max training: one session per week
> Usually 3 to 5 minutes total of fast intervals
> Long recoveries (10 to 20 minutes)
> Recovery runs at lower aerobic training speed
>
> *Note*: The heart rate should be maintained at this lower level after a race because it speeds the removal of lactic acid from the muscles.
>
> Anaerobic training: one session per week
> Usually 12 to 15 minutes of intervals
> Shorter recoveries (4 to 5 minutes)
> Recovery runs at lower aerobic training speed
>
> Aerobic training: five sessions per week
> Steady-state running
> 3 days at the upper limit (such as 160 BPM)
> 2 days at the lower limit (such as 140 BPM)

Note that these training ideas are still experimental. We have *many* gaps in our knowledge. Understanding training is like putting together a huge puzzle; we have the edges formed, with isolated clusters of knowledge in the open middle. Coaching is still far from an exact science. However, all of the training principles in chapter 1 hold firm in the face of newer scientific knowledge.

Research under the USOC's Elite Athlete Project in the early 1980s[7] found that the best indicators of fitness changes from training by elite male runners were percentage of body fat, anaerobic threshold, blood hemoglobin, and serum ferritin and haptoglobin.

As a note on the tests for iron, such as the serum ferritin level, male distance runners were anemic nearly as often as women runners were. The iron level is critical to distance runners because of its part in oxygen transport. Though women runners must be especially careful that a proper iron level is maintained, male runners are also vulnerable to depletion. Tests such as the serum ferritin level show a drop in the iron level much sooner than the blood hemoglobin, which may give little useful indication until the problem is beyond quick remedy. Runners should be aware that a program of taking iron supplements should include regular blood tests, if possible, because different types of supplements are absorbed at different rates. In some cases, no more than 10% of the iron supplement may be absorbed by the body.

Cross Country

Cross country means many things to many people. The primary purpose of the cross country season is to build a cardiovascular base for the spring track season. We consider the big meets in May and June to be the most important of the year.

The cross country season begins after the opening of school, though the first organized practice may be held in early August, depending on the school system's schedule. We begin the program with a "run," not a race. The distance is equal to the racing distance at the end of the season, which (for university competition) is 5km for women and 8 to 10km for men. The male athletes complete this run at a pace of 6 to 7 minutes per mile, aiming for a time of 37 to 43 minutes for 10km. The women run at a pace of 7 to 8 minutes per mile, aiming for a time of 23 to 26 minutes for 5km. This is a submaximal pace, but we want it to be a comfortable, successful run for the athlete.

Before the start of the run, each athlete declares a pace. The times are given at the 1- and 2-mile points to give the runners an idea of how close they are to their paces. If athletes reach a mark in a time much faster than their declared paces, they must stop until their pace times come up on the watch. After the 2-mile point, the next time for men is given at 4 miles, then times are recorded at 5 miles. The athletes are allowed to run the last mile as fast as they wish. When the last mile split is calculated, the athlete's pace for interval training is determined. If the last mile was 4:40, the training pace for intervals will be 70 seconds per 400, as in the case of a runner like Prefontaine. If the last mile was 6:00, the pace will be 90 seconds. The pace is changed as the runner improves during the racing season. The training pace is usually set at an average of the last three times in the cross country runs.

The Oregon cross country pattern is a 14-day cycle based upon years of training patterns. Like any other dynamic training program, it undergoes periodic changes and improvements. The terms used in the training schedule have already been described. The heavy use of fartlek and steady-pace runs is evident. The present system was described by Bill Dellinger as following this pattern:

(1) Sunday: steady-pace run
(2) Monday: fartlek
(3) Tuesday: cutdown intervals; date pace intervals; light fartlek; cutdowns
(4) Wednesday: steady-pace run
(5) Thursday: hill intervals; light fartlek
(6) Friday: light fartlek
(7) Saturday: overdistance; simulated race; fartlek
(8) Sunday: steady-pace run
(9) Monday: fartlek over hills
(10) Tuesday: date pace intervals; steady-pace run; cutdowns
(11) Wednesday: steady-pace run
(12) Thursday: quick; light fartlek; cutdowns
(13) Friday: light fartlek
(14) Saturday: competition or test effort

The athletes need to learn to run on hills as well as on the flat. Their posture should still be relatively upright, as on the track, though the slopes will cause some leaning. Runners should try not to let the slopes cause them to lean too much, though. When they run uphill or downhill, they should keep their legs a bit bent at the knee to allow for more play in a joint in case of unexpected changes in the ground. When going uphill, they should try not to lean too far forward, which could result in back strain and "stabbing" at the ground with the feet. When running downhill, they should try to avoid leaning back because hitting a wet spot might cause a rough landing on the wrong part of the anatomy. Cross country is the season for developing a base that will help the runner throughout the year.

During the cross country season, the training uses more fartlek and steady-pace running than interval training because the primary object is cardiovascular development. Interval training generally is used only 1 day a week, usually Tuesdays, and it is run at the date pace, as explained in chapter 10. The athletes should have a minimum of 3 weeks of training before they compete in any meets. There should be no more than one meet per week. If the athletes race twice a week, they will have a difficult time making any real progress. With such a heavy racing schedule, they would be better off with a bookkeeper than a coach.

The training schedules are at the end of the chapter. The training dates can be changed to reflect the local season.

Racing Tactics in Cross Country

Cross country is a sport that allows runners to use a variety of tactical maneuvers. Because the terrain varies, the course turns, rises, and falls, and the weather and the opponents affect the racing conditions, successful runners must consider many factors before the race. Some examples of cross country tactics follow.[8]

Check the entire course before the race. Ideally, the athletes should see the course before the day of the race so they do not get exhausted by the warm-up. They should learn what dangers and benefits the course has.

Go for position at the start. In dual meets this is rarely so important, but in major races no course is wide enough to allow freedom of movement to slow starters. Some courses turn into narrow trails very soon. Athletes must run fast enough in the first 400m to get into position without risking later oxygen debt. Some long training runs should begin with a fast 400m from a group start, so this skill can be learned.

Surge to get out of heavy traffic. Sometimes runners must use a faster pace to get ahead of the crowd. They should be careful that the pace does not over-extend them, however.

Run against the opponents, not the watch. Because of course conditions, even-pace running may not be possible, as it is in road or track races.

Be ready to take advantage of an opponent's moment of weakness. Some runners slow down at a curve or after reaching the top of a hill. Runners should look for such sudden opportunities to make an effective move.

Make a move just after turning a corner or crossing the top of a hill. Making sudden gains in position while out of sight can be unnerving to an opponent.

Float up the hills, then surge on the downhill. This takes less energy, and most people slow down as they top the hill.

Be careful not to slow down too much after a surge. The surging runner may fall too far off the pace and be caught by an opponent.

Think of strength rather than speed at the end of the race. An opponent's superior 400m or mile speed means nothing. No runner is starting afresh at this point. The finishing kick comes down to who has more strength and determination, not who has greater speed.

The Steeplechase

The steeplechase is the real test of an athlete. The training for the steeplechase is basically the same as that for a 3,000m or 5,000m runner. The only real difference involves the hurdling activities. Ideally, the athlete will run a steeplechase about once a month, or hopefully no more often than every 2 weeks until he gets into a situation where he has to race twice as part of a single meet. Otherwise, running the steeplechase too often can cause the steeplechaser to be "flattened out" from giving too much in his practice and early competitive seasons.

The difference between training for the flat races and for the steeplechase is the hurdle training. We place hurdles and small logs (up to 3 feet in diameter, lying on their sides) around the track and athletics areas of the campus for the runners to use for informal practice. One principle of training is that every male distance runner does some steeplechase training, whether or not he ever runs a steeplechase in competition. This practice helps the teacher discover potential steeplechasers, some of whom might not be inclined to volunteer for such a tough event. The runners practice jumping over the obstacles or stepping on and then over them while running on their own.

Some pace work is done over a distance of 200m on the track over the hurdles. This is done with two arrangements of hurdles. In one case, only two hurdles are used, one set at the end of the first straight and the other at the end of the turn as the second straight begins. In the other case, about five hurdles are run, set 15 to 20m apart and included in a 200m run. In both cases, the athlete runs about four intervals while working on his hurdling. He tries to hurdle as a hurdler would. During the early part of the year, the hurdles are set at 30 inches in height; as the training year progresses, the hurdles are raised to the 3-foot level of the steeplechase barriers.

The steeplechasers practice over the water jump and barrier once a week. Except during regular competitions, the water jump does not have any water in the pit. The athletes run in a loop, going over the barrier or water jump perhaps four times. Except for this practice situation, they practice with the regular hurdles. The reason for this is simple: You can hit the regular hurdles and they move. The water jump barrier does not move at all. The other barriers are over 12 feet long and weigh well over 200 pounds. They do not move too freely, either. Finally, if an athlete prefers to step on the barriers rather than hurdle over them, he must work on this regularly. The athlete may place a barrier at the edge of the long jump pit and practice running down the runway and stepping onto and going over the barrier and into the sand.

The steeplechaser should not compete too much in his event for it causes a lot of wear and tear. Also, he should not hurdle too much, for it can be hard on the legs.

American steeplechasing would be helped greatly if the race were added to the high school competitive schedule. Unfortunately, few athletes are exposed to steeplechasing before college. A short, 2,000m (5-lap) race is an excellent high school event. When the race is longer than a mile, it begins to highlight the experts. This can provide precollege experience to many runners, and it would be one more event for competitors, allowing more participants. This is the real objective of the entire sport: the joy of competition.

The steeplechase training schedules are at the end of the chapter.

Steeplechase Racing Tactics

Most distance running tactics hold true for the steeplechase. However, the hurdles add another dimension to the race: Some runners fall. This is especially true at the first barrier. Athletes should run wide approaching the first hurdle so they have a clear look at where the barrier is. Some runners have run into the barrier, not realizing where it was until the runner ahead of them jumped suddenly. One way to stay safe is to step on the first barrier rather than hurdle it.

At every barrier it is safer to move out to the side and have a clear view than to follow closely behind a runner, for two reasons. First, the athlete needs to judge exactly where the barrier is so he can time the clearance properly. Second, if the runner falls while clearing the barrier, the trailing runners may fall over him or be injured while trying to avoid stepping on him.

The steeplechaser should try to get a straight line for the last three or four steps to the water jump barrier. After the first lap, the feet will be wet and may slip on the barrier if they hit it at an angle. The runner should stride onto the barrier with the heel so that the foot rolls across the top and the toe of the shoe (and some spikes) pushes off from the far side of the barrier, propelling him across the water. One should not try to clear the water completely because it wastes energy. Some athletes hurdle over the barrier rather than step on it. This procedure can be marginally faster, but it may be more stressful on the legs, and the runner may land in deeper water.

The best way to run the race is to begin cautiously, avoiding getting caught in the crowd or following the early leader's pace, which is often too fast. The runner moves into position after four laps, staying in the front three positions just as suggested for the middle distances. He finishes strongly over the last one or two laps but must be especially careful of the barriers on the last lap. Some runners get carried away with the head-to-head competition and hit a barrier. The steeplechase is an event for the more courageous and determined athletes.

The Middle Distances: 2 Miles to 10 Kilometers

The training principles and patterns for the longer distance races are the same as those given for the shorter middle distance runs. The fall training is usually the cross country training described earlier. At the end of the cross country season, in late November, the distance runners switch to training schedules that more specifically apply to their racing distances on the track.

As in other events, we follow the hard-easy principle in planning the athletes' training programs. This is an area of danger if the coach attempts to overwork the athlete. Runners must not be sent beyond their personal tolerance levels in training. The basic cycle used is 1 day of hard or heavy training followed by 1 day of light or easy training. However, this pattern is not universal. Some athletes need 2 light days after each heavy day of training; an example is Kenny Moore, who became an Olympic marathoner after graduating from Oregon. Many athletes are not physically mature until their early or mid-20s, so the teacher/coach should be careful of the work load assigned to young athletes even in college.

Other athletes are extremely strong and can go 2 hard days for every easy day. Examples are Dyrol Burleson, an American record holder and three-time NCAA mile champion as an Oregon undergraduate, and Steve Prefontaine, who set an American record in the 5,000m as an Oregon sophomore. Those runners might even be able to progress on a program of 3 hard days for each easy day, but the coach must be very cautious in following up such possibilities. Each individual has his or her own tolerance level for work. If the athlete is pushed beyond that level, the performance will go into a nosedive. Once this happens, it is very difficult to reverse the process and get the athlete's performances moving in the right direction.

The training patterns for the longer distances are the same as for the shorter distances, but the mileage covered is greater. This does not mean 100 miles a week, which for most athletes is foolish. It means that where a miler or half-miler might run 6 to 10 miles for a long run of the week on Sunday, the 5,000m runner may run as far as 15 miles or more. Interval work is essentially proportionate to the racing distance, varying from 1-1/2 to 3 times the racing distance. Where an 800m runner will cover no more than 1-1/4 to 1-1/2 miles in a long interval session, the 5,000m or longer runner may cover from 3 to 6 miles of intervals. Even so, most male athletes rarely need to cover more than 70 to 80 miles (50 to 70 miles for females) in the longer training weeks of the winter.

Actually, from the 5,000m to the marathon, the training is very similar. A 5,000m runner can train for a marathon by using some longer intervals (but not run any more total miles of intervals), but about the only real change in training would be the addition of a long run of 20 to 30 miles once a month for the Sunday run. Five- and 10km racers have learned that superhigh mileage is not as necessary to successful marathoning as theorists once suggested. Also, running the marathon does not mean that the athlete cannot compete successfully in the track races. Experience has shown that it can be done.

The tactics of the longer distance runs are essentially the same regardless of the racing distance: Find out what the opposition can do, then determine how he or she can be beaten.

The training schedules are given fully at the end of the chapter. They can be adapted by the athlete for almost any racing distance between 1,500m and the marathon because the principles and patterns are the same. Only the paces and the quantities differ.

Training for the Marathon

The marathon is an event for the mature athlete, starting no sooner than their mid-20s. Success at the highest levels requires great talent, just as in the other events. The most influential factors on marathon performance are shown in Table 11.2.[9]

Table 11.2   Performance Factors in the Marathon

Physiological factors
Slow-twitch muscle fiber dominance (genetic)
Relatively large $\dot{V}O_2$max, depending on
 genetic heritage,
 body weight,
 heart volume, and
 blood chemistry
High utilization of the $\dot{V}O_2$max
High level of running economy (limits oxygen
 consumption)
Optimal glycogen storage system
Optimal fluid supply (prevents overheating and
 dehydration)
 Quality and quantity are factors
 Aided by reduced body weight (reduces energy needs)
Training factors
Training structures based on
 sufficiently high total volume and
 principles of periodization and regeneration
Tempo endurance runs that develop the aerobic capacity
 (near the anaerobic threshold)
Sufficiently high volume of single endurance loads (runs
 of 30 km or longer) consolidating aerobic capacity,
 allowing adjustments to overheating and dehydration,
 and assisting in development of willpower
Anaerobic loads adjusted to energy needs of marathon
 short-interval training one or two times per week

From Jurgen Schiffer. (1988). Performance factors in the marathon. *Track Technique*, **105**, 3360. Reprinted with permission.

References

1. Manuel Bueno. (1985). Current conceptions of endurance training. In Jess Jarver (Ed.), *Middle distances: contemporary theory, technique and training* (2nd ed., pp. 10-15). Los Altos, CA: Tafnews.
2. David Hinz. (1986). U.S. Elite Athlete Project. *The Harrier*, **12**(10), 6.
3. Brian J. Sharkey. (1984). *Physiology of fitness* (2nd ed., pp. 10-11). Champaign, IL: Human Kinetics.
4. George A. Brooks & Thomas D. Fahey. (1985). *Exercise physiology: Human bioenergetics and its applications* (pp. 208-213). New York: Macmillan.
5. F. Conconi et al. (1982). Determination of the anaerobic threshold by a noninvasive field test in running. *J. Appl. Physiol. Respirat. Envir. Exercise Physiol.*, **52**, 869-873.
6. John Underwood. (1985). Personal communication.
7. David E. Martin. (1985). Distance running: The Elite Athlete Project. *Track Technique*, **93**, 2969.
8. Tricks of the trail. (1987). *Track and Field Quarterly Review*, **87**(2), 25-27.
9. Jurgen Schiffer. (1988). Performance factors in the marathon. *Track Technique*, **105**, 3360.

Additional Readings

AAA Runner's Guide. (1983). London: William Collins.

Alford, J.W. (Ed.). *Running: The IAAF Symposium.* London: International Amateur Athletic Federation.

Bompa, Tudor O. (1989). Physiological intensity values employed to plan endurance training. *Track Technique,* **108,** 3435-3442.

Bowerman, Bill. (1985). Steeplechase training. *Track and Field Quarterly Review,* **85**(3), 15-17.

Costill, David L. (1986). *Inside running: Basics of sports physiology.* Indianapolis: Benchmark Press.

Dare, Bernie. (1988). V̇O₂max, training, and other factors. *Track and Field Quarterly Review,* **88**(2), 43-44.

Dellinger, Bill, & Freeman, Bill. (1984). *The competitive runner's training book.* New York: Macmillan.

Diemer, Brian. (1988). Progressive training towards a peak. *Track and Field Quarterly Review,* **88**(2), 32-33.

Frederick, Sue. (1987). Why altitude training doesn't work. *Track and Field Quarterly Review,* **87**(2), 30-31.

Freeman, William H. (1985). Concerns in training women distance runners. *Track and Field Quarterly Review,* **85**(3), 29-36.

Freeman, William H. (1985). Pacing chart for the steeplechase. *Track Technique,* **92,** 2930-2931.

Freeman, William. (1989). *Peak when it counts: Periodization for the American coach.* Los Altos, CA: Tafnews.

Hislop, Chick. (1985). Steeplechase technique. *Track and Field Quarterly Review,* **85**(3), 18-22.

Jarver, Jess (Ed.) (1985). *Middle distances: Contemporary theory, technique and training* (2nd ed.). Los Altos, CA: Tafnews.

Lenzi, Giampaolo. (1987). The marathon race: Modern training methodology. *New Studies in Athletics,* **2**(2), 41-50.

Lundin, Phil. (1986). Means of developing specific endurance in middle and long distance running. *Track Technique,* **94,** 2991-2993.

Maulbecker, Klaus, & Kruger, Jobst. (1988). Are long distance runners overworked? *Track Technique,* **104,** 3228.

Pahud, Jean Francois, & Gobbelet, Charles. (1986). Training at altitude: General principles and personal experience. *New Studies in Athletics,* **1**(3), 53-57.

Pohlitz, Lothar. (1986). Practical experiences of altitude training with female middle distance runners. *New Studies in Athletics,* **1**(3), 47-52.

Robertson, John. (1989). Training safety tips for long distance runners. *Track Technique,* **108,** 3453-3455.

Sparks, Ken, & Bjorklund, Garry. (1984). *Long distance runner's guide to training and racing: Build your endurance, strength, and efficiency.* Englewood Cliffs, NJ: Prentice-Hall.

Stevenson, Carol. (1987). Cross country training for women. *Track and Field Quarterly Review,* **87**(2), 19-21.

Stevenson, Carol. (1988). Mileage illusions and limitations in women's distance running. *Track and Field Quarterly Review,* **88**(2), 30-31.

Vigil, Joe. (1987). Distance training. *Track Technique,* **100,** 3189-3192.

Cross Country Training Schedule

ATHLETE _____

1. Warm-up
   A. Jog 1-3 miles, stretch
2. Fartlek
   A. Varied (1) 30 min (2) light
   B. Steady (1) 2-4 miles
      (2) 4-6 miles (3) 6-10 miles
      (4) 3-5 miles (5) easy (6) 8-15 miles
3. Strength & flexibility
   A. Weights and jogging
   B. Jogging and stretching
4. High knee and power run
5. Intervals
   A. 100 (1) 18-16-14 sec (2) 17-15-13 sec
   B. 150 (1) 25 sec (2) 24-26 sec
      (3) 21-22 sec
   C. 200 (1) 35 sec (2) 27 sec (3) 30 sec
   D. 300 (1) 52 sec (2) 48 sec (3) 45 sec
   E. 400 (1) 70-73 sec (2) 72-75 sec
      (3) 66-68 sec (4) 62 sec
   F. 600 (1) 1:45 (2) 1:42 (3)
   G. 800 (1) 70 sec pace (2) 68 sec pace
      (3)
   H. 1200 (1) 70 sec pace (2) 69 sec pace
      (3) 68 sec (4) 66 sec
   J. 1600 (1) 72 sec pace
      (2) 68-70 sec (3) 64-67 sec
   K.
   L.
6. Sets
   A. 600-400-300-200-100
      (1) 1:45-68-49-32-15 sec (2)
   B. 400-600-400-200 (1) 63 sec (2)
   C. 500-150-150 (1) 55 sec pace (2)
   D.
7. Team meeting
8. Special
   A. Sauna   C.
   B. Swim
9. Drills
   A. 150 sprint-float-sprint
   B. 150 middle 1-step acceleration
   C. 40-30 drill (1) 4 laps (2) 6 laps (3)
   D. 70-90 drill
      (1) 1-1 (2) 2-1 (3) 3-1 (4)
   E. Cut-downs
      (1) 100 (2) 150 (3) 200 (4) 300
      (5) 400 (6) 800 (7) mile/1600
   F. Simulated race drills
      (1) 1st 200, last 200
      (2) 2-1/2, 1-1/2 (3) 15km, 1200
   G. 2-4 miles at (1) 80 sec pace (2)
10. Progress assessment
    A. Meet   C. Simulation
    B. Trial   D. Control test
       (1) 3/4 date pace (2) over (3) under
11. Hill intervals
    A. 100   C.
    B. 200
12. With Coach
    A. (name)
    B. Leader
14. A. Wind sprints (1) straight (2) curve
    B. Hurdle X drill
    C. Spring and bound
    D.
15. Plyometrics
    A. Jumps (1) 1 leg (2) both legs (3)
    B. Bounding (1) 1 leg (2) both legs (3)
    C.
16. Finish work
17. Acrobatics or apparatus
18. 3/4 effort
19.
20. Work on second event
21. Visual aids
    A. Videotape   C. Photos
    B. Film
       (1) record performance (2) study
30. Experimental work

DATE September

Day	a.m.	p.m.
M	2B(4)	6x 2A(1)—5A(grass)
Tu	2B(4)	12-16-20x 5E(2)—2B(1)—9E(1) [6x]
W	8x 2B(4)—5A	2B(3)
Th	2B(4)	16-24x 5B(2)—1—7
F	1	1
Sa		6x 5E(3)—2B(3)—9E(4)
Su		2B(5)
M	2B(4)	6x 2B(2)—5A (grass)
Tu	2B(4)	4x 3x 5H(2 or 3)—9E(7)[72-70-68 or 80-75-70]
W	9x 2B(4)—9E(1)	1
Th	2B(4)	12x 5D(grass)
F	1 (grass)	1
Sa		12x 5J(3)—9E(5)[72-70-68]
Su		2B(6)
M	2B(5)	2B(5)
Tu	2B(4)	12x 5D(1)—2B(1)—9E(1) [6x]
W	2B(4)	2B(3)
Th	2B(4)	16x 9E(2)—2B(5)(grass)
F	1 (grass)	1 (grass)
Sa		10B(10 km.)
Su		2B(6)
M	2B(4)	4x 2B(2)—9E(1)
Tu	2B(4)	3x/5H(1-3-4)—3x/9E(3)—1—3x/9E(4)
W	9x 2B(4)—9E(1)	2B(3)
Th	2B(4)	12x 5D(grass)
F	1	1
Sa		3x 9F(3)—5A
Su		1

DATE October

Day	a.m.	p.m.
M	2B(5)	2B(5)
Tu	2B(4)	12x 5D(1)—2B(1)—9E(1) [6x]
W	2B(4)	2B(3)
Th	2B(4)	16x 9E(2)—2B(5)(grass)
F	1 (grass)	1 (grass)
Sa		10B(10 km.)
Su		2B(6)
M	2B(4)	4x 2B(2)—9E (1)
Tu	2B(4)	3x/5H(1-3-4)—3x/9E(6)— 9E(5)—3x/9E(3)—1—3x/9E(4)
W	9x 2B(4)-9E(1)	2B(3)
Th	2B(4)	12x 5D (grass)
F	1	1
Sa		3x 9F(3)—5A
Su		1
M	1	2B(2)
Tu	2B(4)	2x 5H(1)—5G(2)—5D(2)—2A(2)—9E(1) [6x 3x]
W	2B(4)	2A(1)
Th	1	4x 9E(2)—2A(2)—9E(1)—7
F	1	1
Sa		10A—meet
Su		2B(6)
M	2B(4)	2B(4)
Tu	2B(4)	9x 9F(3)—9E(4)
W	2B(4)	9x 2B(2)—9E(1)
Th	12x 9E(4)	2x 5C(2)—2B(2)—5C(1) [6x]
F	1	1
Sa	3x 5J(2)—5D [12x]	2B(2)
Su		2B(6)

DATE November

Day	a.m.	p.m.
M	1	2B(2)
Tu	2B(4)	2x 5H(1)—5G(2)—5D(2)—2A(2)—9E(1) [6x 3x]
W	2B(4)	2A(1)
Th	1	4x 9E(2)—2A(2)—9E(1)—7
F	1	1
Sa		10A—Northern Division Meet
Su		2B(6)
M	2B(4)	2B(4)
Tu	2B(4)	9x 9F(3)—9E(4)
W	2B(4)	9x 2B(2)—9E(1)
Th	12x 9E(4)	2x 5C(3)—2B(2)—5C(1) [6x]
F	1	1
Sa	3x 5J(2)—5D [12x]	2B(2)
Su		2B(6)
M	1	4x 9E(1)
Tu	2B(4)	4x 5F(2)—5E(3)—5D(2)—5C(2)—1 [4x 4x]
W	2B(4)	2B(3)
Th	1	2x 5B(3)—9G(1)—9E(1) [4x]
F		Travel—light over course
Sa		10A—PAC 8 Meet
Su		2B(5)
M		4x 2B(5)(6 miles)—9E(1)
Tu	2B(2)	2-3x 9C(2)—2B(5)—9E(4) [6x]
W	2B(4)	2B(5)(45 min.)
Th	2B(2)	8-12x 5D(1-2)—2B(2)—9E(4) [6x]
F		2B(5)
Sa		Travel
Su	Jog course	Monday—NCAA Meet

Steeplechase Training Schedule

ATHLETE _____

1. Warm-up
   A. Jog 1-3 miles, stretch
2. Fartlek
   A. Varied (1) 30 min (2) 40 min (3) 45 min
   B. Steady (1) 2-4 miles (2) 4-6 miles (3) 6-10 miles (4) 8-15 miles (5) 12-15 miles
3. Strength & flexibility
   A. Weights and jogging
   B. Jogging and stretching
4. High knee and power run
5. Intervals X. Over hurdles
   A. 100 (1) 18-16-14 sec (2) 17-15-13 sec
   B. 150 (1) 25 sec (2)
   C. 200 (1) 35 sec (2) 32 sec (3) 27-29 sec (4) 27 sec
   D. 300 (1) 52 sec (2) 48 sec (3) 45 sec (4) 46 sec
   E. 400 (1) 70-73 sec (2) 68 sec (3) 62 sec
   F. 600 (1) 75 sec (2) 72 sec (3) 68 sec (4)
   G. 800 (1) 72-75 sec (2) 68-70 sec (3) 64 sec (4) 70 sec
   H. 1200 (1) 72-75 sec (2) 69-71 sec (3)
   J. 1600 (1) 72-75 sec (2) 69-72 sec (3)
   K.
6. Sets
   A. 600-400-300-200-100 (1) 1:45-68-49-32-15 sec (2)
   B. 400-600-400-200 (1) 64 sec (2) 62 sec
   C. 600-300-150
   D. 300-200-100
7. Team meeting
8. Special
   A. Sauna   C.
   B. Swim
9. Drills X. Hurdle X drill (1) LH (2) IH (3) water barrier
   A. 150 sprint-float-sprint
   B. 150 middle 1-step acceleration
   C. 40-30 drill (1) 4 laps (2) 6 laps (3)
   D. 70-90 drill (1) 1-1 (2) 2-1 (3) 3-1 (4)
   E. Cut-downs (1) 100 (2) 150 (3) 200 (4) 300 (5) 400 (6) 800 (7)
   F. Simulated race drills (1) 1st 800, last 800 (2) 10 miles, 1200 drill (3) 3200 at 80 sec pace (4) 6 laps at 80 pace (5) 4 miles (6400) at 80 pace
   G. Last 150 (water jump & hurdle) (1) 200
   H. IH (1) 150 (2) 200 (3) 300 (4) 400
   J. 5km: 4 hurdles (1) 90 sec (2) 85 sec (3) 80 sec (4)
   K. Pace over 4 hurdles per 400
10. Progress assessment
    A. Meet   C. Simulation
    B. Trial   D. Control test (1) 3/4 date pace (2) over (3) under
11. Hill intervals   C.
    A. 100
    B. 200
12. With Coach
    A. (name)
    B. Leader
14. A. Wind sprints (1) straight (2) curve
    B. Hurdle X drill
    C. Spring and bound
    D.
15. Plyometrics
    A. Jumps (1) 1 leg (2) both legs (3)
    B. Bounding (1) 1 leg (2) both legs (3)
    C.
16. Finish work
17. Acrobatics or apparatus
18. 3/4 effort
19. Regular steeplechase course
    A. 1600   C. 800
    B. 1200   D. 400
20. Work on second event
21. Visual aids   C. Photos
    A. Videotape
    B. Film (1) record performance (2) study
30. Experimental work

DATE December

M	9X—2A(2)—9E(1) [4x]
Tu	5F—5D—2B(2)—9E(4) [2x ... 4x]
W	2B(3)
Th	5BX—9F(3)—5A(1) [4x]
F	1
Sa	10B(1)(5 km.)—2B(2)—9E(4) [6x]
Su	2B(4)
M	2A(2)
Tu	12-24x 5D
W	2B(3)
Th	2A(2)
F	1
Sa	2B(3)
Su	2B(3)
M	2A(2)
Tu	5H—5G—5E—5D [3x 3x 6x]
W	2B(3)—5A(1)
Th	5C(3)—2B(2)—5A(1) [4x]
F	2B(2)
Sa	9C(2)—2B(1)—5D [6x]
Su	2B(3)
M	
Tu	
W	
Th	
F	
Sa	
Su	

DATE January

M	2A(3)—9X(1)
Tu	1—9J(3)—5A(2)
W	7—9X(3)—2B(2)—5A(1)
Th	5J—5G—9E(4)—1 [2x 3x]
F	1
Sa	5D(1-2-3) [15x]
Su	2B(3)
M	2A(2)—9X(1)
Tu	1—5XG—5E—1—9E(4) [4x 4x]
W	9X(3)—2B(2)—5A(1)
Th	5XC—1—5A(2) [4x]
F	1
Sa	5B(1)—2A(1)—5A(1) [16x]
Su	2B(3)
M	2A(3)—9B(2)
Tu	1—5D—1—5A(1) [8x]
W	9X(3)—2B(2)—5A(1)
Th	9J—5A(1)
F	1
Sa	Oregon Indoor Meet
Su	2B(3)
M	
Tu	
W	
Th	
F	
Sa	
Su	

DATE February

M	9X—2A(3)
Tu	5D—2B(1)—9E(1) [6x]
W	9X(3)—2B(3) [4x]
Th	5XG—5E—2B(1)—9E(4) [4x 6x]
F	1
Sa	5C—10A(2)—9E(1)—10-km run [12x 6x]
Su	2B(5)
M	9H(2)—2A(3) [3x]
Tu	5D—5C—2B(1)—5A(1) [4x 4x]
W	9X(3)—2B(3) [4x]
Th	5H—5XG—5E—2B(1)—9E(1) [2x 2x 4x]
F	1
Sa	5C—2B(2)—9E(4) [8x 6x]
Su	2B(5)
M	9H(2)—2A(3) [2x]
Tu	5D—1A—9E(1) [12x 4x]
W	9X(3)—2B(2) [4x]
Th	5C—9F(3)—9E(1) [2x 4x]
F	1—9X
Sa	19A(72-75)—19C(70-72)—19D(64-66)—2B(1)—5A
Su	2B(5)
M	9X—2A(3)—9E(1) [4x]
Tu	5D—2B(3)—5D [6x]
W	2B(2)
Th	9H(1)—2B(1)—9E(1) [6x]
F	1—9A
Sa	5H—5G—9E(5)—1—9E(3) [2x 3x 4x]
Su	2B(5)

DATE March

M	2A(3)
Tu	4x 4x / 5E—5XD—2B(1)—9E(3)
W	2B(2)
Th	6C—2B(1)—6C
F	1
Sa	4x / 10B(mile)—1—9E(4)
Su	2B(3)
M	2A(3)
Tu	6x / 5D—2B(1)—9E(3)
W	2-4x / 2B(2)
Th	19B(72)—5G—5E—1—9E(1)
F	1
Sa	6x / 5G—2B(2)—9E(4)
Su	2B(3)
M	9X—2A(3)
Tu	4x 6x / 5D—5XD—1—9E(3)
W	4x / 2A(4)
Th	5C—2B(1)—9E(1)
F	1
Sa	10A—Fresno
Su	2B(5)
M	3x 3x 2x 2x 2x / 5XD—5D—2B(1)—5D—5C—9G
Tu	2B(2)
W	2A(1)
Th	5F—5D—5A—1—5A(2)
F	1
Sa	10A
Su	2B(5)

DATE April

M	2A(3)
Tu	6B(2)
W	2B(2)
Th	2x 2x 2x / 5J—5XG—5E—9G(1)
F	1
Sa	6x / 9H(3)—2B(3)—9E(3)
Su	2B(3)
M	2A(3)
Tu	2x 3x 3x / 19B—5G—9E(5)—1—9H(2)
W	7—2B(2)
Th	6D—1—6C
F	1
Sa	10A
Su	2B(5)
M	9X—2A(3)
Tu	3x 3x 3x / 5XD—9E(6)—2B(1)—5XD
W	4x / 2B(2)—9E(1)
Th	9F(5)—9G(1)—9G—5A
F	2B(1)—5A(2)
Sa	1
Su	10A—Twilight meet
M	2B(3)
Tu	2x 4x 2x 2x / 5XG—9E(5)—2B(1)—9G(1)—9B
W	2B(2)
Th	2x 2x 2x 2x / 5D—5C—5A—2B(1)—5A
F	1
Sa	10A—Washington
Su	2B(3)

DATE May _____

Day	a.m.	p.m.
M		2A(2)
Tu		3x/9E(6)—3x/9E(5)—9E(3)—2B(1)—3x/9E(3)
W		2B(2)
Th		2x/9H(2)—2B(1)—2x/9G(1)
F		1
Sa		1,500 trial
Su		2B(3)
M		2A(3)
Tu		5G(3)—9K(800 in 2:20)—5GX(3)—5D(3)—9K(300 in 51)—5D(3)—2A
W		2B(2)
Th		6x/5C(3)—2B(1)—2x/5C(water barrier + 1 hurdle)
F		Light
Sa		10A—Northern Division Meet
Su		2B(3)easy
M	2B(1)	2A(3)
Tu	Light	9K(800 in 2:20)—3x/9E(5)(66-64-62)—1—3x/9E(4)(49-47-45)
W	Light	2x/9X(3)—1
Th	Travel	Light grass
F		10A—PAC 8 Meet
Sa		Light grass—8x/5A
Su		2B(3)easy
M	2B(1)	2A(3)
Tu	2B(1)	6x/5E(3)—2A(1)—9K
W	2B(1)	2B(2)
Th	Light	4x/5G(2-3)—4x/5E(3)—4x/5EX(2)—4x/9E(3)(33-31-29-27)
F	Light	Light
Sa		3x/9E(4)(hurdles in 52-50-48)—2B(3)—3x/9E(4)(48-45-42)
Su		

DATE June _____

Day	a.m.	p.m.
M	Light	Light grass—5A(2)
Tu	Light	5XD(1)—2x/5C(2)—9F(4)
W	Light	1
Th		10A—Trials, NCAA meet
F		1
Sa		10A—Finals, NCAA meet
Su		
M		
Tu		
W		
Th		
F		
Sa		
Su		
M		
Tu		
W		
Th		
F		
Sa		
Su		
M		
Tu		
W		
Th		
F		
Sa		
Su		

Distance Runners' Training Schedule

ATHLETE _____

1. Warm-up
   A. Jog 1-3 miles, stretch
2. Fartlek
   A. Varied (1) 30 min (2) 45 min
   B. Steady (1) 2-4 miles (2) 4-6 miles
      (3) 6-10 miles (4) 8-12 miles a. easy
      (5) 12-15 miles a. easy
      (6) 8-15 miles easy
3. Strength & flexibility
   A. Weights and jogging
   B. Jogging and stretching
4. High knee and power run
5. Intervals
   A. 100 (1) 18-16-14 sec
      (2) 17-16-15-14 sec (3) 16-15-14 sec
      (4) 17-16-14-13 sec (5) 15-14-13 sec
   B. 150 (1) 25 sec (2) 24 sec
      (3) 8-6-8 (50 splits)
   C. 200 (1) 35 sec (2) 28 sec (3) 27 sec
      (4) 27-28 sec (5) 29 sec
      (6) 30 sec (7) 32-34 sec
      (8) 33 sec (9) 31 sec
   D. 300 (1) 52 sec (2) 48 sec
      (3) 45 sec (4) 42 sec (5) 54 sec
      (6) 50 sec (7) 46-47 sec (8) 47 sec
   E. 400 (1) 70-73 sec (2) 68 sec
      (3) 62 sec (4) 66 sec (5) 60-64 sec
   F. 600 (1) 1:45 (2) 1:39
   G. 800 (1) 70 sec (2) 62-64 sec
      (3) 64 sec
   H. 1200 (1) 70 sec (2) 90 sec
      (3) 66 sec (4) 62-68 sec
   J. 1600 (1) 72 sec (2) 68-70 sec
      (3) 64-67 sec (4) 63 sec
   K. 4 miles (1) 6:30-7:00/mile
   L. 10km (1) 6:00/mile or 1600
6. Sets
   A. 600-400-300-200-100
      (1) 1:45-68-49-32-15 sec (2)
   B. 400-600-400-200 (1) 63 sec (2)
   C. 500-300-150-150 (1) 55 pace (2)
   D. 300-200-100 (1) 48-31-14
7. Team meeting
8. Special
   A. Sauna   C.
   B. Swim
9. Drills
   A. 150 sprint-float-sprint
   B. 150 middle 1-step acceleration
   C. 40-30 drill (1) 4 laps (2) 6 laps
      (3) 6-12 laps
   D. 70-90 drill (1) 1-1 (2) 2-1
      (3) 3-1 (4) 2-2
   E. Cut-downs (1) 100 (2) 150
      (3) 200 (4) 300 (5) 400 (6) 800
      (7) 1200 (8) mile
   F. Simulated race drills
      (1) 1st 200, last 200
      (2) 2-1/2, 1-1/2 (3) 15km, 1200 (4)
   G. 2-4 miles at (1) 80 sec (2) 75 sec
10. Progress assessment
    A. Meet   C. Simulation
    B. Trial   D. Control test
       (1) 3/4 date pace (2) over (3) under

11. Hill intervals   C.
    A. 100
    B. 200
12. With Coach
    A. (name)
    B. Leader
14. A. Wind sprints (1) straight (2) curve
    B. Hurdle X drill
    C. Spring and bound
    D.
15. Plyometrics
    A. Jumps (1) 1 leg (2) both legs (3)
    B. Bounding (1) 1 leg (2) both legs (3)
    C.
16. Finish work
17. Acrobatics or apparatus
18. 3/4 effort
    A. 5,000m on date pace
    B. 5km at 70±1 sec/400
19.
20. Work on second event
21. Visual aids
    A. Videotape   C. Photos
    B. Film
       (1) record performance (2) study
30. Experimental work

DATE November

Day	a.m.	p.m.
M	1	2B(2)—5A(2)
Tu	2B(2)	8-12x 5D(on hill)—2B(1)
W	2B(1)	2A(2)
Th	1	3x/9E(7)(67-66-64)— 3x/9E(8)(75-70-68 or 69)—6x/9E(4)—7
F	1	1(grass)
Sa		6x 5D(on hill)—2B(2)—5D(track)
Su		Easy run
M		Light—5A(2)
Tu	2B(1)	2x/5F(1)—2x/5F(2)—2x/5D(1-2)— 2x/5D(3-4)—2x/5D(2)—2B(1)
W	2B(2)	2B(3)
Th	Easy	2x 5C(2)—9G(1)(sawdust)—5A(2)
F	Light	Light
Sa		10B(18A)—2B(2)—6x 9E(4)
Su		Easy run
M		2A(1)—5A(2)
Tu	2B(1)	9C(1)—800 rest— 9C(1)—800 rest—9C(1)—1—6x 9E(4)
W	2B(1)	2B(3)
Th	2B(2)	2x 5C(3)—2B(2)—5A(2)
F	Light	Light
Sa		16-24x 5D(1-2)(sawdust)
Su		Easy—long
M		2A(1)—5A(2)
Tu		2B(3)
W		2A(2)
Th		Light run—Thanksgiving
F		2B(4)
Sa		12-24x 5D(50-52)
Su		Easy running

DATE December

Day	a.m.	p.m.
M	2B(2)	2A(2)
Tu	2B(2)	3x 9D—5K(1)—9E(4)(52-49-46)
W	2B(2)	2B(3)(6:30-7:00 pace)
Th	2B(2)	6x 6x 6x 2A(2)(include 5G—5E—5B)
F	2B(2)	2B(2)
Sa		3x 4x 9F(3)—(5H)—9E(4)—2B(2)
Su		2B(5)
M	2B(2)	2A(2)
Tu	2B(1)	6x 5D(2)—2B(3)—9E(4)
W	2B(2)	2B(3)(easy)
Th	2B(1)	2x 5C(3)—2A(1)—5A(3)
F	Light	Light grass
Sa		6x 10B(18A)—2B(2)—9E(4)
Su		2B(5)
M	2B(1)	2A(2)
Tu	2B(2)	12-24x 5D(1-2)
W	2B(1)	2B(3)
Th	2B(2)	4x 4x 4x 2A(2)(include 5G—5E—5C—5A)
F	2B(1)	Light run
Sa		2B(4)
Su		2B(4)(light)
M	2B(1)	2A(2)
Tu	2B(2)	3x 3x 3x 5H—5G—5E—5C
W	2B(1)	2B(4)—5A(3)
Th	2B(2)	4x 5C(1)—2A(1)—5A(3)
F	2B(2)	Light run(30-40 min.)
Sa		2B(4)
Su		6x 9C(3)—2B(1)—9E(4)

DATE January

Day	a.m.	p.m.
M		2A(2)
Tu	2B(2)	15x 6x 5E(2)—2B(2)—9E(4)
W	2B(2) 5A(2)	2B(2)
Th	2B(2)	4x 5D(3)—2A(1)—7
F	2B(2)	2B(1)
Sa		9D(4)—2(light)
Su		2B(5)
M	2B(2)	2A(2)
Tu	2B(2)	1—9F(1)—5A(1)
W	2B(1)	7—2B(2)
Th	2B(2)	2x 1x 5J(3)—9G(1)—9E(8)(80-75-70-65)
F	1	1
Sa		12x 5D(1-2)—2B(2)—5A(2)
Su		2B(5)
M		2A(2)
Tu	2B(2)	8x 5D(1-2)—2B(2)—5A(2)
W	2B(2)	2A(2)
Th	2B(2)	4x 3x 9E(8)(72-70-68-66)—9E(7)(75-72-68)—1
F	1	1
Sa		22x 5B(2)—9G(1)—5A(2)
Su		2B(5)
M		2A(2)
Tu	2B(2)	6x 6x 6x 5D(5)—5D(6-1)—5D(2-6)—1—5A(2)
W	2B(1)	2(easy—1 hour)
Th	2B(1)	2x 6x 2x 5C(4)—9G(1)—9E(4)(52-50-48-46)
F	1	1
Sa		10A—Portland Indoor
Su		

DATE February

Day	a.m.	p.m.
M		2A(1-2)(light)
Tu	2B(2)	6x 5D(4)—2B(2)—9E(1)
W	2B(2)	2B(3)
Th	2B(1)	4x 8x 5G(2)—1 (light)—9E(4)(50-48-46-44)
F	1	1
Sa	2B(2)	8x 5C(5)—2B(2)—9E(1)
Su		2B(4)
M		2A(2)
Tu	2B(2)	6x 5E(2)—5L(1)—5A(2)
W	1	2B(2)
Th	2B(2)	3-4x 5H(1)—2B(1)
F	2B(1)	2B(1)
Sa		12-20x 5C(6)—1
Su		2B(5a)
M	2B(1)	2A(2)
Tu	2B(2)	4x 8x 5E(3)—5E(2)—2B(1)
W	2B(2)	2B(3)
Th	2B(2)	2x 5C(3)—2B(2)—9E(1)
F	2B(2)	1
Sa		6x 5J(4)—9G(1)—9E(4)—2B(5a)
Su		2B(5a)
M		2A(2)
Tu	2B(2)	6x 5D(4)—2B(2)—9E(1)
W	2B(2)	2B(3)
Th	2B(2)	3-4x 5H(1)—2B(1)
F	2B(2)	2B(1)
Sa		16x 5D—1
Su		2B(5a)

DATE March

Day	a.m.	p.m.
M 1		2A(2)
Tu	2B(2)	6x 5E(2)—9G(1)—5A(2)
W	2B(2)	2B(2)
Th	2B(2)	3-4x 5H(1)—2B(1)
F	1	2B(1)
Sa		12-20x 5C(6)
Su		2B(5a)
M	2B(1)	2A(2)
Tu	2B(2)	6x 5D(7)—2B(2)—9E(4)
W	2B(2)	2B(3)
Th	2B(2)	9D(4)
F	1	1
Sa		6x 10A(800)—2B(3)—9E(4)
Su		2B(5a)
M	2B(1)	2A(1-2)—5A(2)
Tu	2B(1)	6x 9E(4)—2B(1)—9E(3)(32-30-30-28)
W	2B(1)	2B(2)—5A(2)
Th	1	2x 5C(3)—9G(1)(2 mi.)—5A(2)
F	1	1
Sa		10A—Fresno meet
Su		2B(4)
M	2B(1)	2A(2)—5A(2)
Tu	2B(1)	6x 5D(7)—2B(1)—9E(4)
W	2B(1)	2B(2)
Th	1	2x 5C(3)—9G(1)—5A(2)
F	1	1
Sa		10A
Su		2B(5)

DATE April

Day	a.m.	p.m.
M		2B(2)
Tu	2B(2)	4x/5E(4)—rest/5G(2)—4x/5E(4)— 2B(1)—4x/9E(4)(51-49-47-45)
W	2B(2)	2B(2)
Th	2B(1)	5F(1)—5D(8)—5A(14 sec)—1A—5A(4)
F	1	1
Sa		10A(2 mi.)
Su		2B(5)
M	2B(2)	2A(2)
Tu	2B(2)	6x 6B(2)—2B(2)—9E(4)
W	2B(2)	2B(2)
Th	2B(2)	4x 9G(1)—9E(4)(52-50-48-46)
F	2B(2)	2B(1)
Sa		3x 2x 4x 5H(2)—5J(1,2)—1—9E(4)
Su		2B(4)
M	2B(1)	2A(1)
Tu	2B(1)	8x 6x 7—5D(2)—1—9E(3)(34-32-30)
W	1	7—2B(2)
Th	1	2x 6D(1)—1—5A(4)
F	1	1
Sa		10A(3 km. or 5 km.)
Su		2B(5)
M	2B(2)	2A(2)
Tu	2B(2)	4x 3x 5D(8)—9E(8)(70-68-66)
W	2B(1)	2B(2)—9A
Th	2B(1)	2x Light grass—5A(14 sec)
F	1	9G(1)
Sa	1	1
Su		10A—Twilight meet

DATE May

	a.m.	p.m.
M		2A(2)
Tu	2B(1)	8x 5D(2)—2B(2)—5F(1)—5D(7)—5A(13 sec)
W	2B(2)	2B(2)
Th	2B(1)	2x 5B(3)—9G(1)(2 mi.)—5A(2)
F	1	1
Sa		10A—dual meet
Su		2B(5)easy
M		2(light)
Tu	2B(1)	4x 9E(4)(50-48-46)—2B(2)—3x 9E(4)(48-46-44)
W	2B(1)	2B(2)
Th	1	4x 9E(4)(52-50-48-46)—1—5A(2)
F	1	1
Sa		10A—5 km.
Su		2B(5)easy
M	2B(1)	2A(2)
Tu	2B(1)	5H(3)—5G(3)—5E(3)—1—6x 9E(4)(50-48-46)
W	2B(1)	2B(2)
Th	2B(1)	6x 5C(7)—2B(1)—5A(2)
F	1	1
Sa		10A—Northern Division Meet
Su		2B(5)easy
M	2B(1)	2A(2)(easy)
Tu	2B(1)	6x 5D(2)—2B(1)—3x 9E(4)(48-46-43)
W	2B(2)	2B(2)
Th	2B(1)	4x 5C(8)—light grass—3x 9E(3)(31-29-27)
F		Light grass
Sa		10A—PAC 8 Meet
Su		2B(5)easy

DATE June

	a.m.	p.m.
M	2B(1)	2A(2)
Tu	2B(2)	6x 5E(5)—2A(1)—6x 9E(4)
W	2B(2)	2B(2)
Th	2B(2)	4x 5H(4)—12x 5D(1-2)—1
F	2B(2)	Light run
Sa		3x 9E(4)(48-45-43)—5L(1)—3x 9E(4)(48-45-43)
Su		2B(5)
M	2B(1)	Light grass—5A(5)
Tu	2B(1)	1-2x 5C(3)—9G(1)—5A(2)
W		Light grass
Th		10A—5 km. trials or light grass(NCAA)
F		Light grass or 10A—finals—10 km.(NCAA)
Sa		10A—finals—5 km. (NCAA)
Su		
M		
Tu		
W		
Th		
F		
Sa		
Su		
M		
Tu		
W		
Th		
F		
Sa		
Su		

CHAPTER 12	# The High Jump

In 1968 an Oregon State high jumper with an eccentric jumping technique stunned the athletic world by winning the Olympic Games and setting an Olympic record. For almost 30 years, the best jumpers had used the straddle style, facedown to the crossbar and bodies almost parallel to it during their clearance. Dick Fosbury cleared the bar while lying on his back at a right angle to the bar. Today most top jumpers use the Fosbury Flop. Another pioneer of the style, also in 1968, was Canadian jumper Debbie Brill with the "Brill Bend."

Because the flop, or back layout, style dominates high jumping, our theoretical look examines only the flop. The two styles of flop are the *speed flop* and the *power flop*.[1] Thinner jumpers tend to use the speed flop, with its faster approach run, while heavier, slower jumpers rely more on strength development and the power flop (Table 12.1). The speed floppers are concerned with their direction of travel and body lean, with "keeping vertical." Power floppers are more concerned with trying to move faster and apply more force in the jumping action.

Training Theory for the High Jump

Three basic principles should be the focus of training:

- The ratio of strength to body weight is the foremost training factor. This means concerted work

on the takeoff, converting the energy from horizontal to vertical.
- Besides technique, the jumper must develop the speed and power components of training.
- Technical mechanics stay the same at each height. At some height the jumper's technique breaks down. The jumper must train to locate the breakdowns and correct them.

The technical points that jumpers must perfect are the following:

- Make a fast approach; speed is critical.
- The second half of the run-up must be smooth but done without slowing down (done partly with the arms).
- The shoulders and the neck muscles must stay relaxed.
- Plant the foot at a shallow angle (20 to 30 degrees), with the hips at about 45 degrees, and the shoulders at about 90 degrees to the bar.
- Have a strong plant leg, kept straight on the plant.
- Use aggressive knee-drive action.
- The heel is tucked, arching the back over the bar.
- When the head is back, watch the bar for feedback.

Soviet studies suggest that the most effective power training is at 70 to 90% of the athlete's best mark, while speed increases result from weights of 30 to 50% of an athlete's maximum.[2] They used a 4-week weight-training cycle, followed by 3 weeks of the

Table 12.1 Speed Flop Versus Power Flop

Speed flop	Power flop
Run-up at 7.7 to 8.4m/sec	Run-up at 7.0 to 8.0m/sec
8 to 9-stride run-up	10 to 12-stride run-up
Takeoff in 0.13 to 0.18 sec	Takeoff in 0.17 to 0.21 sec
On toes until last step	First half of run-up on toes, then flat-footed footed on heels
High knee lift in run-up	Low trail-leg recovery, especially on last two strides
Fast single-arm action in last stride and takeoff	Wide, very active double-arm action on takeoff
Little speed loss in last stride, center of gravity relatively high and forward	More speed loss on last step, center of gravity lower and back or above plant foot
Farther from bar on takeoff	Closer to bar on takeoff
Less arm and leg action while in the air	More active in air with arms and trail leg
Trail leg rises close to body soon after takeoff	Slow trail leg, conscious effort to lift heel and arch back
Less "head-throwing," look at bar for feedback	Head thrown back, must learn to look at bar
Jumpers talk in terms of upper body, components of direction	Jumpers talk in terms of lower body, components of propulsion
Usually low body weight, ectomorphic, less power weight training	Usually heavier, more mesomorphic, much power weight training
Do much speed work (enjoy it)	Do less speed work (do not enjoy it)

From Patrick Reid. (1986). The high jump. *New Studies in Athletics*, **1**(1), 47-53. Reprinted with permission.

other training. Plyometric training is increasingly used as a part of the training program, though no general agreement exists on the amount or nature of the most effective training.

A double-periodized year for high jumping, with an indoor and an outdoor macrocycle, is the most common training year for older high jumpers.[3] Bob Myers (University of Arizona) suggests a training year with the following six phases, which is consistent with current training trends:[4]

- General conditioning (June/July through November)
- Specific conditioning (Precompetition I) (December through January)
- Competition I (February through March)
- Specific conditioning (Precompetition II) (April)
- Competition II (May through last major meet)
- Active rest (Transition/regeneration)

Athletes break down during heavy load cycles (such as during the general and specific training phases) if all areas of their training have high loads. The peaks should be alternated among strength training, plyometrics, and running. The microcycle (week) should also show the wave pattern of varying loading.

The Athletics Congress's Track and Field Coaching Manual (2nd ed.) suggests this five-phase, single-periodized program training year:[5]

- Maximal loading base (July through September)
- Power development (October through January)

- Power transfer (February through April)
- Transition/precompetition (2 weeks)
- Power retention (Competition peak season)

For young male high jumpers, the rapid growth of muscular strength between ages 17 and 19 can hamper proper technique development if conditioning work is not mixed with the technical training.[6] From 19 to 23 is the "high-performance development phase" for potential elite jumpers, so jumpers should focus on improving their technique and specific fitness, while gaining competitive experience at a high level.

The fastest development for male high jumpers occurs between ages 14 and 15 and between ages 17 and 19, with the "real potential talent" reaching 7'1-1/2" to 7'4" during the latter ages. However, young athletes should not use maximal loads in resistance exercises before age 18 or 19 because growing athletes are more vulnerable to stress injuries.

Applying the Theory

The high jumper is usually average or above average in height and possesses good spring. He or she may be a tenacious worker but not necessarily well coordinated. The general test for high jumpers is the jump and reach, the Sargent jump, but it is not an infallible guide. On that test, Dick Fosbury, who high-jumped over 7'4", was outjumped by some weight men on his college team. Also, there have been world-class male high jumpers no taller than 5'8" tall.

High Jump Tactics

Jumpers must consider their tactics for major and minor competitions. Among the factors that affect the choice of tactics are the following:[7]

- In some tie situations, the smallest total number of jumps decides the winner. Emphasize clearing a height on the first attempt.
- Maximal concentration, speed, and coordination are possible only for 6 to 10 jumps. Plan the best number of jumps and use it to determine your starting height.
- A jumper may wait 45 minutes or more between attempts in high-level meets. This should be practiced on a regular basis.
- Warm-up areas for major meets may be outside the stadium. Practice this situation, with a delay between warm-up and competition.
- Trials and finals are on successive days in major meets. Simulate the meet with 2 hard days or with morning and evening sessions in a single day.
- Passing heights is useful, but risky. Do not do it in a major meet until practiced in training and at smaller meets.
- Opening heights at major meets may be near the athlete's best. Practice at higher heights in some sessions and take more warm-up jumps before the major meet.

- Prepare for all weather conditions, including rain, wind, and sun.
- Only 90 seconds is allowed for a jump. Use a clock in some practice sessions so the time does not seem restrictive.

Major High Jump Styles

There are two major techniques or styles of jumping commonly in use: the straddle and the flop. The straddle, or belly roll, has several variations. It is a very efficient technique, though there may be mechanical advantages for the Fosbury Flop (the center of gravity may not have to rise as far to clear the bar). The *belly roll* may be the best name because it perfectly describes the clearance of the bar. The jumper uses a straight-line approach from the side, taking off from the inside foot and kicking with the outside foot. The athlete clears the bar while facedown atop it, rolling around and over it.

There are variations of this style, such as the true belly roll, with the jumper in a beautiful layout that perfectly parallels the bar. In the dive straddle, the head clears the bar ahead of the leg, which is more efficient than the nose-to-the-bar style. Although the straddle is less popular now, it is still very effective. The gold medalist in the 1988 Olympic decathlon (Christian Schenk) jumped 7'5-1/4" with it.

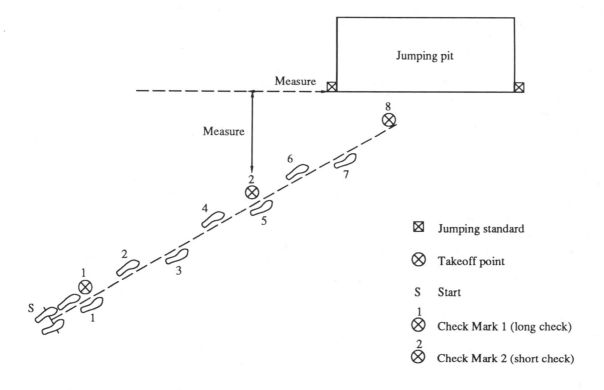

Figure 12.1 Straddle-style approach.

The Straddle Style

The approach for the straddle begins from a check mark about eight strides from the takeoff point (Figure 12.1). Most often the jumper runs toward the bar in a line that forms an angle between 30 and 45 degrees in relation to the crossbar. The speed of the approach varies with the jumper. Some jumpers make a slow approach, relying heavily upon spring for their height, while others make a fast approach, relying on leg strength to enable them to convert their forward momentum to upward momentum. Generally, the last three strides are longer and faster as the athlete lowers the center of gravity and "gathers" for the takeoff. The jumper plants the heel of the takeoff foot solidly, coordinating the "brake" on the forward momentum with a swift upward kick of the lead leg and upward thrust of the arms, designed to divert the momentum upward. On the takeoff, the plant foot is put down out ahead of the jumper's center of gravity. The jump is then coordinated as shown earlier.

The straddle jumper kicks upward, but the lead leg continues over the bar, after which the trail leg clears the bar, so the athlete clears the bar on the stomach. If the height of the jump is great enough, the jumper continues to rotate while falling, landing on the back.

The Fosbury Flop

Four advantages of the Fosbury Flop, or back layout, make it worth the coach's consideration:

- It is very easy to learn.
- It is a simpler technique, thus having fewer problems.
- It permits greater use of the athlete's natural speed.
- It is more fun to many jumpers than other techniques.

Those advantages do not mean that the form has no risks. Do not overlook one risk: Only a good landing pit should ever be used. The risks of back or neck injury are considerable if any landing area other than a large, deep foam rubber pit is used.

The flop style of jumping is much simpler in practice than it appears. Most athletes take an 8- to 12-step approach, the first step being with the right foot if the jumper plants with the left foot on the takeoff. Some jumpers rock into the first step, though it is mostly a technique of mental focus and preparation, or a personal trait that results from nervousness.

The approach run should be fast but relaxed. Too much speed changes the body lean and hampers the smooth transfer from the run-up to the takeoff.[8] Three approaches are recognized, the curved approach, the

Table 12.2   Approach Styles for the Flop

Curved approach
Limited speed
Difficult to develop consistent stride pattern and length of run-up
Easier to maintain on a constant curve through takeoff

J-Approach
Develops more speed
Provides more consistency
Blends speed and centrifugal force

Hook approach
Provides maximum speed without pause when moving into curve
Allows acceleration up to takeoff
Forces emphasis on continual curve running

From Ed Jacoby. (1986). High jump: A technique evaluation. *Track Technique*, **97**, 3089. Reprinted with permission.

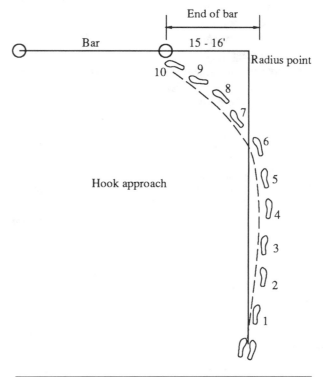

Figure 12.2 Hook approach. From Ed Jacoby. (1986). High jump: A technique evaluation. *Track Technique*, **97**, 3090. Adapted with permission.

J-approach, and the hook approach (Table 12.2).[9]

The curve approach is a continuous curve, commonly used by beginning jumpers. The hook approach curves slightly outward before curving toward the bar. It lies between the other two styles, though it is closest to the J-approach. It helps the jumper avoid losing

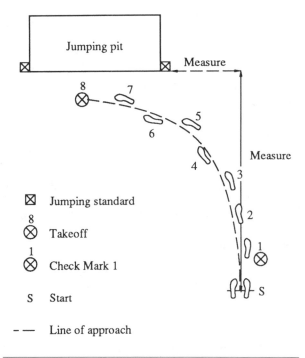

Figure 12.3 Fosbury-style approach.

speed when moving from a straight approach into the curve (Figure 12.2).

The athlete who takes off on the left foot approaches the bar from the right side of the pit (Figure 12.3). The jumper should measure the starting point when the approach run becomes consistent. Measure the distance to the right of the right standard to a point even with the start of the run, then measure out from that point to the actual starting position. Though the measurements are in straight lines, the run is a curving approach, similar to an inverted letter J.

The starting point should be measured carefully, at a right angle to the nearer of the high jump standards (Figure 12.4). Measure in a straight line extended for either 10 meters or 32 feet (depending upon your type of tape measure) from the end of your crossbar. Mark

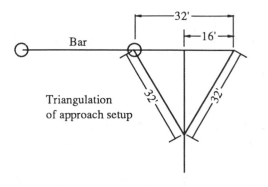

Figure 12.4 Measuring the flop approach. From Ed Jacoby. (1986). High jump: A technique evaluation. *Track Technique*, **97**, 3090.

each end of the line and its midpoint (5 meters or 16 feet). Then make an arc equal to the long line from each end of the baseline. Mark where the arcs cross, then draw your right angle line from the midpoint of the baseline.

The jumper begins by running straight in at a right angle to the front of the pit rather than toward the takeoff point. Around the fourth or fifth step, the run curves to the left until it points at a very shallow angle to the bar. The jumper gradually accelerates during the run, then lowers the center of gravity by stretching the stride around the sixth or seventh step. The takeoff stride, which is shorter, finds the body already starting to move upward in the air.

During the takeoff, the kick is coordinated with an upward swing of both arms. The kick is with the upper part of the leg only, a bent-leg kick that gives the sensation of kicking with the knee rather than the entire leg. That kick, combined with the curving run, causes the athlete's back to rotate toward the bar as he or she rises off the ground. By arching the back, that part of the body clears the bar. The athlete clearing the bar may appear to be lying flat on the back from the head to the knees, with the lower legs still hanging down. The knees and feet are then lifted to clear the bar. An upward swing of both arms can help that movement. The landing in the pit is high on the back or in the upper neck region, and the jumper may do a backward roll when landing. Otherwise, the landing may be flat on the back.

Training Considerations

The first thing for the coach to remember in training high jumpers is that the best style for one athlete is not necessarily best for another jumper. Also, the amount of work that a jumper can tolerate varies greatly from one jumper to the next.

The first thing to do with a group of jumping prospects is to determine their dominant or kicking legs. Have them run over a low hurdle several times, then hand-vault over a sawhorse. This should bring out the kicking leg clearly because each athlete will prefer one leg to the other. Athletes might then be taught the Western roll style of jumping because it is helpful to learn and has great carryover value to the takeoff for the straddle jump. At one time this progression of learning to jump was considered the proper learning sequence. Though it is not emphasized too much today, it is still very helpful.

After the lead foot has been determined, an athlete should work on the check marks. It helps to have two check marks in the approach as a safety factor. The first mark is four steps from the takeoff point, and the second check mark is another four steps out, giving an eight-step approach (Figure 12.1). The last four steps from the check to the takeoff are measured, as is the distance from the check to a line extended from the crossbar and the distance from this juncture to the nearest jumping standard. It is very important to know the jumper's check marks. It is helpful to have a short check mark, in case the jumper has to compete in bad wind conditions. It is easier to vary a short run to hit the takeoff properly than to vary a full run. For floppers, the worst weather condition is rain, making the curved run and takeoff very hazardous.

The jumper warms up, then works on a routine. The jumper first works on the check marks, then on the takeoff, concentrating on the two-count rise. The last two steps of the approach are longer and faster than the preceding steps, lowering the center of gravity. The jumper drops down slightly, then rises over the last two steps to go into the air with increased momentum. The jumper should try to get both arms and the lead leg rising to aid the momentum and raise the center of gravity.

Form work comes next, with the athlete working from 6 to 8 inches below his or her best mark at that time of year. With a best of 6′6″ for the season, the jumper thus does form work at 5′10″ to 6′0″. The jumper might take the last three jumps at increasing heights, but the coach should not permit as many as three misses at a single height: the jumper should be able to finish while feeling that he or she might have cleared the bar. The jumper also needs to get used to seeing the crossbar at higher heights.

Weight lifting is useful in improving the jumper's spring. Some jumpers do much leg work, emphasizing leg presses. The athlete should be sure to exercise the muscles within the usual limits of his or her movement in performing the event. As an example, full squats are risky, and their range of motion is never imitated during high jumping.

Plyometric jumping and bounding exercises have become widespread as a training technique over the last decade. Although a coach should be cautious when first using them, they are extremely valuable exercises.

Training Program for Floppers

The training program for a flop-style jumper can be a problem to plan, not because of the work involved but because the jumper who has mastered the form may prefer to do little jumping. Flop jumpers thrive on little or no jumping during the season. A flopper whose form is good during the meets rarely has any reason to jump during the week. If a form problem does appear in a meet, the jumper might work on that aspect of form by jumping on the Monday or Tuesday before a Friday or Saturday meet.

A jumper whose performances begin to get worse may actually be jumping and practicing too much. A flopper is more likely to flourish under the old-fashioned light-training methods than under the modern hard-training methods. The time for perfecting the form with many jumps is during the fall and the winter, when there is plenty of time and no pressure.

Dick Fosbury's training is a good example of the way an athlete might train for this type of jumping after learning the style well. This schedule is for a typical week during the competitive season, with a meet each Saturday:

(1) Monday: sprints; runs up 80 rows of stadium seats, or hopping halfway up stadium seats

(2) Tuesday: weight training

(3) Wednesday: same as Monday

(4) Thursday: weight training

(5) Friday: usually light (might repeat Monday's workout)

His weight-training program, which he had followed for only 2 years before the Olympic Games, was as follows (on a Universal Gym):

Leg presses: 1 set × 10 at 390 pounds
                     1 × 8 at 450 pounds
                     1 × 6 at 510 pounds
                     1 × 4 at 540 pounds
                     1 × 2 to 3 at 600 pounds
Toe presses: 2 sets × 25 at 150 pounds

During the competitive season, he did no shoulder work, did only some of the leg work, and added partial jumping squats with the feet close together and alternating feet on the landing, usually doing two sets of 15 with 135 pounds.

Other strength-training exercises are suggested by the coaches who produced the high jump chapter in *The Athletics Congress's Track and Field Coaching Manual* (2nd ed.).[5]

The Training Schedules: Special Fundamentals for the High Jump

The common elements of all training schedule sheets are given in chapter 5. Now we need to look briefly at the numbered fundamentals that are specific to the high jump schedules.

4A. Short check mark.   This is used for learning a method of arriving at a takeoff point that achieves maximum height directly over the crossbar. Usually four steps are taken from the one check mark to the takeoff. Standing one or two steps from the check, the jumper thinks through the fundamental, if working on one fundamental, then shuts out the thinking process. The jumper advances the one or two steps to the check, then takes four steps to the takeoff and executes the jump. This distance varies from 18 to 25 feet, depending upon the athlete's needs and stride length. The jumper should take three practice approaches while being observed then average the length of the three runs to determine the short check mark. This mark should be measured daily because better physical conditions and weather differences (heat, cold, etc.) cause variations in the approach.

4B. Long check mark.   The long check mark uses two checks. The jumper begins one or two steps from the first check, then takes four strides to the second check (the short check), then takes another four strides to the takeoff point.

5A. Rhythm jumping (2-4-6-8).   The athlete pays attention only to developing a rhythm. For learning purposes the athlete stands at a long check mark and comes in to the jump either counting or having the coach count the even-numbered strides, "2-4-6-8," with "8" being the takeoff. It is for rhythm, for speed, and to get rid of a jerky or uneven approach. The other fundamentals work more smoothly if a good rhythmical approach is achieved.

5B. Settle and 2-count rise.   This technique is used either consciously or because of the superior coordination of every great high jumper. To acquire this technique, the athlete starts learning with a short check mark. Usually jumpers find that on the second step before the takeoff, they settle and then start to rise on the step before takeoff so that the body weight as well as the momentum is going up at the instant of the takeoff. Some great jumpers have made the settle on the last step before the takeoff, then started to rise on the same step, taking off on the next step.

5C. Lead leg and lead arm.   The lead leg and the lead arm, which are approaching the bar for clearance, should be hurried upward well before the takeoff foot leaves the ground. The lifting of the leg and the arm raises the center of gravity, bringing the total mass of the body nearer the crossbar. The fact that the body mass is going up makes the relative weight of the body mass less. This leg-arm movement must be executed before the takeoff or the physical principle of the "equal and opposite reaction" will tend to destroy the effect of the lift because the movement will not have the strong base of the takeoff and will be negated by the action of the extremities being in motion at this time.

5D.   A vacant space for use when some unlisted specific is needed in an individual's schedule.

6A. Head.   The head is 10 pounds of dead weight that can either help or hinder the jumper. If the chin is raised, the head helps the jumper direct him- or herself upward off the ground. If the chin is dropped, it can hamper the takeoff. If the chin is tipped toward the crossbar, it will lead the body into a premature lean into the bar, a common fault leading to poor jumping.

6B. Layout and bar clearance.   The center of gravity is what rises, and the body and its extremities rotate around it. The first motion is up; then, by the last actions at the point of takeoff, the body coordination is affected by the arms and legs, turning the body and helping it to "lay out" atop the crossbar. The rotation around the bar is accomplished by lowering the head, which is beyond the bar, and lifting the takeoff leg.

6C. Up and down, not up and out.   Jumpers who use more speed than they can control tend to cover space in the wrong direction. The rule is to use as much speed as can be controlled. The jumper who takes off too close with speed uncontrolled goes into the crossbar. The speed jumper should be farther out than the "stroller." The fast jumper who is going into the bar should experiment with a more acute angle, going down more toward the crossbar as do the floppers, using another speed jump.

9A. Takeoff.   An exact takeoff spot is a necessity, and check marks must be made that assist the jumper in hitting that spot on every approach run. When the spot is reached, the most important part of the technique is maintaining body position and lift. An outward lean not only makes for a premature turn and striking the crossbar, but it can make the jumper effectively 2 to 4 inches shorter by lowering the center of gravity by that distance.

9B. Arm lift.   The left arm almost automatically rises with the right leg. The coordination of the double-arm lift (both arms together) is an acquired one. As the right foot is planted on the last step before the final plant and takeoff, both arms drop back only as far as the plane of the body, then both lift vigorously as the lead (right) leg is driven up toward the crossbar. The arms are near bar height as the takeoff foot leaves the ground. As the body rises, the right arm reaches across the bar, and the most natural thing is for the left elbow to smoothly come to the side and proceed to the rear until the hand is near the hip area. It is also believed helpful for takeoff-leg clearance if the right arm rises, lifting to the outside and triggering a compensating action by the takeoff leg.

9C. Center of gravity over takeoff foot.   As the jumper makes the final step of the takeoff, the center of gravity should pass directly over the takeoff foot. If there is to be a fault out of line, it should be in the direction of the bar, not away from the bar. Crossing the right foot across the line of approach (and away from the bar) would lower the center of gravity and cause the jumper to lean into the crossbar.

10B. Trial.   A warm-up procedure should be acquired for trials and experimented with to determine what is best for competition. The trials themselves are learning situations. A competitive trial exists only to eliminate someone if there are more entries available than can be used in the competition. If there is one outstanding jumper, he or she should be an automatic entry but should also compete in the trials for the learning experience. The other jumpers are also learning, but they will also be competing for the other two spots in the dual meet entries.

Let the athletes set the crossbar at a good starting height for each individual, within reason. In Item 10B(1), the athlete raises the bar 2 to 3 inches after clearing the height, and lowers the bar 4 inches after missing. For example, one jumper may start at 5′6″, while another jumper may start at 6′4″. If the weaker jumper misses, he or she will jump next at 5′2″. The better jumper might have the next jump at 6′6″ to 6′7″, depending upon how good he or she is and how early in the season it is.

10B(2). Two jumps 2 inches above average best.   The jumper who has reached the approximate best and has had two misses at a height may have two more jumps at 2 to 3 inches above his or her best seasonal mark. The jumper should not be allowed three misses, for psychological reasons and because it would put him or her out of the competition. In practice, the jumper should never take more than two misses at a submaximal height.

11. Alternate from straddle to Fosbury.   This is an experimental exercise for variety of activity, teaching body control, and perhaps discovering an additional jumping weapon. The jumper works with several different jumping styles, going from the straddle, or belly roll, to the Fosbury Flop style of jumping, learning better body control and perhaps discovering whether he or she can do better with a different form.

16. Easy acrobatics or apparatus.   If possible, have some apparatus in the practice area. Also, take advantage of the usually superior equipment and instruction of a good gymnastics teacher. It is great exercise for body control, as well as pleasurable and a good change of pace.

17. High kicking.   High kicking is used for work on the takeoff and for timing in the leg lift in relation to the takeoff for straddle jumpers. It consists of short approaches followed by high kicks with the lead leg toward a high target of some sort. Floppers might practice kicking with the lifting knee.

18. Form jumping.   Form jumping should be done at a minimal height. It is possible to concentrate on the techniques and mechanics without being concerned about the height of the jump. The jumper should acquire the tools, then do the job in the meet.

19. Speed jumping.   The crossbar is set at an easy height, perhaps a foot under the jumper's best. In rotation the jumpers take their jumps as fast as they can get into the pit and back out again. A miss puts the jumper out. The winner is the last person out. A solo jumper takes four to eight or so speed jumps.

20. Work on second event.   Every athlete should have a second event, if only for a change of scenery. The jumper should also consider him- or herself a part of the team, and may get the extra point that will win a letter or the team's meet. The greatest high jumper in Oregon history, Les Steers, also threw the javelin, hurdled, and pole vaulted. He also held the world record for the high jump for well over a decade.

Interpretation of Week 1 of the Training Schedules

Monday: Class organization is intended for a physical education unit. Squad organization is listed in the event that fall track is conducted. The objectives and goals of the program are covered. Equipment and responsibility for attendance and separate workouts are discussed.

Tuesday: (16) Easy acrobatics might be done in the gymnastics room, where more equipment is available. Such rudimentary activities as the forward roll and cartwheels can be done at the track. (4A) The short check mark is a fundamental drill covered in the previous section. (14D) In the general schedule, run 50m, then jog 50m, and repeat the exercise for a distance of 400 to 800m or more.

Wednesday: (7) Squad meeting, time and place to be written on the board in the squad dressing room. (3) Weight activities of the athlete's choice or according to the suggestions given in the section on weight training. This is followed by jogging and comfortable running.

(8A or B) A sauna or swim, depending upon jumper's preference and pool's availability.

Thursday: (1A) In pairs or threes, take a warm-up jog of 400 to 800m. Each runner handles the baton, passing it forward. When the front runner receives the baton, he or she drops to the rear, and the exercise is continued.

(4A) Short check work, already mentioned.

(19) The superscript 6 means the exercise is done six times. Set the bar at an easily cleared height, such as 5 feet. One or more jumpers go through and jump as fast as they can make their clearance and get back to repeat the jump from one to six times. The jumper who misses is through jumping. This exercise is for conditioning and fun.

(14D) Repeated 50s, already mentioned.

Friday: (3) Weight activities, already mentioned.

(1B) A run through the park (2 to 3 miles), comfortable pace but with some stress for conditioning.

Saturday: (3) A full workout according to the section on weights or the athlete's already established weight-workout activities.

Sunday: Recreational activities should be included on this day. Sunday can also be a very productive practice day and is very useful in bringing to life the athlete who overdoes Saturday night and would otherwise not revive until Tuesday or Wednesday.

References

1. Patrick Reid. (1986). The high jump. *New Studies in Athletics*, **1**(1), 47-53.
2. V. Nedobivailo. (1984). Weight training for high jumpers. *Track Technique*, **87**, 2785.
3. Dragan Tancic. (1986). Organization of high jump training. *Track Technique*, **94**, 3013.
4. Bob Myers. (1988). Periodization for the high jump. In Jess Jarver (Ed.), *The Jumps* (2nd ed.). Los Altos, CA: Tafnews.
5. Berny Wagner, Sue Humphrey, & Don Chu. (1989). The high jump (Fosbury Flop). In Vern Gambetta (Ed.), *The Athletics Congress's Track and Field Coaching Manual* (2nd ed., pp. 105-116). Champaign, IL: Leisure Press.
6. W. Lonskiy & K. Gomberadse. (1981). Long range training plan for high jumpers. In Jess Jarver (Ed.), *The Jumps* (2nd ed., pp. 47-49). Los Altos, CA: Tafnews.
7. Andrei Soran. (1988). High jump tactics. *Track Technique*, **102**, 3267.
8. V. Ambarov. (1988). Looking at the high jump. *Track Technique*, **104**, 3329-3330.
9. Ed Jacoby. (1986). High jump: A technique evaluation. *Track Technique*, **97**, 3089-3093.

Additional Readings

Badon, Tommy. (1988). Constructing and utilizing the "ultimate" jump ramp. *Track Technique*, **106**, 3378-3380.

Boosey, Derek. (1980). *The jumps: Conditioning and technical training*. West Heidelberg, Victoria, Australia: Beatrice.

Chu, Donald A. (1984). The approach pattern in the Fosbury Flop. *Track and Field Quarterly Review*, **84**(4), 15-16.

Dapena, Jesus. (1988). Biomechanical analysis of the Fosbury Flop. Parts 1 and 2. *Track Technique*, **104**, 3307-3317, 3333; **105**, 3343-3350.

Dyatchkov, V.M. (1984). The preparation training phase of top level high jumpers. *Track and Field Quarterly Review*, **84**(4), 26-28.

Freeman, William H. (1971, January). Coaching the Fosbury Flop. *Athletic Journal*, **51**, 16, 71-72.

Hackett, Brad. (1989). Analysis of the high jump crossbar in failed attempts. *Track Technique*, **107**, 3409-3411.

Humphrey, Sue. (1984). Some new thoughts on high jumping. *Track Technique*, **88**, 2808-2810.

Jarver, Jess (Ed.) (1988). *The jumps: Contemporary theory, technique and training* (3rd ed.). Los Altos, CA: Tafnews.

Lohmann, Wolfgang. (1985). Principles of beginners' training in jumping events. *Track Technique*, **91**, 2891-2892, 2899.

Martin, David E., Stones, Dwight, Joy, Greg, & Wszola, Jacek. (1987). *The high jump book* (2nd ed.). Los Altos, CA: Tafnews.

Myers, Bob. (1989). Training for the jumps and multi-events. *Track Technique*, **108**, 3449-3452; **109**, 3492-3493.

Reid, Patrick. (1987). Approach and take-off for the back lay-out high jump. *Track and Field Quarterly Review*, **87**(4), 36-38.

Ritzdorf, Wolfgang. (1986). The practice of strength training in women's high jump. *New Studies in Athletics*, **1**(2), 81-89.

Strischak, A., et al. (1987). Specific exercises for women high jumpers. *Track Technique*, **100**, 3201-3202.

Tancic, Dragan. (1985). Organization and control of high jump training. *Track and Field Quarterly Review*, **85**(4), 17-22.

Tansley, John. (1980). *The flop book*. Santa Monica, CA: Petersen.

High Jump Training Schedule

ATHLETE _____

1. Warm-up
   A. Jog 1-2 laps with relay pass, in 2s or 3s
   B. Hendricks Park
   C. Golf course
   D. Steps
2. Fartlek
   A. Varied pace
   B. Slow, steady pace
3. Strength & flexibility
   A. Weights and jogging
   B. Jogging and stretching
4. Check mark
   A. Short   B. Long
5. A. Rhythm (2-4-6-8)
   B. Settle & 2-count rise
   C. Lead leg & lead arm
   D.
6. A. Head
   B. Layout & bar clearance
   C. Up and down, not up and out
   D.
7. Team meeting

8. Special
   A. Sauna   C. Hill
   B. Swim
9. A. Takeoff
   B. Arm lift
   C. Center of gravity over takeoff foot
   D.
10. Progress assessment
    A. Meet   C. Simulation
    B. Trial   D. Control test
       (1) up 2-3" on make, down 4" on a miss
       (2) 2 jumps at 2" above average best
11. Alternate from straddle to Fosbury
12. With Coach
    A. (name)
    B. Leader
14. A. Wind sprints (1) straight (2) curve
    B. Hurdle drill: 3 LH, 7-9m apart
    C. Spring and bound
    D. Alternate 50m run & jog, at least 800m
    E. Starts (1) 100 (2)
    F. High knee (slow) & fast leg

15. Plyometrics
    A. Jumps (1) 1 leg (2) both legs (3)
    B. Bounding (1) 1 leg (2) both legs (3)
    C.
16. Easy acrobatics or apparatus
17. High kicking (straddle)
    A. Basket   B. Target
18. Form jumping, 6-12" under best
    A. Short run   B. Long run
19. Speed jumping: 4-8 fast, or a miss
20. Work on second event
21. Visual aids
    A. Videotape   C. Photos
    B. Film
       (1) record performance (2) study
30. Experimental work

DATE September/October

M	Class or squad organization
Tu	16—4A—14D
W	7—3—8A or 8B
Th	1A—4A—19—14D (6x)
F	3—1B
Sa	3
Su	Recreation
M	1A—14D—4A—5C—18A (2-4x)
Tu	3—16—14C
W	1A—14D—5A—5B—14B
Th	3—16—17B
F	1—10B—18A—14D
Sa	2B
Su	Recreation
M	1A—14D—4A—5A—18A
Tu	3—16—17—14C
W	1—14D—4B—9A—5B—14B
Th	1—16—17
F	1—10B(1)—18A
Sa	3—14D
Su	Recreation
M	1—14D—4A—4B—9A—18A (2-4x 2-4x)
Tu	3—14C—14B
W	1—4B—9A—5B—14B
Th	3—16—17
F	1—18A—18B—14D (6-10x 6-10x)
Sa	3—14D
Su	Recreation

DATE January

M	New term or start new year
Tu	Class or squad organization
W	Register—11—3—or classes
Th	7—Register—lockers—11—3
F	1—14A—3—1B
Sa	3—11
Su	Recreation
M	1—4A—5B—9A—14D
Tu	1A—3
W	1—5A—5C—6C
Th	1A—3—1B
F	1—14D—5B—5C—9A—14D
Sa	1A—3—14A
Su	Recreation
M	1—3—14B
Tu	1A—5B—4A—4B—5A (2-4x 2-4x)
W	1—3—14D—1B
Th	1—4B—6B—9A
F	1—3—14C—15B
Sa	1—10—6A—14C
Su	Recreation
M	1—3—14D
Tu	1A—4A—4B—5B—5C—6B
W	1—3—14A
Th	1A—5A—5B—5C—14E
F	1—3—14A
Sa	3—14A
Su	Recreation—3

DATE February

M	1—4A—4B—5A—5B—14B—14C
Tu	3—14A
W	1—4A—4B—1B or 1D
Th	14C—3
F	1—4A—5B—9 (2-3x)
Sa	Swim or weights
Su	Recreation
M	1A—14B—5C—14F
Tu	3—8A or B
W	1—5A—5B—5C (3x 3x)
Th	Light
F	1—10
Sa	Sprint and hurdle trials 10:30 a.m.
Su	
M	1A—4B—5C—5B—18—jog
Tu	3
W	1A—18—8C or 1B (6x)
Th	3
F	1A—4A—4B—5B—5C—14C—14D
Sa	Jog and 3
Su	Recreation
M	1A—4A—4B—5A—5B—14C—14D (2x 2x 3x 3-6x)
Tu	3—8A or 8B
W	1B—16
Th	3—16
F	1A—10B(1)—10B(2)
Sa	3 or 14C
Su	Recreation

DATE March

M	1A—8B
Tu	3—8A or B
W	2x 7—1A—4B—9B—9A—19—14B—14D
Th	Light
F	1A—10B(1)—18—1B
Sa	Light
Su	Light
M	4x 10x 1—14C—4B—9B—9C—14C—14B
Tu	3—8B
W	1—4—9A—18—14D
Th	Jog
F	4—10B(1)—17
Sa	3—16—14C
Su	Recreation
M	1A—4—6B—9B—9C—14C—14B
Tu	Easy grass running
W	7—4—18
Th	Light
F	Gear ready and/or travel
Sa	First meet (10A—20)
Su	Light workout
M	a.m. 1A—jog | p.m. Spring trip 1A—4—5B—6C—14D
Tu	1A—3 | Grass running
W	1A—jog | 1A—18
Th	1A—3 | Light
F	Travel home—loosen up
Sa	Division early season relay meet
Su	Loosen up

DATE April

M	1—5B—4B—18—19—14B
Tu	3—17—14C—14D
W	7—1A—5B—9A —18—14C
Th	3
F	Light and gear ready
Sa	Relay meet
Su	Field open 11 to 3
M	1—4B—4A—5B—9A—19—14B
Tu	3—17—14C—14D
W	7—1A—4B—10B(1) and 2-18 jog
Th	3
F	4-6x 1—4B—18—gear ready
Sa	Dual meet
Su	Church—field open 11 to 3
M	1—4A—4B—5B—18—19—14B
Tu	17—3—14C—14D
W	7—1—5B—9A—6B—18—14B
Th	3
F	Gear ready
Sa	Dual meet
Su	Light workout
M	7—1—4A—4B—5B—18—19—14B
Tu	17B—3—14C—14D
W	4-6x 2x 7—1—4—10B(1)—10B(2)—14D
Th	Light
F	Travel
Sa	Dual meet
Su	Home and loosen up

DATE May

M	7—jog
Tu	Light
W	Memorial Day Traditional Dual Meet
Th	1A—4B—10B(1)—14C
F	3—17—14D
Sa	Jog
Su	Field open 11 to 3—Squad picnic 5 p.m.
M	1—14C—14B—14D
Tu	1—4—5C—6B—18—14C
W	Light & jog
Th	Light & jog
F	1—4
Sa	Light
Su	1—5—18—jog
M	7—1—5—18—jog
Tu	Light
W	7—Light
Th	Championship starts
F	Championship high jump qualifying
Sa	Championship high jump finals
Su	
M	
Tu	
W	
Th	
F	
Sa	
Su	

CHAPTER 13	# The Long Jump

"One giant leap for mankind" was taken on the surface of the moon by Neil Armstrong during the summer of 1969. In the Mexico City Summer Olympics in 1968, Bob Beamon made a great leap for posterity when he smashed the world long jump record with a phenomenal leap of 29'2-1/2" (8.90m). How did it happen? A superb athlete, perfect conditions, and great competition combined to produce it. Although altitude is cited as a major factor, in fact only about 2 inches of the leap are a possible effect of altitude. Though the record has been threatened recently, it still stands after 2 decades, a supreme athletic achievement.

Training Theory for the Long Jump

The bottom line for long jumpers is their speed and power at the takeoff board.[1] In fact, as their velocity increases, the height and length of the jump increase even if the takeoff angle is lower.[2] To give an idea of the effect of the length of the approach run, most jumpers approach their maximum velocity (for controlled long jumping speed) at these rates:[3]

- 70 to 75% after 6 steps (10 to 11m)
- 85 to 90% after 10 steps (21 to 22m)
- 96 to 98% after 14 steps (30 to 31m)

- 100% after 17 steps (38 to 39m)
- Takeoff after 19 steps

The two or three strides before the last stride of the approach tend to be longer than average, while the stride into the takeoff is shorter. The two-count rise (raising the center of gravity during the last two steps) starts with a slightly longer step, combined with landing flat-footed. This lowers the center of gravity and results in a rising center of gravity during the last two steps. This gradual rise helps overcome the inertia of the body's horizontal motion, making the transition to vertical motion easier.

The critical element of the approach is proper sprinting technique, beginning with a gradual acceleration. The stride pattern should be very consistent. Though some coaches suggest a flat-footed takeoff, there is only limited evidence of its use by jumpers. The key to the jump is controlled speed. Speed is useful *only* if the jumper can fully control it.

An analysis of world-class women long jumpers shows that the American edge in pure talent, as seen in sprint performances, does not suffice for the long jump.[4] Instead, better planned, more thorough training in the Eastern Bloc has overcome much of the American raw advantage. Besides their more intensive training, Eastern Bloc athletes are tested regularly on a battery of control tests designed to assess their specific conditioning and progress in training, with the records kept for year-to-year comparisons of performance and reaction to training.

Applying the Theory

Training injury is a very real risk in the long jump, so long jumpers should not take too many jumps in any one session, nor should they jump too often. They are athletes blessed with both agility and speed. Speed alone does not make a really good jumper, though most male world-class long jumpers are capable of 10.5 seconds or faster for 100m.

There have been exceptionally speedy runners in the event, such as Jesse Owens and Carl Lewis. As well as being fleet of foot, they were also very agile. Long jumpers should be well coordinated, with explosive reactions. This is also an event that may attract the most strongly competitive athletes.

The basic jump involves a run of 120 feet or more, with relaxation during the last 20 to 30 feet, an attempt to go high into the air after the takeoff, then landing with as much outward reaching of the feet as possible. The jumper tries to go into the air from a gradual rise to the board over the last two steps. This technique is sometimes referred to as the "two-count rise." For example, consider a female jumper who hits the takeoff board with her left foot. On the third and fourth strides before hitting the board, she settles down, lowering her center of gravity to hit a low point when she puts down her left foot two strides before she hits the board. Some jumpers accomplish this settling action by slightly lengthening the stride for a step or two. She then rises, so that her center of gravity has already begun its ascent by the time she hits the board. This overcomes the inertia of horizontal motion. She hits the low point by landing flat on the left foot, then rises onto the right foot, then rises to the left foot, which hits the board, then she drives upward into the air.

Technique Considerations

An excellent training technique is the use of short-run pop-ups. These are done with a run of 50 feet or less, usually taking an eight-step approach. The jumpers work on the two-count rise, doing pop-ups from the area in front of the takeoff board, trying to fly off the runway and get good height in their jumps.

The two biggest problems long jumpers encounter in action are bad check marks and bad takeoffs. Consider the check marks first. How long should a jumper's approach run be? Probably 120 feet or so would be enough. Most world-class jumpers take 120 to 140 feet. Some jumpers who take as much as a 150-foot approach run (there is no legal limit) are probably wasting energy rather than gaining benefits. Jumpers using an overly long approach often do not improve after the second jump, probably because they become fatigued. Most people can reach their top sprinting speed in 40 yards, so a longer run is rarely of any benefit.

There are about as many ideas on the number and location of check marks as there are long jumpers plus coaches. Some jumpers use only one check, located at the start of the full approach, while others use two or three marks. We suggest three marks as the most useful number. The first is at the start of the long approach. The jumper leaves this mark running at half effort for 4 strides. The jumper then hits the second mark, at which point he or she accelerates to 3/4ths or 7/8ths speed, running for the next 6 steps, at which point he or she hits the final check. This mark is 10 steps from the takeoff board. This part of the approach is run at full speed, or as close to it as the jumper can keep under control and convert to upward momentum when the jump occurs.

There are many views of what is desirable in the use of check marks. A jumper can use a 2-4-6 set of checks (similar to Figure 13.2) or any other combination that is found most useful for his or her own particular jumping style. One highly recommended practice is to have two check marks two steps apart (hitting both marks with the same foot) somewhere in the middle of the approach run. If the first mark is missed, any stride adjustment can be checked quickly. If both marks are missed, the jumper can terminate the run at that point rather than risk wasting a jump. However, the jumper should be aware that major meets allow only 90 seconds for the jump.

Some jumpers may have trouble with their check marks in the switch from high school to college jumping. Because some high schools use a 24-inch-wide takeoff board, the switch to hitting the collegiate board, which is only 8 inches wide, is a major adjustment.

A jumper should keep in mind the benefits of the short run (8 to 12 strides) in the competitive situation. If there is a strong head wind, the jumper may find it especially tiring or difficult to jump well after a full approach battling the wind. In this case, the jumper should use the short approach instead. It saves energy on the approach run, energy that can be applied to additional speed to give a jumping edge over those who are sticking with the more exhausting long run. Also, if the jumper has opened with two fouls, leaving only one jump to make the finals, the surer short run is safer to use.

On the takeoff, the jumper should hit the board and pass over the plant foot, not reach out for the board.

Actually, the last stride (onto the board) is slightly shorter than the other approach strides, so essentially the jumper "runs off the board" because he or she is rising through the last two strides. However, some coaches advocate "stamping" the foot on the board.

Also, the jumper should take care not to bring the kicking foot across the body, misdirecting the line of flight to the side. At the takeoff board, the jumper should shift his or her line of sight from the board to the horizon. The chest should be kept up, and the jumper should concentrate on getting knee lift off the board. The movements in the air are done only to keep the body balanced in flight and to prepare for the landing. While in the air, the primary considerations are getting the feet extended forward (not letting them drop toward the pit) and holding the hands up and out.

Putting a mark in the pit is actually of little real benefit (and is also illegal), for after the jumper has left the ground, the laws of physics determine how far he or she will go. Nothing done in the air will cause the body to travel any farther, nor can anything be done to shorten the flight of the center of gravity.

The only effect the jumper has on the distance of the jump after takeoff is the extension of the legs and feet. If they are dropped too quickly, the jumper will land before the center of gravity would have landed, thus getting a poorer jump. If they are kept up and extended perfectly, they can land as much as 2 feet or more ahead of the center of gravity. This, then, is the importance of extending the feet, for it can make a difference of 3 or more feet between the distance achieved by two jumps that are equal in all other respects. This means that although the center of gravity may travel 20 feet, the jump could vary from 17 to 23 feet! Thus, the proper use of arms and legs is extremely important.

The Training Schedules: Special Fundamentals for the Long Jump

A training schedule sheet is used for communication and for the convenience of the long jump coach and athlete. The numbers and common interpretations were explained in chapter 5. The following are used particularly for long jump training:

4. Check marks. The long jump check mark is a critical fundamental. We recommend that the jumper first establish a short check mark to use when jumping against the wind, or when there have been two fouls in the preliminaries and a "must" jump is necessary to qualify for the finals. The short check is important in training for other fundamentals, also.

4A. Short check. The short check is a one-mark approach, the distance being 50 to 70 feet, depending upon the length of the athlete's strides. The approach is 10 strides in most cases, though one variation uses a short check of 8 strides. Figure 13.1 illustrates the stride pattern for a 10-stride short approach for a jumper who steps on the board with the left foot.

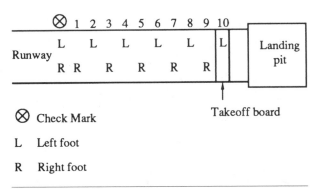

Figure 13.1 Short check approach.

Finding the starting point for a jumper's approach run is like locating a target with mortar fire. Have the jumper start from the takeoff board and run 10 strides up the runway two or three times; mark the location of the 10th stride each time. Then mark the average of the three marks as a starting check mark and have the jumper begin practicing with it. This approach is long enough for practicing most technique work, except for perfecting the full approach run.

4B. Long check mark. This mark has several variations. The most commonly used one is the 4-8-10 pattern. Using "S" for the start (Figure 13.2), Checks 1, 2, and 3, and "T" for takeoff, a procedure for establishing the marks is the following.

Start the athlete at S and the coach or observer on the runway or track about 20 feet away. Two walking steps lead to Check 1 with the left foot.

Running at half speed and gradually speeding up, on the fourth step the jumper is at Check 2. The observer marks the location of this step, and the procedure is repeated for a total of three efforts. The average distance, usually 20 to 25 feet, establishes the first two check marks.

The procedure is repeated for Check 3. The jumper begins at S and reconfirms Checks 1 and 2 while going through three runs, running at 3/4ths effort, gradually increasing the speed. The observer again marks each of the three efforts and takes the average, eight steps being taken from Check 2 to Check 3.

The T mark is established in the same manner, with the speed gradually increasing from 7/8ths to 9/10ths

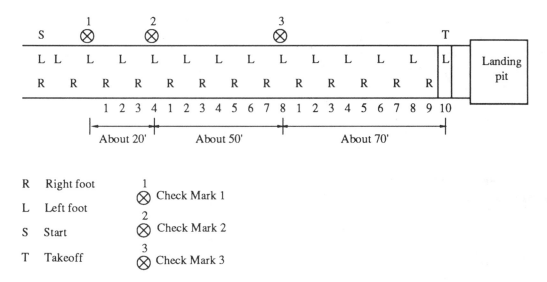

Figure 13.2 Long check approach.

effort. It may be necessary for the jumper to establish the T on another day, particularly if his or her fitness level is low.

4A(1). Short run, height. This is a drill to emphasize the slight settle on the second-to-last step, a slight rise on the next-to-last step, and final lift at the takeoff. The perfect jump would find the jumper's center of gravity rising at an angle of close to 45 degrees, with the maximum height achieved at the midpoint of the jump.

4A(2). Short run, landing. This is a reflex action. The between-the-feet or over-the-feet action is the most common landing. The feet must be dropped soon enough for the forward momentum to carry the jumper over the feet, or a slight spread of the feet should be used to let the jumper go between the feet, forcing the hips forward. This action (the same as in Item 9A) also depends on the jumper's reaching forward and through between the knees.

A second excellent method is landing with one knee slightly stiffened (also used in Item 9B). At the instant of foot contact with the landing surface, the opposite arm and hand reach across the body, while the arm on the same side as the locked knee is moved outward. This action causes a rotation around the feet. This is difficult to coordinate and is only for the very agile athlete.

4C. Takeoff. The takeoff here is for the emphasis of having the takeoff foot under the hip, not across the center of gravity. A cross-step by the takeoff foot (planting the foot across the line of the run to the board) would cause a compensating motion across the body by the arm opposite the takeoff leg. This also

would cause the lead leg to cross over the line of the approach to the pit. Not only would the takeoff be spoiled, but the flight would be a fight for balance, resulting in a poor landing.

5. Height work. Height work is of such importance that not only is it treated within check mark fundamentals, but it is also a separate fundamental requiring special attention. In a 20-foot jump, the center of gravity should reach its peak height at a point 10 feet from the takeoff. The body should be perpendicular to the ground at the midpoint of the jump.

6. Flight. There are two major methods of body control in the air in preparation for landing. Neither propels the center of gravity any farther. The importance of the flight is to gain balance so the feet can be thrust as far forward as possible and so the center of gravity can move forward past the feet at impact without the hands or buttocks making sand marks.

6A. Hitch-kick. As the takeoff foot pushes off the board, the lead knee is brought to hip height, followed by the takeoff leg's coming into a running position, then extending, and the lead leg's coming up into the extended position for a 1-1/2-step "walk in the air." Very long jumpers might use a 2-1/2-step walk. Only those who can benefit from the technique should use it. It is strongly recommended that the 1-1/2-step style be mastered before the athlete even plays with the 2-1/2-step style.

6B. Hang. At the takeoff the lead knee is raised and the arms lift. As the lead knee is lowered, the takeoff leg is brought alongside, but the legs are spread and the knees are slightly bent. The jumper, with arms overhead and the legs hanging down, appears to hang until past the midpoint of the jump, when the legs and arms are brought forward and the jumper awaits the pull of gravity for the landing.

9. Landing.   This work was described with the check mark work. It may be practiced with either the long or the short approach (Items 9A and 9B with 4A and 4B).

10B. Progress assessment, trial.   The coach or the athlete should record the results of this effort in the lower left area of the training sheet. The 3/4ths to 7/8ths effort is a usual procedure for practice. There is no benefit in an athlete's being exhausted on Tuesday or Wednesday. The trials are a learning and technique procedure. Assuming a jumper has an average of 22 feet in competition, we believe a reasonable trial or test jump would be 20 feet. A "hot" practice effort might well equal or better the competitive average, but technique combined with controlled progress should produce the big jumps at the big meets.

11A. Feather the board.   The technique strived for here is to achieve a running up into the air rather than a pounding of the takeoff board. It is believed that an emphasis up, rather than down, gives maximum lift.

11B. Pound the board.   This means exactly what it says. It is a technique used by many fine jumpers and advocated by many coaches. The jumper should use what suits him or her and gets results. Heel bruises and muscle pulls are the great dangers in the pounding technique. In practicing either this or the feathering takeoff technique, the jumper should take off either in front of the board or on the grass, rather than from the board.

11C. Over the foot.   The coach or a teammate should watch the jumper from the rear to determine that the takeoff foot is directly under the hip. Otherwise, a crossover would cause many compensating equilibrium problems that would detract from the jumping distance.

11D. Two-count rise, height.   The two-count rise (Figure 13.3) is a very important technique. The jumper settles on the third-to-last step (left foot for a left-footed takeoff, two steps out), is just barely rising on the next-to-last step, and on the last step gives the final propulsion and lift. Theoretically, if the body is already rising, it not only weighs proportionately less but also utilizes the body's momentum to detract from the body's weight. The jumping leg has a tremendous advantage in lifting a mass that is already moving upward.

11E. Off platform.   A platform of plywood with one edge on a two-by-four makes an inclined plane with a slight elevation, which enables the jumper to artificially attain additional height, giving more time to practice body control in the air.

20. Work on second event.   A secondary event might be the relay, the 100, or sometimes the triple jump. The dangers of the triple jump are the same as those of the long jump: heel bruises, muscle pulls, back problems, and such. If an athlete limits him- or herself to a total of 4 to 6 jumps in both events combined, perhaps it would then be a good double. However, the jumper may turn out to be only fair in both events, yet great if he or she concentrated on only one event.

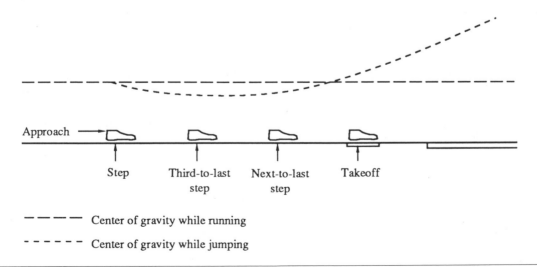

Figure 13.3 Two-count rise.

Interpretation of Week 1 of the Training Schedules

Monday: Organization: The physical education class or squad meets to discuss objectives and goals. The teacher or coach explains responsibilities for regular attendance or for separate individual workouts. Use and care of facilities are also explained.

Tuesday: (1A) In groups of two or three, jog one or two laps of the track. A relay fundamental is used, with the joggers carrying a baton and passing it forward as they jog single file. When the baton reaches the jogger at the head of the line, he or she drops to the rear and begins passing the baton again.

(14D) Run 50m, then jog slowly or walk for 50m, until 400 to 800m or more have been covered.

(3) Weight-training activities according to the schedules or the routine of the athlete.

Wednesday: (1A). Warm-up activities already described.

(4A) Short check mark.

(14F) High knee drill, followed by the fast leg described in detail in the sprint chapter.

Thursday: (3) Weight-training activities.

(16) Acrobatics or apparatus work of a gymnastic nature.

Friday: (1A) Warm-up routine.

(1B) A run to Hendricks Park and two times up the short hill, which is about 50m long.

Saturday: (3) A weight-training session, followed by a jogging session.

(14D) Alternating runs and jogs or walks of 50 meters for 400 to 800m.

Sunday: Recreational activities are recommended. Workout procedures are gradually worked into the program as the year progresses. For those who need training and exercise, this is a day to restore physical well-being.

References

1. Gerd Osenberg. (1983). Performance factors in the long jump. *Track Technique*, **86**, 2754.

2. Tom Tellez. (1980). Long jump. *Track and Field Quarterly Review*, **80**(4), 8-10.

3. Yukio Muraki. (1984). Fundamentals of approach running and takeoff. *Track Technique*, **89**, 2845.

4. Adrian Samungi. (1985). The training of world class women long jumpers. *Track Technique*, **92**, 2922-2927.

Additional Readings

Badon, Tommy. (1988). Constructing and utilizing the "ultimate" jump ramp. *Track Technique*, **106**, 3378-3380.

Boosey, Derek. (1980). *The jumps: Conditioning and technical training*. West Heidelberg, Victoria, Australia: Beatrice.

Clayton, Jerry. (1987). Power development for the long jump. *Track and Field Quarterly Review*, **87**(4), 17-19.

Hay, J.G., Miller, John A., & Canterna, R. W. (1987). Biomechanics of elite long jumping. *Track Technique*, **101**, 3229-3232.

Humphrey, Sue. (1980). Conditioning and training programs for jumpers. *Track and Field Quarterly Review*, **80**(4), 52-55.

Jarver, Jess (Ed.) (1988). *The jumps: Contemporary theory, technique and training* (3rd ed.). Los Altos, CA: Tafnews.

Larkins, Clifford. (1989). The takeoff drill for the long jump. *Track Technique*, **107**, 3415-3418, 3427.

Lohmann, Wolfgang. (1985). Principles of beginners' training in jumping events. *Track Technique*, **91**, 2891-2892, 2899.

Myers, Bob. (1989). Training for the jumps and multi-events. *Track Technique*, **108**, 3449-3452; **109**, 3492-3493.

Rosenthal, John. (1988). Igor Ter-Ovanesyan on the long jump. *Track Technique*, **102**, 3263-3264.

Ter-Ovanesyan, Igor. (1985). Long jump fundamentals. *Track and Field Quarterly Review*, **85**(4), 4-5.

Walker, Joe. (1987). Long jump ideas. *Track and Field Quarterly Review*, **87**(4), 4-8.

Long Jump Training Schedule

ATHLETE

1. Warm-up
   A. Jog 1-2 laps with relay pass, in 2s or 3s
   B. Hendricks Park
   C. Golf course
   D. Steps
2. Fartlek
   A. Varied pace   B. Slow, steady pace
3. Strength & flexibility
   A. Weights and jogging
   B. Jogging and stretching
4. Check marks
   A. Short run   B. Long run   C. Takeoff
      (1) height   (2) landing
5. Height work
   A. Emphasize body control
   B. Apparatus
   C. Takeoff
   D.
6. Flight
   A. Hitch-kick 1-1/2   C.
   B. Hang
7. Team meeting
8. Special
   A. Sauna   C. Hill
   B. Swim
9. Landing
   A. Over the feet   C.
   B. Around the feet
10. Progress assessment
    A. Meet   C. Simulation
    B. Trial   D. Control test
       (1) 3/4 to 7/8 effort   (2) full effort   (3)
11. Short run & jump, relax last 4 steps
    A. Feather the board
    B. Pound the board
    C. Over the foot
    D. 2-count rise: height
    E. Off platform
    F. Landing
12. With Coach
    A. (name)
    B. Leader
14. A. Wind sprints   (1) straight   (2) curve
    B. Hurdle drill: 3LH, 7-9m apart
    C. Spring and bound
    D. Alternate run & jog, at least 800m
    E. Starts   (1) 100   (2)
    F. High knee (slow) & fast leg
15. Plyometrics
    A. Jumps   (1) 1 leg   (2) both legs   (3)
    B. Bounding   (1) 1 leg   (2) both legs   (3)
    C.
16. Easy acrobatics or apparatus
17.
18. A. 300-150-100   B. 100-200-100
19.
20. Work on second event
21. Visual aids
    A. Videotape   C. Photos
    B. Film
       (1) record performance   (2) study
30. Experimental work

DATE September/October

M	Class or squad organization
Tu	1A—14D—3
W	1A—4A—14F
Th	3—16
F	1A—1B—1B (2x)
Sa	3—14D
Su	Weights and long walk
M	1A—9A—14D (4-8x)
Tu	3—jog
W	7—1A—14F—14B—14C—14A
Th	3—jog
F	1A—14D—11F—14D
Sa	3 or 1B
Su	Weights and run
M	1A—14C—1B—14D (3x)
Tu	1A—3—8A
W	1A—14C—14A—14C—14B
Th	1A—3—14D
F	1A—14C—1C—jog (2x)
Sa	Jog Hendricks Park
Su	Jog Hendricks Park
M	1A—14F—9A—8A or B
Tu	3—jog
W	1A—4A—4B—14B—14E—jog (2x 2x)
Th	3—14D—jog
F	1A—4A—10B—jog (3x)
Sa	Help on track trials or run sprint or hurdle
Su	Run

DATE October/November

M	1—14C—18B—100 in 15-16
Tu	1—3—14C
W	7—1—4B—4A—5C—14B—11D—20 (4x)
Th	3—14F
F	1—4A—4B
Sa	1B or C
Su	3
M	1—5—4A—4B—20—11D—jog
Tu	3—16—8A
W	1—14C—4B—10B(1)—18B—jog (2x)
Th	3—8A or B
F	1—14C—4A—4B—14B—18B—jog (2x)
Sa	1B or 3
Su	18A or 3
M	1A—1C—14B—4B—5D (2-4x 2-4x)
Tu	3
W	7—1C—14E—11A—11D—18A
Th	3
F	1—4B—9—1B
Sa	10B and sprint or hurdle trial
Su	3
M	1—14A—14B—4B—11C—11D—14A (2-4x 2-4x)
Tu	3
W	1—14F—4A—4B—11F—11B—jog (2x)
Th	3
F	1—14E—4B—11D—18A
Sa	3
Su	1B or C

DATE January

M	Recheck all gear, squad or class organize
Tu	1—9A—1D—locker arrangements
W	1A—11D—14B—14D
Th	7—3—8A
F	1A—14F—11D—14D
Sa	1A—14A or F
Su	Jog the halls
M	1A—14F—4A—11A—14A
Tu	7—3—14D
W	1A—14F—4A—11D—14D
Th	3—8A or B or jog
F	1A—14F—4B—11A—14A
Sa	3—14B
Su	1 or 8A
M	1—14D—4B—11C—18A
Tu	14D—8A
W	1—14C—4B—10B short run—14A (2-4x)
Th	14D—14F
F	1A—4B—11A—11D—18A
Sa	3—1B—1D
Su	
M	1—4B—4A—9A—11A—14D
Tu	3
W	1A—4B—4A—9D—18B—18C—14D (2x 2x)
Th	Light
F	Gear ready
Sa	Compete indoors
Su	Light

DATE February

M	1—4A (2x)—4B (2x)—5A (6-10x)—5B (3-6x)—14B—14C
Tu	3—14A
W	7—1—4A(1) (3x)—4A(2) (3x)—1B or 1D or 8C
Th	14C—3
F	1—4A (2-3x)—1B or C—14C
Sa	8B or 3
Su	Long walk
M	1A—14B—5C—14F—jog
Tu	3—8A or B
W	1—5A (3x)—5B (3x)—5C
Th	Light
F	1—10B—8C
Sa	Sprint and hurdle trials
Su	
M	1—14A—14F—11D—14C—14F
Tu	3—16
W	7—14E—4B—4A—14D
Th	3—8A or B
F	1—4A (2x)—18A—18B—1B
Sa	8—1B
Su	3
M	1A—14B—5C—14F
Tu	3—8A or C
W	7—5A (3x)—5B (3x)—5C—1B or 1C
Th	3—8A
F	1—10B—run a 250—15
Sa	
Su	

DATE March

M	1A—14E—14C (3-5x)—11D (3-5x)—11A—14D
Tu	3—14D (3x)
W	7—1C (2-4x)—14A (2-4x)—9C (2x)—9A—9B—14B—14D
Th	3—14D or set of 300—200—100
F	1C (3x)—4A (3x)—4B (3-4x)—5A—9A—jog
Sa	3—jog
Su	Park run
M	1A—14F—14C (3x)—14E (3x)—4A (3x)—4B (4x)—run 100
Tu	14A—3
W	7—1C (3x)—4B (3x)—4A(2)—14B
Th	3—14A
F	Gear ready and jog
Sa	Meet routine—compete—after-meet routine
Su	Run
M	a.m. 1A—3 p.m. 1—4A (2x)—4B (2x)—5C (2x)—14D
Tu	Jog 1—14C—20—4A (2x)
W	Light Light
Th	1—14C 1—14C—4B (2x)—4A(1) (2x)—4B(2)—14
F	Jog D Gear ready—light exercise
Sa	Meet routine—compete—after-meet routine
Su	
M	
Tu	
W	
Th	
F	
Sa	
Su	

DATE April

M	7—1—14F—4A—4B—11D—1C
Tu	1—14F—3
W	1—4A—4B—14C—14A
Th	1—4B—jog—3
F	Light
Sa	Meet
Su	Jog and 8A or 8B
M	7—1—14F—5B—14A 7 at 4:45 p.m.
Tu	1—4B—11—14D
W	1—14C—14B
Th	1—4B—11A—11D—14C
F	Light
Sa	Big meet—relay and long jump
Su	Jog
M	7—14F—4B—14A
Tu	1—4B—11D—11F—jog
W	1—14C—11—14D
Th	1—4B—4A—11D
F	Travel and loosen up
Sa	Compete
Su	1—8A—jog
M	7—1—14A—4B—14C—14D
Tu	1—4B—11A—4B(1)—14D
W	3
Th	1—4B—11D
F	Light
Sa	Dual meet—away
Su	Home—8A—jog

DATE May

M	1—4—5A—11D—9A—20—14D
Tu	3—jog
W	1—4—11D—9A—14C—14D
Th	3—jog
F	Travel and loosen up
Sa	Major meet
Su	Home—1—14F—8B—8A
M	Jog
Tu	Jog
W	Twilight meet or trials
Th	11C—11D—11F
F	4A—4B—15A
Sa	Squad picnic
Su	Walk or jog
M	1—4A—4B(1)—11C—14C—jog
Tu	1—4B—14A
W	Jog—3
Th	Jog—4
F	1—4A—4B—jog
Sa	3x / 1—14C—4B—10B(1)
Su	Jog and weights
M	4x / 1—14C—14A—14E—pop-ups—70 m—jog
Tu	2-3x / 1—14C—4A—4B—easy 14B
W	Easy grass running
Th	Easy grass running
F	Qualifying
Sa	Championship
Su	

CHAPTER 14	# The Triple Jump

A prospective triple jumper needs several natural qualities to be successful. Speed and leg strength are essential. The speed is there or it is not. The leg strength can be developed. Perhaps the most important factor in successful triple jumping is balance. Finally, rhythm is necessary because the triple jump is, as its title implies, a series of jumps rather than a single effort.

Analysis of the Triple Jump

The triple jump has been called the "hop, step, and jump." The first part of the action is called the "hop" because the jumper lands on the takeoff foot. This action of taking off and landing on the same foot requires considerable leg strength if the jumper is to continue through the other two phases of the jump. From the landing at the end of the hopping phase, the jumper moves into a step, pushing from the takeoff foot and landing on the opposite foot, preparatory to the last phase of the action, the jump. The jump is simply a normal long jumping action. If the triple jumper takes off on the left foot (placing that foot on the board when beginning the jumping sequence), the step pattern will be takeoff (left foot) to land (left foot) at completion of hop, to land (right foot) at completion of step, to land (both feet) in pit at completion of jumping phase.

The approach run for the triple jump is similar to the run for the long jump, with the primary excep-

tions that it is not generally as long as the long jump run, and the two-count rise is not used. The triple jumper is primarily seeking controlled speed to the point of the takeoff.

At the takeoff the jumper does not want to get much height off the board. The action off the board is very similar to the normal sprinting action. The jumper should try to hit the board with the hips a bit more forward than they would be in the normal sprinting position. The jumper wishes to conserve as much horizontal momentum as possible. This momentum at the time of takeoff must last through all three takeoffs. The jumper must hit the board both balanced and relaxed. Balance at this point is very important because any imbalance at the takeoff would result in a loss of power and control later in the jump.

On each landing, the landing foot should be pulled back quickly just before it strikes the ground. This maneuver allows the jumper to preserve momentum through the landing and the later takeoff actions. If the foot is not pulled backward, it acts as a brake when the jumper lands, lessening potential momentum for the next jumping phase.

The coach and the jumper should listen to the footstep rhythm of the jump as it is performed. It should be regular for all three portions of the jump. If the middle portion sounds too quick, the stepping phase is probably not performed properly.

The step is usually the hardest part of the jump to learn and develop properly. The jumper must try to develop strength equally in each leg. He or she will generally use the same leg for taking off in both the long jump and the triple jump.

Jumpers use the double-arm swing, a coordinated swinging action of both arms in the same direction and at the same time in certain portions of the jump. This consists of a forward and upward swing of both arms at the time of the takeoff of each phase of the jump. It is used by expert jumpers to give additional impetus to each phase of the jump. It requires much practice, but if mastered it benefits the jumper considerably.

Training Theory for the Triple Jump

Just as in the long jump, in the triple jump the operative word is *speed*. The European approach is to find good sprinters and train them as long and triple jumpers.[1] Most important is the takeoff speed, the acceleration across the takeoff board. Next is the rhythm of the jump, distributing a fairly even part to each of the three phases. Coaches and researchers are not completely agreed on the ideal relative distribution of the phases (Table 14.1). Tom Tellez (University of Houston) recommends a ratio of 6:5:6, which is about the same as the Polish school.

Table 14.1 Suggested Triple Jump Phase Percentages

Source	Hop	Step	Jump
Polish	35	30	35
German	37	30	33
Russian	38.5	29.5	32

From Joe Walker. (1987). Triple jump ideas. *Track and Field Quarterly Review*, **87**(4), 16. Reprinted with permission.

However, all jumping schools hold similar views on the critical role of the step phase. They suggest a step equal to 29 to 30% of the total jump (Table 14.2). This focuses the evaluation of the balance of the jumper's style. The step is the most useful part of the jump for beginners to try to improve after they master the approach run. The hop should be the training focus after the step. One reason for this sequence is that the beginner's step is usually far short of optimal, but it can greatly improve the overall distance. Another reason is that when beginners focus on improving the hop, they tend to shorten their step until they are proficient.[2] Although a study of the best American jumpers suggests that their step phase was shorter as their jumps became longer, their steps were within the range suggested by Table 14.2.[3]

Table 14.2 Recommended Triple Jump Step Lengths

Total jump	Step
30′	8′9″ to 9′0″
35′	10′2″ to 10′6″
40′	11′7″ to 12′0″
45′	13′1″ to 13′6″
50′	14′6″ to 15′0″
55′	16′1″ to 16′6″
60′	17′5″ to 18′0″

Technique Training

The basic factors in maintaining horizontal velocity through the three phases of the jump are these:[4]

- A proper ratio between the hop, step, and jump phases
- A low (flat) takeoff angle for the hop and the step
- Using the arms (to maintain velocity and aid balance)
- An erect body posture (and head up) throughout
- Pawing action of the contact leg (landing ahead of the center of gravity and pulling through)

The technical complexity of the triple jump, along with the extreme stretching and landing stresses, make it an event with high injury risk. The high injury rate may result from poor preparation in the first several years of jumping.[5] These training factors help decrease the likelihood of injury:

- Long-term planning is essential.
- Emphasize technique development during the early training years.
- Emphasize quality before quantity.
- Learn correct lifting techniques early (age 15).
- Use stretching exercises to develop muscle elasticity.
- Always jump with an active landing action.
- Adjust the length of the approach to the level of technique (shorter approach for poorer technique).
- Execute large portions of the technique training with jumps that are near competition level (with high horizontal speed).
- Never do technique training when fatigued.

The triple jump is a very complex event, so it has many technical aspects to master. Table 14.3 summarizes the major faults found, along with their causes and how they can be corrected.

Table 14.3   Triple Jump Technique Faults, Causes, and Corrections

Fault	Causes	Corrections
Inconsistent steps	• Overstriding • Looking at the takeoff board • Variation in first 3 to 4 steps (emotion or fatigue)	• Emphasizing high knee action with a stride-length decrease and a stride-rate increase • Focusing the eyes above the head and past the board • Using run-throughs as part of the warm-up on technique days (at least twice a week)
Hop too high	• Flexing the knee too much two steps out • Knee drive and arm blocking past 90 degrees • Arm blocking past shoulder level • Transition problems of using same takeoff foot for long and triple jumps (need different actions)	• Running off the board (forward, not up) • Exaggerating the arm and knee blocking at 90 degrees (for the knee) and at shoulder level (for arms)
Over-rotating	• Too much forward lean at takeoff (places center of gravity ahead of base of support)	• Placing takeoff foot in front of hips, with upper body kept upright
Lateral deviation	• Dropping the shoulder below the level position • Driving the knee and the arms across the body's center line instead of straight ahead	• Keeping the shoulders as level as possible • Moving the arms and knee straight forward and backward
Poor timing of arms to leg	• Coordination problems	• Learning how to use both arms with a jumping motion relative to legs • Using repeated bounding and short-approach drills to imitate the whole motion
Short step	• Too high a hop • Too long a hop	• Emphasizing a controlled hop (about 35% of total jump) • Trying not to go very high (the jarring effect of a high hop makes recovery difficult)
Inability to take off on step or jump	• Landing from a hop or a step that is too high • Landing with the center of gravity too far forward • Not using the arms and free leg forcefully and through the full range of motion • Landing on the ball of the foot	• Emphasizing a flat trajectory • Using the arms and the legs together to develop maximum forward momentum • Landing heel-first or midfoot, followed by a pawing action • Landing with the foot comfortably in front, not directly below the hips
Poor trail-leg position	• Heel never coming close to the hip • Leg angle less than 90 degrees or not parallel to the ground when making contact with the ground	• Holding the leg parallel to the ground until contact, allowing greater range of motion to generate more knee drive to carry to the next phase

(Cont.)

Table 14.3   (Continued)

Fault	Causes	Corrections
Decelerating from phase to phase	• Too high a hop • Too long a hop • Lateral deviation • No control of speed at takeoff	• Emphasizing going out, not up • Keeping the shoulders level through all phases • Practicing approaches, with the hop only into the pit or other soft surface, to learn how long a hop can be handled
Premature landing	• Not keeping the head toward the knees long enough • Not extending the legs or keeping them extended	• Holding the leg extended, with the head close to the knee position until the heels land

From Steve Miller & Scott Bennett. (1989). The triple jump. In Vern Gambetta (Ed.), *The Athletics Congress's track and field coaching manual* (2nd ed., pp. 140-141). Champaign, IL: Leisure Press. Adapted with permission.

Training Considerations

One competitive suggestion for teachers and coaches: Do not use an athlete in both the long jump and the triple jump. There are several reasons for this suggestion, the primary one being that both events are very hard on the athlete's legs. The risk of injury with much jumping is great with either event. If the jumper competes in both events, the risk of injury is more than doubled—as are the coach's chances of losing the athlete.

Also, an athlete tends to be better in one or the other of the two events. Only at a low level of accomplishment would he or she be likely to show equal levels of achievement in the events. Few international-class jumpers in either event have been better than national class (and there is quite a bit of difference) in the other. Generally the long jumpers have better speed, while the triple jumpers have better leg strength, which they can utilize despite their lesser natural speed.

The teacher should watch the prospects, looking for rhythm and balance. Hurdlers are often good prospects because they usually have those traits. Rhythm can be developed by jumping first from standing jumps, then going to jumps taken from a short run of three steps or so. While jumping, the athletes should always wear heel cups or pads for their protection.

Training Drills

Several types of drills are used as vital parts of triple jump training. Three types of drills are rhythm drills, power bounding, and box drills.

The rhythm drills use a 5- to 7-step approach, followed by 10 consecutive jumps, with any combination of landings (i.e., any combination of hops and steps). The primary object of these drills is to work on the rhythm of the hopping and the stepping. The drills are judged by their sound pattern and the distance covered in the 10-step sequence. As athletes improve, the distance they cover increases, while the time needed for the series decreases. Covering 120 feet in 5.5 seconds indicates that a male athlete would be a good triple jumper.

The power-bounding drills can focus on either height or distance. There are several variations of the drill. The athlete does intervals of 50 to 100m, on soft surfaces, hopping on either one leg or the other, working on either the height or the length of the hops. This exercise is performed six to eight times as fast as the athlete can go. The jumper might also work on a hop-step drill. In this drill the jumper also covers 50 to 100m, except that he or she alternates the hopping (H) and stepping (S) (i.e., H S H S H S), working on the double-arm action and trying to develop a more powerful lead leg.

The box drills are done with boxes of various heights, with 18 inches the most common height. Boxes 18 inches high by 20 inches across in the jumping direction by 30 inches wide can be used. Usually three to five boxes are used. They are spaced at intervals along the runway or on the grass. At first the boxes are only a few yards apart. As the jumpers become more adept, the boxes can be moved farther apart.

One drill is to go over the boxes, stepping on the ground with the takeoff leg and stepping on the boxes with the opposite foot. The purpose of the drill is to get the jumper in the habit of raising the stepping leg, which is necessary to get onto the box and also to get a long step in the actual jump. Another drill (with the boxes farther apart) is to work on both hopping and stepping. The athlete hops between the boxes, then steps over a box, hops close to the next box, steps over again, and so forth. If the athlete takes off from the left leg (LL), the pattern would be LL, box, RL, box, LL, box, RL, and so forth, always with a step over and a hop between. Because of the boxes, the jumper learns to get the trail leg up fast. In performing the step, the jumper needs to learn to get both legs up, one forward and one to the rear.

Rope jumping is also a good leg-strengthening exercise. The athlete jumps on one leg for 30 seconds, then rests for 15 seconds or so, then jumps for an equal period of time on the other leg. During the fall training, jumpers generally work on drills 3 days a week, with box drills on Mondays and Fridays and rhythm drills on Wednesdays. Fall is a good time for building the athlete's strength and sense of the general movements, leaving the period immediately before the season for more specific technique work.

A warm-up routine is used for the triple jump, as for the other events. After jogging and flexibility exercises, followed by the high-knee (slow), fast-leg drill, the jumper works on power bounding. This is followed by several series of three triple jumps taken with approaches of varying lengths. The first three jumps are taken from a stand. The next three are taken with a 30-foot approach run. Three jumps are taken from a 60-foot approach, then three are taken with a 90-foot approach. Actually, this is quite enough jumping for a triple jumper, and it may even be more than he or she should do, except on rare occasions. The other workouts consist of drills and selected sprinters' exercises. The coach should be careful not to overwork triple jumpers, exposing them to needless injury.

The most important training principle is one that no triple jumper should forget: "Triple jumpers are made."

References

1. Dave Norris. (1988). Run-ups in the horizontal jumps. *Track Technique*, **104**, 3329.
2. John Crotty. (1988). The hop phase of the triple jump. *Track Technique*, **102**, 3261-3262.
3. Tom Ecker. (1987). Hop, step and jump ratios in world class triple jumping. *Track Technique*, **98**, 3126-3127.
4. Andy Heal. (1985). Horizontal velocity in the triple jump. *Track Technique*, **92**, 2944-2945.
5. Klaus Kubler. (1987). Triple jump injuries. *Track Technique*, **100**, 3202-3203.

Additional Readings

Blumenstein, B., & Hudanov, N. (1981). Psychological preparation for competition in the long and triple jumps. *Track Technique*, **83**, 2644-2646.

Boni, Mario, Benazzo, Francesco, Castelli, Claudio, & Barnabei, Giuseppe. (1986). Jumper's knee. *New Studies in Athletics*, **1**(2), 65-80.

Boosey, Derek. (1980). *The jumps: Conditioning and technical training*. West Heidelberg, Victoria, Australia: Beatrice.

Bullard, Ernie, & Knuth, Larry. (1977). *Triple jump encyclopedia*. Pasadena: Athletic Press.

Hayes, Dean. (1984). The beginning triple jumper. *Track and Field Quarterly Review*, **84**(4), 9-10.

Humphrey, Sue. (1980). Conditioning and training programs for jumpers. *Track and Field Quarterly Review*, **80**(4), 52-55.

Jarver, Jess (Ed.) (1988). *The jumps: Contemporary theory, technique and training* (3rd ed.). Los Altos, CA: Tafnews.

Kreyer, Vitold. (1983). Progressive drills for young triple jumpers. *Track Technique*, **86**, 2730-2731, 2733.

Miller, John A., & Hay, James G. (1987). Triple jumping at its best. *Track Technique*, **100**, 3197-3200, 3205.

Miller, Steve, & Bennett, Scott. (1989). The triple jump. In Vern Gambetta (Ed.), *The Athletics Congress's track and field coaching manual* (2nd ed., pp. 131-144). Champaign, IL: Leisure Press.

Muraki, Yukio. (1984). Fundamentals of approach running and takeoff. *Track Technique*, **89**, 2843-2845.

Myers, Bob. (1989). Training for the jumps and multievents. *Track Technique*, **108**, 3449-3452; **109**, 3492-3493.

Walker, Joe. (1987). Triple jump ideas. *Track and Field Quarterly Review*, **87**(4), 12-16.

Triple Jump Training Schedule

ATHLETE

1. Warm-up
   A. Jogging and flexibility; high knee, fast leg
   B. Hendricks Park
   C. Golf course
   D. Steps
2. Fartlek
   A. Varied pace   B. Slow, steady pace
3. Weights and jogging
4. Bounding drills
   A. Height: LR for 50-100m
      6-8 reps as fast as you can control
   B. Distance:
   C. Hop-step drill, double-arm action, powerful lead leg (50-100m), 6-8 reps
5. Rhythm drills: 5-7-9 step approach
   A. S - S - S - J
   B. H - H - H - S - J
   C. LL RR LLL R LL: 10-step sequence for time & distance; 124'/38m is excellent
   D.
6. Box drills

A.
   Step leg UP to get on box

B.

C.

D.
   13' between boxes
   Reverse RRLRRL to LLRLLR

E.
   10' between boxes
   Reverse RRLRRLRR to LLRLLRLL

F.
   16' to 1st box, 10' between boxes

G.
   Begin 8' between boxes, try for 20'

H.

7. Team meeting
8. Special
   A. Sauna
   B. Swim
   C. Hill
9. Short approach
   A. Standing
   B. 3-step
   C. 5-step
   D. 7-step
   E. 9-step
   F. 11-step
10. Full approach
    A. Meet
    B. Trial
    C. Simulation
    D. Control test
    (1) check marks   (2) jumping
11.

12. With Coach
    A. (name)
    B. Leader
14. A. Wind sprints   (1) straight   (2) curve
    B. Hurdle drills: 3 LH, 7-9m apart
    C. Rope jumping: 30 sec, 15 sec rest
    D. Alternate run & jog, at least 800m
    E. Hill work
15. Intervals
    A. 100
    B. 150
    C. 200
    D. 250
    E. 300
    F. 400
    G. 600-400-300-200-100
20. Work on second event
21. Visual aids
    A. Videotape   C. Photos
    B. Film
       (1) record performance   (2) study
30. Experimental work

DATE September/October

M	1A—15C (6-8x)
Tu	1A—3—2A
W	1B—7
Th	1A—3—2B
F	1A—15G—15A (4x)
Sa	1A—3—2A
Su	
M	1A—15E—15C—15A (3x, 3x)
Tu	1A—3—2A
W	1B
Th	1A—3—2A
F	1A—15D—15A—2B (4x, 4x)
Sa	1A—3—2A
Su	
M	1A—4A,B—15G—15A (6x)
Tu	1A—3—2B
W	1A—12—1B
Th	1A—3—2A
F	1A—4A,B,C—5A,B,C—15D—15A (3x, 4x, 4x)
Sa	1A—3—2B
Su	
M	1A—4A,B,C—5A—5B—5C—15G—15A (5x, 4x, 3x)
Tu	1A—3—2B
W	1A—12—1B—8C
Th	1A—3—2A
F	1A—4A,B,C—5A—5B—5C—15F—15E—15C—15B (4x, 3x, 3x, 2x, 3x, 4x)
Sa	1A—3—2A
Su	

DATE November

M	1A—4A,B—5A,B,C—15C—15G (3x, 4x)
Tu	1A—3
W	1A—12—1B
Th	1A—3
F	1A—4A,B,C—6A,B,C,D—15E—15C—15A (3x, 2x, 2x, 4x)
Sa	1A—3—2A
Su	
M	1A—4A,B,C—5A,B,C—15C (3x, 6x)
Tu	1A—3—2A
W	1B—8C
Th	1A—3—2A
F	1A—4A,B,C—6B,C,D,E—15D—15G (3x, 3x)
Sa	1A—3—2A
Su	
M	1A—4A,B,C—5A,B—5C—15F—15E—15C—15A (5x, 3x, 2x, 3x, 4x)
Tu	1A—3—2B
W	1A—1B—7
Th	1A—3—2B
F	1A—4A,B,C—9A,B,C—15G (3x)
Sa	1A—3—2B
Su	
M	1A—4A,B,C—5A,B—5C—15D—15B—15A (5x, 3x, 3x, 3x)
Tu	1A—3—2B—8C
W	1A—14B—1B
Th	1A—3—2B
F	1A—4A,B,C—6C,D,E,F—15E—15C—15A (3x, 3x, 3x)
Sa	1A—3—2B
Su	

DATE December

M	1A—4A,B,C—5A,B—5C—15G—15A (5x, 3x, 4x)
Tu	1A—3—2A
W	1A—12—1C
Th	1A—3—2A
F	1A—4A,B,C—6D,E,F,G—15D (4x, 5x)
Sa	1A—3—2A
Su	
M	1A—4A,B,C—5A—5B—5C—15G—15A (6x, 5x, 4x, 4x)
Tu	1A—3—2A
W	1A—12—1D (3-5x)
Th	1A—3—2A
F	1A—2B
Sa	1A—4A,C—9B,C,D—15E—15C—15A (2x, 2x, 2x)
Su	
M	
Tu	
W	
Th	
F	
Sa	
Su	
M	
Tu	
W	
Th	
F	
Sa	
Su	

DATE January

M	1A—4A,B—15C (6x)
Tu	1A—3—2B
W	1A—14B—1C—7
Th	1A—3—2A
F	1A—4B,C—6E,F,G,H(4x)—15D(4x)—15A
Sa	1A—3—2B
Su	
M	1A—4A,B,C—5A(4x)—5B(3x)—5C(3x)—15G—15A(4x)
Tu	1A—3—2B
W	1A—10C(1)—1C
Th	1A—3—2A
F	1A—4A,B,C—5A,B(3x)—9A,B,C(3x)—15E(2x)—15C—15A(3x)
Sa	1A—3—2B
Su	
M	1A—4A,B,C—10(1)—5A,B,C(4x)—15G—15A(3x)
Tu	1A—3—2B
W	1A—12—10C(1)—1C
Th	1A—3—2A
F	1A—4A,B,C—10C(1)— 4x/6F,G,H—15F—2x/15E—3x/15C—3x/15A
Sa	1A—3—2B
Su	
M	1A—4A,B—10C(1)—5A,B(3x)—9C,D,E(3x)—15G—15A(4x)
Tu	1A—3—2B
W	1A—10C(1)—1C—7
Th	1A—3—2A
F	1A
Sa	1A—10A(indoors)
Su	

DATE February

M	1A—4A,B,C—5A,B,C—15G—15A(4x)
Tu	1A—3—2B
W	1A—14B—1C
Th	1A—3—2A
F	1A—4A,B,C—6D,E,F,G(4x)—15D(3x)—15A(3x)
Sa	1A—3—2B
Su	
M	1A—4A,B,C—5A,B,C—15G—15A(4x)
Tu	1A—3—2B
W	1A—10C(1)—1C—7
Th	1A—3—2A
F	1A—10C(1)—15C (6-8x)
Sa	1A—4A,C—9D,E,F—2B (3x)
Su	
M	1A—4A,B,C—5A,B,C—15D (3-5x)
Tu	1A—3—2B
W	1A—10C(1)—1C
Th	1A—3—2A
F	1A—4A,C—6E,F,G,H(4x)—15G—15A(4x)
Sa	1A—3—2B
Su	
M	1A—4A,B,C—10C(1)—5A,B,C(3x)—9C,D,E(3x)—15C(4x)—15A(4x)
Tu	1A—3—2B
W	1A—10C(1)—1C
Th	1A—3—2A
F	1A—10C(1)—15B(2x)—15A(3x)
Sa	1A—4A,C—10C(1)—9E,F(2x)—10C(2)(2x)—15G
Su	

DATE March

M	1A—4A,C—10C(1)—5A,B,C—15G—15A(3x)
Tu	1A—3—2B
W	1A—10C(1)—1C—7
Th	1A—3—2A
F	1A—4A,C—6E,F,G,H(4x)—15D(3x)—15A(3x)
Sa	1A—3—2B
Su	
M	1A—4A,C—10C(1)—5A,B,C—15G—15A(3x)
Tu	1A—3—2B—8C
W	1A—10C(1)—1C
Th	1A—3—2A
F	1A—4A,C—9D,E,F(3x)—15D(3x)—15A
Sa	1A—3—15C—15A(3x)
Su	
M	1A—4A,C—10C(1)—5A,B,C—15G—15A(4x)
Tu	1A—3—2B
W	1A—4A,C—10C(1)—9C,D,E(2x)—15C(3x)—15B—15A(3x)—7
Th	1A—3—2A—8C
F	1A
Sa	1A—10A
Su	
M	1A—4A,C—10C(1)—5A,B—15G—15A(3x)
Tu	1A—10C(1)—3—2B
W	1A—10C(1)—9C,D,E(2x)—15D(2x)—15C(3x)—15A—7
Th	1A—10C(1)—3(light)—2A—8C
F	1A
Sa	1A—10A
Su	

DATE April

M	1A—4A,C—10C(1)—6E,F,G—15G—15B—7 (3x, 2x)
Tu	1A—10C(1)—3—2B—8C
W	1A—10C(1)—9C,D,E—15D—15C—15B (2x, 3x)
Th	1A—10C(1)—3(light)—2A—8C
F	1A
Sa	1A—10A—7
Su	
M	1A—4A,C—10C(1)—5A,B,C—15G—7 (3x)
Tu	1A—10C(1)—3—2B—8C
W	1A—4A,C—10C(1)—5A,B,C—15D—15C—15A (2x, 3x, 4x)
Th	1A—10C(1)—3(light)—2A
F	1A
Sa	1A—10A—7
Su	1A—15A (6x)
M	1A—4A,C—10C(1)—6D,E,F—15G—7 (3x)
Tu	1A—10C(1)—3—2B—8C
W	1A—10C(1)—5A,B,C—15C—15A (3x, 3x)
Th	1A—10C(1)—3(light)—2B
F	1A
Sa	1A—10A—7
Su	1A—4A,C—3
M	1A—4A,C—10C(1)—5A,B,C—15G—15B—7 (3x)
Tu	1A—10C(1)—3—2B
W	1A—10C(1)—9C,D,E—15D—15A (2x, 3x, 3x)
Th	1A—10C(1)—3(light)—2B
F	1A
Sa	1A—10A—7
Su	1A—15C—15A (4x, 4x)

DATE May

M	1A—4A,C—10C(1)—6D,E,F,G—15G—7 (2x)
Tu	1A—3—2B
W	1A—10C(1)—9B,C,D—15D—15A (2x, 3x, 3x)
Th	1A—3(light)—2B
F	1A—10C(1)
Sa	1A—10A—7
Su	1A—10C(1)—9D,E,F—2B (2x)
M	1A—10C(1)—15G—15A—7 (3x)
Tu	1A—3—2B—8C
W	1A—4A,C—10C(1)—5A,B,C—15D—15A (2x, 4x)
Th	1A—3(light)—2A
F	1A
Sa	1A—10A—7
Su	1A—10C(1)—14C (5x)
M	1A—4A,C—10C(1)—6D,E,F,G—15G—7 (2x)
Tu	1A—3—2B—8C
W	1A—4A,C—10C(1)—5A,B—15D—15A (3x, 3x)
Th	1A—3(light)—2A
F	1A
Sa	1A—10A—7
Su	1A—10C(1)—9B,C,D—15A (2x, 4x)
M	1A—4A,C—10C(1)—15G—15A—7 (4x)
Tu	1A—3—2B
W	1A—4A,C—10C(1)—5A,B,C—15C (6x)
Th	1A—3(light)—2A
F	1A
Sa	1A—10A—7
Su	1A—10C(1)—4A,B,C—2A

DATE June

M	1A—4A—4C—10C(1)—5A,B,C—3x/15D—3x/15C—3x/15A—7
Tu	1A—3—2B
W	1A—4A—4C—10C(1)—2x/9C,D,E—15F—2x/15E—3x/15C—4x/15A
Th	1A—3—2B
F	1A—4A—4C—10C(1)—5A,B—15A (6x)
Sa	1A—4A—4C—10C(1)—6D,E,F—15G—15A (2x, 4x)
Su	1A—10(1)
M	1A—4A—4C—5A,B,C—9B,C,D—15D—15A (2x, 3x, 3x)
Tu	1A—3—2B—8C
W	1A—10C(1)—5A,B—15C (4x)
Th	1A—10C(1)—15A—8C (3x)
F	10A—qualify
Sa	10A—finals
Su	
M	
Tu	
W	
Th	
F	
Sa	
Su	
M	
Tu	
W	
Th	
F	
Sa	
Su	

CHAPTER 15	# The Pole Vault

Pole vaulters vary in size as much as any other athletes in track. Vaulters are athletes with good speed, superior coordination, and determination. The pole vault's technical components require years of hard work to master. Because of the time requirement, the best vaulters often are athletes who grew up with the pole, so to speak. The youngster who started vaulting at age 10 has a great advantage over the vaulter who started only after entering high school or college. The early beginners have already learned to handle the pole easily, to feel it as an extension of themselves or to feel that they are an extension of the pole.

Most pole vaulters need an approach of over 100 feet; good relaxation prior to the plant; a smooth, well-placed planting of the pole so that the takeoff will be a swift flow off the ground and into position for the swing and rise that precede the turn; and a smooth flow from the turn into the off-the-pole phase. A good landing is also critical because of the height involved.

The technical complexity of pole vaulting makes it one of the most difficult of sports events. It consists of at least six separate "events" that must be combined into a smooth-flowing motion, from the beginning of the run through the planting of the pole, the takeoff, the hang, the turn-rise, the crossing of the bar, and the dismount, or landing.

For those reasons, experience is important in pole vaulting. It has been shown repeatedly that pole vaulters who started practicing this event when they were about 10 years old always have an advantage over those who did not begin until high school or college.

Training for the Pole Vault

The pole vault is the most complex event in track and field. The athlete must try to coordinate two pendulum actions, those of the pole and of his body, which can work at cross-purposes. For decades the leader in vaulting, the United States has been surpassed in the last decade by vaulters from Russia, France, and Poland. Coaches agree that vaulters should begin the event between the ages of 12 and 14. While the Americans have emphasized agility, the Europeans have stressed increased strength and conditioning. These latter factors allow the vaulter to use a faster approach and a higher handhold, reaching higher vaulting heights.

The Russians recommend a high vertical pole carry,[1] while others simply prefer that the end of the pole stay above the vaulter's eye level.[2] Late in the approach run, the pole is lowered gradually toward the level of the vaulting box, which adds to the speed of the approach.

The approach falls into these three phases:[3]

- Start and early acceleration
- Acceleration to top speed
- Pole plant and takeoff foot placement

The first phase, the start and smooth early acceleration, usually has 4 to 6 strides. It must be very consistent, just as initial phases in the other jumps. The second phase, accelerating from the running start to maximum controllable speed, usually has about 10 strides. The pole is usually carried at an angle of 60 to 70 degrees in this phase. The third phase usually has 4 to 6 strides. During this time, the end of the pole is lowered to slide into the box, and the takeoff position is reached.

The higher grips, with much stiffer poles used for higher jumps, put added stresses on the body, especially on the back and the shoulders.[4] This is a major reason for the European emphasis on conditioning and strength. The distance that a vaulter can fly above his handhold has changed little in the last 2 decades. The tale of progress is simply faster approach speeds and higher grips on the pole, which require improved strength.

Although we recommend teaching the vaulter to resist the pole with the lower hand, it may not be entirely possible in a good vault. In fact, some Olympic coaches stress letting the lower arm bend.[5] This is best left to more experienced vaulters who are not concerned with ensuring that the pole does, indeed, bend during their vault. More advanced vaulters bend the pole with the pressure of the body through the upper hand and chest, smoothed by dropping the knee at takeoff to lower the center of gravity.

Though most mechanical concerns are the same for vaulters of all levels, beginners have far less time to complete the vaulting sequence than an athlete who clears 18 to 19 feet. The beginner faces the task of dealing with fast-moving actions, while the elite vaulter must learn to hang back and be patient as he rises through the air. Maurice Houvion (who coaches world-class French vaulters) has given an excellent overview of pole vault training.[6]

Soviet coaches recommend that developing vaulters go through these stages at about these ages:[7]

Introductory Phase: ages 10 to 12

Specialization Phase: ages 13 to 15

Establishment Phase I: ages 16 to 17

Establishment Phase II: ages 18 to 19

Final Development Phase: ages 20 to 23

They give recommended tasks, training loads, numbers of meets, tests, and performance levels for each stage. Their excellent examples show how a coach begins planning the annual training program for a vaulter.

As the athlete becomes more experienced and skilled over a period of years, the proportion of training gradually shifts from more general to more specific conditioning. The components of jumping training and performance are:[8]

Endurance: fartlek and cross country

Speed: intervals, starts, and approach runs

Strength/power: strength training

Bounding: plyometrics and varied jumping activities

Technique: from major to minor skill changes

The preseason training should take at least 3 months, including at least 120 training sessions, over 200 vaults on a softer pole from short approaches, and over 100 full-approach vaults with the regular pole.[9] The length of the competitive season depends largely on the length of the preseason training and the volume of work included. The training load during the season should be controlled carefully, allowing enough recovery for good performances. The training volume should be about 20 to 25% less per week than in preseason training. However, the training load should not be decreased too sharply because the athlete may quickly peak, then decline.

The vaulter may use a phase of 6 to 8 weeks to prepare for a major meet, with a training volume of about 90% of maximum for the first week or two. The emphasis is on quality vaulting, with good recovery between vaulting sessions (2 days of rest after a session of 15 quality vaults, or 3 days of rest after a session of 25 quality vaults).[10]

Speaking of the European coaches' stress on the importance of overall fitness (contrasted to American coaches' emphasis on technique), Andrzej Krzesinski (who coached a Polish Olympic champion and is now an American coach) says, ''Present vaulters ought to be strong and powerful, fast, with jumping ability, agility and nerve.''[11] Table 15.1 summarizes his suggested training loads for a world-class vaulter.

Analysis of Vaulting Technique

The phases of pole vaulting technique that need to be examined here are holding the pole and running (including check marks and how they are set up). In the following discussion, a right-handed vaulter is used as an example, so the pole is held with the right hand up, but not too far out, and the left hand down the pole.

Holding the Pole

Some vaulters have the mistaken notion that the height of the crossbar (the height that the vaulter is attempt-

Table 15.1 Suggested Training Loads for the Elite Pole Vaulter

| Component | Annual load | Emphasis by mesocycles and periods | | |
		General	Special	Component
Fartlek	60 miles	1	1	—
PV pop-ups	1,600 reps	4-3	3	3-2
PV jumps, short run	1,000 reps	3-2	1	—
PV jumps, full run	1,000 reps	—	2	3
Acrobatics	1,000 reps	3	2	1
Hurdle drills	3,500 reps	3-2	2	1
Plyometrics	4,000 reps	1	3	1
Sprint starts	5 miles	1	1	1-0
Games	21 hours	4	3-2	2-1
Weight lifting	150-170 tons	3	3-2	2-1
Abdominals	1,500 reps	3	3	1-0
Shot & medicine ball	3,500 reps	3-2	2	2-1
Knee drills	3,600 reps	5-4	3	—
Apparatus drill	600 reps	2	2	1
Speed	8 miles	—	1-2	1
Speed endurance	10 miles	—	1	1/2
Other running	85 miles	6-5	6-5	5

From Andrzej Krzesinski. (1983). Pole vault: The total program. *Track Technique*, **84**, 2681-2682. Reprinted with permission.

ing to make at any one time) influences the position of their hands on the pole. This is not true. A vaulter holds the pole where it is most advantageous to him, where he feels he has the best possible control of the pole and is himself in a position in relation to the pole to make maximum use of that control.

The position of the hands on the pole, like the number of steps in an approach, is a matter for the individual athlete to decide, based on experimentation. It should not be changed impulsively. Any changes should be made only when there is time to master them before competition. The height of the hold may vary in some conditions. With a strong headwind or crosswind, the vaulter may use a shorter run and a lower hold. If the wind is at his back, he might use a longer run and a higher-than-usual hold.

Approach

The approach is planned for the vaulter to reach maximum speed as closely as possible to the moment the pole is planted in the box, giving explosive power to the takeoff. Perhaps the vaulter should reach maximum speed as soon as possible so that at the plant he is "freewheeling." This approach might contribute to the smoothness of the vault and be a noticeable advantage to some vaulters. The theory advocates getting the most *controlled* momentum possible at Point T because longer maintained speed contributes to *fluidity*.

We teach two types of approaches, the long run and the short run. The long run (100 to 130 feet) is generally favored by vaulters and taught as "normal" technique. However, vaulters should learn the advantages of a short run (50 to 70 feet) and practice it as thoroughly as the long one so they will be able to use it whenever special conditions warrant.

When a strong wind is against the vaulters, it is exhausting to get off the ground with a full run and hold. A short run with a low hold is important for such conditions. For practice sessions, it is possible to take many more vaults with the short run and low hold than with the full run. In big competitive meets, also, when the pole vaulting promises to be a long, drawn-out affair requiring many attempts, the vaulter who can take a short approach and vault from a low hold, at least in the early attempts, will find that he has a great advantage in conserving his energy for his later, higher attempts.

The hand grip is measured from the bottom of the pole to the top of the top hand. The athlete should be vaulting 2 feet or more above his hand grip before raising the grip. Many athletes try to use a higher grip than they can effectively handle, mistakenly believing that it will enable them to vault higher. A good vaulter should be able to clear 14 feet with a grip of no more than 12' to 12'6". The pole is taped, generally made sticky with "firm grip" or a similar substance, giving a more secure handhold. While carrying the pole, the hands are usually gripping the pole about 3 feet apart.

For a short-run approach, the vaulter uses a low hold on the pole, probably at about 12 feet. This hold should be comfortable. In any situation where exhaustion, rather than another competitor, may contribute to defeat, the vaulter who can conserve his energy with a short run and a low hold will turn a disadvantage into an advantage.

Establishing Check Marks

When measuring and establishing check marks, it is not necessary to work on the pole vault runway. It is almost impossible for an athlete to establish his check marks alone. It would be ideal if the coach could help each vaulter with this procedure at the beginning of the season. Remember to have the athlete carry the pole when establishing the marks. If the coach cannot assist the vaulter in establishing his marks, then vaulters should work in groups or pairs, with the experienced vaulters particularly helping the inexperienced ones.

A vaulter whose stride is so erratic that he cannot reach the takeoff point in the 4-6-10 stride pattern might drop down to a shorter approach, such as a 4-4-8 stride pattern.

Sometimes, however, the candidate's stride is so erratic that he simply cannot establish or meet his check marks. What does the coach do? He tries to help the man improve the evenness of his stride. A good drill for this is to set three low (30-inch) hurdles about 9 yards apart and have the vaulter practice hurdling over the side and over the top, not trying for hurdle style but for evenness of stride. It might be very helpful if all vaulters would try competing

in the hurdles. It is hard to tell whether hurdling serves as a particularly good conditioning exercise or whether the benefit comes from improved evenness of stride, but there seems to be a good correlation between excellence in hurdling and excellence in vaulting.

For check marks for the short approach, a single mark suffices. Begin by assuming that the approach will be 50 to 70 feet and should take 8 strides. We measure back 10 feet from the planting box (standing under the hand grip with the pole planted in the box) for the takeoff point. From there we measure back 50 feet (or however far the vaulter travels in his 8 strides) and locate at that point Check Mark 1. The vaulter goes through the short approach three times; average the distances for his measured short-run check mark.

As an athlete becomes more fit, the check marks tend to change. His stride may be as much as 6 inches longer at the end of the season, making his short approach about 4 feet longer. For that reason, check marks should be measured *every day* before practice or competition and changed as necessary. Other factors that influence the stride length, such as the condition of the track and the wind, also vary and need to be considered.

The early-speed approach applies the same principles in setting the marks and measuring the stride (Figure 15.1): From the starting point, two steps to Check Mark 1, then four strides at half speed to Check Mark 2. From Check Mark 2 to Mark 3, the vaulter is going at 7/8ths speed. From Check 3 to the takeoff, he goes another eight steps, at the same speed, then plants the pole. The big advantage of the early-speed approach for the last 100 feet of the approach run is

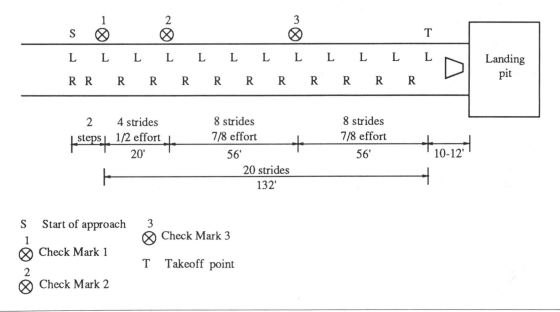

Figure 15.1 Early-speed approach.

that the vaulter may have better control of his speed for the pole plant and therefore have better control for the things that follow through the rest of the vault.

Training Considerations

What do you want the athlete to do, and how do you tell him? The schedule is a continuing line of communication between the teacher and the student, the coach and the athlete. The training schedule lists the fundamentals of pole vaulting and is a day-by-day plan for practicing those items. It also becomes a record of what the athlete did in practice and competition, a diary of his progress and accomplishments.

The patterns that make up the schedules may not all be the best possible for every given individual. However, they provide a plan to work from, a starting point. These schedules have been used successfully by other vaulters. The virtuoso, the truly gifted, may prefer his own adaptations.

The vaulter needs to learn to establish a practice routine. The first step in the routine is work on the short run. Using a run of 50 to 70 feet, the vaulter works at perfecting his technique. He should work on the fundamentals of the pole plant, the takeoff, and the lay back and wait. A general training routine might look like this:

1. Three times a long run (for the steps)
2. Three times a short run (also for the steps)
3. Work with the short run
   1 to 3 times working on the plant
   1 to 3 vaults working on laying back and waiting
   1 to 3 vaults working on coming off the pole

When working with a short run and low hold, the vaulter should use a pole that reacts like the one he uses for the long run and high hold. A long pole (such as 16 feet) does not react the same if a low hold (such as 11 or 12 feet) is used. Also, the vaulter may at times begin to get tired when he is vaulting. If the vaulter is tired and shows it, he should *stop vaulting* for that day. He runs the risk of emphasizing and setting bad habits of vaulting if he continues.

The Training Schedules: Special Fundamentals for the Pole Vault

4A. Short check mark.   A short approach is recommended for early season work because the vaulter can do more vaulting with a shorter run. It is also help-

ful in competitions that have bad weather conditions, such as rain or a strong headwind or crosswind.

An approach of 50 to 70 feet is used to reach the takeoff point, which is 9 feet or more from the vaulting box. The approach is 6 to 10 steps, with a 2-step approach to the one check mark (Figure 15.2). With the short approach, a low hold on the pole is used. It should be low enough for positive control in any conditions and high enough for respectable clearance. A handhold of 11'6'' will permit a clearance up to 13 to 14 feet. A shorter, calibrated pole should be used for this short-check, low-hold vaulting. When the vaulter can consistently clear 14 to 15 feet, he should acquire a pole with a lower calibration for the short-run practice and for bad weather competition.

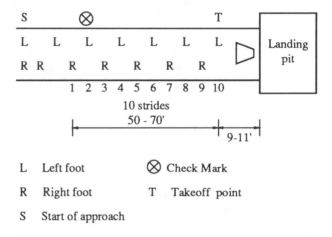

Figure 15.2 Short check mark.

The vaulter stands in a forward-leaning position, pole on the ground or at the ready. He concentrates on his total vault, then with a walking-step approach hits the check mark and gradually accelerates in 10 steps to the T, the takeoff point. When starting fall or winter training, the vaulter can work on the check mark on the runway or on the track. A right-handed vaulter carries the pole, hits the check with his left foot, then accelerates through 10 steps to the takeoff. His observer marks the T spot. This run is repeated two more times, and the T marks are averaged to give the length of the short check. This mark is then transferred to the runway. Ten feet (or the proper distance, according to his handhold) from the box, a T mark is placed. The vaulter can now practice his approaches on the runway.

4B. Long check mark.   The long run and regular high hold are for the time when the parts of the technique, fundamentals, and physical condition are approaching their peak. Having check marks is as important to the vaulter as navigation points are to the astronaut going to the moon.

The right-handed vaulter stands two steps behind Check Mark 1 (Figure 15.3). He stands with both feet together or the right foot forward, whichever is more comfortable for him. He should think through the entire technique of his vault before starting his approach. His second step is with his left foot hitting the first check mark.

Assuming that the stride of the vaulter, going at half-effort at this point, is 5 feet, he would then take 20 feet to reach Check Mark 2 with his left foot. This example is not intended to push the vaulter either to try for any particular stride length or to run through an approach when he is establishing his check marks. He should run through this part of the procedure from his starting point before Check 1 through Check 2 so he can establish the length of his stride and exactly what this distance should be. The vaulter takes three tries, then uses the average of the three results.

After he has established the distance between Checks 1 and 2, the vaulter works at measuring his stride at 3/4ths-effort so he can put in Check Mark 3, which will be 6 strides after Check 2. If his stride is 6 feet, for example, he will cover about 36 feet between Checks 2 and 3. The vaulter now returns to his starting point and runs through Checks 1 and 2 to see how close he comes to Check 3 in six additional strides. Again, the run is done three times, and an average distance is taken.

The next distance is to the T, or takeoff, 10 to 12 feet from the box. If the vaulter has become tired or erratic, the procedure is stopped until the next day.

To zero in on the takeoff, have the vaulter run the complete approach, marking the track or runway each of the three times. After checking through the first three check marks, the vaulter's intent is to reach a speed that might be called 7/8ths-effort while taking 10 strides to Point T. If a vaulter's stride at this speed is 7 feet, for example, this part of the approach will take 70 feet. He will measure it, taking three trials and averaging their lengths.

The technique of setting the check marks must be practiced and rechecked every vaulting day. Measuring is a must. The champion vaulter is not only an artist, he is a careful technician.

5A. The pole plant.
The second phase of the vault consists of planting the pole in the vaulting box. It should be accomplished in two or three counts. The vaulter should look at the box rather than the crossbar as he plants the pole. There are two planting techniques, the overhand and the straight underhand. Choosing one is simply a matter of personal preference. The plant should not be too hurried. The count or steps should be carefully practiced and a rhythm established.

The pole should be aligned straight into the box and along the vaulter's nose. If it is off to the side, it throws him out of line. The delivery of the pole into the box should be smooth and well timed. The vaulter should try to be rising over the last two steps leading into the plant, so he will seem to float off the ground rather than to be pushing off hard. The vaulter should

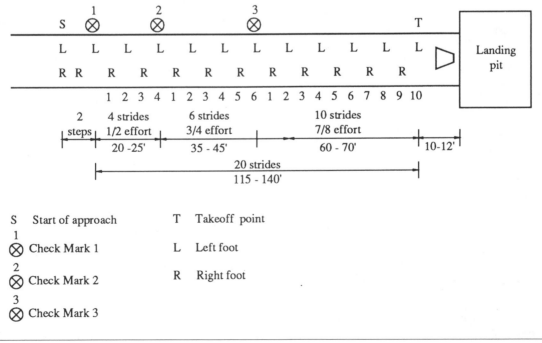

Figure 15.3 Long check mark.

not pull the pole toward himself during the plant or takeoff, but neither should he hold it out to the side because that would throw him off to the side during his rise.

5B. The takeoff.

The pole should be straight overhead during the takeoff, and the head should be hanging in a position about halfway between the hands as they grasp the pole. The lead knee should be quick in leaving the ground. The higher the hold on the pole and the straighter the angle between the pole and the ground, the higher the vaulter will go. The vaulter at this critical stage needs to be on guard against several faults:

- Being off to the side
- Settling down during the last several strides
- Having the arms too bent, which may result in their collapsing as he rises into the air

5C. The lay back and wait (hang).

The vaulter should not pull the pole toward him but should hold the pole away as he rises in order to get into the hang. As the pole bends, he should not sit down because this would put more pressure on the pole, a frequent cause of broken poles. Even if the sitting position does not break the pole, it requires greater exertion to get the man off the ground, which means that he could have gone higher and risen more easily had he not dropped into the sitting position.

6A. Pull when back is parallel and pole up.

A vaulter hangs as the pole continues to move upward. Then he tries to get his center of gravity up in the air. Too often a vaulter watches his feet. When he sees that they are high enough, he believes he is high enough. However, it is not the feet, but the center of gravity, that determines the height of the vault. He should think of the hips or the waist as rising to crossbar height before starting the turn. If he gets the center of gravity up, good things will happen in the pole vault.

6B. The turn and rise.

If the turn comes too soon, the vaulter may stall the pole. He has to stay behind the pole throughout the bend. The action is like simultaneously performing a curl with the right hand and a press with the left hand. When the hips and the center of gravity are at the height of the crossbar and the bottom of the pole is perpendicular to the ground, then the vaulter should pull and turn. This will cause the pole to straighten and the vaulter to rotate around his center of gravity. The lead foot continues up as the turn is completed.

6C. Off the pole.

This is the final stage of the vault, taking place as the hands are rising and the vaulter's body is clearing the crossbar. The vaulter needs to learn to use his feet and legs to clear the upper body, leaving only the problem of a safe landing, which is no problem if a good landing pad is used.

9A. Short-run, low-hold form work.

Using the short approach, the vaulter works on the aspects of form listed by the letters in Item 6 on the training sheet. Many more productive vaults can be made with a short approach than with the long run.

9B. Long-run form work.

This work is done as in Item 9A, practicing on technique, fundamentals, or individual needs, using the full approach with all checks.

10B. Trials.

Trials are meant to give progress reports as well as to be learning situations. The starting level of the competition should be within the capability of the weakest or youngest vaulter. The vaulters should rotate turns, with the crossbar going up or down according to the talent of each vaulter.

10B(1). Up or down 6 inches on a make or a miss.

Move the bar up if the height is cleared and lower the bar if the height is missed. Assume that Vaulter A starts at 12'0" and misses. His next jump is at 11'6". Vaulter B starts at 13'0" (in squad rotation, not according to the height being attempted) and clears it, so his next height will be 13'6". Vaulter A clears 11'6" on his next attempt, so he goes back up to 12'0".

10B(2). Two jumps at 4 inches above average best.

When the vaulters acquire some consistency, which usually takes about 6 weeks, they then occasionally practice above the season's average best mark. Assume that Vaulter B reaches 15'3" and is given two attempts to make the height. He does not get a third attempt, for psychological reasons: Three misses would put him out of the competition, and we prefer that he quit while feeling that he might have made it on that third jump.

10B(3). Establish starting height for good or bad day.

The starting height that the vaulter can use with assurance should be established according to the runway, the weather, and the vaulter's ability. The vaulters should jump in rotation and move the standards to their capability.

11. Higher grip and check mark adjustment.

Some vaulters too easily change their holds. The height of the vaulter's hold should not change until he has mastered the technique to a near-maximum height. The vaulter should especially not vary his hold out of hope or panic in competition. When the vaulter is ready, then he should start with a 3- to 6-inch (possibly as much as 12-inch) increase in the handhold. His routine must be reestablished, including the variations in check marks, the changes in timing to a longer hang, and possibly the delayed releases of the pole's stored energy at the turn and the off-the-pole phases of the vault. Those changes may take several vaulting sessions. They should start with no crossbar, working through to a successful simulated competition.

16. Easy apparatus or acrobatics.   The apparatus room and gymnastic equipment offer great opportunity for variation and pleasant exercise. Vaulting skills can be related to this work, but it is most important that the athlete acquire mastery of his bodily movements. Trampoline activities can be useful for developing body control, but great care should be taken for safety reasons.

20. Work on second event.   The secondary event for the pole vaulter may be for competitive pleasure, conditioning, or team points. Temperament is an ingredient necessary to athletic or any other success. Real champions make it work for them. An athlete should have a secondary event for pleasure as well as self-mastery. The champions do, the losers do not.

Interpretation of Week 1 of the Training Schedules

This is a translation of the first week of training from the vaulting schedules at the end of this chapter. The numbers on the schedule sheets represent the fundamentals of pole vaulting.

Monday: The class or squad meets for the first time. Equipment is discussed, procedures are explained, goals are recommended for individuals, and such things as hard and easy days with test efforts every 7, 10, or 14 days are explained.

Tuesday: (1A) Warm-up with jogging, relay routine, stretching, and flexibility exercises.
(14F) *High knee*, slow running, almost in place, bringing the knees about hip high. Go for 10 meters, then walk for 10m. This is followed by *fast leg*, barely lifting the feet off the ground, gradually increasing the cadence, and bouncing the ball of each foot off the surface in cadence with a short, very rapid arm action. Go about 10m, then rest and repeat the high knee, then the fast leg, for 50 to 100m.
(16) Apparatus work, such as ropes, rings, parallel bars, and other apparatus activities.
(14D) Run 50m, walk 50m to recover, then repeat until 400 to 800m or more have been covered. This is a conditioning activity.

Wednesday: (1A) Warm-up.
(17) Run, carrying the pole. This is for conditioning and learning that the vaulting pole is the vaulter's best friend.
(14B) Set up three low hurdles about 7 to 9 meters apart. This exercise is for evenness of stride.
Thursday: (3) Weight lifting. Most athletes work out weight-training routines of their own. There are suggested exercises in chapter 2.
Friday: (1A) Warm-up.
(14A) Wind sprints, starting slowly, gradually increasing the speed for about 50m, then gradually decreasing to a jog and recovering for 50m. Cover 400 to 800m.
(17) See Wednesday explanation.
(4A) Short check mark drill of 50 to 70 feet. This is explained in the section on pole vaulting fundamentals.
(6A) Another pole vaulting fundamental, explained in the section on fundamentals.
(14D) See Tuesday explanation.
Saturday: (1A) Warm-up.
(3) Weight training.
(17) Running with the pole.
Sunday: (16) See Tuesday explanation.

References

1. Vitaly Petrov & Sergei Bubka. (1985). Pole vault clinic (after the lecture). *Track and Field Quarterly Review*, **85**(4), 33.
2. Rick Attig. (1987). Understanding pole vault mechanics. *Track and Field Quarterly Review*, **87**(4), 25-32.
3. J. Nikolov. (1986). The structure of the pole vault run-up. *Track Technique*, **94**, 3012.
4. J. Nikolov. (1987). The contemporary take-off. *Track Technique*, **98**, 3124-3125.
5. Andrzej Krzesinski. (1983). Mt. SAC Relays pole vault clinic. *Track Technique*, **86**, 2734-2739.
6. Maurice Houvion. (1986). Perfect vaulting technique. *Track Technique*, **95**, 3027-3036. [Very valuable.]
7. V. Jagodin, V. Kurbatov, & J. Volkov. (1981). Systematic development of pole vaulters. In Jess Jarver (Ed.), *The jumps* (2nd ed., pp. 72-74). Los Altos, CA: Tafnews.
8. Derek Boosey. (1980). *The jumps: Conditioning and technical training*. West Heidelberg, Victoria, Australia: Beatrice.
9. V. Jagodin & V. Tshunganov. (1981). Periodization in pole vault training. In Jess Jarver

(Ed.), *The jumps* (2nd ed., pp. 81-82). Los Altos, CA: Tafnews.

10. William H. Freeman. (1989). *Peak when it counts: Periodization for the American track coach.* Los Altos, CA: Tafnews.

11. Andrzej Krzesinski. (1983). Pole vault: The total program. *Track Technique*, **84**, 2679-2682.

Additional Readings

Ashbrook, Dan. (1984). Coaching the beginning pole vaulter. *Track Technique*, **89**, 2827, 2830.

Bubka, Sergei. (1989). My training. *Track Technique*, **108**, 3456.

Cox, Don. (1984). Mechanics of the pole vault. *Track and Field Quarterly Review*, **84**(4), 29-32.

Ganslen, Richard. (1980). *Mechanics of the pole vault* (9th ed.). Published by the author.

Goss, Marshall. (1984). The beginning pole vaulter's start and problem-solving. *Track and Field Quarterly Review*, **84**(4), 33-35.

Hay, James G. (1988). The approach run in the pole vault. *Track Technique*, **106**, 3376-3377, 3396.

Houvion, M. Maurice. (1982). The preparation of the pole vaulter for advanced levels: 6 meters in 2000. *Track and Field Quarterly Review*, **82**(4), 38-41.

Jarver, Jess (Ed.) (1988). *The jumps: Contemporary theory, technique and training* (3rd ed.). Los Altos, CA: Tafnews.

Knapp, Donald. (1983). Drills to improve and simplify the pole vault. *Track Technique*, **85**, 2699-2701.

Kochel, Guy. (1989). Pole vaulting. In Vern Gambetta (Ed.), *The Athletics Congress's track and field coaching manual* (2nd ed., pp. 117-121). Champaign, IL: Human Kinetics.

Krzesinski, Andrzej. (1981). My views on pole vaulting. *Track and Field Quarterly Review*, **81**(4), 42-43.

Kutman, M. (1980). Conditioning for pole vaulters. *Track and Field Quarterly Review*, **80**(4), 50-51.

Kutman, M. (1981). Planning to pole vault training. *Track and Field Quarterly Review*, **81**(4), 47-48.

McGinnis, Peter M. (1986). General pole vault findings: USOC/TAC Elite Athlete Projects. *Track Technique*, **94**, 2994-2997.

McGinnis, Peter. (1989). Pete's pointers for perfect pole vaulting. *Track Technique*, **109**, 3472-3474.

Miller, Steve. (1981). Training program for the prep pole vaulter. *Track and Field Quarterly Review*, **81**(4), 49-50.

Myers, Bob. (1989). Training for the jumps and multi-events. *Track Technique*, **108**, 3449-3452; **109**, 3492-3493.

Paar, Colin. (1988). An analysis of Pierre Quinon's vault technique. *Track Technique*, **104**, 3326-3327.

Smith, Steve. (1982). Pole vault. *Track and Field Quarterly Review*, **82**(4), 44-45.

Pole Vault Training Schedule

ATHLETE _____

1. Warm-up
   A. Jog 1-2 laps with relay pass, in 2s or 3s
   B. Hendricks Park
   C. Golf course
   D. Steps
   E. Vaulting routine
2. Fartlek
   A. Varied pace   B. Slow, steady pace
3. Weights and jogging
4. Check mark
   A. Short   B. Long
5. A. Pole plant
   B. Takeoff UP
   C. Lay back & wait (hang)
   D.
6. A. Pull when back parallel & pole up
   B. Turn & rise, lead foot up
   C. Off the pole
   D.
7. Team meeting
8. Special
   A. Sauna   C. Hill
   B. Swim

9. A. Short-run, low-hold form work
   B. Long-run form work
   C.
10. Progress assessment
    A. Meet   C. Simulation
    B. Trial   D. Control test
       (1) up or down 6" on make or miss
       (2) 2 jumps at 4" above average best
       (3) establish starting height, good or bad
           day
11. Higher grip & check mark adjustment
12. With Coach
    A. (name)
    B. Leader
14. A. Wind sprints (1) straight (2) curve
    B. Hurdle drill: 3 LH, 7-9m apart
    C. Spring & bound
    D. Alternate run & jog, at least 800m
    E. Starts (1) 100 (2)
    F. High knee (slow) & fast leg
15. Plyometrics
    A. Jumps (1) 1 leg (2) both legs (3)
    B. Bounding (1) 1 leg (2) both legs (3)
    C.

16. Easy apparatus or acrobatics
17. Run with the pole 50m, walk 100m,
    go 400m
18.
19.
20. Work on second event
21. Visual aids
    A. Videotape   C. Photos
    B. Film
       (1) record performance (2) study
30. Experimental work

DATE September/October

M	Class or squad organization
Tu	1A—14F—16—14D
W	1A—17—14B
Th	3
F	1A—14A—17—4A—6A—14D
Sa	1A—3—17
Su	16
M	(3x) (3x) (3x) 1A—4A—5A—6A—9A—14A
Tu	1A—3—17
W	(2x) (2x) 7—1A—4B—4A—9A—14A
Th	1A—3—14D
F	(2x) (2x) (2x) 1A—4B—4A—5A—9A—14A
Sa	3
Su	3—16
M	(3x) (2x) 1A—4B—4A—6B—14B—14A
Tu	1A—3—17
W	(2x) (2x) (2x) 1A—4A—4B—5A—5B—9A—14B
Th	1A—3—1C
F	(2x) (2x) 1A—4A—4B—9A—17
Sa	3
Su	3—14B
M	(2x) (2x) (2x) 1A—17—4A—4B—5A—6B—9A—14D
Tu	3—14D
W	(2x) 1A—17—4A—4B—9A—7
Th	1A—3—1C
F	1A—4A—4B—10B(1)—14A
Sa	3
Su	3

DATE October/November

M	1A—14F—17—16
Tu	3—14B—1C
W	(3x) 1A—4B—14C—16
Th	(2x) (2x) 1A—4A—4B—5B—14A—8B
F	1A—3—17
Sa	(2x) (2x) 1A—4B—5A—6B—14B
Su	1B
M	(3x) (2x) (2x) 1A—17—4A—5A—6C—14A
Tu	1A—3 or 1C
W	(2x) 1A—4A—5B—5C—9A—14D
Th	1A—14B
F	3—4B—5C—9A—14D
Sa	3
Su	Jog
M	1A—14B—4A—4B—5C—9B—1B
Tu	1A—1C
W	3—5B—5C—9A—1B or 1C
Th	3—8A
F	1A—10B(1)—10B(2)—14B
Sa	3
Su	
M	1A—14F—4B—6A—6C—9B—2B
Tu	3—8A
W	7—1A—4A—4B—5A—9A—2B
Th	3—8A or B
F	1A—5A—10B(1)—10B(2)—14B
Sa	3
Su	

DATE January

M	(3x) (3x) Register—squad meet—4A—4B—14D
Tu	3
W	1A—14F—16 or 4A—9A—14A
Th	(3x) 7—3
F	(3x) 1A—1E—4B—20—14A
Sa	16
Su	Jog
M	(2-3x) (2-3x) (2-3x) 1A—4A—4B—5A—9A—14D
Tu	3—16
W	(2-3x) (2-3x) 1A—4A—4B—1C(8C) or 1D
Th	3
F	1A—14F—4B—1E—14D
Sa	16 or 3
Su	Jog
M	(2-3x) (2-3x) (2-3x) 1A—14F—16—4B—4A—5B—9—14A
Tu	3—8A or B
W	(2-3x) 1A—4B—1C(8C)
Th	3—1B
F	1A—4B—10B(1)—10B(2)
Sa	3 or form work
Su	Jog
M	(2-3x) (2-3x) 1A—14F—6—4B—4A
Tu	3—8A or B or sun
W	7—1B—5A—6C—1C(8C)
Th	3
F	1B—gear ready
Sa	10A indoors
Su	Jog

DATE February

M	1A—17—9A—4D—jog
Tu	3—8A
W	7—1A—10B—9A—14A
Th	3—8B
F	1A—4A—4B—5C—6A—14D
Sa	3—8A or B
Su	Jog
M	1A—14F—9B—9A—14A
Tu	1A—16—8A or B
W	1A—1E—4B—6C—9A—14A
Th	1A—16
F	1A—10B(1)—10B(2)—14B—14A—jog
Sa	3—1B
Su	Jog
M	1A—4B—6A—14B—17
Tu	16—8A or B
W	1A—17—12—4A—5C—6C—17
Th	3—16
F	1A—4B—6B—9A—14B
Sa	3—14A
Su	Jog
M	1A—4B—5B—6A—9A—14C
Tu	3 or 16
W	1A—10B(1)—10B(2)—14A
Th	1A—16—8A or B
F	1A—4A—4B—5B—9B—14B
Sa	1B or 1C
Su	Jog

DATE March

M	1A—17—1E—5A—9B—14B
Tu	3—16
W	1A—1E—10B(1)—10B(2)—9A—5B—jog
Th	1A—16—14A
F	1A—1E—6B—10—14A
Sa	3—1B or 1C—8A or B
Su	
M	1A—1E—17
Tu	1A—4B—5A—5B—10B(2)
W	1A—gear ready or 3—14A
Th	Travel—1A—14F—4A—4B
F	Meet routine
Sa	Travel home
Su	Loosen up at 1 p.m.—14D
M	7—1A—14A
Tu	1A—4A—4B—9B—14A
W	16
Th	1A—4B—9B—14D
F	Gear ready
Sa	Relay meet
Su	Loosen up at 1 p.m.
M	1A—17—4B—5A—9B—14B
Tu	3—14A
W	1A—1E—9B—10B(2)
Th	16
F	Gear ready
Sa	Travel to meet—10A
Su	Loosen up

DATE April

M		1A—4A—6B—5A—9A—14A (2x / 2-4x)
Tu		1A—3
W		7—1A—4—6A—10B(2)—9A—14B
Th		3—16
F		Meet preparation
Sa		Premeet—compete—after-meet
Su		3 or 1C
M		1A—4—5A—5C—9A—14A (3x / 3x)
Tu		3—8A or B
W		7—1A—4B—10B(1)—9A—14B (3x)
Th		Jog—8A or B
F		Light
Sa		Meet routine
Su		16
M		1A or 17—4B—5A—5C—9A—14C
Tu		1A—14F—14B
W		1A—4B—10B—9A—14D
Th		3—8B—14A grass
F		Light
Sa		Dual meet
Su		1A—11—9B
M		17—16—8A or B
Tu		1A—11—10B—9A—9B
W		3—16—8A or B
Th		1A—1E—11—9B—9A
F		Light
Sa		Compete
Su		1A—recheck grip—11

DATE May

Day	a.m.	p.m.
M	Jog	1A—4B—5A—5C—9A—14B (3x / 3x / 3-6x)
Tu	Jog	3
W	Jog	7—1A—1E—10B(2)—14A(1)
Th	Jog	Light
F		Light
Sa		Be good, be tough, be relaxed / Traditional meet
Su		Pole plant and swing
M		14D—easy 14B
Tu		1A—1E—10B—9A—14F
W		7—1C or grass run
Th		1A—4A—4B—5A—14B (2x 2x 2x)
F		Light
Sa		Dual meet
Su		Grass run
M		1A—4B—5A—5C—9A or B—14C (3x 3x 3-6x)
Tu		3 and light
W		1A—4B—5B—10B(2)
Th		Light
F		Light
Sa		Championship
Su		Grass run
M		
Tu		
W		
Th		
F		
Sa		
Su		

CHAPTER 16	# The Shot Put

Some of the best potential throwers never enjoy the fierce, lonely effort that is the reward for the months and years of preparation, culminating in the explosion that leads to an Olympic gold medal. Football's demands of time and organization consume the best of the physical giants who might otherwise be a Neil Steinhauer, an Al Feuerbach, or a Randy Barnes. Also, many of the team-sport giants may not be psychologically equipped to face the possibility of having their abilities measured with the absolute objectivity of the individual sport.

The shot put is traditionally considered the strong athlete's event in track and field. Collegiate putters are typically big and strong. The bigger and stronger they are, the more likely they are to be successful. This is not as strictly the case with high school shot-putters. Because the high school shot is only 12 pounds for boys and 8 pounds for girls, a smaller athlete who is fast and explosive can compete with the larger athlete at that level of competition. While the college women's shot weight increases only to 4 kilograms (8.8 pounds), the men's weight rises to 16 pounds, a significant increase.

Training Theory for the Shot Put

Spectators think of the shot as a very simple event: The biggest, strongest person wins. However, the technique of putting, as well as the training that prepares an athlete for a supreme effort, is really quite complex. Yet, the basic factors that result in the length of a throw are quite simple:[1]

- release velocity
- angle of release
- height of release

This means that the thrower must develop technique, but the speed-strength factor is extremely important. A thrower must be quick, explosive in movement to accelerate the shot rapidly to an optimal release speed.

The proportionate contributions of the body's muscle groups to a shot put are

- 50% legs,
- 30% trunk, and
- 20% arms.

We make this point to emphasize the importance of proper use of the lower body during the throw. Perhaps the most common fault is "arm throwing," relying on arm strength alone to propel the shot. A throw comes 80% from the legs and trunk.

Leg power is the key to success. Throw from the ground up. Lead the throw with the knees and hips. Energy flows from legs, hips to shoulders, arm and implement in a linked series. Rotation of the right foot-knee-hip is *fundamental* to all throws. . . . The shot is thrown from the *jerk* position—knees bent equally, weight shifting from right to left over the front (left) leg. The left leg exerts most of the explosive power.[2]

Although absolute strength is important, it is not the primary goal. It is useful only as long as it contributes to speed-strength. Specific strength is more important because, although "super strength did not always win, it was explosive strength that produced champions."[3] Explosive strength is developed by using Olympic-style weight lifting (not power lifting) and plyometric jumping exercises.

Better marks in the vertical jump, standing long jump, and 20-meter dash correlate to better performances in the shot put.[4] The most common lifts used by putters are bench press, snatch, power clean, and squat.[5]

Most putters use one of two styles, the glide (O'Brien) or the spin.[6] The optimal release angle, regardless of style, is about 40 to 42 degrees.[7] Each style has its strengths and weaknesses. Although the spin makes higher release velocities possible, it is also less stable, which can result in a poorer release position. Women throwers are still less technically proficient than male throwers,[8] though that may result from the limited depth of competition to date. Varied weight implements (heavier and lighter) can be used to improve technique and release velocity, but there is no general agreement on principles for their use.[9,10] The general trend in training in all events, including the throws, is toward greater quality rather than greater quantity.[11]

A brief word concerning the equipment is necessary because it can affect the distance of the put, though not to the extent possible with different discuses or javelins. The athlete has the choice of iron, steel, or brass instruments. Brass is the smallest shot, but it is not popular with the better putters. Shotputters want the largest legal implement they can get. This gives them greater leverage to exert while throwing. Some high school throwers have gone so far as to use the larger indoor shot outdoors, when it has been allowed. However, a birdshot-filled instrument is not as good as one of solid metal or of rubber-covered solid metal because it gives the effect of trying to throw a beanbag.

Technique of the Shot Put

The shot is held at the base of the fingers, where the pads are at the top of the palm. It is held by four fingers (three fingers and the thumb, with the little finger often curled under). Some putters try to hold the shot on the fingers only, but few are strong enough to keep it there, and throwing it that way can hurt the arm all the way to the elbow. The putter should squeeze the shot a bit, helping to keep better control. The elbow should be parallel to the ground and kept behind the shot at all times. The hand might be turned out to keep the elbow in a good position.

As we said, two styles of throwing are now popular, the glide and the spin. We will look first at a glide thrower who throws with the right hand. He or she begins crouched at the rear of the circle, facing away from the direction of the throw. The shot is cradled in the hand and held alongside the neck at the chin. The athlete's weight is on the right foot, with the left foot reaching back a bit, in preparation for the movement across the ring.

The athlete begins by raising the left hand or extending it to the rear of the circle. This is primarily a matter of attaining balance. The athlete must be in a good state of balance before beginning the movement across the circle.

When the movement begins, the throwing elbow is raised to the side until the arm is parallel to the ground. From this position the putter carries the shot to the front of the ring to add speed to its movement. In the process of crossing the ring, the athlete lifts, turns, pushes the shot upward, and gives a final flip of the wrist to impart the last bit of momentum to the shot as it leaves the hand.

In the spin (discus-turn) technique, the thrower starts in the rear of the circle with the feet in the position for starting a discus throw. The movements are the same as for the discus, except that the shot is carried next to the neck at the jaw, just as in the glide technique. The release is essentially the same for both styles.

The four stages of the shot-putting action are the move to the center of the circle; the lift, changing the direction of the shot; beginning to turn toward the direction of the put; and pushing the shot outward until it leaves the hand. These stages are not as separate as the description may suggest. The movement is a continuous, uninterrupted action. According to the laws of physics, the shot weighs less when it is moving, as long as it is pushed along the same line of travel it is already following.

The Shot Put Routine

The routine is designed to give the shot-putter the feel of what he or she should be doing when going through the entire putting action. It consists of two groups of exercises, the first group performed in the front area of the circle and the other involving crossing the ring. These exercises should help the putter review the basics of the event, progressing in effort from easy to medium to hard. Although the description is for the glide style, it is performed in the same manner by spin throwers.

The first part of the routine is done with the putter in the front of the circle. Actually, this means that the thrower begins at the start of the final phase of the put, with the body over a flexed right leg and the left leg extended back to the toeboard. This part of the exercise is called the *stand*. The shot is held while the athlete goes through the action of the lift and turn, but with one difference: The athlete does not push the shot. The arm goes out to the side, just as though the shot were to be pushed, but the hand stays at the neck area. The shot is allowed to fall from the hand, but it travels only as far as the force of the body, with absolutely no arm action, causes it to go.

The second drill repeats the first one, except that the hand follows (but does not push) the shot as it leaves the hand. The third drill does involve pushing the shot as it leaves, but it is not a hard push. The last standing drill has the athlete lifting, turning, and pushing hard.

The second part of the routine is done by crossing the ring, using the full action of throwing. When crossing the ring in the routine, the thrower should start slow and finish fast. The complete crossing drill is to give the feel of the event rather than to work on the speed of the crossing. The first drill is similar to the second drill from a stand. The athlete crosses the circle, lifts, turns, and lets the shot leave the hand, following it with the hand but not pushing it.

The second, third, and fourth drills with the ring crossing involve pushing the shot at the completion of the action. The second drill has the putter make a medium-effort push. The third drill makes a hard-effort push. On the fourth drill, the athlete tries to explode, unleashing all of his or her force into the put. At all times the feet should be spread enough for the athlete to get the hips into the throw.

Some throwers have worked on the final push of the throwing arm by trying to develop a punching action. One exercise used for this action has been to work at hitting a punching bag while on one's knees, which requires the thrower to push upward at about the angle of the putting action (40 to 42 degrees).

Training Considerations

For the purposes of records, the condensed, coded training sheet shown for the shot put is more practical than one page for every day of training or even every week. Though preparing a written workout may be a bit easier, it can also be sloppier in thought. The workout sheet lists the exercises considered fundamental to training for the shot put. Because all the exercises are listed on the sheet, the coach or teacher is less likely to forget to assign vital portions of the training regime.

The shot put training schedules are organized so that either an individual or a group, such as the members of a physical education class, can devote a unit of 10 weeks to one or more events. The schedule is a guide, not a dictum.

The routines are introduced and repeated regularly. Technique is introduced early in the schedule, and those points that are most basic to the event are repeated with the greatest frequency. Also included are agility drills, speed work, and possibly a secondary event. The program moves from the simple to the more difficult, with a gradual increase in the planned distance of the throws, so the best technique can be acquired as physical condition and strength improve. The schedules are arranged so that 1 month's record is available. There are three particular values to this system:

- A complete "book" may be kept on the athlete.
- Comparisons may be made to previous athletes.
- No fundamentals are overlooked (probably the most important value).

The athlete and the coach should try to follow patterns that have been successful. This is one reason for recording and saving the schedule sheets. In training for the technique of the put, it is best to work on only one technical element or phase of the put at a time. Gradually, multiple elements or phases can be put together into the complete put. On the schedule sheet, those elements of the put are listed by letters under Item 6. This is primarily to avoid confusion and frustration. We have not explained the numbered fundamentals as in the other chapters because they have already been discussed elsewhere in the chapter.

On the fartlek running, we want the putters to be able to run steadily for at least 20 minutes. Fartlek running is good for the cardiovascular system, and a steady run of at least 20 minutes is necessary to gain much cardiovascular benefit from such a run.

The athletes need to use weight-training activities that develop enough body mass for successful putting. Although we suggest training exercises, the athletes should not rigidly follow someone else's weight-training schedule. Each athlete basically needs to develop his or her own program of weight-training activities, though younger athletes need considerable (careful) guidance.

This is in keeping with our belief that the athlete should not be overcoached. By the time athletes are collegians, they should have enough background to know fairly well what activities of this nature are most beneficial for them, if they have been very successful putters. The weight lifters should try to arrange their schedules so they can do their lifting activities together, as they will pick up ideas from each other.

Weight training definitely helps, though it can be overdone. The ultimate object is feet thrown, not pounds lifted. Weight training is done three times a week in the fall, going to two to three sessions per week in the winter, with one (sometimes two) sessions per week in the spring (Tuesday, for a Saturday meet).

The hard-easy schedule is followed to some degree, though not as closely as with running activities. The pattern also varies according to the time of year. For example, in January the putter might go hard on alternating days, such as Monday, Wednesday, and Friday. In February or early March, preparation for future 2-day meets begins. Because the athlete will have to qualify on one day, then throw again the next day in finals, this sequence is simulated in practice. The thrower would go hard on both Monday and Tuesday, with other hard days on Thursday and Saturday. In preparing for a big meet, the thrower might go hard on Monday and Tuesday, then go light until the meet, either on Friday for trials or on Saturday for a 1-day meet.

References

1. Bill Black. (1987). The scientific bases of training for the shot put. *Track and Field Quarterly Review*, **87**(3), 14-17.
2. Harmon Brown. (1985). Some principles of throwing. *Track Technique*, **93**, 2955.
3. George Dunn. (1987). Current trends in shot put training. *Track Technique*, **98**, 3118-3123.
4. Black, *supra* note 1, p. 15.
5. Bogdan Poprawski. (1988). Aspects of strength, power and speed in shot put training. *New Studies in Athletics*, **3**(1), 89-93.
6. John Kenneson. (1987). Rotary shot putting. *Track and Field Quarterly Review*, **87**(3), 5-6.
7. Ken Shannon. (1988). Fundamentals for the throws. *Track and Field Quarterly Review*, **88**(3), 13-14.
8. Max Jones. (1988). Why can't a woman be more like a man? *Track Technique*, **104**, 3331.
9. Ralf Uebel. (1986). The value of different weighted shots in the practice and teaching of shot putters. *Track and Field Quarterly Review*, **86**(1), 18-21.
10. L.A. Vasiliyev. (1985). Varied-weight shots in specific power development. In Jess Jarver (Ed.), *The throws: Contemporary theory, technique and training* (3rd ed., pp. 68-70). Los Altos, CA: Tafnews.
11. Peter Tschiene. (1988). The throwing events: Recent trends in technique and training. *New Studies in Athletics*, **3**(1), 7-17.

Additional Readings

Feuerbach, Al. (1987). Teaching the shot put. *Track and Field Quarterly Review*, **87**(3), 4.

Freeman, William H. (1989). Periodized training for throwers. In *Peak when it counts: Periodization of training for American coaches*. Los Altos, CA: Tafnews.

Jarver, Jess (Ed.) (1985). *The throws: Contemporary theory, technique and training* (3rd ed.). Los Altos, CA: Tafnews.

Jones, Max. (1986). Rotational shot technique. *Track Technique*, **97**, 3096-3097.

Marks, Richard. (1985). Specialized strength and technique training for shot and discus. *Track Technique*, **91**, 2898-2899.

Miller, Brian P. (1985). Psychological factors in competitive throwing. *Track and Field Quarterly Review*, **85**(1), 40-44.

Santos, Jim. (1987). Increasing throwing speed through upper body plyometrics. *Track and Field Quarterly Review*, **87**(3), 29-33.

Sing, Robert O. (1986). Psychological concerns in the throwing events. *Track Technique*, **96**, 3069-3070.

Venegas, Art. (1987). Rotational shot put technique. *Track and Field Quarterly Review*, **87**(3), 7-13.

Shot Put Training Schedule

ATHLETE _____

1. Warm-up
   A. Jog 1-2 laps, easy stretching
   B. Hendricks Park
   C. Golf course
2. Fartlek
   A. Varied pace   B. Slow, steady pace
3. Weights and resistance activities
4. Routine
   A. Stand   B. Crossing
      (1) lift (2) follow (3) push
5. Effort
   A. Stand   B. Crossing
      (1) easy (2) medium (3) hard
6. Technique
   A. Stand, shot almost in palm
   B. Crossing, have speed under control
      (1) comfortable knee bend
      (2) hip push from cocked position
      (3) left arm in position, pull for torque
      (4) eye on ground or target
      (5) explode on every 3rd or 4th throw
      (6) lift well before turn
      (7) squeeze the shot
      (8) right foot in center of ring
      (9) target for 3/4 to 7/8 effort
      (10) left foot timing & position
      (11) reach on put & lean into it

7. Team meeting
8. Special
   A. Sauna   C. Hill
   B. Swim
9. Alternate stand-step-crossing routine
   (same letters/numbers as #6)
10. Progress assessment
    A. Meet   C. Simulation
    B. Trial   D. Control test
11. Cross ring easy; feeling of exploding;
    start slow, finish fast
12. With Coach
    A. (name)
    B. Leader
14. A. Wind sprints (1) straight (2) curve
    B. Hurdle drill: 3 LH, 7-9m apart
    C. Spring & bound
    D. Alternate run & jog, at least 800m
    E. Starts, go 20-25m
    F. High knee (slow) & fast leg
15. Plyometrics
    A. Jumps (1) 1 leg (2) both legs (3)
    B. Bounding (1) 1 leg (2) both legs (3)
    C.

16. Tumbling activities
17. Have feeling of low & relaxed;
    no strain at back or in crossing
18. A. Work on staying in the ring
    B. Lift-turn
19. Ring crossing, feet not too far spread;
    go only as fast as you can control
    (same letters/numbers as #6)
20. Work on second event
21. Visual aids
    A. Videotape   C. Photos
    B. Film
       (1) record performance (2) study
30. Experimental work

DATE September/October

M	Organization—equipment—lockers
Tu	Use of equipment—safety—training times
W	1A—6A(1)—6A(2)—7—14D
Th	(10 a.m.)21A—3
F	1A—6A(1)—6A(3)—8C—14D
Sa	3
Su	3—14A—14D or recreation
M	1A—6A(1)—6B(1)—6A(2)—6B(2)—14A
Tu	7—5A(1,2,3)—3—14A
W	1A—6A(3)—6B(3)—17
Th	3—8B or 8C
F	1A—6B(6)—11—14F
Sa	3—14B—14D
Su	Recreation
M	1A—6A(4)—6B(4)—6A(11)—6B(11)—14A
Tu	3—14D
W	1A—6A(4)—6B(4)—6A(11)—6B(11)—6B(8)—1A
Th	3—14D
F	1A—6A(1)—6B(1)—6A(11)—6B(11)—6B(8)
Sa	3—14D
Su	Recreation
M	1A—6A(11)—6B(11)—6A(1)—6B(1)—17—20
Tu	3—14D
W	1A—6A(2)—6B(2)—6A(4)—6B(4)—14E
Th	3—14D
F	1A—10B—9A(8)
Sa	3—14D
Su	Recreation

DATE October/November

M	1A—3
Tu	1A—6A(1)—6B(1)—6B(2)—9A,B(1)—20
W	3—14D
Th	1A—6A(1)—6B(1)—9A,B(8)—14D
F	3
Sa	
Su	
M	1A—3
Tu	1A—6A(3)—6B(3)—9—14A
W	3—20
Th	1A—4 (for distance)—6A(5)—6B(5)—9A,B(5)—14D
F	1A—3
Sa	
Su	
M	1A—3—14D or 20
Tu	1A—5A(4)—9A,B(4)—14A
W	1A—3
Th	1A—5A(4)—9A,B(4)—17—14D
F	1A—3
Sa	
Su	
M	1A—3
Tu	1A—14D—6A(6)—6B(6)—9A,B(6)—17—14A
W	1A—3—14D
Th	1A—14A—6A(6)—6B(6)—9A,B(6)—11—1A
F	1A—3—14D
Sa	1A—6A(8)—6B(8)—9A,B(8)—11—14A
Su	

DATE November/December

M	1A—14B—6A(6)—6B(6)—9A,B(6)—17
Tu	1A—3—14D
W	1A—14A—6A(6)—6B(6)—9A,B(6)—11
Th	1A—3—14A
F	1A—3—6A(8)—6B(8)—9A,B(8)—11
Sa	
Su	
M	3 (easy and very light)
Tu	6 (form)
W	1A—14A
Th	Light
F	10B—test for distance
Sa	
Su	
M	
Tu	
W	
Th	
F	
Sa	
Su	
M	
Tu	
W	
Th	
F	
Sa	
Su	

DATE January

M	Class or squad organization—3—5A
Tu	1A—5A(1,2,3)[3-6x]—9A,B(1)—17—14A
W	3
Th	7[6-10x]—6B(2)[3-6x]—9A,B(2)—14A
F	3
Sa	1A[6-10x]—6B(5)[2-4x]—9A,B(5)
Su	Recreation
M	3—14B
Tu	1A—5A(1,2,3)[6-10x]—5B(1,2,3)[3-6x]—6B(6)—9A,B(5)—14D
W	3
Th	1A—5B(1,2,3)[6-10x]—6B(6)[3-6x]—9A,B(6)—14A
F	3
Sa	10B(record)—9B(7)—14D
Su	Recreation
M	3—14E—14D
Tu	1A—5A(1,2,3)[6-10x]—6A,B(8)[3-6x]—9A,B(8)—14D
W	3
Th	1A—5B(1,2,3)[6-10x]—6A,B(4)[3-6x]—9A,B(4)—14D
F	3
Sa	1A—5B(1,2,3)[6-10x]—6A(6)[3-6x]—9A,B(6)—19
Su	
M	3
Tu	1A—8A[6-10x]—6A(1)[6-10x]—6A(4)[3-6x]—9A,B(4)—14E
W	3
Th	1A—19A,B(9)[4-6x]—17—14D
F	3
Sa	10B (form work)
Su	

DATE February

M	3—14A
Tu	1A—4—6A(1)—9A,B(1)—17—14D
W	3
Th	1A—4A,B(1,2,3)—9[2x]—14A
F	Gear ready—weigh shot—7
Sa	Indoor meet or 10B
Su	3
M	3—14E or 14D
Tu	1A—6B(1)—19B(3)—14D—8A—14D
W	1A—3
Th	1A—6A(2)—19B(2)—17—19B(8)—11—14A
F	
Sa	1A—6A(4)—19B(4)—9—17—14D
Su	3
M	1A—3
Tu	1A—6A(1)[20x]—6B(1)[20x]—14D
W	1A—3
Th	1A—9B(11)[20x]—18[20x]—6A(3)[20x]—11—14D
F	1A—3
Sa	7—20
Su	3
M	1A—9B(5)[20-40x]—9B(11)[10-20x]—11—14A
Tu	3—14B
W	1A—9B(11)[20x]—18[20x]—5B[20x]—19B(2)—14D
Th	3—14E
F	10B
Sa	3
Su	3

DATE March

M	1A—6A(1)—6B(1)—17—14A—14D—6A(4)—6B(4)
Tu	3—14D—20
W	1A—11—17—10B[4x]—10B[4x]—14A
Th	3—20—14A
F	1A—11—17—10B[4x]—10B[4x]—10B[4x]—14A
Sa	19—20
Su	19—20
M	1A—6A(3)—6B(3)—6B(8)—19—14D
Tu	3—20—14D
W	7—1A—11—6B(8)—17—14A
Th	3—20—14D
F	1A—8B(8)—11—17—14A
Sa	Exams and jog
Su	
M	3—14D—20
Tu	1A—4—4A—4B—5A—5B—17—14A—14D
W	3—20—14D
Th	1A—11—17—10B[4x]—14A
F	Travel
Sa	10A—meet
Su	Settle in—spring trip

Day	a.m.	p.m.
M	1A—3	1A—6B(8)—4A(1,2,3)—4B(1,2,3)—14A
Tu	1A—14D	1A—20—3—14D
W	1A—3	1A—17—6A(8)—6B(8)—14A—14D
Th		1A—6B(8)—4A—4B—11—14D
F	Light	Light
Sa	10A—triangular meet	
Su	Travel home	

April

M	1A—3—14A
Tu	1A—6A(6)—6B(6)—9A(4)—9A(2)—14D (3x 4-6x 4-6x)
W	3—14E
Th	1A—5A—6A(7)—11—20
F	Easy
Sa	10A—dual meet
Su	Your choice
M	3—14E
Tu	7—1A—6A(6)—6A(4)—9 (3-4x 3-4x)
W	3—20
Th	7—1A—6A(1)—6B(1)—11—14A (3-4x 3-4x)
F	Easy jog
Sa	10A—dual meet
Su	Your choice
M	3—14E(easy)
Tu	1A—6A(2)—6A(6)—6A(2)—9—14D (3x 3x)
W	3—20
Th	7—1A—6A(2)—6A(3)—6B(9)—easy 20 (2-3x 3-4x 4x)
F	Travel
Sa	10A—dual meet
Su	Home and loosen up
M	2—14D
Tu	12—21A(1)—5A—6A—6B—9—14D
W	2—20
Th	12—6A(8)—6B(8)—17—19—14A
F	Gear ready
Sa	10A—dual meet
Su	Your choice

May

M	1A—3—14A—14D
Tu	7—12—6A(2)—9A(2)—10—17—14E
W	Form work and 20
Th	1A—distance—11—17—12—distance—11—8 (3x)
F	Travel
Sa	10—dual meet
Su	Home and loosen up
M	1A—3—14D
Tu	12 with Coach—technique and target (10% less than goal)
W	12A—as on Tuesday, (10% less than goal)
Th	Light—3
F	Light—3
Sa	10—twilight meet
Su	Your choice
M	Target 10% less than average—3—14A
Tu	1A—4—9A,B(5)—18A—11—14A
W	3—14A
Th	1A—9(11)
F	Light—gear ready
Sa	10—Northern Division Meet
Su	4 puts—3
M	Light—3
Tu	1A—4—9A,B(5)—17—14D
W	1A—4—11—form work—14A
Th	Light
F	Travel
Sa	10—PAC 8 Meet
Su	

Late May or June

M	1A—2—11—17—14D
Tu	Light
W	10B—14A—14D (3x)
Th	Semicompetition
F	Light
Sa	1A—3—6B(8)—17—10B—14D (3x)
Su	1A—10B—17—14A—14D (3x)
M	Jog
Tu	Jog
W	1A—3—6B(1,2)—17—14A
Th	1A—3—6B(8)—17—10B—14A (2x)
F	Jog
Sa	Jog
Su	1A—6A(1)—6B(1,3)—10B—9A(8)—17—14A (3x)
M	1A—3—9A(8)—17—14D
Tu	Medium—3 puts—14E
W	Light
Th	Light
F	Qualify—NCAA meet
Sa	Finals
Su	Home
M	
Tu	
W	
Th	
F	
Sa	
Su	

CHAPTER 17	# The Discus Throw

Twenty-five years ago any discus throw of 200 feet was considered exceptional, but today the record is into the 240s. How have athletes progressed this far? We see three contributing factors:

1. More athletes are throwing in the schools today, and they compete for many more years than before. Not only was he a four-time Olympic champion, but Al Oerter was probably the best technician the world has ever seen. Certainly he was the best Olympic competitor.

2. The throwing facilities are better, and the discuses are now delicate instruments, well balanced and physically prepared to achieve aerodynamic wonders. All-weather surfaces take most of the chance out of footing. Nonskid shoes take care of some of the disadvantages of rain, and the throwing circles are often placed to take advantage of the prevailing winds.

3. Technique has evolved from the slow turn, through applied speed and agility, to the careful analysis of body mechanics and use of the principles of physics and aerodynamics.

Training Theory for the Discus

There are three styles of discus throwing:[1]

- Torque: Rotate on the turn foot, then rotate the lower body when crossing the ring; this causes increased upper-body torque for the release.

- Linear speed: The arms and the legs stay close to the vertical axis for faster rotation; most momentum comes from the sprint across the ring.
- Lineal-rotary: The arms and the legs are out from the vertical axis at the start, then brought in during the turn; this gives a slow-fast progression.

Mac Wilkins, the 1976 Olympic champion (232′10″), is the best discus thrower from the Oregon program. He stresses the following training points for discus throwers:[2]

- Try to maximize leverage throughout the throw.
- Start with longer, slower movements in the early phases of the throw.
- Learn to block with the left leg and side (for a right-handed thrower).
- Emphasize training and using the lower body.

A top-level male thrower takes 5,000 to 6,000 high-intensity throws in a year, compared to 2,500 to 3,000 for a 17- or 18-year-old thrower and 3,700 to 4,500 for a young (age 18 to 19) male collegian throwing 160 feet.

A high school thrower should take at least 75 to 100 full throws per week, while college throwers should take at least 100 full throws per week.[3] Only 65% of the throws in the preseason should be with the regulation-weight discus.

An example of the training loads at the elite level is that of Luis Delis (233′2″).[4] He can train very intensively only by devoting his full-time energies to training. His training year falls into these four periods (the figures are weekly):

Phase 1: *General physical preparation.* This includes 600 general throws, 40 specific throws, 360 general jumps, sprinting, gymnastics, swimming, and special endurance activities.

Phase 2: *Absolute-strength preparation.* This includes 170 general throws, 375 specific throws, 450 jumps, sprinting, and 6 sessions of absolute-strength training.

Phase 3: *Special-strength preparation.* This includes 270 to 325 specific throws, jumping, sprinting, and 3 sessions of fast-strength training.

Phases 4-5: *Competition.* This includes 60 to 130 specific throws, jumping, sprinting, and 2 sessions of competitive-strength training.

Throwers use implements of different weights, but coaches and athletes are still experimenting to find the most effective combinations. Heavier objects work on strength factors, while lighter implements allow more precise technique adjustments and improve arm speed.

Strength training is very important in training for the discus. These are the most common lifts used by discus throwers:[5]

- squat
- snatch
- clean
- dead lift
- bench press

Wilkins tried to have maximum lifts in the squat 5 weeks before competition, and in the snatch 2 weeks before competition. However, he admits that he tended to do too much upper-body lifting during the season.

Wilkins recommended light lifting on the day before a meet, using 2 sets of 5 reps of light squats, bench press, and snatch.

This practice is becoming widespread among elite throwers because it prepares the body for maximum effort on the following day (assuming the athlete has tapered for the meet).[6] Another suggestion is two or three sets of three or four reps of barbell exercises at 85 to 95% of the thrower's maximum.

Throwers appear to peak at about age 27, when their greatest strength is finally reached.[7] The better junior throwers develop a throwing technique that is slow-fast, that is, they begin the motion slowly through the wind and turn but keep their time in the air (while moving to the front of the ring) very short and accelerate very quickly through the power position and into the release. This maximizes their control in the early stages of the throw while increasing the torque that can be applied to the release velocity.

The more advanced throwers vary the release angle of the discus to adapt to changing wind conditions. The discus is highly affected by the wind's speed and direction. A head wind gives the longest throws. The best throwing angles are shown in Table 17.1.

Table 17.1   Release Angles for the Discus

Wind direction	Release angle*	Angle of attack*
Head wind	About 27	−4 (nose up at 23)
Tail wind	About 43	Even
No wind	36 to 40	To −14 (nose at 22 to 26)

*All angles are given in degrees from horizontal.

From Kim Bukhantsov. (1988). Wind variations in discus training. *Track Technique, **104**, 3329.* Reprinted with permission.

Women throwers may have more technical weaknesses because the level of their competition is not as high.[8] That is, there are fewer competitors at the higher levels, which allows the better athletes to get by more on strength than on careful attention to their technique.

With more advanced throwers, the early training, called *general preparation,* is disappearing from the annual program, except during the *regeneration* or *transition* phase.[9] The importance of specificity plays a vastly increased role in elite training. At the same time, researchers emphasize the need for individualized training, particularly in the late stages of the year. Each athlete reacts differently to training, with possibly as many as seven different types of throwers, depending upon their personal adaptation to training stresses.

The Discus Routine

The training routine for the discus progresses through the standing throw, stepping into the throw, and using the turn.

The first part of this stand-step-turn cycle is throwing from a standing position in the circle. For the right-handed thrower, the right foot (trail leg) is in the center of the circle, pointing at an angle of 120 degrees or so from the direction of the throw. The left foot is in the front of the circle and a bit to the left of center, so the thrower has room to rotate the hips into the throw. The body is back over the trail leg before throwing. The athlete rotates the body into the throw, keeping a long throwing arm (not bending it) and pulling the discus through the throwing position. The body shifts during the throwing action from the right leg to the left leg, throwing over a relatively straight left leg.

The second part of the routine consists of stepping into the final position and throwing. The turn is not used at this time. When stepping into the final portion, the thrower drops down slightly. Thus, while going into the actual throw, he or she lifts and "unwinds," like the outer edge of a screw rising as it rotates.

The final part of the routine uses the full turn and throw. From the starting position in the circle, located in the rear of the circle, with the feet planted comfortably facing away from the throwing direction, the athlete turns, moving into the throwing position, and throws. The progression is turn, step (trail-leg plant), step (lead-leg plant, with both feet now in throwing position), and throw.

The athlete should try to stay close to the center of the ring, allowing room for the follow-through after the throw. When throwing, the athlete should use only as much speed as he or she can control. Otherwise, the athlete would handicap the throw much more than help it. Also, the athlete should drop down only as low as he or she can control, then lift and unwind while throwing.

Basic Discus Throw Technique

When studying throwing sequences, athletes and coaches should remember two particular points:

- A sequence covers only a single throw, which may vary in some respects from the athlete's usual throwing form in the most successful throws.
- Each athlete has facets of form that are personal peculiarities, differences that work for him or her but would not work for many other athletes. A photo sequence is an example of technique, not a law to be rigidly followed.

A right-handed thrower turns on the left foot, keeping the body low and the throwing arm extended and behind the line of the shoulders. While rotating on the foot, the thrower drops the discus down, so it will then rise until it reaches the point of its release. The turn is *very* rapid. The thrower drives off the turning foot, preparing to go into the power position in the center of the ring. At this point the athlete has bent the lead arm considerably, which speeds up the turn. This may or may not be a virtue at this point in the throw because the thrower does not wish to get too much ahead of him- or herself.

The right foot lands and turns into the throwing power position. Then the left foot comes down in the front of the ring as the thrower lands in a strong position for the last phases of the throw. When both feet have touched down, the weight is over the rear (right) foot in the center of the circle, and the thrower is still down a bit in a semicrouch. As the athlete brings the discus around to the release position, the body shifts its weight forward toward the front foot, also straightening the legs, so the body is rising. This causes the discus to move in a pattern like the edge of a screw, circling in an upward direction. After the release, the thrower reverses the foot position (from left-foot to right-foot support) in the front of the circle, preventing a foul.

Discus Throwing Tips

When throwing the discus, using the entire torso and the legs is important. An "arm" thrower succeeds only against poor competition. While moving into the throw, the thrower rises upward, gradually lifting with the legs and adding to the force applied to the discus. When the throw is being made, the hips are cocked. The right hip is thrown forward like a punch, adding to the power of the throw. If the lead foot is placed directly in front of the body, though, the hips cannot be thrown forward because they have nowhere to go. The thrower should lead into the release of the discus with the nose and chin, which should be pointed straight ahead at the release of the discus.

All the unwinding (of hips, chest, and so forth) must precede the arm. This leading motion gives a sling or whip action to the arm. The farther the discus can be pulled in this manner, the greater the velocity that can be imparted to it. Connected with these actions are the left-arm coordination and the footwork of the throw, which are very important. The direction the discus goes depends on where the left foot points when the hips are cocked. The best throws have a low trajectory, which comes through the thrower's shoulder. The athlete wants a "low screamer" into the wind at an angle of about 22 degrees in relation to the ground. Throws using wooden pegs as targets set in different directions from the throwing circle help develop the ability to throw the discus where it should be going for the greatest benefit to the thrower.

A Typical Training Week for the Discus Thrower

Schedules are given for 10 months for the discus thrower, but the basic training principle is the hard-easy training cycle. An example of 1 week of training along the suggested hard-easy cycle is given here and can be considered a "typical" week of training:

Monday: Warm-up routine
    4 standing throws, working on leading with the chest and the nose
    4 throws after a turn, working as above
    4 throws standing, working on a long pull
    4 throws turning, working on a long pull
    4 to 6 throws alternately standing and crossing the ring
    25m wind sprints
Tuesday: Weight-training work
Jogging and flexibility exercises
Wednesday: Same throwing cycles of standing, then turning, as Monday, except working on
- keeping the hips ahead of the arm,
- throwing through the shoulder, and
- left-arm coordination

Thursday: Weight-training work
Jogging and flexibility exercises
Friday (trials):   Find out how many throws it takes for
    the athlete to reach the best mark. Throw in sets of three throws, with 5-minute breaks, as in competition.
- Where do the throws begin to taper off?
- Where are the longer throws?

Might throw three and three, sprint for a bit, throw four and four, sprint again, and so forth.
Saturday (finals):   Repeat Friday's drill. This prepares the thrower for competing in trials on one day and finals on the following day.

References

1. Frank Morris. (1981). The Wilkins style of discus throwing. *Track and Field Quarterly Review*, **81**(1), 22-27.
2. Mac Wilkins. (1987). Technique conditioning drills for the discus throw. *Track and Field Quarterly Review*, **87**(3), 20-23.
3. Vern Gambetta. (1986). TT interview: Mac Wilkins. *Track Technique*, **96**, 3053-3055.
4. Hermes Riveri. (1986). Discus training periodization. *Track Technique*, **96**, 3058-3059.
5. Ross Dallow. (1987). Mac Wilkins on weight training, mental preparation, diet, technique. *Track and Field Quarterly Review*, **87**(3), 24.
6. George Dunn. (1987). Current trends in shot putting. *Track Technique*, **98**, 3123.
7. Jan Stepanek & Petr Susanka. (1987). Discus throw: Results of a biomechanic study. *New Studies in Athletics*, **2**(1), 25-36.
8. Max Jones. (1988). Why can't a woman be more like a man? *Track Technique*, **104**, 3331.
9. Peter Tschiene. (1988). The throwing events: Recent trends in technique and training. *New Studies in Athletics*, **3**(1), 7-17.

Additional Readings

Amundsen, Glenn B. (1987). Analysis of four world class discus throwers. *Track Technique*, **99**, 3159-3160, 3170.

Bosen, Ken O. (1985). Coaching discus throwing technique. *Track and Field Quarterly Review*, **85**(1), 26-28.

Brown, Harmon. (1984). Training women throwers. *Track Technique*, **87**, 2763-2766.

Jarver, Jess (Ed.) (1985). *The throws: Contemporary theory, technique and training* (3rd ed.). Los Altos, CA: Tafnews.

Marks, Richard. (1985). Specialized strength and technique training for shot and discus. *Track Technique*, **91**, 2898-2899.

McGill, Kevin. (1983). Analysis chart for discus. *Track and Field Quarterly Review*, **83**(1), 23.

Miller, Brian P. (1985). Psychological factors in competitive throwing. *Track and Field Quarterly Review*, **85**(1), 40-44.

Naclerio, Anthony. (1987). Steps in teaching the high school discus thrower. *Track and Field Quarterly Review*, **87**(3), 18-19.

Santos, Jim. (1987). Increasing throwing speed through upper body plyometrics. *Track and Field Quarterly Review*, **87**(3), 29-33.

Shannon, Ken. (1988). Fundamentals for the throws. *Track and Field Quarterly Review*, **88**(3), 13-14.

Silvester, Jay. (1986). Points for the discus thrower and coach to ponder. *Track and Field Quarterly Review*, **86**(1), 26-27.

Sing, Robert O. (1986). Psychological concerns in the throwing events. *Track Technique*, **96**, 3069-3070.

The tests of equivalence [throws]. (1984). *Track and Field Quarterly Review*, **84**(1), 50-53.

Vrabel, Jan. (1987). Coaching the final phase of the discus. *Track and Field Quarterly Review*, **87**(3), 25.

Discus Throw Training Schedule

ATHLETE _____

1. Warm-up
   A. Jog 1-2 laps, easy stretching
   B. Hendricks Park
   C. Golf course
2. Fartlek
   A. Varied pace   B. Slow, steady pace
3. Weights and resistance activities
4. Routine
   A. Stand, foot in center of ring
   B. Cross the ring
   C. Stand, step, turn
5. Effort
   A. Stand (1) easy (2) medium (3) hard
   B. Cross (1) easy (2) medium (3) hard
6. Technique
   A. Standing throws
   B. Crossing the ring
      (1) knee bend & lift
      (2) maximum reach-back or torque
      (3) lead with chest and nose
      (4) long pull
      (5) hips cocked to uncocked
      (6) through the shoulder
      (7) other arm coordination
      (8) back knee bend-lift
      (9) discus flight
      (10)

7. Team meeting
8. Special
   A. Sauna   C. Hill
   B. Swim
9. Alternate stand and crossing the ring
   (same letters/numbers as #6)
10. Progress assessment
    A. Meet   C. Simulation
    B. Trial   D. Control test
       (1) 3/4 to 7/8 effort
       (2) 9/10 to full effort
11. Cross ring easy; feeling of exploding;
    start slow, finish fast
12. With Coach
    A. (name)
    B. Leader
14. Wind sprints (1) straight (2) curve
    A.
    B. Hurdle drill: 3 LH, 7-9m apart
    C. Spring & bound
    D. Alternate run & jog, at least 800m
    E. Starts, go 20-25m
    F. High knee (slow) & fast leg
15. Plyometrics
    A. Jumps (1) 1 leg (2) both legs (3)
    B. Bounding (1) 1 leg (2) both legs (3)
    C.

16. Tumbling activities for agility
17. Get over rear leg; lift with legs
18. Position
    A. Staying in the ring
    B. Good position at end of turn;
       lift & unwind
19. A. Throw into net
    B. Throw at target
    C. Ring crossing, feet not too far spread,
       speed you can control
       (same numbers as #6)
20. Work on second event
21. Visual aids
    A. Videotape   C. Photos
    B. Film
       (1) record performance (2) study
22. A. Slow down & be back over rear leg
       for long lift & unwind
    B. Pull the discus; lift & push with toes
30. Experimental work

186 High-Performance Training for Track and Field

DATE September/October

M	Class or squad organization
Tu	3—14D
W	1A—14E—6A(4)—6B(4)—19B—14D
Th	21A—3
F	1—14A—6A(5)—6A(8)—19A—14D
Sa	3—14D
Su	3
M	1—14A—6A(4)—9A(4)—6B(4)—6A(5)—14F $\overset{4x}{}$ $\overset{4x}{}$ $\overset{4x}{}$ $\overset{4x}{}$
Tu	3—14F
W	7—14A—9A(5)—19B—11
Th	3—14A
F	1—14A—6A(1)—19C(5)
Sa	Choice
Su	3
M	1—14A—4C—6A(7)—6B(7)—19—14A $\overset{4x}{}$ $\overset{4x}{}$
Tu	3—2A
W	1—14D—6A(3)—6B(3)—6A(8)—6B(8)—14A
Th	3—8A or 8B
F	1—14A—6A(9)—19B—19C—14D
Sa	7
Su	
M	1—14A—19C(5)—19C(2)—17—14D $\overset{5\text{-}10x}{}$ $\overset{5\text{-}10x}{}$
Tu	2B—14A
W	7—1—14A—10B—12—9A(9)—14A
Th	3—8
F	1—19C—10B—19B—14A
Sa	3
Su	1—19B

DATE October/November

M	1A—4—6A(7)—9A(7)—19B—2B
Tu	7—1A—20
W	1A—5A—5B—9A(4)—9A(5)—14A
Th	1A—3
F	10—20—14D
Sa	3
Su	3
M	1A—14A—6A(4)—6B(4)—9A(4)—2A $\overset{4x}{}$ $\overset{4x}{}$ $\overset{4\text{-}8x}{}$
Tu	3
W	1A—9A(3)—11—14D
Th	3
F	1A—20
Sa	3
Su	3
M	1A—14A—9A(2)—14A $\overset{3x}{}$
Tu	10B—20
W	7—3
Th	1A—14D—4A
F	1A—4—5—11—18A—14D
Sa	3
Su	3
M	1—14A—19C(5)—19C(2)—22A—14A $\overset{5\text{-}10x}{}$ $\overset{5\text{-}10x}{}$
Tu	3
W	1—4A—4B—5A,B—9A(5)
Th	Light—3
F	1—14A—10B—14A—10B—19C—jog $\overset{3x}{}$ $\overset{3x}{}$
Sa	3
Su	3

DATE November/December

M	1A—6A(4)—6A(5)—6B(3)—9—14D
Tu	3
W	1A—21A—17—11
Th	3
F	1—14A
Sa	3
Su	Recreation
M	1—14D—6A(2)—6B(2)—11—14A
Tu	3—8A or 8B
W	1—14D—6B(4)—11
Th	
F	10B(1)—10B(2)
Sa	Assist with cross-country
Su	Recreation
M	
Tu	
W	
Th	
F	
Sa	
Su	
M	
Tu	
W	
Th	
F	
Sa	
Su	

DATE January

M	Week of class organization—3
Tu	Squad organization—3
W	Registration—1—3—16
Th	7—1A—4A,B—6A(7)—6B(7)—4A,B
F	3—5
Sa	1A—4A,B—6A(6)—11—14A
Su	
M	1A—3—14A—6A(5)—6B(5)—11—14A
Tu	1A—3
W	1A—6A(4)—6B(4)—11—4A,B—14D
Th	1A—3
F	1A—4A,B—5—10B—4A,B—14D
Sa	3
Su	3
M	1A—4A,B—9A(8)—17—14A
Tu	3
W	1A—14A—4A,B—6A(1)—6B(1)—11—18A—14D
Th	3
F	10B(4 to 6 throws)—4A,B—14A
Sa	3
Su	3
M	1A—3—14A
Tu	1A—4A,B—9A(1)—14A—14D
W	7—1A—3—14D
Th	1A—6A—11—22—14A
F	3—14A
Sa	1A—4A,B—9A(8)—18B—22—14D
Su	3—14D

DATE February

M	6-10x 1—6A(9)—17—9A(1)—6A(6)—14A
Tu	3—1A
W	6-10x 6-10x 1—14A—6A(6)—6B(6)—19B—14D
Th	3—1A
F	1—21—10B—9A(6)
Sa	3
Su	
M	1—14A—3
Tu	6-10x 6-10x 1—14A—19B—6A(5)—9A(5)—14A
W	3
Th	4-6x 6-10x 1—14A—19A—6A(3)—10B(today or Sat.)—14D
F	3
Sa	10—20
Su	
M	1—3—14A
Tu	6-10x 6-10x 1—14A—6A(3)—9A(8)—9A(6)—14A
W	1—3—8A or 8B
Th	4-8x 1—14A—9B—6A(6)—14A
F	Jog—3
Sa	1—14A—19B—10B—14C
Su	
M	1A—3—14B
Tu	6-10x 6-10x 1A—14A—6A(6)—6B(6)—11—19A
W	3
Th	1A—10—20—16
F	3
Sa	3
Su	

DATE March

M	3—14D
Tu	10-20x 1A—6A(9)—11A(1)—11A(5)—14D
W	1A—3—14A
Th	1A—22A—20—14A—gear ready
F	Gear ready
Sa	10—meet or trials
Su	
M	a.m. Jog p.m. 1A—3
Tu	Jog 1A—6A(2)—9A(2)—22
W	Jog 3 3
Th	Jog 4x 1A—10B—11—14A
F	Light—gear ready
Sa	10—meet
Su	Home
M	1—14A—6A(6)—6B(6)—11—19B—14D
Tu	1A—3
W	1—10B or 20—19B—18B
Th	1—16—14D
F	1—18B—9A(2)—11—14D—9A(3)—18B
Sa	1A—3—14D
Su	1A—14D
M	1A—14D—18B—19B—9A(4)—18B—19A
Tu	1A—3
W	1A—6A(3)—19B
Th	1—3
F	Gear ready
Sa	10—meet
Su	Jog or recreation

DATE April

M	1A—9A(4)—11—19B—14A—14D
Tu	1—9A(5)—11—19A—14D—14A
W	7—1A—3—grass
Th	1—22A—18B
F	Light and gear ready
Sa	10—meet
Su	3—10B—14B
M	Light
Tu	1A—6A(8)—6B(8)—22B—19B—14D
W	7—light
Th	1—6A(6)—6B(6)—18B—11—14D
F	Gear ready
Sa	10—meet
Su	3—1A
M	1A—18B—9A(5)—11—14A—14E
Tu	1A(light)
W	1—6A(3)—18B—11—14A—14E
Th	Light
F	Gear ready
Sa	10—meet
Su	1A—18B—9A(3)—11—10—14D
M	Light
Tu	1—6A(4)—6B(4)—19B—11—3
W	7—light
Th	Gear ready
F	Jog
Sa	10—meet
Su	3

DATE May

M	Light
Tu	Light
W	7—10 (meet-night)
Th	1A—9A(7)—18B—22B—14E—14A
F	Light
Sa	Light
Su	Squad picnic
M	1A—10B
Tu	3x 1—19B—3
W	Light
Th	Light
F	1—9A(6)—18B—19B—14A—14D
Sa	1—9A(8)—18B—17—14D—14A
Su	3x 1—19B—3 or form work
M	1—3(light)—14E
Tu	3-6x 11—jog
W	Light
Th	Light
F	Qualifying, PAC 8 Meet
Sa	Finals, PAC 8 Meet
Su	

DATE June

M	Exams start—3
Tu	1A—6A(6)—11A—17—18B—14D
W	Light
Th	3x 1A—10B as in trials
F	3x 1A—10B as in finals
Sa	Final exams completed
Su	1A—Form work or loosen up
M	17—18B
Tu	Easy form work
W	Travel and loosen up
Th	1st day prelims, NCAA Meet
F	2nd day prelims, NCAA Meet
Sa	Finals, NCAA Meet
Su	

CHAPTER 18	# The Javelin Throw

The javelin throw is perhaps the most military of track and field events. To the ancient Greeks the ability to throw the javelin well was a mark of military prowess, for the javelin was an important weapon of their golden age. Many children still play at throwing spears, then graduate to the intricacies of the javelin. Technique becomes all-important, for the throwing form used with the javelin is not a natural motion. Though the military value of the javelin throw has passed, the beauty of a good throw survives.

Training Theory for the Javelin

The javelin is a complicated event because it is highly affected by a mixture of aerodynamic factors. At one time the javelin was little more than a long, unwieldy stick. Now it is an aerodynamically designed precision tool continually undergoing further advances in its design. As a result of the length of the world record (approaching 350 feet), in 1985 the balancing point of the men's javelin was moved forward. The result was a javelin that noses down sooner, giving shorter throws but also easing the official's job (fewer flat throws).

The East Germans test potential javelin throwers between the ages of 12 and 14, looking for the performances shown in Table 18.1. As with other tests, these are only guidelines. The East German goal is to have 5 years of directed training before the athlete can compete in the World Junior Championships (ages 18 to 19).[1] They predict records of 90 meters

(295 feet) and 80 meters (262 feet) for men and women, respectively.

Early research on the new men's javelin suggests that the primary change is in its downward flight.[2] The float largely disappears. The primary factor in the length of the throw is the speed at the release,[3] though that factor is not as great as before.[4] The new javelin appears to require more technical precision than the old one.

When the javelin is released, two angles are factors:

- Angle of release, the path that the throwing hand travels in relation to the ground
- Angle of attack, the angle of the javelin in relation to the path that the throwing hand travels

Most throwers release the javelin with a positive angle of attack (the nose is higher than the path of the hand). A higher angle of attack may be more a characteristic of lower level throwers. Indeed, with the new javelin, the ideal throw appears to be "through the point," as we suggest in the training schedules. Coaches are not completely agreed on this, however.[5] Nor is there consensus on the ideal angle of release, though the mid- to upper-30s seems most widely accepted. One study suggests 37.5 degrees as the ideal.[6]

A common weakness of poorer throwers on the braking step with the lead leg is to take too short a stride, making it impossible to transfer the momentum fully to the throw. Interestingly, one authority suggests that the new javelin's flight characteristics might

Table 18.1   East German Youth-Selection Age-Group Standards for Javelin

	Girls		Boys	
Exercise	12-13	13-14	12-13	13-14
Height	5′7″	5′7″	5′7″	5′9″
Baseball throw	180′-197′	197′-213′	213′-230′	230′-246′
60m dash	8.50	8.40	8.30	8.20
30m flying start	4.25	4.15	4.00	3.90
3 hops, right leg	21′4″	22′4″-23′0″	21′4″	23′0″
3 hops, left leg	21′4″	22′4″-23′0″	21′4″	23′0″
Shot put*	32′10″	36′1″	36′1″	39′4″
800m	2:35.0	2:32.0	2:30.0	2:25.0

*3 kilograms for girls, 4 for boys.

From E. Arbeit, K. Bartonietz, P. Borner, K. Hellmann, & W. Skibbia. (1988). The javelin: The view of the DVfL of the GDR on talent selection, technique and main training contents of the training phases from beginner to top-level athlete. *New Studies in Athletics*, **3**(1), 57-74. Reprinted with permission.

make the old fork grip (described later) a good technical choice.[7]

An example of training loads is the Finnish program, which includes the following during the training year:[8]

- 7,000 to 13,000 total throws
    30 to 50% with the javelin
    Others with a variety of weights
- Throwing weights for men
    Regular javelin (800 grams)
    800- to 1,000-gram weights
    400- to 700-gram balls for specific speed
    1- to 1.5-kilogram javelins for specific strength
- Throwing weights for women
    Regular javelin (600 grams)
    700- to 900-gram weights (10 to 15% of throws)
    400- to 600-gram balls for specific speed
    1- to 1.5-kilogram javelins for specific strength

The bottom line for survival as a javelin thrower is a good base of conditioning, strength, and flexibility.[9] A high throwing volume can lead to spine, shoulder, and elbow injuries. Technique training and the throwing load should increase gradually during the training year, as the conditioning and strength program advances. As an example of the conditioning required for elite performance, these are the recommended performance levels for a Soviet female who throws 70m (230 feet):

- Snatch: 176 to 187 pounds
- Clean: 220 to 243 pounds
- Squat: 309 to 353 pounds
- 60-meter dash: 7.5 to 7.6 seconds
- Short-approach long jump: 18′0″

Analysis of the Javelin Throw

The thrower begins with a running approach of not more than 120 feet, going into a cross-step on Step 2 of the final five steps. The thrower should accelerate into the cross-step, then plant the right foot (for a right-handed thrower) to begin the actual throw. The throwing arm is extended back, and the lead arm is across the body. The thrower brings the lead arm around to provide more pull for the throw. The left leg is extended to plant and provide a break on the forward momentum, which will be transferred to the javelin.

When the thrower plants the heel of the left foot, he or she is already pulling the javelin forward and bringing the left arm around to provide additional pull. The right leg provides additional push, and the torso rotates into the throw. The lead leg is kept rigid, forcing the body to go over it. As the thrower releases the javelin, the pushing right foot is still in contact with the ground, with the thrower continuing forward over the left foot. The thrower lands on the right foot, the fifth step of the final five, stopping his or her forward movement short of the foul line.

Common Faults of Javelin Throwers

One of the greatest faults, especially with American throwers, is the tendency to throw the javelin to the side rather than bring it across the shoulder. This probably results from the common throwing technique used with a baseball, which may be delivered over the elbow, held out to the side of the shoulder, or even

The Javelin Throw   191

thrown sidearm. This throwing form not only results in a poorer throw but also puts a much greater strain on the arm and elbow than the correct over-the-shoulder delivery.

Another fault is throwing the javelin rather than pulling it. Most of the work in a good javelin throw is done before the hand comes over the shoulder, rather than after the hand has passed the shoulder and is in the process of throwing. Much better results are gained by concentrating on pulling the javelin through the throw.

A great weakness in many throwers is the lack of body pull. The arm is not everything in throwing the javelin. The thrower must coordinate the entire body into the throw. When the athlete learns to throw with the arms, the legs, and the body, he or she is beginning to develop from a learner to a thrower.

Premature lift of the left foot (if the thrower is right-handed) also hampers good throwing considerably. This problem may also develop from American ball games, which use a "reverse" of the feet after throwing, much as the shot does. The thrower should stay on the left leg until going over it. The leg should not be pulled out at any stage of the throw because it contributes to the shifting of the athlete's momentum from straight ahead to the launching of the javelin itself.

A final fault is not technical: throwing the javelin hard too often in practice. Notice that all the training described here consists of throwing at levels varying from easy throwing to 7/8ths-effort, but never at full effort. Frequent full-effort throwing usually has one result: injuries, most frequently to the elbow region.

Holding back the effort of the throws does not hamper the success of the thrower. In 1964 Oregon had a thrower with a very bad elbow, Gary Reddaway. In the first meet of the season, in late March, he threw well enough to qualify for the NCAA Meet. He was then held out of all other meets until the NCAA Meet in mid-June. He went through his practice routines doing only easy throwing, using a tennis ball. He qualified for the NCAA finals with a single throw of 219'10". He made a vast improvement on his second throw in the finals to 246'1-1/2" and finished second as Oregon swept the first three places.

Training Considerations

There is no ideal size to look for in the prospective javelin thrower. Top male throwers have been as tall as 6'6", yet the world record has been held by men as small as 5'7" and 165 pounds. The coach is looking for the well-coordinated male or female with a good throwing arm. Tests such as the softball or football throw have been used for locating prospects, but

perhaps the most accurate indicator is throwing a ball the same weight as the javelin, 800 grams for men, 600 grams for women.

There are two major ways of holding the javelin, the fork grip and the Finnish grip. The fork grip is a simple style, consisting of holding the javelin between the index and middle fingers, with the fingers against the rear of the cord grip of the javelin. This style has been used partly because of its simplicity and partly for other reasons (Oregon's Boyd Brown, who set an American record at 234'1-1/2" in 1940, used the fork grip because he had lost his thumb in an accident). However, it is rarely seen today.

The Finnish grip consists of laying the cord grip of the javelin through the palm at the middle of the hand, the middle finger encircling the spear at the rear of the cord grip, the thumb around the opposite side of the grip, and the index finger extended back and to the same side of the javelin as the middle finger. Keep in mind that the object is to see how far one can throw the javelin, not how prettily it can be held.

The Finnish approach run, or variations of it, is the most commonly used style in the world today. When reaching the final steps of the approach, the thrower gradually turns the feet slightly to the side of the throwing arm and goes into a fast cross-step or series of cross-steps to get into a powerful throwing position. Although this style is not easy to learn, it allows great use of the thrower's speed. The basic throwing motion, regardless of the grip or approach style, is over the shoulder and close to the ear.

The Javelin Routine

In training, the thrower should progress from standing throws to throws with a short run, then to throws with a full run. This is done in a regular routine that is repeated before every workout in which any throwing is done. The standing technique can be done by replacing the javelin with a ball of the same weight.

The first step of the routine is throwing three times from a stand at a target about 30 feet away. The thrower begins with the weight back over the rear leg and the knee bent (the right leg, for a right-handed thrower). The front (left) leg is extended well to the front, pointing in the direction of the throw. The hips are turned at an angle of about 30 degrees away from the line of direction of the throw. The torso is back, with the hips over the rear leg. The right arm (throwing arm) is extended to the rear comfortably, but it is not stretched. The left arm is usually across the chest, leading the torso in rotating into the throw. The hips and legs are used to give additional thrusting power and rotation to the body to impart to the javelin. The javelin is thrown when maximum pull, rotation, and whip of the body have been applied. The thrower works at this last phase of the throw from the standing position for 5 to 10 throws, then progresses to the trotting throws.

The next step in the routine is the 3-4-5 exercise, which consists of going through the last three steps of the approach and throwing the weight or javelin three times at a target about 60 feet away. This gives the feel of moving the body into the final stages of the throw.

The last step in the routine is taking three throws while going through the approach from the last check mark through the last five steps of the approach. These throws are aimed at a target about 90 feet away. After the routine is completed, the thrower may move on to more warm-up throws with an approach run.

The thrower may work with the trotting throws next. The purpose of the trotting throw is to add momentum to the other mechanics of the throw. With an easy trot of 10 to 20 steps, the javelin or weighted ball is brought back into throwing position, then thrown easily for 50 to 100 feet. This exercise is repeated about five times.

The final stage of the warm-up might be taking several throws, usually about five, with the full-approach run. This is especially important for getting the approach pattern and check marks perfected. Three check marks are recommended, though some throwers may use two marks or only one. The first mark is 90 to 110 feet from the rear of the throwing arc, keeping in mind that the rules do not allow a run exceeding 120 feet. From the starting check mark to the second check should be 4 strides, then another 10 strides to the final check, at the point where the last 5 strides, including the cross-stepping, begin. The thrower wants to reach the throwing point with as much speed as he or she can control, though excessive speed hinders successful throwing more than it assists it. We want to reach the throwing point with good position and control. The last check mark, 5 strides from the completion of the throw, is about 30 feet or so behind the throwing arc.

After the check marks have been practiced, nine throws with the javelin are taken, but none of them is a hard throw at full effort. Three throws are made at half effort, followed by three throws at 3/4ths-effort, and finally three throws at 7/8ths-effort.

For the progression of throwing in a competitive situation, the check marks should be set up first, then the warm-up cycle taken, followed by one or two throws. The good throws should not be wasted; they should be saved for the competition. The thrower may find it helpful to follow a cycle or pattern like this with the competitive throws:

- *First throw*: medium effort only. The primary object of this throw is to get a safe throw, qualifying for the finals at the start of the competition.

- *Second throw*: relatively hard (7/8ths to 9/10ths effort), a bit of a gamble.
- *Third throw*: attempt to explode with a full effort, a "big" throw.

The same cycle is recommended for the final three throws: medium to hard to explosion.

For a general pattern of training, a good practice for the preseason is to throw on Monday, Wednesday, and Friday. When the season arrives, if the meets are on Saturdays, the throwers throw on Saturday, are off (from throwing) on Sunday and Monday, then throw again on both Tuesday and Wednesday (to help prepare for the experience of 2-day competitions later in the season). They do not throw on the Thursday and Friday leading into the next Saturday's competition. For a very big meet, there should be no throwing after Monday.

Javelin Technical Points

Several technical points of the approach and throw should be noted at this point. The lead foot comes into the throwing position pointed straight ahead or slightly to the right of the direction of the throw, while the trail foot is pointed slightly to the side. This allows the thrower to rotate the hips into the throw. The lead foot is not moved until the body passes over it.

The lead foot should come down flat. If the landing is made on the heel, the knee is more likely to collapse and absorb much of the momentum of the approach run. Rather, the knee should force the body to pass up and over the leg, passing the body's momentum on to the throw as a summation of forces. The lead arm should not be brought through too fast, or it will get too far ahead of the throw, limiting its effectiveness.

The head should continue looking straight ahead throughout the throwing action, though there is a tendency to pull it down to the left while making the throw. The thrower should try either to look ahead or to watch the tip of the javelin. If the head is turned aside, the shoulders may not be squared to the throw, or the legs may not be properly utilized. A very common throwing fault is pulling the front leg from under the body and executing a reverse, rather than going over the leg.

Finally, the faster the javelin is thrown, the lower the trajectory can be. A bit over 30 degrees is considered ideal with the newer javelins. The athlete should always throw through the shaft and to the point of the javelin, trying to send it off at the optimum angle.

Weight training is advantageous for the javelin thrower, as it is for most other athletes. The use of balls of various weights is very beneficial. Some throwers recommend throwing javelins or balls of various weights above and below the javelin weight. Theory suggests that the lighter implement permits faster arm movement, gradually increasing the speed of the arm strike, which is then applied to the regulation-weight javelin.

The Training Schedules: Special Fundamentals for the Javelin Throw

4A. Short check mark.   The check marks for the javelin thrower are as important as those used in the jumping events. The elite thrower knows almost to the inch how close he or she will come to the scratch line. This technique should be practiced on every throwing day.

To establish a short check mark, which is used for technique throwing, for bad weather conditions, or for when the thrower is having a bad competitive day, the thrower begins 2 steps before the first check mark (Figure 18.1). The first check mark is hit with

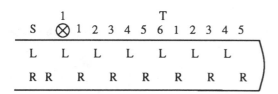

L   Left foot

R   Right foot

S   Start of approach run

1
⊗   Check Mark 1

T   Start of five-count final approach
Step 3 (right foot) is the cross-step
The throw is over the plant of Step 4
Step 5 is the reverse, to keep from
crossing the scratch line

Figure 18.1 Short check mark.

the left foot (for a right-handed thrower), then the thrower continues for 6 steps to hit the T with the left foot. The T point is the start of the five-count final approach, which includes the cross-step.

4B. Long check mark.   The long check marks are for competitive throwing. The more speed at which the javelin thrower can use control and still get an effective throwing position, the farther the throws should travel. This technique is not easily acquired, so it should be started early in the year and practiced

regularly. The rules do not permit an approach longer than 120 feet. Most elite throwers use from 90 feet to the 120-foot maximum.

The athlete stands at the rear of the approach (Figure 18.2), then takes a four-step trotting start from S, the start of the run, to the first check mark. An observer marks the last step while the thrower repeats the 4 steps twice. The average for this first part of the approach is about 20 feet. The average of the thrower's three trials is the first check mark.

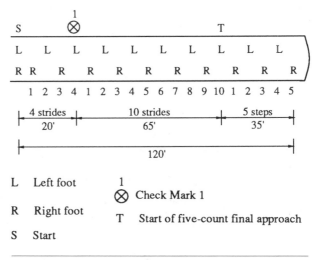

L   Left foot

R   Right foot

S   Start

1
⊗   Check Mark 1

T   Start of five-count final approach

Figure 18.2 Long check mark.

The same procedure is followed to establish the distance from the first check mark to T, with three trials made and the distances averaged. However, the athlete runs through the approach from the start, S, through Check 1 and on through the 10 steps to T, rather than running only the 10 steps. This part of the approach usually averages around 55 to 65 feet.

The final measurement adds the last 5 steps, including the follow-through. From the starting point, the thrower takes 4 steps to Check 1; 10 steps to T, the start of the final approach; and the final 5 steps, which include the throw and the follow-through. This long run is also done three times for an average. The 5-count, or last 5 steps of the approach, varies from 25 to 35 feet in most cases.

The type of approach as well as the wind and weather conditions can make a great difference in the length of the short approach, and even more dramatic variations in the long approach. Competitive areas vary from soft grass, cinders, and mud to all-weather materials. It is imperative that athletes who aspire to be the best should have among their tools a short as well as a long approach and a full knowledge of their distances on different kinds of approach surfaces.

5A. Stand, throw 10 to 30 times.   This is a routine warm-up drill. From a standing position, the athlete throws the javelin from 10 to 30 feet into a soft surface, gradually increasing the effort of the throws. This is also an opportunity to work on technical procedures. The lengths of throws suggested here and later are for male college throwers and should be modified according to the age, the sex, and the experience level of the individual thrower.

5B. Routine.   This is a continuation of the warm-up, but it is also a technique drill.

5B(1). 3-steps, throw 45 to 90 feet.   The javelin is already held back in the throwing position. The athlete takes two approach steps (Figure 18.3), then executes Steps 3, 4, and 5 of the final approach, throwing over the left foot on Step 4.

```
            S        3   4   5
          ┌─────────────────────
          │  L     L    L          ⟩
          │     R  R    R    R
          └─────────────────────
```

S   Start of two-step approach

R   Right foot

L   Left foot

3-4-5   Throwing approach

Figure 18.3 Three-step routine.

Three easy throws are taken with this approach, with the athlete trying to throw only in the range between 45 and 90 feet. The emphasis is upon perfecting the technique of the approach and the throw, not on distance achieved.

5B(1). 3-steps, throw 45 to 90 feet.   The javelin is already held back in the throwing position. The athlete takes two approach steps (Figure 18.3), then executes Steps 3, 4, and 5 of the final approach, throwing over the left foot on Step 4.

Three easy throws are taken with this approach, with the athlete trying to throw only in the range between 45 and 90 feet. The emphasis is upon perfecting the technique of the approach and the throw, not on distance achieved.

5B(2). 5-steps, throw 90 to 150 feet.   The athlete takes two approach steps to the final check mark, then executes the five-step final approach and delivery, taking three easy throws (Figure 18.4). The approach should be rhythmical, hitting the check with the left foot (for a right-handed thrower) and going through the final 5 steps, with Step 3 the cross-step, Step 4 (the left foot) being the plant leg over which the throw is made, and Step 5 the follow-through step.

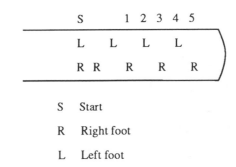

```
    S        1   2   3   4   5
  ┌──────────────────────────────
  │  L     L    L    L             ⟩
  │     R  R    R    R    R
  └──────────────────────────────
```

S   Start

R   Right foot

L   Left foot

1-2-3-4-5   Throwing approach

Figure 18.4 Five-step routine.

6A. Short approach and 6B. Long approach.   As with all other events, we believe that concentration on one part of the technique at a time produces the best results. Eventually the athlete, like a well-timed machine, fits all cogs of the meshing gears together. He or she then produces gradually increasing efforts as the season progresses. The numbers listed below, such as ''1'' beside 6A, are the numbers of the individual techniques listed under 6A and 6B (and also used in Number 9).

6A(1). Position of feet, keep lead foot down.   This drill's purpose is to provide a throwing foundation while maintaining motion. Starting from the T mark in Figure 18.5, the first step of the 5-count approach is a rhythmical, slightly longer, straight-ahead step. At the same time, the javelin starts back toward the throwing position. On the second step, the left foot turns slightly to the right, the javelin is now almost back in the throwing position, and the torso is turned partially to the right. On the third step, the right foot is turned slightly to the right (this is the cross-step), the javelin reaches its final throwing position, and the torso is turned as far to the right as is practical for the individual. The final left-foot position (Step 4) is almost straight ahead, but it is still slightly to the right in its aim. The right-leg momentum is increased by a slight push, the left foot remains planted, and the final step or reverse (Step 5) is made to the final position on the right foot.

6A(2). Rear foot under—be over it.   On the third step of the final approach, the torso should be turned as far toward a right angle to the throwing direction as the javelin thrower can reach and still be able to pull back into the delivery. This position varies with some individuals. Some excellent throwers keep the torso almost directly ahead, getting a ''bow'' effect, rather than a ''lay back'' over the back (right) leg, which is the method most commonly used. The action starts from a slightly bent right knee, and the

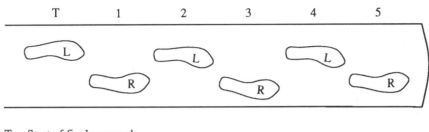

T   Start of final approach

R   Right foot

L   Left foot

Figure 18.5 Foot position in the final approach.

hip has also been cocked. The torso is turned to the right, and the javelin is back, with the thrower's left arm across the chest or pointed in the direction of the throw. The head and nose are aimed in the direction of the throw. The right knee straightens; the hip thrusts the torso back to a position "across" the direction of the throw (this is a turn of 45 degrees, not 90 degrees).

6A(3). Body to right, body precedes arm.
This position is taken on the third step and continues into the fourth step. The torso is turned to the right to make it easier to pull the javelin back to the throwing position. The left arm should be across the chest or, as some athletes carry it, pointed toward the throwing direction. As the left foot comes down (Step 4), the left arm swings in an arc below shoulder height and comes to the direction of the throw. The torso is turned quickly to the direction of the throw, and the throwing arm flows into the throw.

6A(4). Good (long) pull.
The javelin is pulled, as one would pull on a rope. The pull of the body's turn and momentum, which is transferred from the feet to the hips to the torso and finally to the pulling arm, adds momentum to the javelin before the actual throw is made.

6A(5). Cock the hand, rotate palm up.
The throwing hand should be rotated up (palm up) as the arm is cocked for the throw. The emphasis on the throwing hand should be "palm up at the start of the throw, palm down at the finish."

6A(6). Over the shoulder, close to the ear.
The javelin on delivery should pass over the shoulder and close enough to the head that the head tilts slightly to the left during the delivery. Beware! The sidearm delivery is the most certain way to have elbow injuries.

6A(7). Through the shaft, keep tip low.
The shaft should be delivered a bit above 30 degrees. In deliver-

ing it, the thrower should watch the point to see that it does not wander to the right or tip up on delivery. As the javelin leaves, all the thrower should be able to see is the "tail-tip," which should appear no larger than a silver dollar. A tipped-up shaft would show the whole javelin and result in a high, bad flight.

6A(8). Lead foot down quickly, pass over it.
The lead foot (Step 4 in Figure 18.5) should come down quickly. The thrower should keep the power and momentum flowing. The left leg is planted quickly, the foot pointed slightly to the right, and the knee almost straight and straightening up into the throw as the body passes over it.

10AB. Test or compete.
The number indicates a trial or an actual throwing all-out. 10B(1) is a trial throw of 1/2- to 3/4ths-effort, 10B(2) is a trial throw at 3/4ths- to 7/8ths-effort, and 10B(3) is a trial throw at 9/10ths-effort. The best throw is recorded, along with the date, at the bottom of the training sheet.

11A. Start slow, finish fast.
The emphasis on the approach run should be to gain momentum with relaxed speed at the end of the throw. The beginner tends to slow down at the end, not only stopping the feet but also stopping the torso. A thrower gains very little from such an approach. It is true, though, that the feet stop in a good approach. The feet stopping at the end of a fast approach make the body a catapult or a whip, which increases the momentum of the javelin before the final throwing motion.

11B. Explosion.
The athlete is trying to explode with a burst of energy at the end of the throw. If done well and timed perfectly, the explosion can help the thrower put more into the throw.

11C. Easy, medium, hard.
This is work on a throwing cycle for competition. The first throw is relatively easy, in other words, a "safe" throw, a sure

mark. The second throw in the qualifying round would be a bit harder, a medium throw. The last throw is hard, an attempt to explode and get a big improvement in the mark. The same throwing cycle is used in the final round of three throws.

17. Have feeling of being back and relaxed over rear leg, no strain.
The final throwing position (Steps 3 and 4 in Figure 18.5) is one of a slight lean back over the right or rear leg, which is bent. As the body is turned into the throw, it makes a bow or sling for shooting the "arrow."

18. Work on staying behind the scratch line.
All javelin throwers need some practice in staying behind the scratch line, some because after good throws they wander over the line, causing fouls. A thrower also needs to know how much momentum he or she can use and still have room for the follow-through.

19A. Throw ball into net.
If a net is available, a softball or weighted ball up to 3 pounds can be used to work on technique as well as arm strength and flexibility.

19B. Throw at target.
Target throwing is used to keep the athlete from competing every practice day. It is also used so the athlete can learn to use the wind by varying the direction of approach in the throwing area.

19C. Approach speed.
The thrower should constantly be working for more approach speed. How much speed? Armas Valste of Finland said, "As much speed as you can control." Work regularly to attain greater controlled speed.

20. Work on second event.
A secondary event should be a pleasurable diversion. It may also be a team point winner. Les Tipton, Oregon and Olympic athlete, helped win a dual track meet with a third in the high hurdles.

Interpretation of Week 1 of the Training Schedules

The first week of the javelin throw training schedules are translated here from the numbers to show how the charts are interpreted. The training week begins on Monday and ends on the following Sunday.

Monday: The first week of training in the javelin, as with the other events, leads off with the organization of the class, if it is for physical education or the squad. It concerns equipment, practice periods, principles, squad meetings, and so forth.
Tuesday: (1A) This number represents the usual warm-up jog and flexibility exercises.
(5A) Starting in a standing position, the athlete throws into the grass nearby (15 to 30 feet away) or into a sand pit or other soft surface, gradually increasing the effort of the throws.
(16) Simple acrobatic activities not only are excellent conditioners but also teach body control.
(14D) When time permits, every workout should be concluded with easy running.
Wednesday: (3) Weight-training activities. In the section on weight training, resistance exercises are suggested. Most athletes develop their own weight-training routines.
(14D) Running activities, alternating 50-meter intervals of running and walking or jogging for 800m or more.
(7) Squad meeting. The meeting time will be posted on the blackboard in the team dressing room.
Thursday: (1A) Warming-up activities already described.
(4A) Short check mark establishment is a critical and technical exercise.
(19A) A softball or a weighted ball of 1 to 3 pounds is an excellent substitute for the javelin. It does not put the same pressure on the arm as a javelin held in a bad position. Emphasize the same techniques as for the javelin. If no net is available, throw up and down a field.
(14A) Wind sprints are short dashes of 25 to 50m with a recovery of 50 to 100m—whatever is needed. The thrower starts slowly, gradually increases to almost full effort, then slows down to recovery pace.
Friday: All of Friday's activities have been described.
Saturday: Weight-training or some special activity. A sauna, if available, is recommended, as are many other healthful activities.
Sunday: What better way to finish a week or start a new one than in light recreation? We also use workout activities on occasion for the athlete who needs special attention on technique. It is also a great way to bring back to life those who spend much of the weekend in extracurricular expression of their personalities.

References

1. E. Arbeit, K. Bartonietz, P. Borner, K. Hellmann, & W. Skibbia. (1988). The javelin: The view of the DVfL of the GDR on talent selection, technique and main training contents of the training phases from beginner to top-level athlete. *New Studies in Athletics*, **3**(1), 57-74.

2. Wilf Paish. (1986). Some initial observations on the new men's javelin. *New Studies in Athletics*, **1**(3), 81-84.

3. Hans-Joachim Menzel. (1986). Biomechanics of javelin throwing. *New Studies in Athletics*, **1**(3), 85-98.

4. Anders Borgstrom. (1988). Two years with the new javelin. *New Studies in Athletics*, **3**(1), 85-88.

5. Glenn DiGiorgio. (1988). Coaching insights for the new javelin. *Track Technique*, **104**, 3318.

6. Randolf Peukert. (1987). Training and biomechanical factors in the development of the javelin throw technique. *Track and Field Quarterly Review*, **87**(1), 37-44.

7. DiGiorgio, *supra* note 5, p. 3318.

8. Esa Utriainen. (1988). Javelin periodization. *Track Technique*, **103**, 3296.

9. O. Ditrusyenko. (1986). New approaches to javelin training. *Track Technique*, **95**, 3041.

Additional Readings

Brown, Harmon. (1984). Training women throwers. *Track Technique*, **87**, 2763-2766.

Calvert, Sherry. (1982). Throwing the javelin. *Track and Field Quarterly Review*, **82**(1), 23-26.

DiGiorgio, Glenn. (1985). Javelin training: The dynamic approach. *Track Technique*, **93**, 2970-2973.

Irving, Scott. (1988). Putting some flex into your throws. *Track Technique*, **102**, 3246-3249.

Jarver, Jess (Ed.) (1985). *The throws: Contemporary theory, technique and training* (3rd ed.). Los Altos, CA: Tafnews.

Kovacs, Etele. (1987). Complex development of strength, velocity and technique of young javelin throwers. *New Studies in Athletics*, **2**(1), 43-45.

Mazzalitis, V. (1985). Observations of javelin trajectory. *Track Technique*, **91**, 2908.

McGill, Kevin. (1982). Analysis chart for the javelin throw. *Track and Field Quarterly Review*, **82**(1), 39-42.

Miller, Brian P. (1985). Psychological factors in competitive throwing. *Track and Field Quarterly Review*, **85**(1), 40-44.

Nazarenko, E. (1988). Evaluation of women javelin throwers. *Track Technique*, **102**, 3266-3267.

Santos, Jim. (1987). Increasing throwing speed through upper body plyometrics. *Track and Field Quarterly Review*, **87**(3), 29-33.

Sing, Robert O. (1984). *The dynamics of the javelin throw*. Cherry Hill, NJ: Reynolds.

Sing, Robert O. (1986). Psychological concerns in the throwing events. *Track Technique*, **96**, 3069-3070.

The tests of equivalence [throws]. (1984). *Track and Field Quarterly Review*, **84**(1), 50-53.

Tschiene, Peter. (1988). The throwing events: Recent trends in technique and training. *New Studies in Athletics*, **3**(1), 7-17.

Webb, Bill, & Sing, Bob. (1989). The javelin throw. In Vern Gambetta (Ed.), *The Athletics Congress's track and field coaching manual* (2nd ed., pp. 189-199). Champaign, IL: Leisure Press.

White, Scott C. (1986). Introducing the essentials of javelin throwing to beginners. *Track and Field Quarterly Review*, **86**(1), 29-34.

Javelin Throw Training Schedule

ATHLETE _____

1. Warm-up
   A. Jog 1-2 laps, easy stretching
   B. Hendricks Park
   C. Golf course
2. Fartlek
   A. Varied pace   B. Slow, steady pace
3. Weights and jogging
4. Check mark
   A. Short   B. Long
5. A. Stand: throw 10 to 30 times
   B. Routine: throw 3 of each—easy, medium, hard
      (1) 3 steps, throw 45-90'
      (2) 5 steps, throw 90-150'
      (3) run & throw, 150-180'
6. Technique
   A. Short approach   B. Long approach
      (1) position of feet—keep lead foot down
      (2) rear foot under—be over it
      (3) body to right, body precedes arm
      (4) good (long) pull
      (5) cock the hand, rotate palm up
      (6) over the shoulder, close to ear
      (7) through the shaft, keep tip low
      (8) lead foot down quickly, pass over it
      (9)

7. Team meeting
8. Special
   A. Sauna   C. Steps or hill
   B. Swim
9. Full run and form throws (same numbers as #6)
10. Progress assessment
    A. Meet   C. Simulation
    B. Trial   D. Control test
       (1) 1/2 to 3/4 effort
       (2) 3/4 to 7/8 effort   (3) 9/10 effort
11. A. Start slow, finish fast
    B. Explosion
    C. Easy, medium, hard
    D.
12. With Coach
    A. (name)
    B. Leader
14. A. Wind sprints (1) straight (2) curve
    B. Hurdle drill: 3 LH, 7-9m apart
    C. Spring & bound
    D. Alternate run & jog, at least 800m
    E. Starts, go 20-40m
    F. High knee (slow) & fast leg

15. Plyometrics
    A. Jumps (1) 1 leg (2) both legs (3)
    B. Bounding (1) 1 leg (2) both legs (3)
    C.
16. Tumbling activities for agility
17. Have feeling of being back & relaxed over rear leg, no strain
18. Work on staying behind scratch line
19. A. Throw ball into net
    B. Throw at target C. Approach speed
20. Work on second event
21. Visual aids
    A. Videotape   C. Photos
    B. Film
       (1) record performance (2) study
30. Experimental work

DATE September/October

M	Class or squad organization
Tu	1A—5A—16—14D
W	3—14D—7
Th	1A—4A—19A—14A
F	1A—5A—16—14D
Sa	3 or 8A
Su	Recreation
M	3—8A or B
Tu	1A—5A—6A(7)—4—7 at Student Union
W	3—4 or 8A
Th	4—3—16
F	1A—5A—5B—14A
Sa	3—14B—8A or B
Su	Recreation—study
M	3—14A—Tuesday 12:30 S.U.
Tu	1A—5A—5B—14A—12:30 S.U.
W	3—8B
Th	1A—4A—3—16
F	1A—check gear—easy jog
Sa	1A—4A—4B—10B—14B
Su	Usual
M	3—14A
Tu	1A—6A(2)—6B(2)—5B—4B—14B
W	3—14B
Th	14A—3—16
F	1A—6A(2)—6B(2)—19A—14B
Sa	3
Su	Usual

DATE October/November

M	1A—3
Tu	Choice
W	1A—4A—5A(1)—5A(2)—5A(3)—19B—14B
Th	3
F	1A—4A—4B—10B(1)—14A—10B(2)
Sa	3
Su	Choice
M	1A—3
Tu	Choice
W	1A—4A—4B—5A—6A(8)—6A(7)—14B
Th	3
F	1A—4A—4B—5A—6A(3)—17—14B
Sa	3—16
Su	Usual
M	1A—3
Tu	3 or choice
W	1A—4A—4B—21—10B(1)—19A—14A or 14B
Th	Choice
F	1A—19A—19B—2A or 2B
Sa	3
Su	Choice
M	1A—3—14A—8
Tu	3
W	1A—4A—4B—6A(8)—6B(8)—18—14F—2B
Th	3—8A
F	1A—4A—4B—10B(3 short run—3 long run)
Sa	3
Su	Choice

DATE January

M	Reorganize class or squad
Tu	3—8B
W	1A—5A—6B—6A—2
Th	3—8A or B
F	1A—5A—6B(1)—6A(8)—14A
Sa	3
Su	Walk or recreation
M	3—8A
Tu	3—16—8B
W	1A—5A—12—6A(5)—6A(3)—19A—14B
Th	3—8A
F	1A—5A—6A(5)—6A(7)—14A
Sa	3
Su	2 or good walk
M	3
Tu	16
W	1A—12(4 p.m.)—5A—6B(6)—6B(8)—5A
Th	3—8A or B
F	1A—14A—6A(1)—6B(1)—6B(7)—14B
Sa	3
Su	3
M	1A—3—14A
Tu	3—16
W	1A—5A—6A(6)—6A(3)—19A—14B
Th	1A—3—14A
F	1A—5A—5B—easy 11A and B—14F
Sa	3—2
Su	Choice

DATE February

M	1A—3—14A or 14B
Tu	1A—6B(5)—6B(2)—6B(6)—14A
W	3
Th	1A—5A—5B—4A—4B—14B
F	3—8A or B
Sa	
Su	Study and recreation
M	1A—3—14A
Tu	1A—4A—4B—6B(2)³ˣ—6B(6)—5B—14A
W	3
Th	1A—4A—4B—5A—5B—6A(2)—19A—14A
F	3
Sa	1A—5A—6B(2)—11B—14B
Su	Study or recreation
M	1A—3
Tu	1A—4A—4B—5A—5B—19B—14B
W	7—1A—3
Th	1A—5A—6B(2)—6A(1)—5B—14B
F	3—8A or 8B or 16
Sa	1A—12—10B(1)—5B—14A or B
Su	Usual
M	1A—3—16
Tu	1A—5A—6B(6)—6B(7)—19B—14A
W	2—8A or B
Th	1A—10B(1)—12—4B—10B(2)—5B
F	3—8A or B
Sa	3
Su	Usual

DATE March

M	2—14A
Tu	1A—5A—6A(9)—6A(6)—4B—19B(150-180')—14D
W	1A—3
Th	1A—12—10B(190-210')—target at 200 ft.—14B
F	1A—3—14F
Sa	Secondary event test
Su	Usual
M	3—14A
Tu	1A—4A—4B—5A—6B(2)—6B(1)—5B—14B
W	3—8A or B
Th	1A—12—6A(8)—6B(8)—19B—20—8A or B
F	3
Sa	1A—10A—14B
Su	Study
M	3—8A or B
Tu	1A—4A—4B—5A—5B—6B(2)—6B(1)—17—14A
W	3—8A or B
Th	1A—5A—5B—6B(3)—6B(5)—19A
F	3
Sa	3 or 14A
Su	Study
M	1A—3—2
Tu	1A—4A—4B—5A—5B—17—14A
W	1A—4A—4B—3 medium throws—8A
Th	3—14B
F	Light and gear ready
Sa	Travel and compete
Su	Recreation

DATE April

M	3—14A or 14B
Tu	1A—4A—4B—5A— 6A(2)—6A(6)—3x/6B(2)—3x/6B(6)—19B—14B
W	2—8B
Th	1A—12—5A—3x/6A(2)— 3x/6B(2)—3x/6B(2)—4A—4B—19B
F	Gear ready—jog and stretch—no javelin
Sa	Compete
Su	Form work
M	2—4
Tu	7—1A—5A— 3x/6A(6)—3x/6B(6)—6A(3)—4A—4B—14E
W	1A—4A—4B—3 medium throws—3
Th	2—8
F	Jog and stretch
Sa	Compete
Su	Travel home and loosen up
M	1A—3
Tu	1A—3—14A
W	1A—4—5—6A(1)—6A(3) 3x —9B(2)—9B(6) 3x —14B
Th	1A—3
F	Light—all gear ready
Sa	Compete
Su	Home and loosen up
M	3—14A
Tu	7—1A—4A—4B—3x/6A(8)— 3x/6A(6)—3x/9A(2)—3x/9A(6)—19A—14B
W	2—8
Th	1A—12—5A—4A—4B—9A(2) 3x —jog
F	Gear ready and travel
Sa	Compete
Su	Loosen up—4—5A

DATE May/June

M	Light 2—14A
Tu	1A—6A(8)— 3x 3x 6A(3)—4A—4B—6A(2)—6A(6)—5B—jog
W	2—21A
Th	Gear ready
F	Preliminaries, Regional or Conference
Sa	Finals
Su	Home and loosen up
M	Easy
Tu	2x 3x 1A—5B—4A—4B—10B(2)—14A or 14B
W	Help with frosh or JV meet—jog
Th	1A—5B—14A
F	Invitational meet, travel and loosen up
Sa	Invitational meet, or simulate
Su	Usual Sunday routine
M	Runway and form work at championship area
Tu	Light
W	Light
Th	Qualify for championship
F	Light
Sa	Championship finals
Su	Usual
M	
Tu	
W	
Th	
F	
Sa	
Su	

CHAPTER 19	# The Hammer Throw

People have used the hammer as both tool and weapon for thousands of years. The first known competition was in the Aenoch Taillteann Games in Ireland about 500 B.C. The hammer has been thrown in Scotland since about 300 A.D. From Scotland the event was introduced into England, where it was a popular sport during the 16th century. The implement of that time was either a blacksmith's hammer or a round stone with a wooden handle.

In the 1860s the hammer throw was introduced into university sports. The implement evolved into a metal ball at the end of a chain with an attached handgrip. Figure 19.1 shows how the hammer is held with an overlapping grip. The early Olympic champions were Irish or Irish-Americans. Though the hammer throw is an Olympic event of great popularity in the Soviet Union, it has long been the orphan stepchild of American track and field.

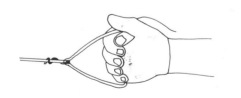

Figure 19.1 Proper hammer grip.

Training Theory for the Hammer

For some years now, the leading hammer throwers have come from Eastern Europe. The world record has decisively passed the 80-meter (262′5″) range. Throwing distance is affected by three factors:[1]

- Release velocity
- Release angle
- Release height

The release velocity appears to be the most important factor. For a 75m thrower, a 5% speed increase adds 7m to the throw, while a 5% change in the release angle changes the distance by only 60cm. The ideal release angle is 44 degrees, though most elite throwers achieve an angle of 38 to 40 degrees. It may be that a thrower cannot rise to the same release speed with a steeper release angle.

Maximum release velocity is achieved by lengthening the path that the hammer follows until it is released. The path is made longer by having a longer radius of rotation. This is done by the counterposition of the pelvis, and extended arms and a relaxed shoulder girdle.

By bending the knees, thereby dropping to more of a sitting position during the turns, the thrower makes the radius of rotation longer. When the thrower extends the arms to their maximum length, while relaxing the shoulder girdle, the arms seem to "stretch" to more than their usual length. The result is a longer radius, a longer pull, and faster velocity of the hammer. Wide winds (preliminary swings) help to set the stage for this movement.

The thrower must minimize the single-support time (when one foot is off the ground during rotation). The hammer is accelerated during the double support, pulled strongly downward as the thrower collapses the knee while the hammer is high in the air. On each turn the trail leg (the right leg for a right-handed thrower) is picked up and touches down earlier than in the previous turn (Figure 19.2).

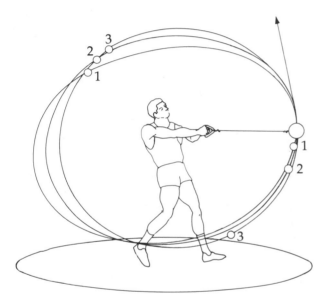

Figure 19.2 Movement path of the hammer. From K. Bartonietz, L. Hinz, D. Lorenz, and G. Lunau. (1988). The hammer: The view of the DVfL of the GDR on talent selection, technique and training of throwers from beginner to top level athlete. *New Studies in Athletics*, **3**(1), 44. Adapted with permission.

Efficient movement with today's technique shows these elements:[2]

- The trail leg is swung closely around the pivot leg.
- The distance between the feet decreases as the turn progress (from about 2 feet to about 1 foot).
- During all turns there is a relatively stable triangle between the arms and the shoulder axis.
- The position of the shoulder axis relative to the hip axis is relatively stable.
- The athlete's eyes are focused on the hammerhead.

- The stable rhythmic organization of the first to the last turn is characterized by these points:
    The position of the hammerhead during the trail foot's touchdown gradually shifts toward the high point.

    As the turns progress, the low point of the hammerhead moves toward the final release path (lower at the low point).

The hammer throw is very technically complex. The East Germans test prospects at age 13 (Table 19.1). They believe that an athlete must train for 10 to 12 years to become an elite thrower.

Table 19.1 East German Standards for 13-Year-Old Hammer Prospects

Height: 5'7"
Weight: 121 to 137 pounds
Arm span: At least 2 inches more than height
30m (crouch start): 4.8 sec
30m (flying start): 4.0 sec
60m (crouch start): 8.8 sec
3 two-footed hops: 22'4"
3-kilogram (6.6-pound) shot: 37'9"

Note. They also test the flexibility of the shoulder girdle.
From K. Bartonietz, L. Hinz, D. Lorenz, and G. Lunau. (1988). The hammer: The view of the DVfL of the GDR on talent selection, technique and training of throwers from beginner to top level athlete. *New Studies in Athletics*, **3**(1), 50. Reprinted with permission.

For the athlete to make long throws as an adult, the technique must be engrained. To do this, lighter hammers are used, so the best junior throwers can reach 80 to 90m by age 17 (using a 3-kilogram hammer, compared to 7.25 kilograms for the regular hammer). The reason is that the mechanical factors for an 80-meter throw are the same, regardless of the weight of the implement. Thus, the athlete learns the technique of the throw by repeating it with an implement that is light enough to allow him to throw 80m, if his technique is correct.

The East Germans note that "the experiences of the world's best hammer throwers show the great advantages of light implements as far as the perfection of the specific movement capacities and technique are concerned. The aim of the training of young hammer throwers is to achieve long throwing distances without a marked degree of strength development."[3] Table 19.2 shows the youth throwing goals.

Table 19.2 East German Performance Goals for Young Throwers

Age	Meet hammer weight (kg)	Distance in meters (feet)	Light hammer weight (kg)	Distance in meters (feet)
13	3	55 (180)	2	60 (197)
14	4	60 (197)	3	66 (217)
15	5	62 (203)	3	74 (243)
16	6.25	62 (203)	3	80 (252)
17	6.25	68 (223)	3	86-90 (282-295)

From K. Bartonietz, L. Hinz, D. Lorenz, and G. Lunau. (1988). The hammer: The view of the DVfL of the GDR on talent selection, technique and training of throwers from beginner to top level athlete. *New Studies in Athletics*, **3**(1), 50. Reprinted with permission.

Training uses technique units with drills using wooden sticks, leather balls with straps or wires, medicine balls, and light (2-kilogram) hammers. Each technical unit must be mastered before the next is attempted, with much use of part-whole learning. Sprint and jump training are used, along with event-specific conditioning and stretching exercises.

For adults, more use is made of strength and speed-strength training. Specific strength training falls into three categories:

- Throwing hammers: different weights, one to four turns
- Strength exercises for shoulder, trunk, and legs (similar to event movements):
      Standing diagonal throws
      Jumps with extra loads
      Trunk exercises with extra loads in swings and turns
- Forms of pulling and leg-strength exercises with barbells, major exercises being the snatch, clean, pull, and squats

Throwers use a double-periodized year, as shown in Figure 19.3. Anatoliy Bondarchuk, the most successful Soviet hammer coach, divides the development of hammer throwers into three stages:[4]

Initial preparation level: ages 12 to 14. Three or four sessions per week, 90 to 120 minutes each, including

- all-around development exercises, sprinting, jumping
- using light implements (3 to 5 kilograms)
- shot putting (4 to 6 kilograms) from different positions
- weight training

Maximum training load for single session:

- 2 tons of weight lifted
- 15 to 20 hammer throws
- 25 throws with the shot
- 500m of sprinting
- most training in first (50 to 80%) and second (80 to 90%) zones of intensity
- 5% of training load in higher zones

Special fundamental preparation level: ages 14 to 18. Five to eight sessions per week, 120 to 150 minutes each, including

- all-around development exercises, sprinting, jumping
- using light (5 to 6 kilogram), normal, and heavy (8 kilogram) hammers
- shot-putting (6 to 16 kilograms) from different positions
- weight training and special exercises

Maximum training load for single session:

- 5 to 6 tons of weight lifted
- 25 hammer throws
- 25 throws with the shot
- 1,000m of sprinting
- 60 to 70% of weights in second zone (80 to 90%)
- 25% of weights in first (50 to 80%) zone of intensity
- 10 to 15% of training load in higher zone (90 to 100%)

Perfecting acquired skill level: ages 18 and over. Can reach 200 throws a day, but have found that 30 to 40 (sometimes 50 to 60) throws are sufficient.

The Soviet throwers mix light and heavy implements with the regulation-weight implement in all of

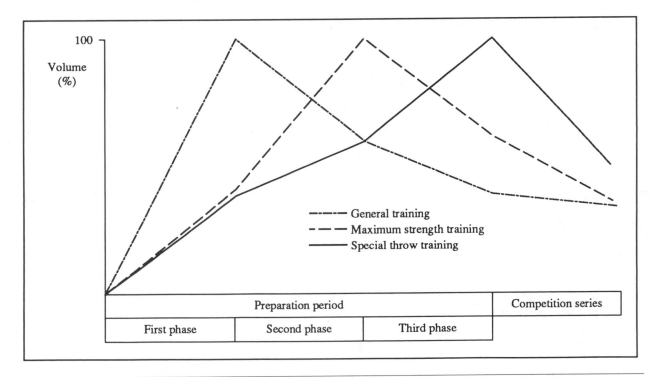

Figure 19.3 Periodized training year for the hammer. From K. Bartonietz, L. Hinz, D. Lorenz, and G. Lunau. (1988). The hammer: The view of the DVfL of the GDR on talent selection, technique and training of throwers from beginner to top level athlete. *New Studies in Athletics*, **3**(1), 53. Adapted with permission.

their throwing events. Figure 19.4 shows a single-period macrocycle and the changing training emphasis of the different weights. Figure 19.5 shows a double-period pattern, again one that is appropriate for athletes competing indoors.

Table 19.3 (p. 208) shows two variations of training by Bondarchuk for elite throwers.[5]

Table 19.4 (p. 208) gives another example of elite training loads, with the Soviet use of precise measurement of the training load. The athlete is Yuriy Syedikh, a world-record holder and Olympic champion coached by Bondarchuk.[6]

Figure 19.6 (p. 209) shows the relative emphases of types of training across the year, based on Soviet training theory.[7]

The Eastern European sport bodies emphasize modeling in developing the training program for each event. This means developing a model of the specific skill patterns, along with tests and standards, that are needed to reach set levels of elite performance. Then the training program is designed to develop those traits, with the standard tests repeated regularly to measure the athlete's progress toward the standard. Table 19.5 (p. 209) shows the East German model for the hammer throw.[8]

Ladislav Pataki has worked with SyberVision to develop a training videotape that uses visualization techniques and sound imagery as a major part of training

for hammer throwers.[9] Together with Ed Burke and Stewart Togher, he developed a highly useful training booklet for learning the hammer throw.[10] It gives one of the clearest programs for learning the hammer, with appropriate skill-training drills.

Technical Components of the Throw

The length of a throw depends upon two things, the speed of the hammer at the moment of the release, and the angle of release. There are no significant aerodynamic factors, as there are with the javelin and the discus. The speed of the hammer results from the thrower's muscular power, reaction time, coordination, and physical stature. His ability to use this biophysical background to increase the hammer's speed from the winds through the turns until the release constitutes his technique. The angle of release also depends on the thrower's technique.

From a theoretical point of view, a tall man with a heavy build has the advantage in the hammer, but a small, powerful thrower can also succeed. The hammer thrower must develop optimal muscular power as a base for advanced technique, which takes years of daily training. Even then, he must continue to train

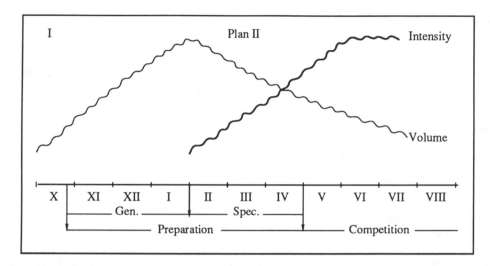

Figure 19.4 Single-periodized year for the hammer. From Kevin McGill. (1984). Hammer clinic. *Track and Field Quarterly Review*, **84**(1), 49. Adapted with permission.

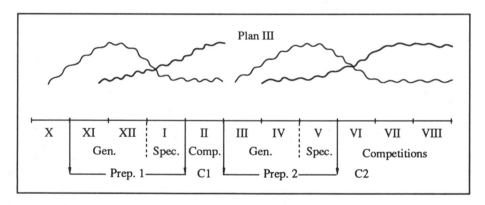

Figure 19.5 Double-periodized year for the hammer. From Kevin McGill. (1984). Hammer clinic. *Track and Field Quarterly Review*, **84**(1), 49. Adapted with permission.

to maintain his strengths and to try to overcome weaknesses.

Physical Strength Background

The hammer thrower must have overall strength, but these muscle groups should have special consideration in the power training:

Legs. The extensors of the hip (the gluteals and others), the extensors of the knee (the femoris group), and the plantar flexors (gastrocnemius and soleus).

Lower body. The twisters of the trunk (obliquis abdominis externis and internis), the muscles controlling the shoulders and arms (trapezius, rhomboids, deltoids, latissimus), the extensors of the trunk (erector spinae, quadratus lumborum), and the finger flexors.

The Mechanical Background

If we look at technique as measured in terms of physical principles, the key word is *speed*, or *velocity*. The thrower tries to build up a high central speed, or angular velocity, during the turns (Figure 19.7 on p. 210) by means of fast footwork. At the same time, he tries to maximize the hammer's peripheral, or linear, velocity by combining the central speed with a long radius. That requires long arms and a relaxed upper body. The body's axis of rotation is always moving forward in the circle and describing the outline of a cone (circumduction) (Figure 19.8 on p. 210).

The fastest central speed and the longest arms give not only the highest speed to the hammer but also the greatest pull outward (centrifugal force), up to 700 pounds for a throw of 200 feet. To control this force during the turns, the thrower must produce an equal

Table 19.3 Weekly Cycle for Elite Hammer Thrower

Variant I: 5 days, 10 sessions

M, Tu, F

Morning session
- 10 minutes warming up
- 12 throws with light hammer (6kg)
- 15 throws with regular hammer (7.25kg)
- 10 throws with heavier (9kg) implement

Evening session
- 10 minutes warming up
- Weight exercises: 10 tons total
  - snatch—1.5 tons
  - twisting—1 ton
  - good morning—1.5 tons
  - half squat—4 tons
  - jumping from half squat—2 tons

W, Sa

Morning session
- 10 minutes warming up
- 30 throws with 16kg weight (50cm handle), 1 or 2 turns
- 15 standing long jumps
- 50 throws
- 10 standing triple jumps

Evening session
- 10 minutes warming up
- Weight exercises: 5 tons total
  - twisting—2 tons
  - jumps from half squat—1 ton
  - half squat—2 tons

Variant II: 6 days, 12 sessions

M, W, F

Morning session
- 10 minutes warming up
- 10 throws with light hammer (6.5kg)
- 10 throws with regular hammer (7.25kg)
- 10 throws with heavier hammer (8.5kg)

Evening session
- 10 minutes warming up
- Weight exercises: 8 tons total
  - twisting—2 tons
  - step test on bench with barbell—3.5 tons
  - cleans without splitting—2.5 tons

Tu, Th, Sa

Morning session
- 10 minutes warming up
- 100 throws with 16kg implement of different kind
- 30 standing long jumps

Evening session
- 10 minutes warming up
- Weight exercises—5 tons
  - twisting—1.5 tons
  - good morning—1.5 tons
  - jumping from half squat—2 tons
- Playing games (basketball, volleyball)—20 minutes

Su Rest

Table 19.4 Increase in Load Volumes for Hammer Thrower

Factor	Year volume*			
	1976	1980	1984	1984†
Training days	100	125	138	222
Total throws	100	118	151	6,332
Barbell training	100	170	198	1,402 tons

*Relative to 1976, except for the last column.

†Absolute values for 9 months.

(centripetal) force pulling in the opposite direction. He must keep his knees bent and his lower back straight to control the centrifugal force exerted by the pull of the hammer.

To understand the relationship between the hammer's speed and the angle of delivery, refer to the nomograph that Russian hammer thrower and engineer Anatoliy Samotsvetov constructed (Figure 19.9 on p. 211). Such nomographs can help coaches discover their throwers' potential and correct their faults.

In Samotsvetov's case, he had measured a 200-foot throw. With a stopwatch he had timed the flight of the hammer, from the release to the landing, as 2.9 seconds. From the nomograph he can determine that the angle of the release was 33 degrees and the velocity was 82 feet per second. However, using the nomograph, he can also see that if his thrower increased his angle of release to 43 degrees, with the same speed of release, he would have thrown 215 feet!

Common Faults of Hammer Throwers

In the starting position

- Placing the wrong hand on the grip
- Not starting with the hammerhead far enough behind

In the preliminary swings

- Bending the elbows and lifting the shoulders
- Bending the trunk forward
- Not bending the knees
- The lowest point of the hammer's swing being too far in front of the athlete
- Not emphasizing the forward and upward part of the swing
- Going too far left with the hands when passing over the head
- Not countering the hips in relation to the shoulders

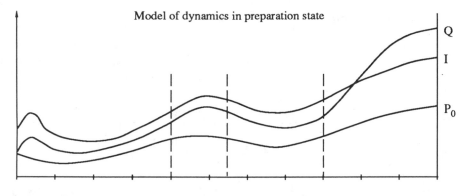

Q—initial power of muscles; I—explosive power (i.e., acceleration); P_0—absolute strength

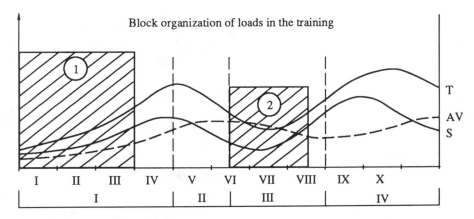

T—technique; AV—general conditioning; S—speed work; 1,2—power blocks

Figure 19.6 Periodized training emphases for the hammer.

From Peter Tschiene. (1988). The throwing events: Recent trends in technique and training. *New Studies in Athletics*, **3**(1), 14. Adapted with permission.

Table 19.5 Model Items in Preparation of Hammer Throwers

| | Desired distance* | |
Measured item	Meters	Feet and inches
Throws		
16kg (or 10kg) weight	20-24	65'7"-78'9"
18kg hammer	48-50	158'-164'
6kg hammer	88-89	289'-292'
5kg hammer	93-95	305'-312'
7.25kg shot, backward	21-22	68'11"-72'2"
Jumps		
Standing long jump	3.40-3.50	11'2"-11'6"
Standing triple jump	9.50-9.80	31'2"-32'2"
Sargent jump (jump and reach)	0.95-1.00	37"-39"
Weights		
Squats	260-280kg	573-617 lbs

*Squats have weight measures.

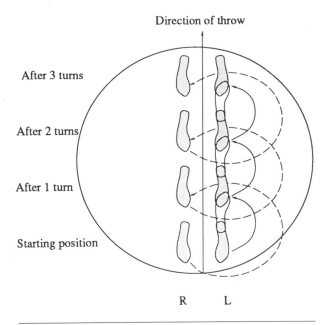

Figure 19.7 Footwork in the hammer throw.

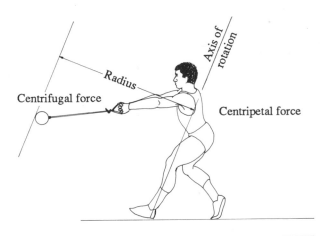

Figure 19.8 Body's axis of rotation during the hammer throw.

• Not raising the left heel when turning the trunk right to "meet" the hammer

In the turns

• Starting the turning of the feet too late and too slow, so the hammer takes the lead
• Not placing the body weight over the bent right leg
• Moving the right leg too slowly and too far from the left in the turn
• Bending the head and upper body forward
• Bending the elbows
• Not turning the left foot 180 degrees, so the thrower ends on the left side of the circle
• Stretching the left knee so the thrower gets too long a turn and ends on the right side of the circle
• The trail of the hammer being too steep

In the delivery

• The body being too far to the right
• The legs being too extended, so the thrower does not get any power from them and the delivery is too flat
• Using only the upper body in the delivery
• Bending the upper body, the hammerhead touching the ground

After the delivery

• Stopping the rotation instead of following through
• Stepping out of the front half of the circle

Training Considerations

The main goals of training for the hammer throw are to build up general and specific strength and to develop good technique. One can say that roughly one quarter of the training will be allotted to developing technique and the other three quarters to general and special conditioning, using a variety of methods, such as running, games, jumping, flexibility, technical training, and barbell work. The training can be done both indoors and outdoors, depending on local conditions.

Types of Training

Running. There are several types of running, and each has its purpose: Jogging is done to warm up; fartlek and long, slow runs develop stamina or cool one off after a hard practice; and sprinting 20 to 40m builds up speed.

Games. Games are a combination of running and jumping, but they are more fun. Basketball, volleyball, and soccer are fine for warming up and for recreation.

Flexibility. This training consists of all kinds of arm swings and hip circling to improve these movements and to develop flexibility in the shoulders and the hip region.

Jumping. Jumping is an important training activity because it develops explosive power and speed in the lower extremities. Specifically, broad and high jumps, continuous hops and steps, step-jumping, and rope-skipping develop these skills.

Technical training. This training is important both to the novice, to learn good technique, and to the champion, to try to improve pattern and speed. Technical training can be done best outdoors, but it is also possible indoors. If the athlete cannot train at the main stadium, it would be worth the effort for him to construct a concrete circle in a quiet place out of the way of activity. Indoors, the athlete can train for technique with sandbags on a rope or with a hammer thrown into a nylon net or a canvas "wall."

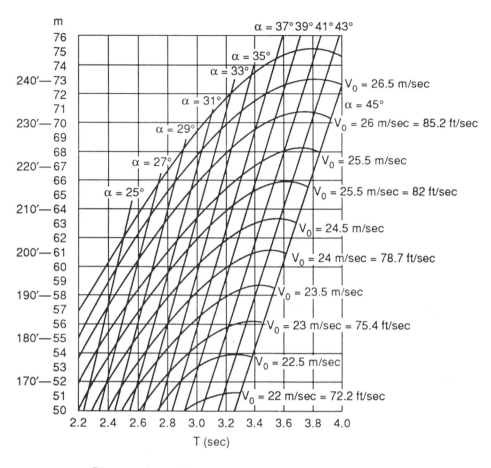

m   Distance thrown in meters
V_0 Velocity of hammer at release
α Release angle
T   Flight time of hammer

Figure 19.9 Relationship between speed and angle of delivery of the hammer.

Technical training for the hammer throw consists of countless swings and turns and releases, practiced in various combinations, with hammers of ordinary weights as well as heavier and lighter implements.

Weight training. Strength is a must for a hammer thrower, and the only way to develop strength is to work against resistance. Of the two types of resistance training, isotonic and isometric, we advocate the isotonic (dynamic). The exercises included here (Figures 19.10 and 19.11) are for only that type of training. Strength training can be divided into basic training, with heavy weights, and specific training, with smaller weights. The basic training concentrates on the muscles in the legs, the back, and the arms. The weights used are 70 to 90% of the maximum that can be lifted. One to six repetitions are done in three sets. The pauses between the sets are from 2 to 3 minutes.

Figure 19.12 shows examples of Soviet exercises. In the specific training, smaller implements and lighter weights are used, such as sandbags, medicine balls, shots, barbell discs, and light and heavy hammers (Fig. 19.13). They are all used in exercises that follow the same pattern as the swings, the turns, and the delivery. They are executed as fast as possible and with adequate rest between tries.

Planning the Training Schedule

In all training programs, the athlete must have one plan that encompasses goals over the long term, such as a year; and one or more plans geared toward short-range goals, such as plans for the preseason months, for competition season, and for days and weeks. All these plans must be flexible enough to accommodate the unpredictable: sickness, injuries, stress from studies, special events, or personal problems.

Without weights

Hops   Knee-lifts   Steps   Steps and jumps

With heavy weights

Squat   Clean   Step-up   Jumps   Leg press

Figure 19.10 Exercises for the lower body.

In planning a long-term training program, the athlete should keep certain points in mind:

1. In the *off-season* the aim is to build up and maintain overall physical fitness and strength. At least 3 days a week should be devoted to this kind of training, and at least 1 day to technical and more specific training.

2. In the *competitive season*, the athlete still requires 2 days of all-around training, mixed with auxiliary exercises more specific to the hammer. Technical training should be done 2 or 3 days a week.

3. The training schedule's ratio of general conditioning to specific training depends largely on the athlete's stage of development. A beginner must spend more time on the basic training than the thrower who has years of practice and several competitions behind him. The experienced thrower must reduce the basic weight training to a level sufficient only to maintain basic strength and should spend most of his training time on technique and special weight training.

4. The thrower chooses his weights and numbers of repetitions and sets according to his level of development (but within the bounds of accepted training methods).

5. Besides weight training and throwing, the athlete should always try to fit in sprints, jumps, and flexibility training. It is best to do this training on the same day as the technical training.

6. The number of throws during one "practice day" must never be over 40, and 30 to 40% of the throws should be for distance.

7. One of the days of technical training should concentrate on special problems of technique, such as winds and turns without throwing, continuous turns (5 to 10) with the hammer or a shot in the hands, and easy turns with stress on the release.

8. Warm-up exercises are essential for physical and mental preparedness. The warm-up should always move from slow movements to more vigorous movements; for example, jogging and wind sprints should be followed by calisthenics.

With heavy weights

Forward raise   Good morning   Rowing   Twist and bend

Curls   Lateral raise   Pull   Bench press

In stallbar without weights   **In stallbar with weights**

Arm-bending in stallbar and on bar   Twisting

Figure 19.11 Exercises for the upper body.

Figure 19.12 Power exercises. From Peter Tschiene. (1988). The throwing events: Recent trends in technique and training. *New Studies in Athletics*, **3**(1), 12. Adapted with permission.

The training load before a major meet is very important, especially during the last 2 weeks. It determines not only the readiness of the athlete for competition but also his rate of recovery after competition. We recommend that the training load for the last 8 to 12 days before competition be decreased by 50 to 60%. During the last week, the number of throws should be reduced to half the number of the previous weeks, and the intensity of the throws should be only 80 to 90% of maximum. In short, you should reduce both load and intensity of training before a meet.

Before the meet, the following warm-up is suggested:

- Slow run for 10 to 20 minutes
- Short wind sprints, 20 to 40m
- General calisthenics
- Winding the hammer and slow turns
- Two or three easy throws
- One or two harder throws (still not maximum)

Table 19.6 gives a sample year plan. Tables 19.7 and 19.8 give sample training weeks for the preseason and the competitive season. As always, these training plans are guidelines, not laws. For this reason, there is no training schedule for the hammer provided in this chapter. The training schedule fundamentals, however, appear at the end of the chapter.

Figure 19.13 Training exercises with small weights.

Table 19.6 Sample 1-Year Training Schedule for the Hammer Throw

	Preseason		Competitive season
	Sept Oct Nov Dec	Jan Feb March	Apr May June July Aug
	(4-5 days a week)	(5-6 days a week)	(4-5 days a week)
M	Basic strength training	Fartlek	Basic strength training; long, slow run
Tu		General fitness	Throwing and specific strength training
W	Basic strength training	Games	Specific strength: light throwing and basic strength, jumps, sprints
Th	Technical training	Throwing	Throwing—sprints
F	Basic strength training	Specific strength	
Sa			Competition or throwing; sprints and jumps
Su	Throwing, sprints, jumps		
Aim	All-around strength	Specific strength	Preparation for competition—technique
Type of work	Increasing the weights	Same weights Increasing the speed	Reducing the weights Increasing the speed

From Arne Nytro. (1974). The hammer throw. In William J. Bowerman & William H. Freeman. *Coaching track and field* (p. 322). Boston: Houghton Mifflin. Reprinted with permission of editors.

Table 19.7   Sample Week of Preseason Training

M 1. Warm-up
    2. Barbell work
      a. Squats, 3 sets of 6
      b. Two-handed curls, 2 sets of 10
      c. Dead lift, 3 sets of 4
      d. Sit-ups, with twist, 3 sets of 10
      e. Clean, 3 sets of 6
      f. Rowing, flat back, 2 sets of 6
      g. Leg press (in machine), 2 sets of 6
      h. Pull (in machine), 2 sets of 6
    3. Exercise for flexibility
    4. 1- to 2-mile slow run
Tu No training
W 1. Warm-up
    2. Barbell work
      a. Squats, 3 sets of 6
      b. Clean, 3 sets of 6
      c. Dead lift, 3 sets of 4
      d. Good morning, flat back, 3 sets of 4
      e. Forward, upward raise, 2 sets of 4
      f. Standing, trunk twist and bend, 2 sets of 8
      g. Rowing, flat back, 3 sets of 6
    3. Exercise for flexibility
    4. 1- to 2-mile slow run
Th 1. Warm-up: one-handed winds
    2. Technical training
      a. 5 to 10 winds and throws with two hammers or a 25- or 50-pound weight
      b. Winds, three turns and throw, with regular hammer: 15 throws with 70% intensity, 10 throws with medium effort
    3. Jumps
      a. 5 to 10 × 20 to 40m sprint, standing start
      b. 5 series of hops, 15m on each leg
      c. 5 series of steps, 25m long
    4. Auxiliary exercises
      a. Arm bending on stallbar or beam, 3 sets of 10
      b. Twisting exercises with small weights
    5. Exercise for flexibility
    6. Slow run
F 1. Warm-up
    2. Barbell work
      a. Squats, 3 sets of 6
      b. Bench press, 3 sets of 6
      c. Good morning, 2 sets of 6
      d. Clean, 3 sets of 6
      e. Shoulder shrug, 2 sets of 10
      f. Arm circling and swinging
      g. Lying on bench, extended arms twisting
      h. Lying down, leg raise and twist
      i. Pull (in machine), 2 sets of 6
    3. Exercise for flexibility
    4. 1- to 2-mile slow run
Sa No training
Su Same as Thursday

From Arne Nytro. (1974). The hammer throw. In William J. Bowerman & William H. Freeman. *Coaching track and field* (p. 322). Boston: Houghton Mifflin.

Table 19.8   Sample Week of Competitive Training

M 1. Warm-up
    2. Barbell work
      a. One-half squat, 3 sets of 6
      b. Clean and jerk, 3 sets of 6
      c. Sit-ups with twist incline board
      d. Step up and down on a box, 20 times
      e. Rowing, flat back, 3 sets of 6
      f. Leg press (in machine), 2 sets of 6
      g. Pull (in machine), 3 sets of 6
    3. Exercise for flexibility
    4. Jog
Tu 1. Warm-up
    2. Barbell work
      a. Throwing with weights (25 to 50 pounds)
      b. Throwing a shot backward, forward, and sideways
      c. Pull-ups on bar
      d. Twisting exercises with the shot in sitting and lying positions
    3. 2- to 3-mile slow run
W 1. Warm-up
    2. Throwing
      a. Continuous turns
      b. 20 easy throws
      c. 10 throws at maximum effort
    3. Exercises for flexibility
    4. Jog
Th 1. Warm-up
    2. Throwing
      a. Winds and throws without turns
      b. 20 throws with 3 turns for style
    3. Jumps
      a. 5 series of hops, 15m on each leg
      b. 5 series of steps, 25m long
    4. Runs
      a. Standing start, 5 reps of 30m sprints
      b. 1-mile slow run
F No training
Sa Competition, or
    1. Warm-up
    2. 6 throws, maximum effort, with 3 to 5 minutes between throws
    3. 15 minutes jogging
    4. 6 more throws at maximum effort, as before
    5. Wind sprints
    6. Exercises for flexibility
    7. Jogging
Su No training

From Arne Nytro. (1974). The hammer throw. In William J. Bowerman & William H. Freeman. *Coaching track and field* (p. 322). Boston: Houghton Mifflin.

References

1. K. Bartonietz, L. Hinz, D. Lorenz, & G. Lunau. (1988). The hammer: The view of the DVfL of the GDR on talent selection, technique and training of throwers from beginner to top level athlete. *New Studies in Athletics*, 3(1), 39-56.
2. *Ibid.*, p. 47.
3. *Ibid.*, p. 51.
4. William H. Freeman. (1989). *Peak when it counts: Periodization for the American coach.* Los Altos, CA: Tafnews.
5. Peter Tschiene. (1988). The throwing events: Recent trends in technique and training. *New Studies in Athletics*, 3(1), 14.
6. Bartonietz, et al., *supra* note 1, p. 55.
7. Tschiene, *supra* note 5, p. 16.
8. *Ibid.*, p. 10.
9. Ladislav Pataki. (1986). *Hammer throwing.* Newark, CA: SyberVision.
10. Ladislav Pataki, Ed Burke, & Stewart Togher. (1989). The hammer throw. In Vern Gambetta (Ed.), *The Athletics Congress's track and field coaching manual* (2nd ed., pp. 177-188). Champaign, IL: Leisure Press.

Additional Readings

Bakarinov, Y., Fantalis, & Tshehotaryov. (1986). Contemporary views: Hammer technique. *Track and Field Quarterly Review*, 86(1), 45-46.

Bakarinov, Y., & Ozerov, V. (1988). Varied weight hammers. *Track Technique*, 103, 3300.

Bondarchuk, Anatoliy P. (1980). Modern trends in hammer technique. *Track and Field Quarterly Review*, 80(1), 39-40.

Bondarchuk, Anatoliy. (1988). Constructing a training system. Parts 1 and 2. *Track Technique*, 102, 3254-3259, 3268; 103, 3286-3288.

Bosen, Ken O. (1985). Coaching hammer throwing technique. *Track and Field Quarterly Review*, 85(1), 36-39.

Chuman, Valentin. (1986). Starting position of a hammer thrower. *Track and Field Quarterly Review*, 86(1), 47.

Connolly, Harold. (1988). What makes Syedikh's technique so effective? *Track Technique*, 102, 3260.

Dapena, Jesús. (1990). Some biomechanical aspects of hammer throwing. *Track Technique*, 111, 3535-3539.

Goldhammer, John. (1984). Post 1976 hammer technique changes. *Track and Field Quarterly Review*, 84(1), 38-40.

Jarver, Jess (Ed.) (1985). *The throws: Contemporary theory, technique and training* (3rd ed.). Los Altos, CA: Tafnews.

Joch, Winfried. (1988). Increase in release velocity as the main objective in the throwing events. *New Studies in Athletics*, 3(1), 35-38.

Johnson, Carl. (1984). *Hammer throwing* (7th ed.). London: British Amateur Athletic Board.

McGill, Kevin. (1983). Analysis chart for hammer. *Track and Field Quarterly Review*, 83(1), 55.

McGill, Kevin. (1984). Teaching the hammer. *Track and Field Quarterly Review*, 84(1), 41-42.

McGill, Kevin. (1989). Hammer. *Track and Field Quarterly Review*, 89(3), 27-47.

Miller, Brian P. (1985). Psychological factors in competitive throwing. *Track and Field Quarterly Review*, 85(1), 40-44.

Pedemonte, Jimmy. (1981). Technical-conditioning training of young hammer throwers. *Track and Field Quarterly Review*, 81(1), 48-49.

Perkins, Rich. (1980). Degree positioning for the hammer. *Track and Field Quarterly Review*, 80(1), 52-56.

Shurina, O., & Shurina, A. (1981). Strength training of young hammer throwers. *Track and Field Quarterly Review*, 81(1), 50-51.

Sing, Robert O. (1986). Psychological concerns in the throwing events. *Track Technique*, 96, 3069-3070.

TT interview: Yuriy Syedikh. (1988). *Track Technique*, 105, 3357, 3362.

Uebel, Ralf. (1986). Teaching methodology for the beginning hammer thrower. *Track and Field Quarterly Review*, 86(1), 39-44.

Hammer Throw Training Schedule

ATHLETE _____

1. Warm-up
   A. Jog 1-2 laps, easy stretching
   B. Hendricks Park
   C. Golf course
2. Fartlek
   A. Varied pace   B. Slow, steady pace
3. Weights and jogging
4. A. Winds   C. Release
   B. Turns
5. Routine
   A. Turn & throw   B. Cross ring & throw
      (1) one hand   (2) hammer in each hand
      (3) regular
      a. heavy hammer   b. light hammer
6. Technique
   A. Control of winds
   B. Lift & turn toward front of circle
   C. Collapse knee & drop toward back of circle
   D. Hips back, arms extended; long radius of rotation
   E. Explode on every 3rd or 4th throw
   F. Direction across circle
   G. Lift, pull, & explode on release
   H. Target for 3/4 to 7/8 effort
   J. Angle of release
   K.
      (1) stand
      (2) crossing, have speed under control
      a. easy b. medium c. hard
7. Team meeting
8. Special
   A. Sauna   C. Steps or hill
   B. Swim
9. Special implements
   A. Light hammer   B. Heavy hammer

   C. Shot   D. Medicine ball
      (1) 4kg   (2) 5kg   (3) 6kg
      (4) 16 lb   (5) 8kg   (6) 9kg   (7)
10. Progress assessment
    A. Meet   C. Simulation
    B. Trial   D. Control test
11. Cross circle easy; feeling of exploding; start slow, finish fast
12. With Coach
    A. (name)
    B. Leader
14. A. Wind sprints   (1) straight   (2) curve
    B. Hurdle drill: 3 LH, 7-9m apart
    C. Spring & bound
    D. Alternate run & jog, at least 800m
    E. Starts, go 20-25m
    F. High knee (slow) & fast leg
15. Plyometrics
    A. Jumps   (1) 1 leg   (2) both legs   (3)
    B. Bounding   (1) 1 leg   (2) both legs   (3)
    C.
16. Tumbling activities
17. Jumping drills
    A. High jump   D. Hops & steps
    B. Long jump   E. Step jumping
    C. Plyometrics   F. Rope skipping
18. Work on staying in the circle
19. Games
    A. Basketball   C. Soccer
    B. Volleyball
20. Work on second event
21. Visual aids
    A. Videotape   C. Photos
    B. Film
       (1) record performance   (2) study
30. Experimental work

CHAPTER 20	# The Combined
	# Events: Heptathlon and
	## Decathlon

The combined events, the heptathlon and the decathlon, might be called the "acid tests of athletics," for their demands upon the participants are great. The name *decathlon* comes from the Greek *deca*, meaning "ten," because it includes ten separate events, while *heptathlon* refers to seven events. The competitions last for 2 days, with the events in the order shown in Table 20.1.

Both competitions are scored by tables devised by the IAAF on a range of 1 to 1,200 points per separate event, with the 1,000-point level roughly equivalent to the "decathlon world record" for that event (no *official* records are awarded, but these are the best marks made in decathlon competition). A score for an inexperienced person of 5,000 total points in the decathlon or 3,000 points in the heptathlon shows potential, provided the weaknesses in any individual event are not too glaring. For men, a score of 7,000 points is beginning to reach national class; the world-class level begins around 8,000 points. For women, 5,000 points is national class, and 6,000 points is world class.

The training for the individual events within the combined events follows the same patterns as for those separate events.[1] However, the sequence of the events in a combined meet affects the performance of the events that follow. For example, going from the shot put to the high jump is not the same as warming up and competing in the high jump as the first or only event of the day.

Americans no longer dominate in the decathlon. Their recent success in the heptathlon is very unusual.

Table 20.1 The Combined Events

Decathlon	Heptathlon
Day 1	Day 1
100m	100m hurdles
Long jump	High jump
Shot put	Shot put
High jump	200m
400m	
Day 2	Day 2
110m hurdles	Long jump
Discus throw	Javelin throw
Pole vault	800m
Javelin throw	
1,500m	

The reason lies in two major changes in international training. Compared to American training systems, the foreign programs carefully plan and record training plans and results and increase the training loads for both men and women. The result is a gradually developing superiority in the strength and technical events, which reflects more effective training methods.

Table 20.2 shows an example of the increasing training loads. It gives the recommended annual training load for male and female combined-event athletes in the Soviet Union.

Table 20.2 Recommended Training Loads for Soviet Combined Events

	Women	Men
Training days	280	280
Training sessions	420	420
Training hours	1,120	1,120
Running at max speed (km)	35	40
Repetition runs, 100-600m (km)	85	75
Steady running (km)	1,100	1,200
Hurdling (number of hurdles)	4,000	3,100
Long jumps	900	700
High jumps	1,100	800
Shot puts	2,600	2,300
Javelin throws	3,100	3,000
Weight training (tons)	240	300
Jumping exercises (takeoffs)	11,000	11,000

From Fred Kudu. (1984). Training load in the heptathlon. *Track Technique*, **90**, 2883. Reprinted with permission.

Training Theory for Decathlon

Basic training goals for the younger male athlete (after a sub-4:40 1,500m) might be 700 points for each of the other events, along with 800 points for two to four high-point events. For more advanced athletes, the goals should rise gradually to 800 points per event, with some events ranging toward the 900 to 1,000-point level. This approach has been popular for several decades.

Though the most common training pattern is to practice each event in the order that it occurs in competition, that training pattern needs changes.[2] Recent studies suggest that is not the most efficient way to train.

Polish studies show that greater gains are made by more general training, developing the traits and skills that are shared by several events, thus making more efficient use of training time.[3] For example, aspects of speed training and technique are involved in 7 of the 10 events. The start from blocks occurs three times. Certain basic takeoff patterns are found in all three jumps.

Decathlon training should fall into three stages:[4]

Ages 14 to 17: beginning training. Stresses building endurance (rather than speed), strength, and mobility.

Ages 18 to 20: developing specialized motor skills. Mastering the technique of the events.

After age 20: specialized training. Emphasizes dynamic training and making the technical skills automatic.

The first stage uses general physical training to aid the body's growth and development with effective training, rather than overloading it and interfering with the growth process. Endurance (rather than speed) is emphasized because it provides a base for developing speed and strength later. Flexibility and dexterity are developed across a wide range of motor skills. The hurdles and the pole vault are emphasized because they are the most complex events in the decathlon.

During the second stage, the foundations for elite-level motor skills are developed. The training volume is very high, with optimal volumes in running, jumping, strength training, and the mastery of the skills of each individual event. Absolute strength is emphasized, using 75 to 90% of maximum in most exercises. Jumping exercises are used, including single-legged and double-legged jumps, along with jumps from a run and over hurdles.

The overall training program uses more intense, complex training methods and higher volumes to improve the athlete's capabilities. The ability to relax is needed because of the length of decathlon competitions. The athlete must conserve his reserves during the intervals between peak efforts.

The third stage uses strength training (to develop speed-strength qualities), jumping exercises, and technical training with more advanced skills. Psychological preparation becomes more important. Both coach and athlete must be careful not to overuse jumping exercises or plyometrics; otherwise, the athlete may suffer frequent injuries.

The coach should stress that improvements are gradual. The new decathlete should not expect radical improvements except in new events. A study of elite athletes showed that they averaged 7,600 points (1962 tables) at age 20.[5] From that point, in 4 years of competitive growth, they reached a mean score of 8,350 points between ages 24 and 25. Most athletes had explosive improvements in their scores only where attaining their full growth was a factor. For many of the athletes, there were no improvements in some of their high-scoring events.

The composition of the scoring tables is a major factor in planning training. Decathletes perform in a highly subjective environment; the IAAF scoring tables give an edge to the sprinter-jumper. The coach must study the point tables and the athlete's best marks in each event, then plan the training in relation to the tables, trying for the most effective use of training time for potential scoring improvements. Though the scoring tables were revised in 1985, they still favor the sprinter-jumper.

As an old study pointed out, more points are lost than are gained in a major competition.[6] For this reason, the most important goal of a young athlete should be to eliminate low-scoring performances in any events. After a stable skill base is developed, the tables can be restudied to probe for potential "easy" events, sometimes easy relative to the scoring table, sometimes relative to the athlete's talents.

Decathlon performances have improved sharply over the last decade. Elite decathlon performers do not develop from untalented youths who became decathletes because they had no single strong event.[7] Those who reach the top are generally among the cream of the crop even as junior-level athletes.

At the same time, as Table 20.3 shows, performance improvement is not a series of big jumps. It is made up of regular small improvements, a gradual rise in performance over several years (usually 4 to 5 years from the national to the elite level).

For the young athlete at the national level (7,500 to 7,700 points), very gradual improvements in performance are the norm for most events, and balance across the events is a clear criterion of success at the highest level. In short, there are no weak events among elite decathletes.

The performances of elite athletes show that the events that improve the least are the high jump and the flat runs (100, 400, and 1,500m). This is not because little training time went into those events. Rather, they are the simplest events in terms of technique. The technical events yield larger point increases as they are mastered. Still, we must require a certain minimal level of skill in every event because those events (except for the 1,500) are the earliest "big score" events for juniors.

We still have much to learn about effective training methods in the decathlon because it involves the interaction of training for events whose major performance traits are not completely compatible.[8] The strength needs for the shot put clash with the body size need for jumping and vaulting, for example. Although the training pattern follows that of the individual events, the coach might prefer a pattern that places the emphasis upon only two or three events during a given phase, allowing more concentrated skill development.

The practice of competing in many individual events during the early season should be limited. The athlete should never compete in an event if he does not have time for a proper warm-up and for concentrating on achieving his goal for that single event in that meet. Rushing from one event to the next results in poor habits of concentration, less effective technique, and an unrealistic sense of what the decathlon is like. In most combined-event competitions, the athlete has from 30 minutes to an hour or more between events (the Olympic Games takes a 2-hour "lunch break" after the second event each day). Competition in individual events should simulate the specific needs of the decathlete, not the needs of a team for an extra few points.

Training Theory for Heptathlon

The points just made about competing in individual events for the decathlon also hold for the heptathlon. Coaches tend to use the talented multi-event athlete as a big "point-man" (or "-woman") for the team,

Table 20.3   Annual Elite Improvement in the Decathlon

Event	Early marks	Peak marks	Improvement	Annual gain
100m	11.17	10.96	0.21 sec	0.05 sec
Long jump	23' 4.75"	24' 6.25"	1' 1.75"	3.5"
Shot put	43' 10.75"	49' 5.25"	4' 6.5"	1' 1.5"
High jump	6' 6"	6' 8"	2.0"	0.5"
400m	50.02	48.68	1.34 sec	0.34 sec
110m hurdles	15.34	14.68	0.66 sec	0.16 sec
Discus throw	134' 3"	152' 4.25"	18' 1"	4' 6"
Pole vault	13' 9"	15' 4.25"	7.25"	1.75"
Javelin throw	187' 6"	208' 2"	20' 8"	5' 2"
1,500m	4:36.12	4:26.88	9.24 sec	2.31 sec
Score	7,595.51	8,352.97	757.46 pts.	198.36 pts.
Age	20.36	24.51	4.15 years	

From William H. Freeman. (1986). Decathlon performance success: Progress and age factors. *Track Technique*, **96**, 3051. Reprinted with permission.

but it is detrimental to his or her chance to become a truly elite combined-event athlete.

The developmental process in the heptathlon falls into these two stages:[9]

Learning Stage. Emphasize the performance balance across the events and the improvement of conditioning, speed, strength, and endurance.

Specificity Stage. Emphasize increasing the speed, specific strength, speed endurance, and specific endurance.

Bob Myers (University of Arizona) recommends stressing the following training components in planning the heptathlon training program:[10]

- Speed training: needed for four of the seven events
- Technique training: stresses the common technique factors, as mentioned for the decathlon
- Strength training

1. General strength—Olympic lifts and power lifts
2. Specific strength—power or speed-strength, including plyometrics and high-volume technique drills

- Endurance training: base for 800m and for work capacity for extensive training and competition
- Mobility (flexibility): increases the range of motion, improving technique and decreasing the risk of injury
- Recovery: extremely important because of high training volume; includes mental and physical recovery, restoration, active rest, and complete rest (active rest is preferred)

All training should be classified and recorded. An example is the classification of work for combined events, shown in Table 20.4. American heptathletes tend to be deficient in special endurance and strength (both general and specific) compared to their foreign

Table 20.4 Classification of Work for Combined Events

Type of training	Intensity (%)	Notes
1. Speed 1-4 sets of 1-4 × 20-60m 1-5 minutes recovery per rep 5-10 minutes recovery per set	95-100	Run on track from different starting positions.
2. Speed endurance 1-3 sets of 2-5 × 60-150m (400-600m total) 2-5 minutes recovery per rep 8-10 minutes recovery per set	90-100	Run on track.
3. Special endurance 1-5 × 150-600m (300-1,800m total) 5 minutes to full recovery per rep	90-100	Run on track.
4. Plyometrics	80-100	Do on grass for multiple contacts, or on track for high intensity.
5. Intensive tempo 1-4 sets of 2-6 × 100-1,000m Recovery to 110-115 HR	80-90	Run on grass, if possible.
6. Extensive tempo 1-3 × 1-3km Recovery to 120 HR	40-80	Run on grass.
7. Technique	Varies	
8. Circuit training	Varies	
9. Weight lifting	Varies	

From Bob Myers. (1989). The heptathlon. In Vern Gambetta (Ed.), *The Athletics Congress's track and field coaching manual* (2nd ed., p. 214). Champaign, IL: Leisure Press. Reprinted with permission.

opponents. This shows in weaker performances in the 800m, the shot put, and the long jump.

A broad weekly pattern or microcycle might look like this:

Monday and Tuesday: high-volume training
Wednesday and Thursday: lower-volume training (higher quality; sprinting)
Friday and Saturday: medium-volume training
Sunday: total rest or restoration

Within a training session, training should follow this rough order:

- Technique work
- Sprinting and explosive activities
- Strength training
- Endurance training

Myers's recommendations for a general annual plan are shown in Table 20.5.

As noted in a research study of heptathlon performances,[11] "A willingness to train our women more at the level of the men in intensity, with loadings in proportion to their relative body-sizes, will pay many benefits in the coming years; for in the revolution in women's track and field, the United States has been largely content to follow sluggishly along some distance behind the leaders. The talent has always been there; it is time for American coaches to work at a more thorough development of it."

Table 20.5 Annual Training for the Heptathlon

General preparation (Sept, Oct, Nov)	Special preparation (Dec, Jan, Feb)	Early competition (Mar, Apr, May)	Peak (June)	Transition (July, Aug)
Beginner				
Flexibility, intensive tempo, speed, running and lifting, technique work, circuits (weights), Mach drills, extensive tempo, basic drill work	Speed, speed endurance, special endurance, jump circuits, extensive tempo for recovery, total technique work, lifting (lower volume, higher intensity)	Speed, special endurance, very specific drill work, total technique refinement	Sound mechanics, speed, special endurance, competitive-style training	1 month rest, fun and game-type activities 1 month active rest (basketball, volleyball); begin lifting, easy circuits, intensive tempo
Intermediate				
Flexibility, intensive tempo, speed, speed endurance, fartlek, running and lifting technique, circuits (weights), throws, hurdle, medicine ball, Mach drills, basic drill work, long bounding	Speed endurance, special endurance, lifting (high intensity), intensive technique work, high-volume plyometrics	Special endurance, speed blocks, low-volume lifting maintenance, speed strength or fast lifting plyometrics until crucial meets	Competition technique, speed, special endurance, competition-specific training	2 weeks rest; 2 weeks active rest; 1 month weights (circuits or stage), intensive tempo, sprinting
Elite				
Speed, intensive tempo, speed endurance, Olympic lifting technique, circuits, weights, throws and hurdle and jump circuits, corrective drill work (problem solving), long bounding	Speed, special endurance, speed endurance, lower volume of lifting and plyometrics, high volume of special strength drills, restorative work	Special endurance, speed, high volume of event-specific work, maintenance lifting and easy lifting plyometrics up until crucial meets, maintaining high volume of training until end of phase	Speed, special endurance, competition-specific work, lower volume training	2 weeks rest; 2 weeks active rest (basketball, volleyball, swimming); 1 month circuits, technique revamping, intensive tempo, speed endurance

From Bob Myers. (1989). The heptathlon. In Vern Gambetta (Ed.), *The Athletics Congress's track and field coaching manual* (2nd ed., p. 215). Champaign, IL: Leisure Press. Reprinted with permission.

Short versions of the official decathlon and heptathlon scoring tables are shown in Tables 20.7 and 20.8 at the end of the chapter. All implements are official, and all international rules apply, except these:

- Only three attempts are allowed in the throwing events and the long jump.
- A runner is not disqualified until the third false start.
- If the athlete does not start in every event, he or she is disqualified.
- Records cannot be set if the wind exceeds 4m per second in the events with wind-velocity limits.

Applied Training for the Combined Events

Few references give details of decathlon training in actual practice. We will describe decathlon training at Oregon, which has produced two world-class decathletes. Coaches often fail to realize the potential all-around training that can be gained from decathlon training. Training for the combined events often produces improvements in the specialty events.

Using the Combined Events in Physical Education

Potential for the combined events can be tested with modified competitions, such as the one by Robert Parks[12] for an indoor activity with elementary and junior high school students, or that by Alfred Sylvia[13] for use in high school and college physical education classes. Bowerman used a variation called the "three-quarter decathlon" in classes for almost 20 years. The most recent version of the scoring table is closely related to the international tables, so it is indicative of genuine decathlon or heptathlon potential. The combined events are strenuous activities (we might even call each a "sport" because they include 7 or 10 events). The short time in which the athletes must produce major efforts creates a need for stamina. The psychological considerations are many because the athlete needs long-term powers of concentration to endure the mental strain of up-and-down competition spread over 2 days.

In any combined event, points are more easily lost than gained, so the key to success is a balance of skill across the range of events. This touches upon the old argument of whether the athlete should concentrate on his or her specialty event or events to make up for the weak events, or concentrate on the weaker

events to not detract so much from the final score. Until the 1960s the common approach was to focus on one or two "big" events to accumulate a mass of points. This idea is no longer accepted, probably because the opponents are far more talented than in the past.

Also, what happens if the athlete does not come through in the big-point event? He or she will probably lose. One approach to counteract that risk is to train in all of the events until every event reaches an acceptable bottom-range score. After that, the athlete can work to develop one or more big-point events. If there are no obvious weak events, the athlete will not suffer so greatly from an off day.

The Oregon Test: The Three-Quarters Decathlon and Heptathlon

The Oregon Test can be used as a class activity, and it also indicates talent for the combined events. A special scoring table is used because it is a "three-quarter" event: All the running events are about three quarters of the usual distances:

- 100m is now 55m
- 200m becomes 150m
- 400m becomes 300m
- 800m becomes 600m
- 1,500m becomes 1,200m
- Men's high hurdles become the 80m hurdles
- Women's high hurdles become the 55m hurdles

Both hurdle events are set at the high school heights. All other events use standard conditions and implements of the standard size and weight. The student may skip 1 of the 10 events, taking an automatic 100 points for that event.

The old scoring tables were revised in 1971 and 1988 to be very close to the values of the IAAF tables, giving greater predictive value to potential achievement in a real competition. The tests are spread over 3 days instead of 2, covering a 5-day period, with testing on Monday, Wednesday, and Friday.

The decathlon event order might be rearranged on the 2nd day, if wished, such as opening with the hurdles, then the discus, then concluding with the 300m run. Starts are without blocks and running from a three- or four-point start (see chapter 4 on testing), with the clock begun when the hand is lifted from the track. The long jump is measured from the takeoff point, so all jumps count. The Bowerman tables for both combined events are reproduced in Tables 20.9 and 20.10 at the end of the chapter.

A simpler, quicker scale, but one that cannot be compared to the IAAF tables, is the one compiled by

Sylvia. His tables were amended to cover 14 events because he suggested that the student be allowed to substitute 1 of the additional events for 1 of the 10 regulation events (or his variations of them), usually replacing the javelin, which is not allowed in most states in high school competition, or the pole vault. The range of events allows it to be used for the heptathlon, though the scoring table may have to be modified. Throwing the softball, the football, or the 800-gram weighted ball can be substituted for throwing the javelin, using the same scoring tables. Thus, any of these versions of the combined events might be used in physical education classes (or as an interest-getter for the track team in the fall, in the preseason, or just after the competitive season has been concluded). The events are shown in Table 20.6.

The Sylvia version can also use the informal aspects of the Bowerman version. No stated length of time is offered for completing this decathlon. The low hurdles are used, set at the low-hurdle spacings (20 yards apart), though the hurdles might be set at the low height with the high-hurdle spacings. One event may be substituted for an additional event, the choices being the 200m and the 800m (scored by Sylvia) and the 3,200m and the triple jump (scored by the authors). Sylvia's revised scoring tables are reprinted in Table 20.11 at the end of the chapter.

Each of the versions has its advantages, with the primary advantage of the Sylvia version being its scoring simplicity, while the primary advantage of the Bowerman version is its similarity to the IAAF tables, giving predictive value without requiring the more exhausting full running distances or metric conversions. In all cases, the IAAF competition rules are generally followed, with the modifications mentioned above.

Training Pattern for the Decathlon

We do not give detailed training schedules for the heptathlon because we have not worked extensively with heptathletes. However, Figure 20.2 gives a suggested form for a heptathlon training schedule sheet. The decathlon training follows the hard-easy principle. Because there are always 2 consecutive days of competition, the training pattern has 2 hard days followed by 2 easy days. The events are practiced in the order in which they are encountered in competition.

On the first hard day, the athlete warms up, then takes four to six sprint starts. He then does a few short sprints, going 30, then 50 meters, possibly adding a 70-meter sprint. He then proceeds to the long jump, where he first works on his check marks, then works on pop-ups. He next follows the shot put routine, first putting from a stand, then crossing the ring and putting, all while working on one aspect of the technique. He then moves to the high jump area, working first on his check marks, then taking about six jumps working on one of the techniques. He then concludes the workout with 4 × 100m and a fartlek run.

On the second hard day, the decathlete warms up, goes through several sprint starts, then goes to the hurdles. He goes through the X drill, then runs a set of either back-to-back 5s or first 3, last 3s. He then moves to the discus, where he works on one aspect of his technique, first throwing from a stand (with his back foot in the center of the ring rather than hanging over the front of the ring), then working with the turn. He then works on the pole vault, first setting his check marks, then working on his pole plant, then the takeoff, and finishing with perhaps half a dozen vaults. He then runs through the javelin routine, first throwing the weighted balls from a stand, then going

Table 20.6 Modified Decathlons

IAAF official	Three-quarter college	Sylvia high school
100m	55m	100m
Long jump	Long jump	Long jump
Shot put (16 pounds)	Shot put (16 pounds)	Shot put (12 pounds)
High jump	High jump	High jump
400m	300m	400m
110m highs (42 inches)	80m highs (39 inches)	110m lows (30 inches)
Discus (2 kilograms)	Discus (2 kilograms)	Discus (h.s.)
Pole vault	Pole vault	Pole vault
Javelin	Javelin	Javelin or ball
1,500m run	1,200m run	1,600m run

to the 3-4-5 throwing sequence, then the full-count check, then moving several times through the full run. The full-run work is done last during the early season training, but it is done first during the late season training. Finally, the decathlete does what he can handle from a distance workout, usually about a mile of intervals (such as 8 × 200m, 6 × 300m, or 4 × 400m). He then concludes the second hard day with a fartlek run.

The third and fourth days are easy days, with activities such as jogging and stretching, with perhaps some swimming or weight training. Day 5 is a return to the first day of hard training, beginning the cycle again.

For more specialized training suggestions, or for clarification of the workout sequence above, study the chapters on the individual events. The decathlon and the heptathlon are indeed the champion's events, the supreme tests of the true athlete.

The Training Schedules: Special Fundamentals of the Combined Events

The fall training schedules show workouts for only 3 days per week (see end of this chapter). During that part of the year, the decathlon is offered as a physical education class. On the days that list no workouts, the track team follows the workouts for each athlete's specialty events. Figure 20.1 is an abbreviated form of these schedules. Figure 20.2 is similar in appearance but is a suggested training format for the heptathlon. Due to space limitations, the schedule sheet at the end of this chapter is also abbreviated. However, on the schedules themselves we have retained the original numbering for technique emphasis.

Almost no new activities appear on the combined-event training sheet that have not already been described in the chapters devoted to the individual events. The events are listed in the order in which they appear in the decathlon competition. For an explanation of the fundamentals of each event, the chapter on that event should be consulted. The few new descriptions that appear here are explained below.

10. Test effort. These are the trials used in the other events. They will be encountered every 2 to 3 weeks during training. They are never full efforts but are attempts at controlled improvement.

10A(1). 100m, 3/4 racing distance. The running events will rarely be contested over the full racing distance. The early trials will be at 60m. The later trials may be longer, moving up to 70m and then 80m.

10E(1). 400m, 3/4 racing distance. This racing distance will also generally be run at less than the full distance in trials. The most common distance is 300m, though later trials may be at other fractional distances, such as 250 or 350m.

10F(1). High hurdles, 3/4 racing distance. For the decathlon classes, the usual trial (and the final exam) is 80m. For other nonclass trials, other distances may be used, such as 60, 70, and 75m. For the class, the first trial is over the 30-inch (low) hurdles, the midterm is over the 36-inch (intermediate) hurdles, and the final exam is over the 39-inch (high school) hurdles. The hurdle spacings are not changed, 15 yards to the first barrier and 10 yards between each hurdle. Few trials will ever be at the full 42-inch international height.

10K(1). 1,500m, 3/4 racing distance. This race will usually be tested either for 1,200m or for the full distance. For the decathlon class, the distance is always 1,200m.

11A(1). Intervals, goal pace. The distance given is merely an example. The "1" notation for either Number 11 (intervals) or Number 18 (sets) means that the distance is to be run at the athlete's goal pace.

11A(2). Intervals, date pace. The distance is again an example. The "2" notation means that the given interval or set is to be run at the athlete's current date pace.

11X. Intervals, over hurdles. This notation may be used if the decathlete is also training for the 400m hurdles as a dual meet event. A notation of "11EX" means run 300m over the hurdles (set at the intermediate hurdle spacings).

11Y. Intervals, easy. The intervals listed are to be run at a comfortable, relatively easy pace. A listing of "3 times 11CY" means to run three times an easy 150m.

11Z. Intervals, fast 20 to 50m in the middle of each interval. This notation is used for a short interval, such as 100 or 150m, and is an exercise to increase the speed or to learn to accelerate quickly in a race.

18AX. Sets, over hurdles. The "A" notation is only an example. The "X" notation, meaning to run over the hurdles, is used if the athlete is training for the intermediate hurdles.

18AX(1). Sets, over 30-inch hurdles. The "X1" notation means that the set is run over 30-inch (low) hurdles set at the intermediate hurdle spacings.

DECATHLON   NAME _____   __/__ to __/__ 19__

1. A. Jog 1 to 2 laps, easy stretching; high knee (slow), fast leg
    B. Relay
2. Fartlek
    A. Varied pace
    B. Slow, steady pace
    C. Light fartlek
3. A. Jogging and stretching
    B. Weights and jogging
    C. Easy jogging
4. Sprints
    A. High knee, fast leg
    B. Starts: 3 at 1/2, 3 at 7/8; 30m
        (1) Straight   (2) Curve
    C. Finish work: 40-60 at 3/4 last 25-40 at 9/10
        (1) 20-40-60m
5. Long jump
    A. Check marks   (1) Short   (2) Long
    B. Pop-ups, 2-count rise
    C.
6. Shot put
    A. Routine
    B. Standing Put (1) Easy   (2) Medium
                      (3) Hard   (4) Explode
        a. Lift   b. Turn   c. Push
    C. Across the ring
7. Team Meeting
8. Special
    A. Sauna   b. Swim   c. Steps or hill
9. High jump
    A. Check marks (1) Short   (2) Long, 2
    B. Takeoff
    C. Clearance
    D. Jumping   (1) Low, easy (2) 4-6 in. below
                         height   best
                     (3)
    E. HJ rhythm 2-4-6-8   F.
10. Test effort   (1) 3/4 distance
    A. 100   B. LJ   C. SP
    D. HJ   E. 400   F. HH
    G. DT   H. PV   J. JT
    K. 1500   L.
11. Intervals   X. Hurdles   Y. Easy
        Z. Fast 20-50 in middle
    A. 50   B. 100   C. 150   D. 200
    E. 300   F. 400   G. 500   H. 600
    (1) Goal pace   (2) Date pace   (3)
12. With Coach A.   B.
14. 110m Hurdles

        A. X Drill (1) 30 in. (2) 36 in. (3) 39 in. (4) 42 in.
15. Discus throw
    A. Routine
    B. Standing throws (center of ring)
        1. Chest and nose lead
        2. Long pull
        3. Hips (cocked to uncocked) ahead of arm
        4. Through the shoulder
        5. Left-arm coordination
        6. Left-arm reach back   7.
           a. Easy   b. Medium   c. Hard
           d. Explode
    C. Across the ring, numbers as in B
    D. Alternate stand and across
    E.
16. Pole Vault
    A. Check marks   (1) Short   (2) Long
    B. Approach
    C. Pole plant
    D. Takeoff
    E. Vaulting (1) Low hold   (2) High hold
        a. 12 in. below best   b.
17. Javelin throw
    A. Standing throws
    B. Trot and throw   (1) 345   (2) Full count
        a. Over the shoulder   b. Close to ear
        c. Good pull   d. Cock the hand
        e. Lead foot down   f. Trail foot under
        g. Body turned to side, then precede arm with body
        h. Through shaft; don't tip it up
        i.
    C. Full run X. Check mark
        (1) 1/2   (2) 2/3   (3) 7/8–9/10
    D. Technique target throws
        (1) Standing at 30-60 ft.
        (2) 3-step and throw at 45-90 ft.
        (3) 5-step and throw at 120-150 ft.
        (4) Full run and checks at 150-180 ft.
    E.
18. Sets   X. Hurdles   (1) 30 in.   (3) 36 in.
    A. 100-200-100   1. Goal pace
    B. 150-100-50   2. Date pace
    C. 300-200-100   3.
    D. 600-400-200
19. Weak event work
    A. Throw   B. Jump   C. Run
    1. Weakest   2. 2nd weakest
20.

Figure 20.1 Abbreviated training schedule for the decathlon.

HEPTATHLON   NAME _____   __/__ to __/__ 19__

1. A. Jog 1 to 2 laps, easy stretching; high knee
        (slow), fast leg
    B. Relay
2. Fartlek
    A. Varied pace
    B. Slow, steady pace
    C. Light fartlek
3. A. Jogging and stretching
    B. Weights and jogging
    C. Easy jogging
4. Sprints
    A. High knee, fast leg
    B. Starts: 30m, 3 at 1/2, 3 at 7/8
        (1) Straight   (2) Curve
    C. Finish Work: 40-60 at 3/4, last 25-40 at 9/10
        (1) 20-40-60m
5. Long jump
    A. Check marks   (1) Short   (2) Long
    B. Pop-ups, 2-count rise
    C.
6. Shot put
    A. Routine
    B. Standing put (1) Easy   (2) Medium
                      (3) Hard   (4) Explode
        a. Lift   b. Turn   c. Push
    C. Across the ring
7. Team Meeting
8. Special
    A. Sauna   b. Swim   c. Steps or hill
9. High jump
    A. Check marks (1) Short   (2) Long–2
    B. Takeoff
    C. Clearance
    D. Jumping   (1) Low, easy (2) 4-6 in. below
                          height   best
                      (3)
    E. HJ rhythm 2-4-6-8   F.
10. Test effort   (1) 3/4 distance
    A. 100H   B. HJ   C. SP
    D. 100   E. LJ   F. JT
    G. 800   H.
11. Intervals   X. Hurdles   Y. Easy
        Z. Fast 20-50 in middle
    A. 50   B. 100   C. 150   D. 200
    E. 300   F. 400   G. 500   H. 600
    (1) Goal pace (2) Date pace   (3)

12. With Coach A.   B.
14. 100m hurdles
    A. X Drill (1) 24 in. (2) 27 in. (3) 30 in. (4) 33 in.
        a. Lean   b. Trail leg   c. Lead leg
        d. Trail arm   e. Lead arm   f.
    B. Hurdle Starts: (1) 2 at 1/2, 2 at 7/8
                         (2) Back-to-back 5s
                         (3) First 3, last 3
    C.
15.
16.
17. Javelin throw
    A. Standing throws
    B. Trot and throw   (1) 345 (2) Full count
        a. Over the shoulder   b. Close to ear
        c. Good pull   d. Cock the hand
        e. Lead foot down   f. Trail foot under
        g. Body turned to side, then precede arm with
           body
        h. Through shaft; don't tip it up
        i.
    C. Full run X. Check mark
        (1) 1/2   (2) 2/3   (3) 7/8–9/10
    D. Technique target throws
        (1) Standing at 30-60 ft.
        (2) 3-step and throw at 45-90 ft.
        (3) 5-step and throw at 120-150 ft.
        (4) Full run and checks at 150-180 ft.
    E.
18. Sets   X. Hurdles   (1) 24 in.   (3) 30 in.
    A. 100-200-100   1. Goal pace
    B. 150-100-50   2. Date pace
    C. 300-200-100   3.
    D. 600-400-200
19. Weak event work
    A. Throw   B. Jump   C. Run
    1. Weakest   2. 2nd weakest
20.
21. A. Videotape   B. Film   C. Pictures
    (1) Record performance   (2) Study
22. Plyometrics   A. Jumps   B. Bounding
    C.
    (1) 1 leg   (2) Both legs   (3)
30. Experimental work

Figure 20.2 Sample training schedule for the heptathlon.

18AX(2). Sets, over 36-inch hurdles. The "X2" notation means that the set is run over the regular intermediate-height hurdles at the intermediate hurdle spacings.

19. Weak event work. On occasion, the athlete will be told to use some of his time in training in one of his weaker events.

19A. Weak event work, throw. Work on one of the weaker throwing events: the shot, the discus, or the javelin.

19B. Weak event work, jump. Work on one of the weaker jumping events: the high jump, the long jump, or the pole vault.

19C. Weak event work, run. Work on one of the weaker running events: the two sprints, the distance run, or the hurdles.

19A(1). Weak event work, [throw], weakest event. The choice of the throws is only an example. The "1" notation means to work in the athlete's weakest event in that group of events.

19A(2). Weak event work, [throw], second-weakest event. The "2" notation means to work on the athlete's second-weakest event in that group of events.

References

1. William H. Freeman. (1989). Periodized training for the combined events. In *Peak when it counts: Periodized training for American track and field*. Los Altos, CA: Tafnews.
2. William H. Freeman. (1986). Decathlon performance success: Progress and age factors. *Track Technique*, **96**, 3050-3052.
3. Andrzej Krzesenski. (1984). The specific features of the decathlon. *Track Technique*, **89**, 2828-2830.
4. A. Rudski & B. Aptekman. (1986). Stages in the training of decathloners. *Track and Field Quarterly Review*, **86**(2), 16-17.
5. Freeman, *supra* note 2, p. 3050.
6. Robin C. Sykes. (1971). Balance: The decathlon keyword. *Track Technique*, **45**, 1442-1443.
7. Freeman, *supra* note 2, p. 3051.
8. Freeman, *supra* note 1, p. 82.
9. Bob Myers. (1986). Periodization for the heptathlon: A practical training theory. *Track and Field Quarterly Review*, **86**(2), 34-36.
10. Bob Myers. (1989). The heptathlon. In Vern Gambetta (Ed.), *The Athletics Congress's track and field coaching manual* (2nd ed., pp. 209-218). Champaign, IL: Leisure Press.
11. William H. Freeman. (1986). An analysis of heptathlon performance and training. *Track and Field Quarterly Review*, **86**(2), 30-34.
12. Robert C. Parks. (1971). Organizing an indoor decathlon in elementary or junior high school physical education classes. *Track and Field Quarterly Review*, **71**(4), 34-35.
13. Alfred J. Sylvia. (1964, April). A decathlon for high school and college. *Athletic Journal*, **44**, 38, 40.

Additional Readings

Dick, Frank W. (1986). Jumps and the combined events. *Track and Field Quarterly Review*, **86**(2), 50-54

Freeman, William H. (1976, April). Decathlon competition organization. *Scholastic Coach*, **45**, 34ff.

Freeman, William H. (1986). Factors of decathlon performance success. *Track and Field Quarterly Review*, **86**(2), 4-11.

Gehrke, Klaus. (1986). Training for take-off with girl athletes in the junior categories for jumping and combined events. *New Studies in Athletics*, **1**(2), 95-100.

Henson, Phillip L. (1986). Coaching athletes for multiple events. *Track and Field Quarterly Review*, **86**(2), 48-49.

Jenner, Bruce. (1986). Bruce Jenner on the decathlon. *Track and Field Quarterly Review*, **86**(2), 26-29.

Knudson, Lyle. (1984). Total training/competition program (heptathlon). Paper presented at the 1984 Heptathlon Camp.

Kudu, Fred. (1984). Training loads in the heptathlon. *Track Technique*, **90**, 2883.

Lawler, Peter. (1988). Chasing decathlon points. *Track Technique*, **103**, 3297.

Marra, Harry. (1986). The decathlon. *Track and Field Quarterly Review*, **86**(2), 12-15.

Marra, Harry, & Freeman, Bill. (1989). The decathlon. In Vern Gambetta (Ed.), *The Athletic Congress's track and field coaching manual* (2nd ed., pp. 203-208). Champaign, IL: Leisure Press.

Moore, Timothy. (1986). Heptathlon training. *Track and Field Quarterly Review*, **86**(2), 37-39.

Myers, Bob. (1986, May). Testing for field and multi-event athletes. *Athletic Journal*, **66**, 10-12.

Myers, Bob. (1989). Training for the jumps and multi-events. *Track Technique*, **108**, 3449-3452; **109**, 3492-3493.

Tolsma, Brant. (1984). A scientific view of decathlon training. In George W. Dales (Ed.), *Proceedings of the International Track and Field Coaches Association IX Congress* (pp. 121-124). Kalamazoo, MI: NCAA Division I Track Coaches Association.

Ushakov, A. (1986). From quantity to quality. *Track Technique*, **95**, 3041.

Verhoshanski, Y., et al. (1989). Decathlon features. *Track Technique*, **108**, 3458.

Yang, C.K. (1987). Decathlon training in preparation for competition. *Track and Field Quarterly Review*, **87**(2), 57-58.

Table 20.7   Summary of IAAF 1985 Decathlon Scoring Tables, Day 1

Points	100m	Long jump		Shot put		High jump		400m
1,000	10.30	7.76	25' 5.5"	18.40	60' 4.5"	2.21	7' 3"	46.17
950	10.60	7.56	24' 9.75"	17.59	57' 8.5"	2.16	7' 1"	47.17
900	10.82	7.36	24' 1.75"	16.79	55' 1"	2.11	6'11"	48.19
850	11.05	7.15	23' 5.5"	15.98	52' 5.25"	2.05	6' 8.75"	49.24
800	11.27	6.95	22' 9.75"	15.16	49' 9"	2.00	6' 6.75"	50.32
750	11.51	6.73	22' 1"	14.35	47' 1"	1.95	6' 4.75"	51.43
700	11.75	6.51	21' 4.25"	13.53	44' 4.75"	1.89	6' 2.25"	52.58
650	12.00	6.29	20' 7.75"	12.71	41' 8.5"	1.83	6' 0"	53.76
600	12.26	6.06	19'10.5"	11.89	39' 0.75"	1.77	5' 9.75"	54.98
550	12.53	5.83	19' 1.5"	11.07	36' 4"	1.71	5' 7.25"	56.25
500	12.81	5.59	18' 4"	10.24	33' 7.25"	1.65	5' 5"	57.57
450	13.10	5.35	17' 6.5"	9.40	30'10.25"	1.59	5' 2.5"	58.95
400	13.41	5.09	16' 8.25"	8.56	28' 1"	1.52	4'11.75"	60.40
350	13.74	4.83	15'10"	7.72	25' 4"	1.45	4' 9"	61.94
300	14.09	4.56	14'11.5"	6.87	22' 6.5"	1.38	4' 6.25"	63.57
250	14.46	4.27	14' 0"	6.02	19' 9"	1.30	4' 3.25"	65.34
200	14.87	3.97	13' 0.25"	5.15	16'10.75"	1.22	4' 0"	67.27
150	15.33	3.64	11'11.25"	4.28	14' 0.5"	1.14	3' 8.75"	69.43
100	15.86	3.28	10' 9"	3.39	11' 1.5"	1.04	3' 5"	71.96
50	16.54	2.86	9' 4.5"	2.48	8' 1.5"	0.93	3' 0.5"	75.15
1	17.83	2.25	7' 4.5"	1.53	5' 0.25"	0.77	2' 6.25"	81.21

Summary of IAAF 1985 Decathlon Scoring Tables, Day 2

Points	110mH	Discus throw		Pole vault		Javelin throw		1,500m
1,000	13.80	56.18	184' 4"	5.29	17' 4.25"	77.20	253' 3"	3:53.79
950	14.19	53.80	176' 6"	5.13	16'10"	73.94	242' 7"	4:00.53
900	14.59	51.40	168' 8"	4.97	16' 3.5"	70.68	231'11"	4:07.42
850	15.00	49.00	160' 9"	4.81	15' 9.25"	67.40	221' 1"	4:14.50
800	15.41	46.60	152'11"	4.64	15' 2.75"	64.10	210' 4"	4:21.77
750	15.85	44.16	144'10"	4.47	14' 8"	60.78	199' 5"	4:29.25
700	16.29	41.72	136'10"	4.30	14' 1.25"	57.46	188' 6"	4:36.96
650	16.76	39.26	128'10"	4.12	13' 6.25"	54.12	177' 7"	4:44.94
600	17.23	36.80	120' 9"	3.94	12'11"	50.74	166' 6"	4:53.20
550	17.73	34.30	112' 6"	3.76	12' 4"	47.36	155' 4"	5:01.78
500	18.25	31.78	104' 3"	3.57	11' 8.5"	43.96	144' 3"	5:10.73
450	18.80	29.24	95'11"	3.38	11' 1"	40.52	132'11"	5:20.10

Summary of IAAF 1985 Decathlon Scoring Tables, Day 2

Points	110mH	Discus throw		Pole vault		Javelin throw		1,500m
400	19.38	26.68	87′ 6″	3.18	10′ 5.25″	37.06	121′ 7″	5:29.96
350	19.99	24.10	79′ 1″	2.97	9′ 9″	33.56	110′ 1″	5:40.41
300	20.65	21.46	70′ 5″	2.76	9′ 0.5″	30.04	98′ 7″	5:51.57
250	21.36	18.80	61′ 8″	2.54	8′ 4″	26.46	86′10″	6:03.62
200	22.14	16.08	52′ 9″	2.31	7′ 7″	22.82	74′10″	6:16.84
150	23.03	13.30	43′ 7″	2.06	6′ 9″	19.12	62′ 8″	6:31.70
100	24.07	10.44	34′ 3″	1.78	5′10″	15.34	50′ 4″	6:49.08
50	25.41	7.44	24′ 5″	1.47	4′ 9.75″	11.40	37′ 5″	7:11.24
1	28.09	4.10	13′ 5″	1.03	3′ 4.5″	7.12	23′ 4″	7:54.11

Notes. To correct the score for a hand-time, ADD 0.24 seconds to the time. Also, each measure for jumps and throws is given first in meters, then in equivalent feet and inches.

Table 20.8   Summary of IAAF 1981 Heptathlon Scoring Tables, Day 1

Points	100mH*	High jump		Shot put		200m*
1,000	13.85	1.82	5′11.5″	17.07	56′ 0″	23.80
950	14.20	1.78	5′10″	16.32	53′ 6.5″	24.32
900	14.56	1.74	5′ 8.5″	15.58	51′ 1.5″	24.86
850	14.94	1.70	5′ 7″	14.83	48′ 8″	25.41
800	15.32	1.66	5′ 5.25″	14.09	46′ 2.75″	25.97
750	15.71	1.62	5′ 3.75″	13.34	43′ 9.25″	26.55
700	16.12	1.57	5′ 1.75″	12.58	41′ 3.25″	27.14
650	16.53	1.53	5′ 0.25″	11.83	38′ 9.75″	27.76
600	16.97	1.49	4′10.5″	11.07	36′ 4″	28.40
550	17.42	1.44	4′ 8.75″	10.31	33′10″	29.06
500	17.89	1.39	4′ 6.75″	9.55	31′ 4″	29.75
450	18.38	1.34	4′ 4.75″	8.78	28′ 9.75″	30.47
400	18.90	1.29	4′ 2.75″	8.01	26′ 3.5″	31.23
350	19.44	1.24	4′ 0.75″	7.23	23′ 8.75″	32.03
300	20.03	1.19	3′10.75″	6.45	21′ 2″	32.88
250	20.66	1.14	3′ 8.75″	5.66	18′ 6.75″	33.80
200	21.35	1.08	3′ 6.5″	4.87	15′11.75″	34.81
150	22.13	1.01	3′ 3.75″	4.06	13′ 3.75″	35.94
100	23.03	0.95	3′ 1.25″	3.24	10′ 7.5″	37.26
50	24.18	0.87	2′10.25″	2.40	7′ 10.5″	38.92
1	26.40	0.76	2′ 6″	1.53	5′ 0.25″	42.08

Summary of IAAF 1981 Heptathlon Scoring Tables, Day 2

Points	Long jump		Javelin throw		800m
1,000	6.48	21′ 3.5″	57.18	189′11″	2:07.63
950	6.33	20′ 9.25″	54.62	179′ 2″	2:11.03
900	6.17	20′ 3″	52.04	170′ 9″	2:14.52
850	6.00	19′ 8.25″	49.46	162′ 3″	2:18.10
800	5.84	19′ 2″	46.88	153′10″	2:21.77

(Cont.)

Table 20.8 Summary of IAAF 1981 Heptathlon Scoring Tables, Day 2 (Continued)

Points	Long jump		Javelin throw		800m
750	5.67	18′ 7.25″	44.28	145′ 3″	2:25.56
700	5.50	18′ 0.5″	41.68	136′ 9″	2:29.47
650	5.33	17′ 5.75″	39.08	128′ 2″	2:33.51
600	5.15	16′10.75″	36.46	119′ 7″	2:37.70
550	4.97	16′ 3.5″	33.84	111′ 0″	2:42.05
500	4.78	15′ 8.25″	31.22	102′ 5″	2:46.60
450	4.59	15′ 0.75″	28.58	93′ 9″	2:51.36
400	4.39	14′ 4.75″	25.92	85′ 0″	2:56.38
350	4.18	13′ 8.5″	23.26	76′ 3″	3:01.70
300	3.97	13′ 0.25″	20.58	67′ 6″	3:07.39
250	3.74	12′ 3.25″	17.88	58′ 8″	3:13.55
200	3.50	11′ 5.75″	15.16	49′ 9″	3:20.31
150	3.24	10′ 7.5″	12.42	40′ 9″	3:27.93
100	2.96	9′ 8.5″	9.64	31′ 7″	3:36.87
50	2.63	8′ 7.5″	6.80	22′ 3″	3:48.32
1	2.14	7′ 0.25″	3.88	12′ 8″	4:10.79

Notes. To correct the score for a hand-time, ADD 0.24 sec to the time (0.14 sec for the 800m). Also, each measure for jumps and throws is given first in meters, then in equivalent feet and inches.

Table 20.9 Bowerman Three-Quarters Decathlon Tables, Part 1
(1985 revision by Freeman)

55m		Long jump			Shot put			High jump			300m		
Seconds	Points	Feet	Points	A	Feet	Points	A	Feet	Points	A	Seconds	Points	B
5.9	990	26′	1042	7	60′	976	1.5	7′ 2″	980	25	34	1040	7
6.0	960	25′6″	1000	7	55′	886	1.5	7′	930	25	35	970	7
6.1	920	25′	958	7	50′	796	1.5	6′10″	880	25	36	900	7
6.2	870	24′6″	922	6	45′	706	1.5	6′ 8″	832	24	37	840	6
6.3	820	24′	886	6	40′	616	1.5	6′ 6″	786	23	38	780	6
6.4	770	23′6″	850	6	35′	526	1.5	6′ 4″	740	23	39	720	6
6.5	720	23′	814	6	34′	508	1.5	6′ 2″	696	22	40	660	6
6.6	680	22′6″	778	6	33′	490	1.5	6′	652	22	41	600	6
6.7	640	22′	742	6	32′	472	1.5	5′10″	610	21	42	550	5
6.8	600	21′6″	706	6	31′	454	1.5	5′ 8″	570	20	43	500	5
6.9	560	21′	670	6	30′	436	1.5	5′ 6″	530	20	44	450	5
7.0	510	20′6″	634	6	29′	418	1.5	5′ 4″	490	20	45	400	5
7.1	480	20′	604	5	28′	400	1.5	5′ 2″	450	20	46	360	4
7.2	440	19′6″	574	5	27′	382	1.5	5′	412	19	47	320	4
7.3	400	19′	544	5	26′	364	1.5	4′10″	374	19	48	280	4
7.4	370	18′6″	514	5	25′	346	1.5	4′ 8″	336	19	49	240	4
7.5	340	18′	484	5	24′	328	1.5	4′ 6″	300	18	50	210	3
7.6	310	17′	424	5	23′	310	1.5	4′ 4″	266	17	51	180	3
7.7	280	16′	364	5	22′	292	1.5	4′ 2″	232	17	52	150	3
7.8	250	15′	304	5	21′	274	1.5	4′	200	16	53	120	3
7.9	220	14′	244	5	20′	256	1.5						
8.0	190	13′	196	4									
8.1	170	12′	148	4									

Key
A—points per inch
B—points per 1/10 second

Bowerman Three-Quarters Decathlon Tables, Part 2

80m HH Seconds	Points	B	Discus Feet	Points	C	Pole vault Feet	Points	A	Javelin Feet	Points	C	1,200m Time	Points	D
10.0	975	18	180'	980	7	17'	970	8	250'	1,000	5	3:00	1065	10
10.5	890	17	170'	910	7	16'6"	922	8	240'	950	5	3:05	1015	10
11.0	810	16	160'	840	7	16'	874	8	230'	900	5	3:10	970	9
11.5	730	16	150'	780	6	15'6"	826	8	220'	850	5	3:15	925	9
12.0	655	15	140'	720	6	15'	778	8	210'	800	5	3:20	880	9
12.5	585	14	135'	690	6	14'6"	736	7	200'	750	5	3:25	835	9
13.0	515	14	130'	660	6	14'	694	7	190'	700	5	3:30	790	9
13.5	450	13	125'	630	6	13'6"	652	7	180'	650	5	3:35	750	8
14.0	390	12	120'	600	6	13'	610	7	170'	600	5	3:40	710	8
14.5	335	11	115'	570	6	12'6"	568	7	160'	560	4	3:45	670	8
15.0	285	10	110'	540	6	12'	526	7	150'	520	4	3:50	630	8
16.0	195	9	105'	510	6	11'6"	484	7	140'	480	4	3:55	595	7
			100'	480	6	11'	442	7	130'	440	4	4:00	560	7
			95'	450	6	10'6"	406	6	120'	400	4	4:05	525	7
			90'	420	6	10'	370	6	110'	360	4	4:10	490	7
			85'	390	6	9'6"	334	6	100'	320	4	4:15	455	7
			80'	360	6	9'	298	6	90'	280	4	4:20	425	6
			75'	330	6	8'6"	262	6	80'	240	4	4:25	395	6
			70'	300	6	8'	226	6	70'	190	3	4:30	365	6
			65'	270	6	7'	166	5	60'	140	2	4:40	305	6
			60'	240	6							4:50	255	5
			55'	210	6							5:00	205	5
			50'	180	6							5:10	165	4
			45'	155	5									

Key

A—points per inch
B—points per 1/10 second
C—points per foot
D—points per second

Table 20.10   Bowerman-Freeman Three-Quarters Heptathlon Tables, Part 1

55m HH Seconds	Points	High jump Feet	Points	A	Shot put Feet	Points	B	150m Seconds	Points	C
7.4	1,030	6' 2"	1,080	30	55'	990	18	18	960	12
7.5	1,000	6'	1,020	30	50'	880	18	19	840	12
7.6	970	5'10"	960	30	45'	770	17	20	720	12
7.7	940	5' 8"	900	30	40'	670	17	21	610	11
7.8	910	5' 6"	840	30	35'	570	17	22	510	10
7.9	880	5' 4"	780	30	34'	550	17	23	420	9
8.0	850	5' 2"	720	30	33'	530	17	24	340	8
8.1	820	5'	660	30	32'	510	16	25	260	8
8.2	790	4'10"	600	30	31'	490	16	26	190	7
8.3	760	4' 8"	540	30	30'	470	16			
8.4	735	4' 6"	480	30	29'	450	16			
8.5	710	4' 4"	430	25	28'	430	16			
8.6	685	4' 2"	380	25	27'	410	15			
8.7	660	4'	330	25	26'	390	15			
8.8	635	3'10"	280	25	25'	370	15			

(Cont.)

Table 20.10   Bowerman-Freeman Three-Quarters Heptathlon Tables, Part 1   (Continued)

55m HH		High jump			Shot put			150m		
Seconds	Points	Feet	Points	A	Feet	Points	B	Seconds	Points	C
8.9	610	3′ 8″	240	20	24′	350	14			
9.0	585	3′ 6″	200	20	23′	330	14			
9.1	560	3′ 4″	160	20	22′	310	13			
9.2	535				21′	290	13			
9.3	510				20′	270	13			
9.4	485				19′	250				
9.5	465				18′	230				
9.6	445				17′	210				
9.7	425				16′	190				
9.8	405				15′	170				
9.9	385									
10.0	365									
10.1	345									
10.2	325									
10.3	305									
10.4	285									
10.5	265									
10.6	245									
10.7	230									
10.8	215									
10.9	200									
11.0	185									

Key
A—points per inch
B—points per foot
C—points per 1/10 second

Bowerman-Freeman Three-Quarters Heptathlon Tables, Part 2

Long jump			Javelin			600m		
Feet	Points	A	Feet	Points	B	Time	Points	D
21′6″	1,042	8	190′	1,020	6	1:35	1,020	20
21′	980	8	180′	960	6	1:40	920	20
20′6″	932	8	170′	900	6	1:45	830	18
20′	884	8	160′	840	6	1:50	740	18
19′6″	836	8	150′	780	6	1:55	655	17
19′	788	8	140′	720	6	2:00	575	16
18′6″	740	8	130′	660	6	2:05	500	15
18′	692	8	125′	630	6	2:10	430	14
17′6″	650	7	120′	600	6	2:15	365	13
17′	608	7	115′	570	6	2:20	305	12
16′6″	566	7	110′	540	6	2:25	250	11
16′	524	7	105′	510	6	2:30	200	10
15′6″	482	7	100′	490	6	2:35	155	9
15′	440	7	95′	460	6			
14′6″	404	6	90′	430	6			
14′	368	6	85′	400	6			
13′6″	332	6	80′	370	6			
13′	296	6	75′	340	6			

Long jump			Javelin			600m		
Feet	Points	A	Feet	Points	B	Time	Points	D
12′6″	260	6	70′	310	6			
12′	230	5	65′	280	6			
11′6″	200	5	60′	250	6			
11′	170	5	55′	230	6			
			50′	200	6			
			45′	170	6			

Key

A—points per inch
B—points per foot
D—points per second

Table 20.11 Sylvia High School-College Decathlon Tables, Part 1
(Modified by Freeman, 1986)

100m		Long jump		Shot put		High jump		400m	
Seconds	Points	Feet	Points	Feet	Points	Feet	Points	Seconds	Points
10.8	1,200	23′	1,200	55′	1,200	6′ 4″	1,200	49	1,200
11.0	1,100	22′	1,150	50′	1,150	6′ 2″	1,150	50	1,100
11.2	1,000	21′	1,100	45′	1,100	6′	1,100	51	1,000
11.4	950	20′	1,000	40′	1,000	5′10″	1,000	52	950
11.6	900	19′	900	39′	900	5′ 8″	900	53	900
11.8	850	18′	800	38′	800	5′ 6″	800	54	850
12.0	800	17′	700	37′	700	5′ 4″	700	55	800
12.2	700	16′6″	600	36′	600	5′ 2″	600	56	750
12.4	600	16′	550	35′	500	5′	500	57	700
12.6	500	15′6″	500	34′	450	4′10″	400	58	650
12.8	400	15′	450	33′	400	4′ 8″	300	59	600
13.0	300	14′6″	400	32′	350	4′ 6″	250	60	550
13.2	250	14′	350	31′	300	4′ 4″	200	61	500
13.4	200	13′6″	300	30′	250	4′ 2″	150	62	450
13.6	150	13′	200	29′	200	4′	100	63	400
13.8	100	12′6″	100	28′	150			64	350
14.0	50	12′	50	27′	100			65	300
				26′	50			66	250
								67	200
								68	150
								70	100

Sylvia Tables, Part 2

110m LH		Discus		Pole vault		Javelin		1,600m	
Seconds	Points	Feet	Points	Feet	Points	Feet	Points	Time	Points
13.4	1,200	165′	1,200	14′	1,200	200′	1,200	4:25	1,200
13.8	1,100	150′	1,100	13′6″	1,150	180′	1,100	4:35	1,150
14.2	1,050	135′	1,050	13′	1,100	160′	1,000	4:40	1,100
14.6	1,000	120′	1,000	12′6″	1,050	140′	900	4:45	1,050

(Cont.)

Table 20.11   Sylvia Tables, Part 2   (Continued)

110m LH		Discus		Pole vault		Javelin		1,600m	
Seconds	Points	Feet	Points	Feet	Points	Feet	Points	Time	Points
15.0	950	105'	900	12'	1,000	120'	800	4:50	1,000
15.3	900	95'	800	11'6"	950	105'	750	4:55	900
15.6	800	90'	700	11'	900	95'	700	5:00	800
15.9	700	85'	600	10'6"	800	90'	650	5:05	700
16.2	600	80'	500	10'	700	85'	600	5:10	650
16.5	500	75'	450	9'6"	600	80'	500	5:15	600
16.8	400	70'	400	9'	500	75'	400	5:20	550
17.1	350	65'	350	8'6"	400	70'	300	5:25	500
17.4	300	60'	300	8'	300	65'	200	5:30	450
17.7	250	55'	250	7'6"	200	60'	150	5:45	350
18.0	200	50'	200	7'	100	55'	100	6:00	250
18.3	150	45'	150			50'	50	6:15	150
18.6	100	40'	100					6:30	50

Sylvia Tables, Part 3: Alternate events

200m		800m		3,200m		Triple jump	
Seconds	Points	Time	Points	Time	Points	Feet	Points
21.0	1,200	1:55	1,200	9:30	1,200	48'	1,200
22.0	1,150	1:58	1,150	9:50	1,150	46'	1,150
22.5	1,100	2:00	1,100	10:00	1,100	44'	1,100
23.0	1,000	2:05	1,000	10:10	1,050	42'	1,000
23.5	900	2:10	950	10:20	1,000	40'	900
24.0	850	2:15	900	10:30	900	38'	800
24.5	800	2:20	800	10:40	800	36'	700
25.0	700	2:25	700	10:50	700	35'	600
25.5	600	2:30	600	11:00	650	34'	550
26.0	500	2:35	500	11:10	600	33'	500
26.5	450	2:40	450	11:20	550	32'	450
27.0	400	2:45	400	11:30	500	31'	400
27.5	350	2:50	350	11:40	450	30'	350
28.0	300	2:55	300	12:10	350	29'	300
28.5	250	3:00	250	12:40	250	28'	200
29.0	200	3:05	200	13:10	150	27'	100
29.5	150	3:10	150	13:40	50	26'	50
30.0	100	3:15	100				

Decathlon Training Schedule

ATHLETE

1. Warm-up
   A. Jogging and stretching
   B. Relay work
2. Fartlek
   A. Varied pace   C. Light
   B. Slow, steady pace
3. A. Jogging & stretching
   B. Weights and jogging
   C. Easy jogging
4. 100m
   A. High knee, fast leg
   B. Starts
   C. Finish work
5. Long jump
   A. Check marks   (1) short   (2) long
   B. Pop-ups, 2-count rise
   C. Across the ring
6. Shot put
   A. Routine
   B. Standing
7. Team meeting
8. Special
   A. Sauna
   B. Swim   C. Steps or hills
9. High jump
   A. Check marks   D. Jumping
   B. Takeoff   E. Rhythm
   C. Clearance

10. Test effort
    A. 100m   F. 110m HH
    B. Long jump   G. Discus
    C. Shot   H. Pole vault
    D. High jump   J. Javelin
    E. 400m   K. 1500m
       (1) 3/4 racing distance
11. Intervals   X. Hurdles   Y. Easy
    Z. Fast in middle 20-50m
    A. 50   E. 300
    B. 100   F. 400
    C. 150   G. 500
    D. 200   H. 600
       (1) goal pace   (2) date pace
12. With Coach
    A. (name)
    B. Leader
14. 110m hurdles
    A. X drill   (1) 30"   (2) 36"   (3) 39"   (4) 42"
       a. buck   b. trail leg   c. lead leg
       d. off arm   e. lead arm
    B. Starts
       (1) 2 at 1/2 speed, 2 at 7/8 speed
       (2) back-to-back 5s   (3) first 3, last 3
15. Discus throw
    A. Routine
    B. Standing
    C. Across the ring
    D. Alternate stand & across
    E.
16. Pole vault
    A. Check marks   D. Takeoff
    B. Approach   E. Vaulting
    C. Pole plant   F.
17. Javelin
    A. Standing throws   D. Technique throws
    B. Trot & throw   E.
    C. Full run   X. Check marks
18. Sets   X. Over hurdles
    A. 100-200-100   (1) goal pace
    B. 150-100-50   (2) goal pace
    C. 300-200-100   (3)
    D. 600-400-200
19. Weak event work
    A. Throw
    B. Jump
    C. Run
       (1) weakest   (2) 2nd weakest
20.
21. Visual aids
    A. Videotape   C. Photos
    B. Film
       (1) record performance   (2) study
30. Experimental work

DATE September/October

M	Class organization—1A—2B(1)
Tu	
W	1A—10A(1)—10C—10B
Th	
F	1A—10D—10E(1)
Sa	
Su	
M	1A—10F(1)—10J—2A(1) or 11D(35-40) [8x]
Tu	
W	1A—2B
Th	
F	1A—10G—10H—2A or 11D(35-40) [8x]
Sa	
Su	
M	1A—14A(1)—9A—9D(1)—5A(1)—5B—2C
Tu	
W	1A—14A(1)—14B(3)—5B—6A—2B(1)
Th	
F	1A—14A(1)—14B(2)—9A—9C—6B—2A(1)
Sa	
Su	
M	1A—14A(1)—15A(1)—15E(1)—17B(1)—2C
Tu	
W	1A—14A(1)—17A—9A—9D—11C—2C [3x]
Th	
F	1A—10F(1)(30 in.)—9D—15B—2B(1)
Sa	
Su	

DATE October/November

M	1A—14A(2)—4B—15D—9D—2C
Tu	
W	1A—14A(2)—9D—6A—2A(1)
Th	
F	1A—14A(2)—5A—5B—6B—6C—2B(2)
Sa	
Su	
M	1A—10A(1)—10C—10D—2C
Tu	
W	1A—10B—10E(1)—2B(2)
Th	
F	1A—10F(1)(36 in.)—10G—10H
Sa	
Su	
M	1A—14A(2,3)—5B(1)—10J—10K—3C
Tu	
W	1A—14A(2,3)—5B—16A—16E—6A—2C
Th	
F	1A—14A(2,3)—16E—9D or 6B—6A or 17D
Sa	
Su	
M	
Tu	
W	
Th	
F	
Sa	
Su	

DATE November/December

M	1A—14A(2,3)—5A—5B—9D—15D—2A(1)
Tu	
W	1A—14A(2,3)—9D—17D(2)—17D(4)—16E—11D(35-40) [4x]
Th	
F	1A—14A(2,3)—6B—6C—5A—15D—2B(2)
Sa	
Su	
M	1A—14A(2,3)—5 or 9 or 16—6 or 15 or 17—2C
Tu	
W	Choice
Th	
F	Choice
Sa	
Su	
M	1A—10A(1)—10B—10C—10J—3C
Tu	
W	1A—10C—10D—10E(1)—3C
Th	
F	1A—10F(1)(39 in.)—10H—10K(1)—3C
Sa	
Su	
M	
Tu	
W	
Th	
F	
Sa	
Su	

DATE January

M	Squad organization—4A—4B—5B (3-6x)—11C (3x)—2A(1)
Tu	1A—14A(1)—9E (3x)—11C (4x)—11F (75-80)—2B(1)
W	7—3B
Th	1A—4A—4B—5B (3-6x)—6B(1)—11C (3x)—2A(1)
F	1A—14A(1)—9E (3x)—11C (4x)—11F (75-80)—2B(1)
Sa	3B
Su	3A
M	1A—14A(2)—14B(2)—15D—16A(1) (10-15x)—6x/11E (50-52)—2B (3x)—3B
Tu	1A—14A(2)—14B(2) (10-15x)—17A (10-15x)—17B (3x)—18B—18C
W	7—3B
Th	1A—14A(2)—14B(2)—15D—16A(1)—6x/11E (50-52)—2B
F	1A—14A(2)—14B(2) (10-15x)—17A (10-15x)—17B (3x)—18B—18C
Sa	3B
Su	3A
M	1A—4A—4B—5B (3-6x)—6B(1)—11C (3x)—2A(1)
Tu	1A—10A(1) or 10F (55m)—14A(1)—9E—4x/11F (4x)—2B(1)
W	7—3B
Th	1A—10A(1) or 10F (55m)—4A—4B—5B (3-6x 3x)—11C—2A(1)
F	1A—14A(1)—9E (4x)—11F (75-80)—2B(1)
Sa	3B
Su	3A
M	1A—14A(2)—16A(1)—16B(1)—16E(1) (6x/11E (50-52))—2A(1) (10-15x/17A)—3B
Tu	1A—14A(2)—15B (10-15x/17B(1))—18C—4x/11B—2B(1)
W	3B
Th	1A—14A(2)—16A(1)—16B(1)—10-15x/17A—17B—18C—4x/11B
F	1A—14A(2)—3-6x/15B (3-6x)—16A(1)—16E(1)—6x/11E—2A(1)
Sa	3B
Su	3A

DATE February

M	1A—4A—5B—6A—6B (3x)—11C—2A(1)—3B
Tu	1A—14A(2)—15B—16A(1)—10-15x/17B(1)—18C—4x/11B—2B(1)
W	7—3B
Th	1A—14A(2)—16A(1)—16B(1)—16E(1)—1B(1)
F	1A—6A—6C—9A—9D—18C—3C (4x)—11B
Sa	2A(1)—3B
Su	19—2B(2) or 3A
M	1A—14A(2,3)—15A—4-6x/15B—16A(1)—10K(1)—3C—3B
Tu	1A—14A(2)—14B(2)—16A(1) (10-15x)—17A (10-15x 4x)—17B—11F
W	1A—10D—2A(2)—3B
Th	1A—14A(2,3)—14B(1)—6x/15D—6x/15C—16A (2x)—16E—4x/11F (3x)—2B
F	1A—14A(2)—14B(3)—10G—16A—16C (2x)—17C—11C (3x)—3C
Sa	1A—10F(1)—2A(1)—3B
Su	19—2B(2) or 3A
M	1A—4A—10A—5A—5B—6A—4x/11C(2)—2B(1)—3B
Tu	1A—14A(2)—6A—6B—9A—9E—2x/18B(2)—4x/11B—2B
W	7—1A—10B—2A(2)—3B
Th	1A—4A—4B—5A—5B—6A—11G—2B(1) (4x)—11B
F	1A—14A(2)—5A—10C—9A—9E—11E(2) (6x)—3C
Sa	2A(1)—3B
Su	19—2B(2) or 3A
M	1A—14A(2,3)—15A—15B—16A—10E (4x)—2B—3B
Tu	1A—14A(2,3)—14B(2)—16A(1)—16B—17A—17B (4x)—11F(1)
W	1A—10H—2A(2)—3B
Th	1A—14A(2,3)—14B(1)—6x/15D—6x/15C—16A (10-15x)—16E—6x/11E(2)—2B
F	1A—4A—16A—17B—10J—2B
Sa	10F—3B
Su	19—2B(2) or 3A

DATE March

M	1A—14A(2,3)—4A—5A(2)—5B(1)—6A—11G—3C—3x/11CX—3B
Tu	1A—4C—3x/6B—3x/6C—9A(2)—9D—3x/11B(1)—18B(2)—2B
W	7—1A—14A(2)—19A(1)—3B
Th	1A—4B—19A(2)—2A(1)
F	1A—14A(2)—15A—16A(1)—16A(2) (3x)—17CX—3C (4x)—11B
Sa	10:00-10:30 11:00-11:30 12:00-12:30; 1A—10A 10B—10C 10D—10E—3C
Su	3C
M	1A—14A(2,3)—14B(2)—15A—18C(2)—2B—11B (4x)—3B
Tu	1A—10A(2,3)—16A (10-15x)—16E—17A (6x)—17B—11E(2)—2B
W	7—1A—19A(1)—3B
Th	1A—14A(2)—14B(1)—2A(1)
F	1A—5A—5B(1)—6A—9A(2) (4x)—3C—11B
Sa	10:00-10:30 11:00-11:30 12:15-12:45; 1A—10F 10G—10H 10J—10K—3C
Su	3C
M	14A—19—16—2A(1)—3B
Tu	1A—4B—5A—5B (3-6x)—6A—9A (3-6x)—9D(2) (3x)—11C—3C
W	14A(2,3)—14B(1)—15A—4-6x/15D—16A—16E—17D—6x/11E—3B
Th	1A—19—3A
F	3C—gear ready
Sa	10—early-season meet
Su	3A
M	14A—19—16—2A(1)—3B
Tu	1A—4A—5A—5B (3-6x)—6A—9A (3-6x)—9B (4x)—11D(2)—2B
W	1A—15D—16A (3-6x)—16C (10-15x)—17X (2-3x)—17D—18C
Th	1A—19—4B or 14B(1) (2x)—11C—3B(light)
F	3C—gear ready
Sa	Dual meet
Su	3C

DATE April

M	7—14A(2,3,4)—4B— 5A—5B—6B—6C—9A—9D—11C—3C [3-4x]
Tu	14A—14B(2)—3-6x/15D— 16A—16E—17X—17D—18D(1)—4x/11B
W	1A—14B(1)—19—3C
Th	3C—gear ready
F	10—decathlon, 1st day
Sa	10—decathlon, 2nd day
Su	3C
M	14A—4A—5A—5B—6B—6C—9A—9D—11E—3B [3-4x]
Tu	3A—19A—19B—19C—3C
W	14A—15B(2)—15D—16A—16E—17X—17D—6x/11E(2)—3B [4x]
Th	14A—14B(1)—19—3C
F	3C—gear ready
Sa	Dual meet
Su	3A
M	14A—4A—5A—5B—6B—6C—9A—9E—18B—3C—3B [2-3x]
Tu	3A—19A—19B—19C—3C
W	14A—14B(3)—15D—16A—16D—17X—17C—11F(1)—3B [4x]
Th	14A—14B(1) or 4B—19—3C
F	3C—gear ready
Sa	Dual meet
Su	3A
M	1A—14A—4B—6A—6C—9A—9B—11C(1)—3C—3B [2-3x]
Tu	14A—14B(1)—15A—15C—16A—16C—17X—17D—11E(1) [6x]
W	1A—19B—19A—19C—3B—3C
Th	3C—gear ready
F	10—decathlon, 1st day
Sa	10—decathlon, 2nd day
Su	3A

DATE May/June

M	1A—4A—4B—5A—5B—6A—9A—9E—18B—3B—3C [2-3x]
Tu	14A—14B(1)—15A—16A—16B—17X—17D—11E—2B [4-6x]
W	1A—4B or 14B(1)—19A(1)—19B(1)—3C
Th	3C—gear ready
F	Qualify, division or conference
Sa	Finals, division or conference
Su	3A
M	1A—19B—19A—19C—3B—2B(1)
Tu	14A—19B(1)—19C(1)—19A(1)—3C
W	1A—4A—4B—5A—5B—6A—9A—9D—18C(1)—3C
Th	14A—14B(1)—15A—16A—16E—17X—3x/17B—18D(1)—4x/11B—3C
F	3A—3B—2B(1)
Sa	3A
Su	1A—4A—4B—4C—5A—5B—6A—3x/6C—9A—9B—18C(1)—3B—3C
M	14A—14B(1)—15A—3x/15C—16A—16C—17X—3x/17B—4-6x/11E(1)—3C
Tu	3C
W	3C—gear ready
Th	NCAA—decathlon, 1st day
F	NCAA—decathlon, 2nd day
Sa	3A
Su	3A
M	
Tu	
W	
Th	
F	
Sa	
Su	

APPENDIX	Sources for Track
	and Field Athletics

Many valuable publications are devoted to our sport. They will expose the coach and athlete to new ideas, while telling you what is happening in the sport. This bibliography lists some of those publications, divided into categories by emphasis. Most publications are either American or Canadian, though other useful publications can be found in almost every other nation of the world.

What Is Going On in Track and Field

Athletics. Published 9 times a year. 1220 Sheppard Ave. East, Willowdale, ON M2K 2X1, Canada.

IAAF Bulletin. Published 6 times a year by the International Amateur Athletic Federation (IAAF), 3 Hans Crescent, London SW1X 0LN, England.

IAAF Magazine. Published 10 times a year by the IAAF, 3 Hans Crescent, London SW1X 0LN, England.

Olympian. Published 10 times a year by the U.S. Olympic Committee, 1750 East Boulder St., Colorado Springs, CO 80909-5760.

Track and Field News. This monthly publication is absolutely essential to any person interested in what is happening in the world in track and field. 2570 El Camino Real, Suite 606, Mountain View, CA 94040.

Training and Technique Periodicals

Coaching Science Update. Published 6 times a year. 333 River Road, Ottawa, ON K1L 8H9, Canada.

National Strength Coaches Association Journal. Published 6 times a year. 251 Capitol Beach Blvd., Lincoln, NE 68528.

New Studies in Athletics. Published 4 times per year by the IAAF, 3 Hans Crescent, London SW1X 0LN, England.

Runner's World. Monthly publication devoted primarily to distance running. Rodale Press, 33 E. Minor St., Emmaus, PA 18049.

Running Times. Monthly publication devoted primarily to road racing. 9171 Wilshire Blvd., Suite 300, Beverly Hills, CA 90210.

Scholastic Coach. Published 10 times a year, covering all sports during their preseasons. 730 Broadway, New York City, NY 10003.

Soviet Sports Review. Formerly *Yessis Review*. Published 4 times per year by Michael Yessis, P.O. Box 2878, Escondido, CA 92025.

Track and Field Quarterly Review. Publication of NCAA Division I Track Coaches Association. Sent to all members. Covers a different set of events each quarter, with 48-64 pp. Extremely useful. 1705 Evanson St., Kalamazoo, MI 49008.

Track Technique. Quarterly magazine that is now the coaching periodical of The Athletics Congress (TAC). Articles tend to be quite short (1 to 3 pages). Includes digests of some foreign coaching articles. Available through *Track and Field News.*

Sport Science Periodicals

The American Journal of Sports Medicine. Published 6 times a year by Williams & Wilkins, 428 East Preston St., Baltimore, MD 21202.

Athletic Training. Published 4 times a year. 1001 East 4th St., Greenville, NC 27834.

Canadian Journal of Applied Sport Sciences. Published 4 times a year. Box 2274, Windsor, ON N8Y 4R8, Canada.

Clinics in Sports Medicine. Published 4 times a year by W.B. Saunders, West Washington Square, Philadelphia, PA 19005.

Exercise and Sports Sciences Reviews. Published 4 times a year by Macmillan Publishing, 866 Third Ave., New York, NY 10022.

International Journal of Sport Biomechanics. Published quarterly by Human Kinetics Publishers, P.O. Box 5076, Champaign, IL 61825-5076.

Journal of Sport Behavior. Published quarterly by the U.S. Sports Academy, P.O. Box 8650, Mobile, AL 36608.

Journal of Sport Psychology. Published quarterly by Human Kinetics Publishers, P.O. Box 5076, Champaign, IL 61825-5076.

Medicine and Science in Sports and Exercise. Six-times-a-year journal for the ACSM (American College of Sports Medicine), 401 West Michigan St., Indianapolis, IN 46202.

The Physician and Sportsmedicine. Monthly journal for sports medicine specialists, but with topics of practical application to specific training problems. McGraw-Hill Inc., 4530 West 77th St., Minneapolis, MN 55435.

Research Quarterly for Exercise and Sport. Sport science journal for the American Alliance for Health, Physical Education, Recreation and Dance, 1900 Association Drive, Reston, VA 22091.

Sportsmedicine. Published 6 times annually. Offers surveys of research literature on a topic, giving a clearer understanding of the current state of knowledge. Adis Press International, Suite 830, Oxford Court Business Center, 982 Middletown Blvd., Langhorne, PA 19047.

Sports Science Periodical on Research and Technology in Sport. Published 12 times a year. 333 River Road, Ottawa, ON K1L 8H9, Canada.

Rule Books

Handbook of the IAAF. The official international rule book, source of all track rule books, revised every 2 years by the International Amateur Athletic Federation, 13 Hans Crescent, London SW1X 0LN, England.

National Alliance Edition of Track and Field Rules and Records. Rules for high schools, NAIA schools, and junior colleges. Published annually by the National Federation of State High School Associations, 400 Leslie Street, Elgin, IL 60120.

Official Collegiate Track and Field Guide. Rules of the National Collegiate Athletic Association, published annually and distributed through the Collegiate Athletics Publishing Service, 349 East Thomas Road, Phoenix, AZ.

Scoring Tables for Men's and Women's Combined Events Competitions. (1985). The *International Edition of the Metric Conversion Tables* should be purchased at the same time. Available through the IAAF address or for a bit more from *Track and Field News,* which also produces its own conversion and information tables in *Track and Field News' Little Blue Book.* Tafnews, 2570 El Camino Real, Suite 606, Mountain View, CA 94040.

TAC Rule Book. Rules of competition of The Athletics Congress, 200 S. Capital Ave., Suite 140, Indianapolis, IN 46225.

MONTHLY TRAINING PLAN

Date_____   Athlete_____   Event_____

Monday	
Tuesday	
Wednesday	
Thursday	
Friday	
Saturday	
Sunday	
Monday	
Tuesday	
Wednesday	
Thursday	
Friday	
Saturday	
Sunday	
Monday	
Tuesday	
Wednesday	
Thursday	
Friday	
Saturday	
Sunday	
Monday	
Tuesday	
Wednesday	
Thursday	
Friday	
Saturday	
Sunday	